HISPANIC
NOTES & MONOGRAPHS

ESSAYS, STUDIES, AND BRIEF
BIOGRAPHIES ISSUED BY THE
HISPANIC SOCIETY OF AMERICA

PENINSULAR SERIES

HISPANIC
COSTUME
1480-1530

by RUTH MATILDA ANDERSON

WITH 569 ILLUSTRATIONS IN BLACK AND WHITE
AND 8 IN FULL COLOR

PRINTED BY ORDER OF THE TRUSTEES
THE HISPANIC SOCIETY OF AMERICA
NEW YORK 1979

LIBRARY OF CONGRESS CATALOGING IN PUBLICATION DATA

Anderson, Ruth Matilda.
  Hispanic costume, 1480–1530.

  (Hispanic notes & monographs, essays, studies, brief bibliographies : Peninsular series)
  Bibliography: p. 265
  Includes index.
  1. Costume—Spain—History. 2. Costume—Portugal—History. I. Title. II. Series.

GT1190.A52   391'.00946   78–66880
ISBN 87535-126-3

Typography by Peter Oldenburg
Composition by Kingsport Press
Printed and bound by Halliday Lithograph

Contents

List of Illustrations

WOMEN AND THEIR DRESS OCCASIONS

WOMEN'S DRESS

Foreword

THIS BOOK begins with costume of the Iberian Peninsula in about 1480, when the Catholic Kings were well established, and continues until after their grandson's coronation (1530) as Emperor Charles V of the Holy Roman Empire. The period includes, besides the subjugation of the Moors (Fig. 1), culminating in the conquest of Granada (1492), the discovery of the New World (1492), Vasco da Gama's first voyage to India (1497–1498), clashes of France and Spain in Italy (1495–1504, 1512, 1525), the conquest of Mexico (1519–1520), the sack of Rome (1527), and Pizarro's advance against Peru (1531–1532).

It was a time of great changes and dress responded. The fashionable silhouette, which had been columnar (Fig. 10), broadened to a rectangle (Fig. 4), to a wide rectangle (Figs. 6, 13) top heavy on the legs. Breadth-building features of masculine dress were reflected in the feminine.

Changes did not move along a solid front. In working to determine the date of an effigy or a portrait, the author has often found the costume to be an assemblage of elements, each of which seems to run a course of its own. The problem is to fix a place where the several lines converge. In this book a few full-length illustrations show whole complexes, while component parts are presented separately—hair styles, headgear, garments, footgear—each with its own development. It is hoped that this method will aid in dating pictured costumes of the period and will enable theater designers to proceed in something of the assured freedom with which Renaissance tailors, furriers, and shoemakers cut and sewed to please the taste of their clients.

Pictures have been drawn mostly from representations of the nobility, Portuguese as well as Spanish. But as noble gentlemen generally do not reveal their inner garments, illustrations of shirts, doublets, and other details have been taken from figures stripped for action, such as executioners, flagellators, soldiers, and farmers.

Names are given in the native form, except those of emperors—Charles, Ferdinand, and Maximilian. Philip the Handsome's name appears in the form current in his time—Phelipe. Fernando V and Isabel I were known as the Catholic Kings *(Reyes Católicos)*.

In the long course of making this book I have been helped by many individuals: by Carmen Bernis, Madrid, who preceded me in the field; by my sisters who motored across Britain, France, and Spain that I might see relevant paintings and sculptures.

Colonel Stopford Sackville and the Conde de Mayalde welcomed me to visit their paintings. At Solsona (Lérida), Don Antonio Lloréns Solé and at Granada, Don Jesús Bermúdez Pareja and Dr. José Manuel Pita Andrade let me handle chopines in their care. Don Manuel Rocamora, a well-known collector of Barcelona, Don Francisco Torrella Niubó, director of the Museo Provincial Textil, Tarrasa, and Srta. Pilar Tomás i Farrell of the Museo Textil, Barcelona, granted access to their material. At The Metropolitan Museum of Art, New York, Dr. Helmut Nickel and Miss Jean Mailey opened cupboards for my benefit.

Any mistakes in this book must be credited to my own efforts; colleagues at The Hispanic Society of America have done their best to prevent error. For the illustrations, the Curators of Sculpture and of Painting took seriously the problems of dating and attribution. Generous help in defining terms was given by the Curator of Textiles. The Director of the Society and the Curator of the Library brought to bear their exact knowledge of Spanish and Portuguese and their wide range of reading. The example of the President—his felicity of phrase, his fund of allusions—helped to ease the task of writing. Special appreciation is due to the Associate Curator of Iconography who joined the staff in time to deal graciously and competently with the questions that arose during publication. This cooperation witnesses to the enduring vitality of the structure that Archer M. Huntington bequeathed to The Hispanic Society of America.

R.M.A., *Curator of Costume*
The Hispanic Society of America

I MEN AND THEIR DRESS OCCASIONS

1 Moorish Surrender of Ronda (1485) 1489–1495

Assault and Surrender at Ronda, choir stall, by Master Rodrigo (Toledo. Cathedral)

2 ROYAL HEIRS APPARENT ON A DAIS ca. 1502

The Very Excellent Princes of Castilla and Aragón in Marcuello, Pedro. *Devocionario de la Reyna d.ª Juana, à quien llamaron la Loca. vºf*4 (Chantilly. Musée Condé)

3 BULLFIGHT 1506

Bullfight in Honor of Phelipe el Hermoso at Benavente (Écaussines. Château de la Follie, Collection of Comte Charles-Albert de Lichtervelde)

4 NOBLEMAN 1508

Saint Julian, retable center, by Juan Gascó (Vich. Finca del Pradell, Collection of Ramón d'Abadal i de Vinyals)

5 SAINT, LANSQUENET, AND NOBLEMAN ca. 1520

The Nobleman Gothard Finding Saint Roch, retable from Corbillos, attributed to Juan Rodríguez de Solís (León. Cathedral)

6 CONQUISTADOR 1529

Don Hernán Cortés in Weiditz, Christoph. *Das Trachtenbuch.* *f*77 (Nürnberg. Germanisches
Nationalmuseum)

7 CAPTURE OF A KING 1525

Capture of François I at Pavia, cartoon for *Battle of Pavia* tapestry series, by Bernart van Orley (Paris. Musée National du Louvre, Cabinet des Dessins)

8   POPE AND EMPEROR IN PROCESSION   1530

Procession of Pope Clement VII and Emperor Charles V after the Imperial Coronation at Bologna by Nicolas Hogenberg. [Malines? 1530?] *f*EE, [FF] (New York. Spencer Collection, The New York Public Library, Astor, Lenox and Tilden Foundations)

9 REED-SPEAR TOURNAMENT 1538

The Game of Canes by Jan Cornelisz Vermeyen (Drayton House, Nr. Kettering, Northamptonshire. Collection of L. G. Stopford Sackville)

Men and
Their Dress Occasions

Prince Juan (Fig. 311) at the age of eighteen (1496) was set up with an establishment of his own in the Mendoza palace at Almazán, just south of Soria.[1] Besides chosen grandees, his companions were noble pages who came in successive groups of six to help him increase his friendships among gilded youth of the realm. His principal attendant was a chamberlain under whom served valets of the chamber, some of them armed. There were also guards, *monteros de Espinosa* and *reposteros de camas,* who watched over the Prince's person night or day, respectively. Each night, as he went to bed, he gave the chamberlain an order for the next day's clothes, which was passed on to the valet in charge of keys.

The chamberlain's wife at their apartment in the palace took care of the royal shirts, handkerchiefs, and cauls of silk net. In the morning her husband, accompanied by valets—one of them carrying a clean shirt and handkerchief wrapped in a towel—went to dress his master. An armed man also was in the party. The valets bore the clothes of the day to the door of the Prince's chamber and waited while their superior entered with the shirt, which the Prince put on. Then the chamberlain came out and superintended the changing of the guard. *Monteros* made sure they had heard the royal voice before departing.

After the Prince had donned his hose and the chamberlain had helped him tie them to his doublet, the valets entered the chamber, appearing without cloak, bonnet, or pantofles. *Reposteros,* wearing capes, came in and guarded the door from the inside. Meanwhile, the valet of the closet *(retrete)* had prepared a towel, a silver basin, and a pitcher of water. If a great noble happened to be present, he would pour the water over the Prince's hands, from which it dripped into the basin offered by a kneeling valet. The towel was held by the chamberlain who kissed it and gave it to the noble who also kissed it and laid it over the royal hands. Next, shoeman and barber were called in. The barber had a ready wit which the Prince enjoyed while his hair was being dressed. Then the shoeman, bracing himself against the Prince's chair which was kept upright and in place by two valets kneeling, tugged on the royal buskins. Barber and shoeman gone, the chamberlain helped the Prince to finish dressing in garments handed over with proper respect by the valets.

At night the ceremony was simpler. The chamberlain helped his master off with his clothes until he had reached doublet and hose, over which he put on a gown lined with pine marten, or a lighter garment according to the season. Seated in a chair, the Prince presented his buskins to be removed by a single valet. Day guards and other attendants withdrew, leaving the chamberlain alone to take off the Prince's shirt and hose, hand him his nightshirt, and discuss the morrow's costume. The Prince decided how much cash he would like to carry, and the chamberlain placed it in a pouch *(escarcela)* to be worn on band or baldric.

Each morning valets with small brushes cleaned the clothes, buskins, hose, and cork-soled shoes the Prince had worn the day before. When he went hunting, a valet carried a scarlet bag containing handkerchiefs, towels, and a suit of brown or green; another carried buskins, shoes, pantofles, and sword, knife, or javelin. Hunting togs certainly had to be cleaned after a day in the field. The keeper of the keys, a polished and well-dressed gentleman who wrote a good hand, was vigilant in the duty of airing and cleaning clothes. He had two assistants to tie and untie boxes, to take out and fold garments, and to sweep the chamber. Lamps and torches were never lighted in a room where the wardrobe was kept.

When new clothes were needed, a tailor was summoned and ordered to search out materials for Juan to select from—brocades, silks, handsome red cloths, fine linens. The Prince responded, "So many varas of brocaded satin, of cloth of drawn gold, for a short gown *(ropa bastarda)* . . . so many pieces of good green cloth for cloaks or tabards for my hunters."[2] Each month usually he had two pairs of new hose and every week at least two pairs each of pantofles, shoes, and buskins. Footgear discarded by the Prince was the perquisite of the chamberlain who received also, after the third wearing, caps, hats, and body garments. If, as was quite proper, the Prince should wish to present clothes to others of his household, the chamberlain was recompensed for their value in money or in favors. A formal distribution came about in the following manner.

When the Prince was little more than eight years old, Queen Isabel asked what had become of a certain suit of his, whether he had given it away. The reply was that he was not accustomed to give away anything. His mother, concerned at this defect of character, instructed the official to see to it that each year on the Prince's birthday, June thirtieth, there would be listed and brought to her all his doublets, jerkins, capes, gowns, and bonnets, his horse, mule, and pony trappings and harnesses—in short, all his personal gear except hose and shoes. And on that day, having the clothes before her and the list in her hand, the Queen sent for the Prince.

"Son, my Angel," said she, "princes should not be old-clothes men or keep their arcas full." A thriving business was the selling of used clothing, even of that obtained by robbery, and her listeners would understand vividly what she meant.

"Henceforth, each year on this day, I wish you to distribute before me all such things among your servants and those whom you would like to favor."

The Prince kissed the Queen's hand, took the list, and bent to his task.

"That gown, that cape, that doublet with that jerkin, present them to Don Alonso de Aragón, duke of Villahermosa,"[3] the second duke, a cousin of about the Prince's age.

When personal friends had been remembered, the Prince directed the chamberlain to take the rest and give what he liked to the valets; the keeper of the keys got the largest share.

The Queen was pleased with her son's distribution and commanded the chamberlain at the beginning of each month, and any other time that the Prince needed clothes, to consult him as to the color he preferred and whether he would like silk or brocade. For hose it was not necessary to refer to him; there should always be on hand fine red and black cloths for making as many hose as he required. Each Sunday and each feast day he should have new buskins, not too tight-fitting because of his youth. Cork-soled shoes and pantofles were to be of velvet.

Isabel provided clothes and attendants also for young sons of the Portuguese Duke of Bragança who, suspected of being too friendly with the Catholic Kings, had lost his head in 1483. The boys were conveyed to Castilla and brought up with Prince Juan, who was a little older. They are still mentioned as pensioners of Isabel in 1496. Another pair of brothers she maintained from 1492 to 1504, the year of her death. These were half-Moorish princes who turned Christian, half brothers of the last Moorish king, Boabdil.

On her son's wardrobe the Queen began to spend money in earnest in 1493, the year that he was fifteen, when her treasurer Baeza recorded a total expenditure for him of 805,790 maravedis.[4] In 1494 the outlay was almost a million. Plans for the marriages of Prince Juan and Infanta Juana with Emperor Maximilian's daughter and son, projected as early as 1486, flickered under the pressure of rival schemes until a firm contract was signed on January 20th, 1495.

Over two years later Juan's bride, Margarita de Austria, arrived by ship at Santander. Three days out from Burgos the bridegroom and his father, on horseback, met the Princess in the Valle de Mena [Toranzo]. For the Spanish betrothal ceremony they stopped at the village of Villasenil [Villasevil], where the Prince put on a cloth-of-gold doublet and a jerkin of white satin slashed over cloth of gold and lined with sable. It was quite cold, having snowed the day before, and he wore in addition a hooded cloak *(capuz)* of crimson velvet open at the sides, lined with crimson satin and trimmed with hammered-gold marguerites in compliment to his bride. His cap of crimson-mulberry velvet glittered with enameled aglets. Night having fallen, he rode by torchlight to the Princess's lodging.

In an upper room—too small to accommodate all the attending notables, even though they stood—Margarita, dressed in French style, was betrothed to the Prince by the Archbishop of Sevilla. Then the Spaniards departed for supper. Afterward, Juan came back and with two attendants went up to a chamber lighted with a single torch. There he stayed with his bride and her ladies until, after two hours, her chief escort begged his Highness to go and give the Princess leave to rest.[5]

The bridal party arrived at Burgos on March 18th, 1497. Queen Isabel with her ladies awaited them in the palace of the Constable de Velasco, where the Queen was lodged. At a splendid reception, among knights in lustrous armor, ambassadors laden with gold, city magistrates in heavy gold chains and crimson satin gowns lined with marten, the Princess began her education in the minutiae of Spanish etiquette, simple and somewhat rigid in contrast with the easy splendor of the Burgundian court.

The next day being Palm Sunday, the eager bridegroom had to postpone his wedding until the demands of Holy Week should have been fully served. Meanwhile massive preparations began, and on Easter Day a banquet was held in the Velasco palace for all the notables assembled. On a dais *(estrado)* in the principal hall was set a table for the Princess and the royal family; guests were seated at floor level. Many sideboards groaned under great table services of silver. Trumpets and other instruments blared; nothing else could be heard. The guest most gorgeously arrayed was the Duke of Béjar, who swept the floor with a long gown bearing valuable gold ornaments as well as precious stones and pearls. After the banquet Isabel and Fernando danced, as did also the guests.

The wedding, held in private on Easter Monday morning, and the grand nuptial Mass on the following Sunday were supplemented with spectacular festivities: a bullfight, jousts, tournaments, and games of reed-spears *(juegos de cañas)*. Before joy could really develop, however, a young nobleman, racing through the streets of Burgos, was thrown from his horse; he died soon after. The court put on mourning to condole with the stricken father and then went back to the wedding celebrations, but without the first enthusiasm.[6]

All the complacent hopes for Juan's future came to an end with his death at Salamanca six months later (October sixth). Funeral expenses were faithfully recorded. A wooden tomb was laid atop a stepped wooden catafalque inside a wooden railing. Moorish carpenters made the railing, which was painted black, and the catafalque, which was hidden beneath 45 varas of black velvet. The tomb, set about with four iron candelabra, was covered with burlap, with a 22-vara cloth of black velvet lined with linen *(lienzo),* and over that with a sheet of Breton linen. Mourners included a hundred poor, each of whom was given a pair of shoes and two garments made of *jerga,* a coarse, heavy, woolen material often mentioned as white.[7]

Ambassadors brought the sad news to France. "Truly, I never heard of such grief and mourning as prevailed in all the kingdoms of Spain: trades and workshops ceased operation for forty days. . . . Every man put on black sackcloth. Nobles and other important persons had their horses and mules covered with mourning cloths to below the knees, leaving only the eyes uncovered. Cities and villages spread black flags across the gates of their walls."[8] The Prince's marble effigy, executed (1511–1513) by an Italian, is clad in armor under a sleeveless cloak—plain material bordered with a Greek fret—which in no way suggests the silks and brocades that Isabel had lavished upon him.

The death of Crown Prince Juan devolved the inheritance upon his oldest sister Isabel (Fig. 311), now married to Manuel I, king of Portugal. In March 1498 they set out from Lisbon, richly dressed though still in mourning for the Prince, to be sworn in as heirs to the Spanish thrones. At the border they were met with music by retainers of the Duke of Medina Sidonia. When the monarchs were within a stone's throw of him, the Duke and his attendants dismounted. He made three reverences, knee to ground, and then with cap in hand went to kiss the royal hands. After him went all his company. King Manuel's gesture in return was to put his hand to his hat and lift it slightly, but not to take it off.

Arrived in Castilla la Nueva, the Portuguese spent three days at a village near Toledo, preparing their entrance into the city. Fernando came outside to meet them. All the Portuguese dismounted; Fernando remained on horseback. Dom Jorge, seventeen-year-old bastard of King João II, took off the hat he wore over a scarf *(touca)* and approached, making three reverences. Still Fernando did not respond. As the lad was small, the majordomo and a captain took him in their arms and raised him to kiss the King's hand.

Informed who he was, Fernando took off his hat with much ceremony and said, "Pardon me for not knowing you; if I had known you, I should have got down." And then with great courtesy he had him mount and ride at his right. As all the principal persons on both sides wished to kiss all the royal hands, three hours passed before the Kings could come together. Fernando insisted on yielding precedence to Manuel as a king until the ceremonies were over and then treated him as a son.[9]

The young Isabel gave the Portuguese a prince and died. Her son Miguel died before he was two years old, and thus the lot fell upon Juana living in Flanders with her handsome but lightweight husband, Archduke Phelipe. Summoned to be sworn in as heirs to the crowns of Castilla and Aragón, they set out from Brussels on November 4th, 1501, passing through Paris and arriving at Bayonne in late January 1502. The carts and wagons that had brought them, the Basques must have thought incapable of traversing their mountain roads, for the wheeled vehicles were sent back and the baggage was transferred to great mules of Vizcaya. Through Burgos, Valladolid, Segovia—entertained with bullfights, reed-spear tournaments, or deer hunting—they arrived on April thirtieth at Olías del Rey (Toledo), where Phelipe came down with measles. Fernando journeyed the ten kilometers from Toledo to visit him. Though ill and in bed, Phelipe must have been wearing a bonnet, for the Flemish chronicler makes a point of his taking it off and of the King's holding his own bonnet, all the while that Phelipe was seizing the royal hand and kissing it by force, Fernando putting on a show of reluctance.[10] At Juana's meeting with her parents the Catholic Kings wore woolen cloth; one feels the icy hand of winter lingering upon that stony capital. Immediately came frustrating news: the Prince of Wales, the English son-in-law, had died, which put the court into mourning. While the King and the Queen kept their chambers for a week, Phelipe went to Aranjuez and hunted. Finally, on May twenty-second in the cathedral of Toledo, he and Juana (Fig. 2) were recognized as heirs to the crown, that is, princes of Asturias.

The King celebrated the event by giving a supper at the castle, served with thousands of gold or silver-gilt vessels—his own and those of four great nobles—that were reckoned "very magnificent" even by a Fleming.

On June twenty-fourth, also at Toledo, Phelipe and Fernando got up early and took horse to attend a celebration of the city's conquest from the Moors. The Prince, the Admiral, and masters of horse were dressed in Moorish style with turbans on their heads. Their long garments of crimson or blue velvet, with crimson satin in the lower part of the sleeves, were worked with Moresque embroidery. Each participant had also a red cloak and a great scimitar, hanging probably from a baldric. The chronicler does not use the word *marlota,* but that is the garment they must have worn, together with a *capellar* or an *albornoz.* A quarter league outside the city four hundred horsemen, also dressed as Moors, rushed out of ambush and, throwing reed-spears, skirmished about the royal spectators. Thus in former days Moors had attacked Christians.

Phelipe again dressed in Moorish clothes to watch a bullfight (Fig. 3) and to tilt with reed-spears. This exercise (Fig. 9) was carried on by two bands *(cuadrillas)* of horsemen, each flourishing its own color and caracoling elegantly. Introduced into Spain by the Moors and considered proper only to the nobility, the exercise had for its object the gaining of skill in the use of arms and in the manège of a horse in battle. Mounted in a saddle with short stirrups, the richly dressed horseman carried on his left arm a shield with the device and motto of his *cuadrilla*. Taking their reed-spears, three or four meters long, horsemen rode the length of a plaza and, as the two bands passed, threw their weapons, at the same time raising their shields to ward off the spears of their opponents. Spaniards at Naples praised the reed-tournament extravagantly. An Italian there took the game seriously until he had seen one; then—confessedly he was a silly fellow—he scorned it. "There is nothing in it but certain shrill, Arabic outcries, a prescribed form of bandage, peaked cap, and beard, 'You pursue while I flee,' and 'You flee while I pursue.' The shield is placed not before the breast, as is proper, but at the back. Fleeing or pursuing a fugitive—one is worthy of a vile man, the other is no indication of strength—both are doings of the light-minded Moors."[11]

In October, when Juana and Phelipe entered Zaragoza, the Prince again was handsomely dressed, this time in Castilian fashion. Officials meeting them were in red gowns with cloth of gold at the collar and a lining of black damask. Two officials, each wearing a gold chain, led the royal horses through streets hung with tapestries and past merchants' houses festooned with silks. But the next day, October 27th, 1502, when the couple swore to maintain the rights, liberties, and privileges of the Aragonese, Phelipe chose Flemish dress to accompany Juana's Castilian. In the miniature of Figure 2, Carmen Bernis suggests,[12] he wears the sumptuous style to which he was accustomed, and which made striking contrast to the rich but restrained outer garment *(loba)*, affected by Spanish royalty (Fig. 283) and assumed by Phelipe in another miniature of the *Devocionario*.

Expecting a fourth child, Juana was forced to remain behind when her husband insisted on returning home, and only after many months was she permitted to rejoin him. Proceeding through Huesca Province toward France, Phelipe (early January 1503) was entertained at Ribagorza Castle, where the Duke of Nájera put on a gown of crimson velvet rich *(plaine)* with ermine and wore a "rather" good chain in "our", that is, the Flemish fashion. The gown of his son, the Admiral, was cloth of gold with tufted nap *(frisé)*, rich with sables, also a fashion of "ours". In Phelipe's suite two beds were hung with cloth of gold *frisé* or with crimson velvet heavily embroidered; the third had a hanging of embroidered satin and a coverlet of sables.

Isabel and Fernando for some time had been issuing decrees *(pragmáticas)*, those chilly stimulants to prudence, restraining everyone who did not own a horse from wearing expensive materials. By prodding ambitious wives, the monarchs doubtless hoped to induce beleaguered husbands to increase the number of horses available for war service. When Isabel died on November 26th, 1504, mourning once more paralyzed the country—except for Fernando. His scheming mind immediately cast about for means to checkmate the prospective power of his deeply distrusted Flemish son-in-law.

Again Phelipe and Juana were called to Spain. In early January 1506 they took ship, but a storm drove them ashore in England, and not until April twenty-sixth did they arrive at La Coruña. Besides princes, gentlemen, and officers, Phelipe had with him six hundred Germans, a hundred mounted archers, and a hundred foot guards. Stewards had difficulty in hiring oxcarts to convey the baggage of this company, and when they did succeed, the drivers might serve only two or three days and then by night take off with their oxen, leaving behind the carts and all those boxes of clothes. It was decided to avoid Villafranca del Bierzo (León), where Fernando was thought to be waiting, and to follow a more westerly course southward through Galicia. As they labored through the mountains, several travelers lost baggage. "Do not doubt that *gallegos* are inclined to larceny," carps the chronicler.[13]

On few occasions now did Phelipe cut a gallant figure; suddenly everything was over for him. An hour after noon on September twenty-fifth at Burgos he died. Juana had his body dressed in a gown of brocade lined with ermine, a jeweled bonnet placed on his head, a cross of precious stones hung on his breast, his feet shod in buskins and shoes in the Flemish fashion. Then she had the corpse brought into a spacious hall and laid on a rich bed. The heart was sent to Flanders in a vial of balsam; the entrails were buried at Burgos. The body, royally embalmed, Juana kept with her.[14]

At this time her father was out of the country. In the hope of achieving an heir to use in his moves against Phelipe, Fernando had married Germaine de Foix, granddaughter of his half sister, and was on the way with her to Naples, still a dependency of Spain thanks to the brilliant campaigns of Gonzalo Fernández de Córdoba. Son of a distinguished house, Gonzalo in his middle teens had entered the service of Queen Isabel soon after her marriage (1469). In knightly games he carried off many prizes and won the good will of the people with his splendid liberality, outshining contemporaries with a magnificence rather beyond his means. Even on a day of no particular importance he would appear in a crimson gown, lined with sables, that had cost 2,000 ducats. When an elder brother tried to temper his extravagance, he defied "this vain fear of poverty to come"[15] and prophesied that one day he would have riches enough to satisfy the desires of both his liberality and his magnificence. Gonzalo fought against the Moors and helped to negotiate the surrender of Granada. Glorious eminence and the title of *Gran Capitán* he earned by success in Italy (1495–1498, 1500–1507), whither Fernando sent him to fight the French in defense of Naples.

During a siege, he might be seen in the vanguard, armed with sword and shield, clad only in doublet and hose, encouraging his men and doing more than any. Money for his soldiers was hard to find, but after one success the booty gained from the French—whose leaders dined in camp on silver gilt and went to battle in jerkins of rich brocade and crimson velvet—inspired them to more ambitious enterprises. Conspicuous luxury served as insurance for fighters. A well-dressed man on the losing side hoped to become a target for ransom instead of slaughter. To Barletta, where in 1502 the Great Captain himself was under siege, a Venetian merchant brought thousands of pairs of hose and shoes which Gonzalo bought for his men, paying for them with funds extracted from his friends and captains. Leaving Barletta, he ordered his arcas—eighteen of them filled with gold and silver jewels, with gowns of silk and brocade—to be brought along to suffer the same fate as himself and his soldiers. "Let it not be said that I took out my men to fight in the field and left my rags under a roof."[16]

To Cerignola, scene of the ultimate French disaster (1503), venders expecting the French to win had brought quantities of rich merchandise, to which the Great Captain, victorious, let his people help themselves. At Naples, after treasures stored at the Castel Nuovo by the French and by expectant merchants had been looted by his Spaniards, the soldiers who had obtained nothing he satisfied by letting them clean out his own quarters. He was generous to defeated foes as well: a Frenchman was given gold and silver tumblers and gowns of silk or brocade lined with sables or with lynxes of great price. It is difficult to see how anything could have been left for the hero himself.

When the fighting was over, or nearly over, he made a triumphal entry into Naples (May 17th, 1503), where he reorganized the government, distributing honors and estates to his auxiliaries with a liberality little to the taste of King Fernando, for whom ostensibly the victories had been won. An embassy sent by the Turks included a Jewish painter to do Gonzalo's portrait. The artist, confused by his constant change of dress, begged him to wear the same clothes three days in succession. He complied and for that time appeared faithfully in his Spanish cape, a black velvet jerkin, and a half cap with medallion, his sword girded. To thirty of the Turks' Janizaries he gave Moorish gowns *(marlotas),* parti-colored of green and brown damask with buttons down to the hem, besides buskins and red bonnets.

Fernando with his new wife arrived at Naples (late October 1506) in a galley *muy ruín* to receive the territory secured for him. The King, who as Isabel's bridegroom entered Castilla in the guise of a muleteer, has been described so far only as dressed in wool. An account of his youth says that he wore good clothes well and praises the grace of his legs, which in a period of long, tight-fitting hose had seductive value. But now the Great Captain persuaded him to remain in seclusion at the Castel Nuovo until truly regal clothes could be assembled, sending thither his own tailors, together with silks and brocades of many kinds, precious stones, rich jewels, and necessary trimmings for the King's use. As a result, when Fernando stepped into a handsome galley to make the royal entry, he was wearing a gown of brocade lined with marten and trimmed with precious stones. His bonnet carried a jewel for which Gonzalo had paid 20,000 ducats. Queen Germana, as she was called in Spain, wore French clothes. They put out from the castle with an escort of twenty-two other galleys beautifully decorated and equipped with more than two thousand men in silk and brocade, most of them wearing a gold collar and many precious stones.

Gonzalo received the sovereigns on an artificial bridge and accompanied them through the city, clad in a crimson gown open at the sides and lined with rich brocade. Yellow cloth of gold made his jerkin; a marvelous jewel hung from his collar of gold and handsome pearls. The halberdiers wore silks of his colors. Gonzalo provided thirty pages in livery carrying tapers which were kindled at midday to insure that the royal pair would have light to enter the palace. These great expenditures he made in order to cover up the small liberality of his king.

At Naples also Fernando put on black to mourn Phelipe's death, of which the King had learned at one of his nightly landfalls during the voyage from Barcelona.

The Great Captain left Italy with the understanding that he was to become Master of the Order of Santiago. Arrived at Valencia in June 1507, he commanded his men to prepare themselves for attending court at Burgos and ordered five thousand varas of silks to clothe them. To pay the bill he had to sell much of the silver plate he had brought from Italy. The knights and soldiers who marched with him in a splendid progress across country, overflowing the roads, wore gowns of different silks, brocades, and cloths, with gold chains hanging over the shoulder and under the left arm. Their bonnets were trimmed with plumes and gold aglets.

Fernando failed to keep the promise about the mastership, and Gonzalo retired to his estate at Loja, near Granada, enjoying the wealth brought home from his wars. In 1512, having been denied a return to Italy after the battle lost at Ravenna, he made a farewell to his soldiers at Antequera (Málaga). Merchants from Valencia, Córdoba, Toledo, Medina del Campo, Sevilla, Granada, and many other places, in expectation of his going back to Italy, had brought thither more than a hundred thousand ducats' worth of merchandise which the Great Captain bought and distributed among his knights—brocades, cloths of gold, silks, satins, damasks, and red woolens; also handsome horses, gilded weapons, silk campaign beds, and embroidered tents. To the common soldiers he gave money. Besides what he had purchased, he dispensed finery and jewels of his own. A servant said to him, "What more could you do in the house of an enemy than you have done today in your own house?"[17]

His foes in Spain, jealous of his great deeds, laughed at such munificence. King Fernando hoped, "Some day, if we live, we shall see the liberality of the Great Captain become shallow enough to ford."[18]

The King outlived him. In 1515 at Granada Gonzalo put on his knight-of-Santiago gear—the great white cape marked with a red sword-cross—and lay down to die upon a heraldic wall hanging *(repostero)* spread over the floor. His household raised the body and set it in a chair, and thus for a day he was visited by his people. "He was most liberal and extremely elegant in his apparel, very much of the palace, a gallant and fluent speaker, never offending with his witticisms and well beloved of the ladies."[19]

Back in Flanders, Juana's children—except Ferdinand who was in Spain—had been left under the guardianship of Phelipe's sister Margarita, widowed the second time. Thus Charles, born in 1500 and made prince of Castilla after his father's death, during the most impressionable years was nourished on the Burgundian ideas of luxury and display natural to his aunt, whose court was considered "ostentatious but not lax". The Prince was to enter Spain only after King Fernando should have left the scene. That event occurred in January 1516, but for various reasons Charles's going was delayed for twenty months. Funds for the journey were eventually provided by Henry VIII of England, uncle by marriage of the young King.

On September 7th, 1517, Charles and his older sister Leonor took ship. Charles had remained at or near Middelburg for weeks, awaiting a proper wind and uneasy lest moves against his interest be set afoot in Castilla: it seemed possible that his brother Ferdinand, brought up by the old King and popular among his subjects, might be set on the Spanish throne. The voyage from Vlissingen, Holland, is described by Laurent Vital, a Fleming who had the royal baggage in his care. The decision to embark came suddenly, and all at once so many people and so many chests had to be put aboard that money could hardly procure carts to take them to the water. Vital finally got the chests containing

Charles's best clothes into a boat which then went off without him towards a place he calls Ermue. Following, he could not find the boat and was almost crazed with fear. There had been eight chests, not one of them valued at less than eight or nine thousand florins at least. He wished he were dead. Standing on the shore in the misty night, through which he could see nothing but the stars shining overhead, he finally perceived a boat coming near with a little sail in a good wind. The boatman, moved by his prayers and by the offer of half again the usual fee, agreed to take him on to Vlissingen, two leagues away. Being intoxicated, the man did not realize what a dangerous journey it was, but they safely reached the harbor where the fleet was still at anchor. Try as they would, Vital and the boatman could not locate Charles's ship, so they went to that assigned to the chamberlains. When the moon had risen, after midnight, Vital was taken to the royal vessel where he must have found his chests.

At sea in the morning Charles was fortified against cold winds with a crimson satin doublet having a high collar lined with scarlet. Next he put on a sleeveless garment rich with martens; closed with an aglet, it extended only a good palm's length beyond the belt. Over hose of scarlet cloth he had great knitted hose, like the sailors', and high shoes lined with scarlet. A double bonnet of scarlet buckled under the chin held his hair in place. Last he put on a high-collared belted gown of delicate velvet lined with Rumanian lambskins, inside which he was so comfortable that it did not seem heavy. Thus clad, he left his cabin every day and proceeded to bid good morning to his sister and her ladies. Then he went to the deck where he knelt on cushions to say his prayers.

After twelve days of stomach-churning waves as well as of great calms, the pilots were chagrined to find themselves only off the coast of Asturias, instead of at Santander. Charles decided to disembark at once, and on September nineteenth a certain number came ashore near Villaviciosa. An English ambassador, like Charles and Leonor, walked the mile into town. Asturians beholding forty powerful ships in their waters thought at first they must be enemies, French or Turks, but when they saw gentlemen unarmed, accompanied by ladies, and when they noted the escutcheon of Castilla among the great banners, their alarm subsided. The wind changing, orders were given the ships to depart for Santander, and they went, taking beds, horses, and baggage with them. That first night ashore many lords and ladies slept on straw or benches. As little food was available in the neighborhood, the company on the third day set out overland for Santander, Charles riding a "hobby" provided by the English ambassador. Most of the attendants walked; a few were carried on pack horses, the ladies in oxcarts, over the difficult Asturian roads. Charles advised local lords not to attend him, because his goods and clothes were at Santander and, besides, the region could not, according to Burgundian standards, care adequately for a large gathering. Towns he passed through did their best, putting on bullfights (see Fig. 3) for his entertainment. At San Vicente de la Barquera the situation improved: mules and horses had arrived from Santander. Rumors of a plague at Burgos decided the company to head for Valladolid.

By the time they arrived, Charles had been reunited with his clothes, and on November eighteenth a brilliant company entered the city. Three hundred of the six thousand horsemen wore gowns of cloth of gold; others appeared in silk, brocade, cloth of silver, crimson velvet, satin, or damask of various colors. Many grand masters and gentlemen displayed a gold chain worth in some cases six thousand ducats. Charles was handsomely dressed in his own colors, yellow, white, and red, expressed in gold and silver cloth and crimson satin. "It is my belief," says the warmly partisan Vital, "that never has a king so noble and triumphant as this one entered Castilla, as indeed several old townsmen and merchants of Valladolid have admitted. . . . The precious stones he wore were worth the ransom of a great prince."[20] Of the same gold and silver stuff as his large jerkin were the trappings of his beautiful but nervous horse, which Charles handled with notable mastery. Following the ladies and his brother Ferdinand who had arrived, he rode at the end of the procession under a canopy of cloth of gold carried on four poles, silver-plated. For a week Castilian lords, displaying great pomp, poured into Valladolid, accompanied by friends, relations, and allies.

There, in November and later, courtiers organized tournaments, and for the silks, brocades, and cloths of gold used in the liveries that were issued Charles ordered 40,000 ducats to be paid. "His Highness began to show himself very generous," his Spanish chronicler dryly records.[21] One can imagine the stricken rage with which his grandfather Fernando would have regarded such easy spending of royal capital. Streets giving on the market place were fenced off with great tubs, except for a gate at each end of the plaza. Behind the tubs, viewing stands were erected and hung with tapestries to accommodate ladies of high rank. Wives of merchants and artisans found places in chambers and attics of surrounding houses; roofs swarmed with men. Vital estimates that 80,000 persons saw the first spectacle. Eight or nine horses were killed, but no contender was injured to the degree that he could not be up and ready to begin again in a fortnight.

Before leaving Brussels, Charles had assumed the kingship of Spain. Now the Cortes at Valladolid was to confirm his title. They remembered, however, that his mother was queen, and insisted, ineffectually as it proved, that Doña Juana's name precede his in all public documents. On February 5th, 1518, he took his oath and on the seventh at nine o'clock in the morning received the clergy and the nobles. Spaniards wore cloth of gold, cloth of silver, handsome silks. Gowns were bordered with motifs of gold plate, adorned with pieces of beaten gold, enriched with furs—sables, ermines, leopard skins, pony skins, lambskins. The ceremony took place in the church of San Pablo, a few hundred feet from the palace. Rain and snow fell from the sky; underfoot was mud and filth. Nevertheless, noble gentlemen insisted on leading their horses and walking, with no more care for their costly habits than if they had been made of canvas. Into the mire they sank up to their ankles, spoiling pantofles and scarlet hose. Preceded by the Count of Oropesa carrying the sword of justice, Charles on a Spanish jennet followed the nobles. Near him rode ambassadors—of the Pope, the Emperor Maximilian, and various kings. Dripping and muddy, they passed through the florid Gothic portal of San Pablo and disposed themselves inside, so that sixty of their number might kiss the hand of the young sovereign.

Of the clothes and events of the tournament on February twenty-fifth Vital's doting account was lost at sea during his voyage back to Flanders with Infante Ferdinand. But he remembered, "There were hardly any Spaniards taking part; whether they found the play too rough, I do not know. But I think they did wisely. . . . Many contenders exposed their good horses with regret, fearing to waste them. They would rather use them later in the service of the King."[22] As knights grew more considerate of their safety, taking fewer risks, tournaments lost their attraction for the people. Then the aristocracy, moved by vanity, turned to the bullfight, becoming public entertainers by lancing bulls, not in the wild in the knightly tradition, but within a city plaza (where they could await an easy opening to attack) for the praise of a noisy crowd.[23]

The imperial grandfather died in January 1519, and against a field that included Henry VIII and François I, Charles was the successful candidate to follow him. Word of the election reached Spain in early July. Henceforth the new Emperor required to be addressed as "Majesty", which rather shocked the Spaniards to whom it seemed a form of address more suited to Almighty God than to a mortal man, "Highness" *(Alteza)* having been the traditional form of address for Castilian kings. Beginning the long trip to secure the German crown, Charles sailed from La Coruña on May 20th, 1520. On the way he spent four days visiting his aunt and uncle in England, where courtiers found his dress and equipage moderate for his rank and unlike the magnificence they were accustomed to see among themselves. Bust portraits of the young Emperor began to hang in European palaces, carefully detailing for him a hat with wide jeweled brim, hair hanging to below the ears, an exquisitely embroidered shirt, a fur-collared gown. Hardly had he left Spain when Castilians rose in arms, declining to pay taxes, resentful that he had placed a foreigner, the Flemish Cardinal Adrian, as regent over them. In August when royal forces set fire to the great warehouses of Medina del Campo, the famous market town lost gold, silver, silks, brocades, pearls, "riches . . . that no tongue can speak, nor pen write, nor heart think of, nor eyes look at without tears."[24] Charles refused to let this unpleasantness distract him, refused also to let François I lure him to the Field of the Cloth of Gold. At Charlemagne's capital, Aachen, on October twenty-third he was crowned emperor, dressed in a floor-length gown of brocade.

Returning to Spain in 1522, the Emperor was still at home when François crossed the Alps into Italy (1524) and besieged Pavia, held by the Spaniards. Their general, Pescara, got money through the French lines to his German lansquenets, and in the battle they held. As the dissatisfied Swiss mercenaries of François failed to advance, the French king was captured (Fig. 7) and shipped to Spain for imprisonment (1525). Part of his ransom price was a promise to marry Leonor de Austria, Charles's elder sister.

An important event of 1526 was the imperial wedding. Years before, Charles had been betrothed to his English cousin, Mary Tudor, but since her dowry could be expected to consist largely of cancellation of the debts he owed her father, the Emperor got himself released from that obligation and sought a princess with a fortune he could spend. He found her in a Portuguese cousin, daughter of Manuel the Fortunate. King João III was prepared to furnish with his sister Isabel a dowry of 900,000 doblas, a good part of which the bridegroom could use for an Italian journey to be crowned by the Pope.

The celebration of the imperial marriage was brief and simple. Charles chose Sevilla, convenient to Portugal, as the scene of the wedding. Arriving a week later than Isabel, he was met outside the city by resplendent prelates, nobles, and officials. It was March tenth, and he rode without cape or gown, dressed in a black velvet jerkin with gold

10 KINGS 1490

Figures of Magi in *Epiphany*, retable from Enviny, by Pere Espalargues (The Hispanic Society of America)

11 WEDDING BANQUET 1496–1497

The Marriage at Cana by Master of the Retable of the Reyes Católicos (Washington, D.C. National Gallery of Art, Samuel H. Kress Collection)

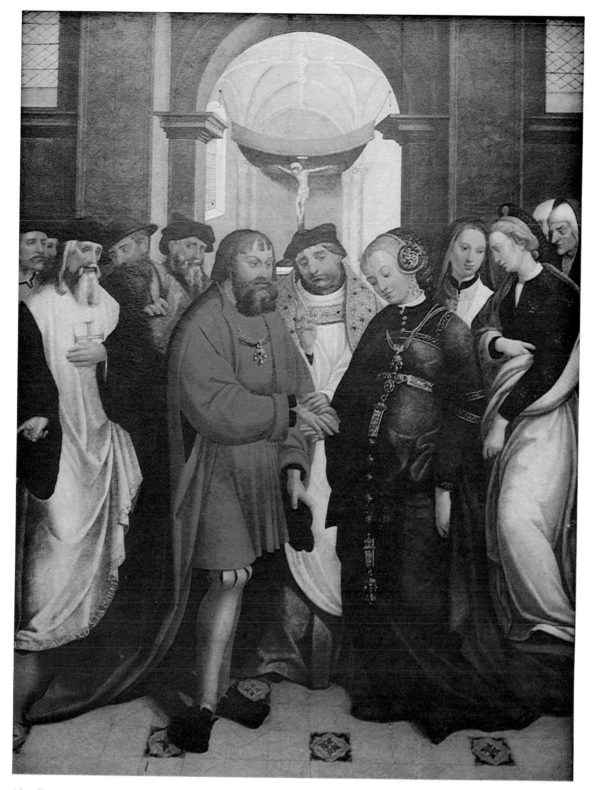

12 ROYAL WEDDING 1518 or 1525

Wedding of Manuel I (or of João III) and a Spanish Infanta by Garcia Fernandes, 1541 (Lisboa, Museu de São Roque)

13 EMPEROR 1532

Charles V, Emperor of the Holy Roman Empire, by Jakob Seisenegger (Wien. Kunsthistorisches Museum)

trimmings and mounted on a dappled horse. City officials wore long gowns of crimson satin and heavy chains of gold marvelously wrought. Red fabrics appeared in a regimental livery, and yellow in the capes and hoods of Sevillian villagers who had been summoned to attend, also on horseback. Admitted to the city, the bridegroom proceeded under a handsome canopy to the cathedral.

Isabel was staying at the Alcázar where Charles arrived two hours after dark, his way lit with torches. Upon seeing him, the Princess knelt and tried to kiss his hand. He bent down and raised her, embracing and kissing his bride. Then he led her by the hand into another chamber where they sat for a quarter of an hour among the many grandees present. Withdrawing, the bridegroom changed his traveling clothes for a rich costume in which he returned to be betrothed in person by the papal legate. After half an hour Charles again withdrew, and the grandees went to their lodgings. When the clock had struck twelve, an altar was prepared in Isabel's chamber, and about 2:00 A.M. the marriage ceremony was performed by the Archbishop of Toledo, witnesses being the Duke of Calabria and the Countess of Haro. Isabel's ladies also were present, but few gentlemen, as the thing was done "unexpectedly, although astutely". Charles went back to his chamber until Isabel should have disrobed. After she was in bed, he went in "to consummate the marriage like a Catholic prince".[25]

As Easter followed hard after, secular festivities were postponed while Holy Week was celebrated with great pomp. Several days of mourning ensued to honor the death of Charles's unfortunate sister Isabel, queen of Denmark. An English ambassador found the Emperor "marvelously altered since his marriage . . . 'full of dumps and solitary musings' ",[26] but this mood must have been swept away by April fifteenth when traditional gaiety took over—jousts on foot, tournaments, reed tilts, and other entertainments, including a third wedding for King Fernando's widow.

Two obstructions in the path to a papal coronation had been surmounted: the Emperor had a wife to leave in charge of the country and her dowry would be coming in. But remembering the explosion that had followed his previous absence, Charles felt that he needed an heir as well as an empress to leave behind him. That contingency was taken care of with the birth of Felipe on May 21st, 1527, at Valladolid. All Spain celebrated the happy event. Reed-spear tilters (see Fig. 9) at Valladolid rode in velvet *marlotas* and damask burnooses (Figs. 236, 244)—an orange-colored burnoose over a green *marlota*, a yellow over a brown, or matched garments in tawny. The exultant father appeared in white satin and velvet, accompanied by three noblemen also in white, except that they had combined with it details in his colors, red, silver, and yellow or gold. In a bullfight the Emperor himself lanced mightily at an attacking beast. It was during a tournament at this time that news arrived of his troops' brutal sack of Rome.

The Emperor was expected to take 10,000 foot soldiers and 500 noble horsemen with him into Italy. Wolsey in England was informed that Spain was unwilling to provide money, that both nobles and people opposed the trip. Biscuit and victuals for the voyage were assembled early in 1529 but had to be sold in March because Charles was not ready to sail. Also in March, at Toledo, he possessed himself of the Empress's best jewels to the value of 90,000 ducats, promising to pay for those lost or spent. The Emperor's funds were mainly those of his wife's dowry—forty mules laden with gold from Portugal and Castilla finally arrived at Barcelona—and he hoped to extract further sums from his ex-prisoner, François I. Meanwhile, he set men to search for horses with which to reward his servitors in Italy, and silversmiths and embroiderers to work on the cape and the crown he should wear, using gold, pearls, and precious stones in such quantity that no one could estimate how much they weighed or what they were worth. The Empress made the alb of very cunning and handsome workmanship in which he would be consecrated. Other necessities for the coronation were gold for the Pope and coins for the populace.

The Emperor finally got off on July 27th, 1529, from Palamós on the Costa Brava of Cataluña. For the ceremony he decided not to appear at the Pope's capital—that Clement and that Rome which had been so roughly treated by his lansquenets—but to have the Pope come to him at Bologna. Charles made his entrance early on November fifth, riding a dapple-gray horse, wearing complete armor except for a black velvet bonnet on his head and over the armor a gown of handsome gold brocade. The center of a great procession, he made his way to the plaza where Clement VII in full pontificals awaited him, seated on a spacious platform and attended by his clergy.

Proud Emperor and scheming Pope sparred for weeks—their apartments had connecting private doors—while the coronations waited. The iron crown of Lombardy was finally bestowed early on the morning of February 22nd, 1530, privately so far as the public was concerned, in the Palazzo chapel. Two mornings later, Charles's birthday and the anniversary of Pavia, the imperial coronation took place in the great church of San Petronio. Here the jewel-laden cape brought from Spain made its expected effect. After the ceremony, wearing the imperial crown and robes except for a cape of lighter weight, Charles rode forth with the Pope in the customary procession. A king-of-arms went before, tossing gold and silver to the crowd. Dukes, a Savoyard and a Bavarian, displayed the dress of their rank—a long gown of crimson velvet, a cloak of the same material, and a ducal hat garnished with rich stones. An Italian marquis had similar clothes and a jewel-trimmed marquis's hat. But it was the Spaniards who made the show. Among them, 150 in number, cloths of gold and silver were so common that to make any impression they had to be embroidered. The Marquis of Astorga, bearer of the scepter, had his gown and jerkin of crimson satin so heavily encrusted with gems and pearls in a design of plumes and dolphins that little satin could be seen.

Etchings by Nicholas Hogenberg present details of this extraordinary progress—banners bearing the Austrian double-eagle, trumpeters on horseback; macers, heralds, ambassadors, cardinals, dukes, other titulars, and infantry afoot or ahorse; Captain Antonio de Leiva borne in a chair. Pope and Emperor are there under a handsome canopy (Fig. 8), each in cope or cape riding a spirited horse. Between edges of the Emperor's cape appear folds of an alb, possibly that worked by the Empress. Mantles and gowns worn by Charles V at great ceremonies were kept for a time, and Felipe II's third wife, Isabel de Valois, was taken to see them displayed in the Alcázar at Toledo.

A full-length portrait (Fig. 13) records a costume in white and gold, richly furred with sable, believed by the Prado Museum to be that worn by the Emperor when he received the Lombardic crown. Single, full-length standing portraits had been known in

Northern Europe from the beginning of the sixteenth century. Also somewhat familiar was the exposure of aristocratic upperstocks, as in the portrait of Duke Heinrich the Pious of Saxony (1514) by Lucas Cranach the Elder (Dresden. Gemäldegalerie), and in that of an Italian nobleman (1526) by Moretto da Brescia (London. National Gallery). Duke Heinrich, standing with torso slightly twisted and about to draw his sword, wears gown, doublet, and upperstocks of dark material slashed in horizontal rows over lighter linings. The Italian leans on an elbow; his dark clothes are not completely explained, but one can distinguish upperstocks opened in cuts over a dark lining. In contrast, the Emperor (1532) stands erect, all details, including his upperstocks, clearly delineated. The left hand rests on the collar of a huge dog; the other on a dagger. Here is majesty at ease. In pose, proportions, and dress the figure is instinct with elegance, especially in the Titian version (Madrid. Museo del Prado), which is elongated. It is thought that François I left no standing full-length portrait, perhaps because his legs were not impressively designed.[27] In the famous cartoon of 1537 by Hans Holbein (London. National Portrait Gallery), Henry VIII still confronts his viewers from behind a skirt. The Emperor's portrait must have appeared as a splendid fashion plate, of some novelty to his contemporaries.

The change in costume silhouette, from column to broad rectangle, occurred throughout western Europe; it may have been due in a measure to the adoption of gunpowder. Well-aimed shots applied to the armored knight on horseback convinced others and finally persuaded him of what he had certainly become, a ponderous anachronism powerless to deal with the new realities. Foot soldiers began to be recognized as the important factor in battle. The Great Captain perceived this change and developed his infantry, insisting that a country to be strong must rely on native forces. He saw also the wisdom of a commander paying troops regularly, with his own coin or goods if necessary.

For those with vision less clear in this matter—for example, Emperor Maximilian who seldom had funds to match his schemes—there were made to order the thousands of tough, foot-loose, greedy men willing to enter military service without pay, on the prospect of the loot they could "liberate". These were the conspicuous foot soldiers of the day—Swiss who had defeated the Burgundians (1477) and Germans from the flatlands who became known (ca. 1486) as "lansquenets" *(Landsknechte).* The Swiss fought in breast plate and jambs, but the lansquenet abandoned armor in favor of stout padding, which increased the bulk of his garments. Furthermore, both Swiss and Germans decorated their clothing, to the limit of extravagance, with slashes over linings of contrasting color.[28]

"From all sides lords and noblemen crowded into the troop of lansquenets and fought in the foremost ranks, earning double wages, honor and cash."[29] Slashing soon found its way into courtiers' dress, as Duke Heinrich's portrait shows. It has been the custom to credit the invention of slashing to the foot soldier. Boehn quotes a chronicle from Switzerland, which reports that in 1490 tailors were having to learn the new "art of patching" introduced by returned fighting men. However, it seems that slashing already had been established in Italy,[30] that fecund inventor of fashions. A lady's figure by Ghirlandaio (1488) shows, between puffs of chemise sleeve at shoulder and sleeve back, a vertical line on the sleeve side, near the top, of five tiny puffs which can only be pull-outs of the white chemise sleeve through openings in the red, gold, and black dress sleeve (Firenze.

Church of Santa Maria Novella). While the Italians were taking their time about developing the slash, the Germans seized it and ran away with it. Phelipe el Hermoso brought Germans into Spain (1506), but cuts already had appeared a decade or more earlier in Spanish sleeves (Figs. 78, 84). Attending a tournament at Valladolid (1517), Charles V wore an elaborately slashed jerkin. The lansquenet occasionally seen in Spanish art (Fig. 5) is a modest creature in comparison with the flamboyant warriors portrayed in prints by Peter Flötner (?) and Daniel Hopfer.[31]

Together with slashing there came into style broad shoes and wide shoulders augmented by full sleeves. Thus was extinguished the Gothic constriction of the fifteenth-century figure (Fig. 10) and there flourished instead the expansive silhouette of Renaissance man (Fig. 6), who was breaking forth on all sides into new concepts of space.

In succeeding pages clothes of the period will be considered in detail. The gentlemen who wore them, how did they move? Proudly, to judge by Lazarillo's master, the squire. "Erect, with reposeful step, head and body swaying gently, cape end thrown over one shoulder or under an arm, right hand put to his side, he went out the door. . . . Up the street he walked with an aspect so genteel, and so self-controlled that anyone not an acquaintance would have thought him a near relative of the Count of Arcos, or at least the valet who dressed him."[32]

The Spaniard, using unguents, perfumes, and gloves, fussy about keeping his clothes clean, was thought by Italians to be pompous and fastidious, almost effeminate. "Neatly dressed, odoriferous . . . swaggering, with moustache erect . . . and with other niceties of his person" are the more attractive strokes in a description of the 1530's.[33] He demanded deference and respect; grave, composed, he was willing to accord them. Italians satirized the ceremonious reverences of the Spaniards, their interminable back-bendings and formal salutations, as Castilian longwindedness *(lungherias castiglianas),* but at the same time imitated their impressive way of taking off a hat and also their precise rules for determining who should take precedence in entering or leaving a house.

Apparent contradictions are resolved by Croce: "The *galas,* the ceremonies, the sighs, the luxury, and the pomp were in the Spaniards aspects of the smiling face of a warlike personality, of a triumphant, powerful, and almost fierce military society."[34]

II MEN'S DRESS

14   ca. 1497   **15**   1502–1506   **16**   1499–1513

17   1488–1495   **18**   ca. 1516   **19**   1518

20   ca. 1510   **21**   1518   **22**   1543

Hair Styles

"UNTIL THE DEATH of the Catholic King, Don Fernando of glorious memory [1516], all Spaniards wore their hair long and the beard shaven," says a faithful and observant contemporary.[35] The persistence of the caul into the late twenties argues for the continuance of long hair into the reign of Charles V.

Hair

The demand for handsome luxuriant hair was met in one way or another. At Naples (1504–1505) elderly men were dyeing their hair or "embellish-

Long hair trimmed diagonally

14 MARQUIS ca. 1497, detail from medal of Don Rodrigo de Bivar y Mendoza [1st marquis of El Cenete], Roman School under Innocent VIII, Alexander VI, and Julius II (Washington, D.C. National Gallery of Art, Samuel H. Kress Collection)

15 GENTLEMAN 1502–1506, from figure of bystander in *Martyrdom of St. Cucufas* by Anye Bru (Barcelona. Museo de Arte de Cataluña)

16 TOWNSMAN 1499–1513, from figure of bystander in *The Deposition* by Felipe Vigarny (Burgos. Cathedral, Trasaltar)

Long hair trimmed horizontally

17 YOUNG DANDY 1488–1495, from tomb of Pedro Martínez Gadea (Burgos. Cathedral, Cloister)

18 DUKE ca. 1516, from portrait of Juan de Aragón, 1st duke of Luna; later 16th-century copy by Roland de Mois (Madrid. Palace of the Duke of Villahermosa)

19 SWORDSMAN 1518, from pinnacle figure on silver *custodia* by Enrique de Arfe (Córdoba. Cathedral)

Bobbed hair

20 ARCHDUKE ca. 1510, detail of portrait of Charles V, emperor of the Holy Roman Empire as archduke of Austria (Edinburgh. The National Gallery of Scotland)

21 BOY 1518, from figure of bystander in the Tostado monument by Vasco de la Zarza (Avila. Cathedral, Trasaltar)

22 KING 1543, from figure of Ferdinand I, emperor of the Holy Roman Empire as king of the Romans, in commemorative plaque by Veit Arnberger (Innsbruck. Tiroler Landesmuseum Ferdinandeum)

ing" it, probably with false pieces.[36] Saint Teresa's father (1507) had false hair *(cabelleras postizas)* which he stored in molds *(moldes)* or in linen cases. For dressing his hair, which fell to the shoulder, he had curling irons *(tenacillas)* and many combs— one small, one of bone, two large and gilded.[37]

One phase of this style is illustrated in Figures 14–16. The hair from a straight fringe over the brow hangs in a long diagonal to the shoulders at back, the edge of the mass being rolled under. A shorter cut tending to this line can be seen in Italian medals from the mid-fifteenth century onward, but few there have the length and the luxuriance of hair that characterize Spaniards. Striking use was made of the style by Rodrigo de Mendoza (Fig. 14), who in 1497 was courting Lucrezia Borgia. His medal, thought to have been struck at that time, portrays him with a large cap. That the hair style required a generous growth is confirmed by the picture of a middle-aged spectator who in black cap and scarlet cape (Fig. 15) is watching an executioner at work. Further into the sixteenth century a townsman wearing this cut (Fig. 16) is carved with a brimless cap and jeweled band. Other good examples are a donor and his son who kneel, bareheaded, on the predella of a retable at Burgos (Church of San Gil, Chapel of Los Reyes).

Long hair was trimmed also to a horizontal line. A fashionable youth (Fig. 17) permits his locks, loosely waved, to stray over his shoulders. King Fernando's cousin, Juan de Aragón, who died at seventy-one in 1528, and who in his copied portrait (Fig. 18) looks at least ten years younger, keeps his hair neatly compacted, while that of a swordsman (Fig. 19) is twisted into long separate curls.

Some change in style may have come about soon after Charles V's arrival in Spain. He probably appeared wearing his hair cut to a little below the ears, much as Flemish barbers had kept it when he was ten (Fig. 20). Early evidence of such a trim being used in Spain is that of a boy (Fig. 21) who kneels beside a young man outside the main group in an important monument. Style changes did not escape the eye of the Emperor's buffoon, who found hair a fertile subject for comment—about a captain of the guard (1522) ardently wishing hair to stay long, about men-at-arms (1523) being dismissed for

23   1526–1529   **24**   ca. 1540   **25**   1568

Beard

23 EMPEROR 1526–1529, from double portrait of Charles V and Isabel de Portugal by Jean Mone (near Bruxelles. Staatsdomein van Gaasbeek)

24 EMPEROR ca. 1540, from bronze bust (cast) of Charles V, emperor of the Holy Roman Empire (The Hispanic Society of America)

25 ELDERLY HIDALGO 1568, from miniature of Foli del Burgo Canaus and Family in Philip II. *Carta ejecutoria.* Granada, 1568 (The Hispanic Society of America)

---

wearing long locks *(cabelleras).*[38] Returning to the bob, one is carried by a late example beyond the Peninsula to Charles's brother King Ferdinand (Fig. 22), an incorrigible conservative who at forty and even with an incipient ruff about his neck was still wearing the bob of his youth. Brantôme tells that when Emperor and King were reviewing troops together, a Spanish soldier called out, "Holy Majesty! I give you my pay. Have them shear your brother Ferdinand!"[39]

In the bridal relief of Charles V and Isabel de Portugal, dated 1526, the Emperor's hair is clipped short (Fig. 23), whereas a sculptured medallion at Palma de Mallorca, dated 1529, shows him still with a bob. Sandoval reports that it was in that year at Barcelona, before sailing to Italy, that the Emperor had his hair cropped in order to relieve head pains. All those in his company were shorn at the same time, some weeping over the loss of cherished locks.[40] Short hair continued to be worn in Spain until Felipe IV began to pair long sidelocks with the stiff, flat collar called *golilla.*

Beard

Face hair was a matter of interest. In an archbishop's house (1492–1507) men were commanded to shave every two weeks.[41] For such a purpose Saint Teresa's father owned half a barber's mirror, good scissors, and a new box of knives.[42] The subject comes up in a poem mourning the death of Fernando el Católico:

> Shed tears, gentlemen,
> They will be well employed.
> Let your beards grow. . .
> Nor leave your hair long.[43]

Charles V's countenance, with its prognathous jaw and ever-open mouth, was much improved in looks with the addition of a beard, a reddish-brown growth rather sparse at first. Opinions differ as to when this addition took place. Sánchez Cantón says that the Emperor did not cease to shave until 1529 and thinks that the earliest portrait showing him bearded is that (Fig. 151) at Chantilly.[44] But a German eyewitness in Sevilla at the time of the imperial wedding states that then Charles had a becoming beard,[45] and two documents dated 1526 show it— a portrait in a private collection and the sculptured relief (Fig. 23). Even in 1524 a correspondent had written to Infante Ferdinand that his brother Charles was "well-bearded" *(bien barbado).*[46]

The buffoon Francesillo implies that face hair was much discussed. He says that the Emperor and his grandees (1523) wished that one gentleman would not wear a beard like a bridle plume *(pluma de cabezal),* that two would not dye theirs, that another would thicken his for it looked like a pestilence-emptied town, and that a further pair would not kill each other over which had the fiercer one.[47]

Fully developed (Fig. 24), the beard stood out like a shovel with square corners. According to Norris, it was the custom for "many gentlemen on the Continent to dress the beard with warm wax to stiffen and thicken it and make it spread out broad at the bottom."[48] A late example of this form can be found in a Spanish patent of nobility (carta ejecutoria), a white-haired old gentleman (Fig. 25) wearing the broad, squarish style while another man of the family has his beard divided into the two points then fashionable.

Headgear

HEADGEAR FIGURED prominently in rites of courtesy. By uncovering his head (Fig. 26) a Spanish gentleman honored his betters and his equals or flattered his inferiors with unexpected flourishes. Celestina, on entering a church, found gentlemen old and young, abbots of every degree, ecclesiasticals from bishop to sacristan tearing off their bonnets in her honor, as though she had been a duchess.[49] The Great Captain never let baldness prevent him from paying this attention to those who spoke with him. But sometimes the demands of convention rankled: one of Lazarillo's masters had left Castilla la Vieja to avoid taking off his bonnet to a count, his neighbor.

"Sir, I said, if he was as you say and had more than you, you made no mistake in taking off your bonnet first, since you say that he also took off his to you.

". . . But considering the many times that I took off mine first, it would not have been amiss had he once been civil and anticipated me.

"It seems to me, Sir, said I to him, that I should not consider it so, especially with my betters and those who have more.

"You are a lad, he responded, and do not feel matters of honor. . . . Let me inform you that I am, as you see, a squire. But I vow to God that if I meet the Count in a street and he does not take off his bonnet to me, quite off, then the next time I come, I will enter a house pretending to have business there, or cross into another street if there is one, before he gets near me rather than take off my bonnet to him."[50]

Cap

Several types of headgear were worn in our period, though styles were settling down after the extravagances of the fifteenth century. A small, fitted cap (carmeñola), mentioned as early as 1464,[51] can be identified by a sculptor's contract (1489) and the corresponding effigy of Don Alvaro de Luna—"a carmeñola on the head and a rich jewel upon it".[52] In the worn stone the cap curves smoothly over the top of the head and carries, at its right side, the suggestion of an agleted lace. The cap of Juan de Padilla (Fig. 28) has a slit at front. Its right side, shaped into a point, is secured with an agleted lace over the left, which turns back in a jaunty curve. Another slit at its right edge is secured with a further lace. This treatment is more easily seen in Figure 27. For the Velasco effigy at Guadalupe (Cáceres) the contract (1467) specifies a carmeñola slit just above the ears so that front (delantera) or back (zaguera) can be turned up;[53] in Figure 26 the back has been so raised. The 1464 carmeñola is described as of white damask, but later ones were red as were those of Prince Juan; in 1488 he had five of the woolen fabric known as grana.[54] Seventeen of the same fabric were provided (1493) for the Prince's mozos de espuelas, footmen who accompanied a horseman to care for his animals.

For other headgear the terms most often used were gorra and bonete, which the early sixteenth century found distinct in their meanings: in 1525 two dozen red bonetes and four gorras, also red, had been exported from Sevilla to Santo Domingo.[55] At Toledo a candidate for membership in the boneteros' guild (1531) had to submit two perfect gorras, a blue and a white, and four bonetes, a blue, a white, a simple blue, and a simple white.[56] Carmen Bernis says that bonete was the generic term and gorra the specific. In actual practice she captions most pieces of sixteenth-century headgear as gorra, applying bonete to rather tall, brimless caps, especially those of physicians. Cunnington indicates that in sixteenth-century English usage "bonnet" and "cap" were alternative terms. "Cap" he applies to illustrations of soft headgear and "bonnet" to those showing a complete brim, especially the "halo" and the "slashed".[57] I shall follow his usage in captions but from Spanish texts translate bonete as "bonnet" and gorra as "cap", even though Brantôme says that for the French term bonnet, gorra was the Spanish equivalent.[58]

26   1496–1497   **27**   1499–1513   **28**   1500–1505

29   ca. 1492   **30**   ca. 1516   **31**   ca. 1524

32   ca. 1498   **33**   ca. 1500–1520   **34**   ca. 1520

Designated as "half caps" *(medias gorras)* were those with ample crown and partial brim or flap. The first illustration (Fig. 29) serves a double purpose: it shows the cap, blocked with narrow ridges at front and sides and probably at top and back also, that is frequently provided for late-Gothic effigies. It has also fairly deep side flaps turned up and standing apparently without support (see also Fig. 58). In later half caps, the flaps are secured at each side with a button (Fig. 30) or with ties across the front (Fig. 31). A painting (Fig. 55) shows a larger half cap with ties run through a slit in each vertical edge of the flaps and tied at the top of the front; this cap is worn over a roundlet. Sectioned flaps could surround the crown completely. A velvet *gorra* of the color of wine dregs (Fig. 32) has the sections turned up all round and secured with agleted laces. That a young knight could appear with front flap section raised, sides and back turned down, is seen in a red cap with gold medallion and black feather (Fig. 33). In a more elaborate

treatment (Fig. 34) the front section is divided into two, raised and buttoned together, while the rest of the brim, slit in short cuts, hangs loosely about the ears. Unslit, the back section hanging down could keep the nape warm in winter.

The headpiece called "flat cap" in England—a flat crown combined with a very narrow, flat brim—is illustrated not only for Charles V (Fig. 23) but also for his subjects. On an effigy (Fig. 35) the brim consists of two sections overlapped at the sides. As for the crown, a stalk *(rabito)* is pressed down at the top, while a cabochon jewel framed with pearls is fastened at one side. The same type was worn by Charles's son Felipe when a lad (Fig. 36). Here the ornament, a cluster of large pearls and perhaps a flower form, is placed on the brim-facing at front.

Bonnet

Turning to the bonnet, which had a continuous brim, one finds cuts making a battlemented edge on a brim which turns up off the face (Fig. 37). With brim also deeply cut—front turned down and sides raised—another bonnet looks soft and without spirit (Fig. 38); it is tied to the head with a narrow ribbon under the chin. A dashing example hangs, undoubtedly from a stout cord or ribbon, down the back of a Portuguese soldier (Fig. 39); grayish rose (in a color reproduction), it is trimmed with a violet and a yellow plume. About the crown, which shows a center stalk and four ridges bespeaking felt, the slashed brim forms wide loops except for a longer, straight portion at the back. Another battlemented brim is shown in Figure 56.

In 1493 twenty bonnets were provided for Prince Juan; after he had worn one three times, it became the perquisite of his chamberlain. Velvets often used were black, crimson, or mulberry-colored; crimson satin *(raso)* and *cebtí*, a popular silk as yet undefined, also were favored. Tawny were three bonnets of wool, one of velvet, and one of satin. An unspecified fabric, doubtless wool, was supplied in red, green, or black. The usual allowances of material were ¼ or ⅓ vara. A Segovia inventory (1503) lists a black bonnet ½ vara long, lined with red and green cloth. One of red wool knitted *(hecho de aguja),* more than ½ vara wide and 3 ¼ varas long, could have been a sort of stocking cap to be wound about the neck as a scarf or about the head as a turban.[59]

Ordinances for the trade have to do with bonnets made of wool. At Sevilla (1499) bonnet makers were to be examined in the making, from "the beginning

---

Cap *(Carmeñola)*

26 GUESTS AT A WEDDING FEAST 1496–1497, detail from *The Marriage at Cana* by Master of the Retable of the Reyes Católicos (Washington, D.C. National Gallery of Art, Samuel H. Kress Collection)

27 TOWNSMAN 1499–1513, from figure of bystander holding pincers in *The Deposition* by Felipe Vigarny (Burgos. Cathedral, Trasaltar)

28 YOUNG KNIGHT 1500–1505, from effigy of Juan de Padilla, School of Gil de Siloe (Burgos. Museo Arqueológico Provincial)

Half cap *(Media gorra)*

29 GENTLEMAN ca. 1492, from effigy of Juan García de Covarrubias (Covarrubias. Collegiate Church)

30 KING ca. 1516, from medal of Fernando V, king of Castilla and Aragón (Madrid. Museo Arqueológico Nacional)

31 GENTLEMAN ca. 1524, from effigy of Velasco de Béjar (Covarrubias. Collegiate Church)

Cap *(Gorra)*

32 ARCHDUKE ca. 1498, from portrait of Phelipe el Hermoso, king of Castilla as archduke of Austria (Paris. Musée National du Louvre)

33 KNIGHT ca. 1500–1520, from central figure, *Warrior Saint,* in retable by the Girard, or Gualba, Master (Montserrat. Monastery, Sala Gótica)

34 BOATMAN ca. 1520, from *St. Felix Cast into the Sea,* retable of St. Felix, by Joan de Burgunya (Gerona. Church of San Félix, Sala de Museo)

35   ca. 1520

36   ca. 1539

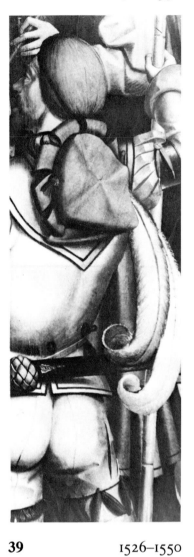

37   1514

38   ca. 1520

39   1526–1550

40   1493

41   ca. 1520

42   1526

with a needle" to the end, of two double bonnets (lined?), two simple ones, two *carmeñolas,* a double cap *(gorra)* with two turnbacks *(vueltas),* and a double *galota,* a sort of calotte with ear pieces.[60] Toledo in 1531—because of its good water and prime materials (the wool had to be shorn from a live animal and not from a dead one) and because the reverse side of its headgear was red deemed good for health—claimed to make the best bonnets and caps in Spain or anywhere else. To become a master *bonetero* required eight years of training. A man had to know the different kinds of wool and to be able to separate the four parts of a fleece, to know carding combs and the carding process, spinning, the proper shapes of bonnets when they were knitted *(enagujados),* how to do fulling—cleaning, shrinking, and thickening wool—to block *(amoldar)* bonnets and make them even *(aparejar),* to dye in red and in black. And to repair and press and line with paper. Eight years were really not enough time to learn it all. Each bonnet had to bear the device of

---

Flat cap

35 KNIGHT OF SANTIAGO ca. 1520, from effigy of Rodrigo de Cárdenas from Ocaña (The Hispanic Society of America)

36 YOUNG PRINCE ca. 1539, from portrait medallion of Felipe II, king of Spain as prince of Asturias (The Hispanic Society of America)

Bonnet with slashed brim

37 RUFFIAN 1514, from figure of Centurio in *Tragicomedia de Calisto y Melibea.* Valēcia, 1514. XVIII auto (Madrid. Biblioteca Nacional)

38 TOWNSMAN ca. 1520, from figure of bystander in *St. Felix Arraigned before Rufinus,* retable of St. Felix, by Joan de Burgunya (Gerona. Church of San Félix, Sala de Museo)

39 SOLDIER 1526–1550, from *Calvary,* retable of Setúbal (Setúbal. Museu Municipal)

Bonnet with brim partly extended

40 VINE PRUNER 1493, from *April* in Li, Andrés de. *Reportorio de los tiempos.* Burgos, 1493. sig.diiij (The Hispanic Society of America)

41 STONE THROWER ca. 1520, from *Martyrdom of St. Stephen,* retable of the Martyrs, attributed to Juan Ramírez (Granada. Museo Provincial de Bellas Artes, Palacio de Carlos V, Alhambra)

42 TOWNSMAN 1526, from figure of bystander in *St. Mary Magdalene Preaching,* retable of St. Mary Magdalene, by Pere Mates (Gerona. Cathedral, Tesoro)

---

the city and a distinctive one of the maker. A master recorded his trademark in a book at the time of his guild examination. Sometimes one would take the mark of a famous master, dead, and thereby profit unfairly.[61] An eighteenth-century book shows as trademarks a flask, an initial, a bird, the sword-cross of Santiago.[62] Sevilla, which also thought well of its bonnets, ruled that those entering from the world outside must be inspected, approved, and labeled with a wax seal before they could be sold in the city. Toledo is said to have exported bonnets beyond the Peninsula, those of red especially to Africa and Turkey, but an Italian merchant figured in early trade with the Indies. Masters of Spanish ships bought of a Genoese ten dozen bonnets in September 1508 and twenty dozen in November to carry to the port of Santo Domingo in the Island of Hispaniola.[63]

Bonnets could be handsomely adorned with ribbon, feathers, aglets, a badge, jewels. When Cortés became general of the Armada and began to spruce up, he set, presumably on his bonnet, a gold medallion and plumes very becoming to him.[64] The bonnet ornament for King Fernando at Naples, which cost the Great Captain so many ducats, consisted of a ruby and one of the largest pearls ever seen. A single white ostrich plume trimmed the black velvet bonnet of Charles V as he traveled towards Valladolid in 1517, and similar plumes the red bonnets of his brother's attendants. The feather that drooped over a bonnet brim of 1488–1495 (Fig. 17), projected horizontally in 1499 and 1508 (Figs. 46, 4), or rose vertically in the next decade (Fig. 41) was later superseded by curly tips (Figs. 13, 48, 51), which continued to be favored well into the next period.

Hat

A large black hat, for which no specific term has yet been found and which has been called "Flemish", was popular for portraits of the young Charles and his brother Ferdinand. Slightly upturned, the brim revealed its underside decoration of gold badge and aglets (Fig. 132) and sometimes of ribbon threaded in and out through slits. Certain woodcuts show the brim divided and overlapped at the slit, which turns it even more off the face; royalty should not hide its countenance. In a small portrait of the Emperor, itself a hat badge (Fig. 44), the brim remains level and the whole crown can be seen, large and flat. Similar hats are found

43   ca. 1515–1530

44   ca. 1520

45   1526

46   1499

47   1527

48   ca. 1530

49   ca. 1500–1510

50   1506

51   ca. 1530

in Spain. The brim of a Magus (Sevilla. Cathedral, Puerta de los Palos, 1520) is upturned all round; that of a handsome youth (Fig. 43) rises in front only. A modestly sized version—the brim faced with crimson velvet and decorated with a hat badge and buttons of gold (Fig. 45)—is worn by a courtier whose figure was recorded by a Portuguese working at Barcelona.

A hat with smaller crown had a broad, continuous brim curved up on all sides. In 1499 such a hat, carrying extravagantly long plumes and a round medallion, is cocked to one side over a *carmeñola* (Fig. 46). A tremendous black hat, almost Mexican in its proportions (Fig. 47), has a peaked crown. The brim edge is stitched with gold and further stitching adorns the peak. Climax of this series is the broad gray (Fig. 48) covered with black and

___

Hat with large crown

43 YOUTH ca. 1515–1530, from *Marriage of the Virgin,* retable of the Virgin (Burgos. Church of San Gil, Chapel of La Natividad)

44 YOUNG EMPEROR ca. 1520, from portrait (hat badge) of Charles V, emperor of the Holy Roman Empire (Wien. Kunsthistorisches Museum)

45 COURTIER 1526, from figure of king's entourage in *St. Eligius Weighs a Saddle* by Pedro Nunyes (Barcelona. Museo de Arte de Cataluña)

Hat with upturned brim

46 KNIGHT 1499, from *Artus Conquers the King who Holds Oliveros Imprisoned* in *La historia delos nobles caualleros oliueros de castilla y artus dalgarbe.* Burgos, 1499. sig.fiiij (The Hispanic Society of America)

47 GENTLEMAN 1527, from figure of bystander in *La Piedad* (Sevilla. Cathedral, Chapel of Santa Cruz)

48 NOBLEMAN ON HORSEBACK ca. 1530, from figure of Saint in *St. Julian Hunting,* main retable, by the Ororbia Master (Ororbia. Parish Church)

Wide-brimmed hat

49 OFFICIAL ON HORSEBACK ca. 1500–1510, from figure of Roman prefect in *St. Margaret Keeping Sheep,* retable of St. Margaret, by the Paredes Master (Paredes de Nava. Church of Santa Eulalia)

50 KING ON HORSEBACK 1506, from figure of Fernando V, king of Castilla and Aragón, in *Meeting of Fernando el Católico and Phelipe el Hermoso at Remesal de Sanabria* (Écaussines. Château de la Folie, Collection of Comte Charles-Albert de Lichtervelde)

51 NOBLEMAN ca. 1530, from figure of Saint in *St. Julian after Killing His Parents,* main retable, by the Ororbia Master (Ororbia. Parish Church)

white feather tips and secured with a black chin strap. Dark scallops, very likely velvet, lie along the brim edge. A similar exuberance of feather tips is illustrated in the Toledo *Celestina* of 1526.

Under Spain's insistent sun, protection from glare would be essential, and hats with shady brims *(sombreros)* are illustrated. The first example shown here (Fig. 49), brown in color and strangely perched atop a dark cap, bears a strong resemblance to the black felt worn with nineteenth-century regional dress in Extremadura, which had a moderately high, sharp-edged crown, encircled with a band of black velvet, and a brim with turned-up edge, crown and brim each carrying a black silk pompon. Here the pompon lies at the crown center. A similar hat, carried by Baltasar (Fig. 71), has a brown crown and a crimson brim, adorned with a gold band and round jewels set with pearls and emeralds. Berruguete shows a red-capped young man with a crimson hat hanging at his back, a pompon on the flat brim (Fig. 302), and a hat not unlike it can be seen in the Valencia *Celestina* of 1514. King Fernando, as he met his uncongenial son-in-law in open country, looked out from under a broad, drooping brim (Fig. 50); the painter, though generally observant, erred in making it dark, for according to an eyewitness the King wore that day, as he did every day, a white hat.[65] A large black one with gray crown and flat brim carrying black and white feather tips it secured with a black chin band (Fig. 51).

Sombreros appear in the documents. A man's inventory of 1490 lists one of straw trimmed with velvet and another of palm leaf, with silk.[66] Beginning at age seven, Prince Juan had a few *sombreros,* new or retrimmed, almost every year. Baeza mentions hats as made of straw or palm leaf, also of cotton, wool, or felt. Several were trimmed with black silk braids and cords; one with peacock feathers. Silk *cebtí* was used, black in trimming, crimson in facing. For the Prince in 1492 six ounces of gold worth 2,400 maravedis were lavished on a shape costing but 93; the making cost a ducat (375 maravedis). (A sculptor's salary for a year (1511, 1513) might be 1,200.)[67] Two white hats of the Prince's (1494) were trimmed not only with gold but also with blue and red braids, tassels, and buttons.

In order to enter the hatters' guild at Sevilla a candidate had to present a plain *(raso)* hat and another frizzed *(frisado)* of 32 ounces of wool, felted apparently, sound and whole with no needle stitching. A maker was not to add oil, bacon, or any grease, coal dust, goat's hair, or any blacking *(betún)*

52   1495   **53**   1496–1499   **54**   1498–1499

55   1526   **56**   1526   **57**   ca. 1530

58   1509–1515   **59**   ca. 1520   **60**   ca. 1521

whatsoever, but was to turn out his hats white or brown as the wool grew on the sheep.[68]

Another word for hat, *chapeo* (derived from the French), was used in the time of the Emperor. Calling on François I, captive at Madrid (1525), Charles took off a *chapeo* as he entered the King's presence, but—with what nuance of intent?—he kept on, as they embraced, a little red bonnet with *gualteras* (side pieces?). Meeting Leonor de Austria at Illescas (Toledo), the sovereigns entered her lodgings hats in hand but soon had them on again. Before the Queens, Leonor and Germana, Charles removed his *chapeo* and made them grand reverences. François stood by, hatted, until he was noticed, when he took off his *chapeo* and bowed deeply.[69]

Remaining covered in the royal presence was a privilege jealously prized by Spanish grandees. To Leiva, who had traveled in an armchair to meet his sovereign (Piacenza, 1529), Charles V insisted that the old soldier remain seated and keep on his hat. " 'What,' said the Emperor, 'shall the Grandees of Spain surround my throne with their hats on, whilst the veteran of seventy years, who has faced sixty battles for his lord, stand [!] before me a man of thirty, bare headed [?]' "[70]

Fiber headgear

Inasmuch as straw and palm leaf are mentioned in the documents, it appears safe to interpret a few illustrations as representing such materials. In one bonnet (Fig. 52) the low crown and inside of the upturned brim are woven continuously of palm-leaf strips, while the outside of the brim is faced with a fabric, perhaps felt. A bonnet entirely of palm leaf, decorated with miniature staves and gourd (Fig. 53), hangs by a cord on the back of the Pilgrim Saint. Another misericord of the Nájera choir shows in both crown and brim rows of hatchings that suggest coarse straw braids. In a half cap (Fig. 54) the tall crown is rendered as of fine straw braids, and the shallow partial brim, turned up, as of a plain-surfaced textile or felt.

Roundlet

A headdress worn in Spain more often by women than by men is the roundlet *(rollo)*, which seems to be the fifteenth-century chaperon stripped of crest and tippet. The roll is stuffed, probably with wool or goat's hair, and covered with a brilliantly patterned fabric. The front carries a prominent circular ornament. At Gerona the roundlet is illustrated under a large half cap (Fig. 55) and also under a bonnet (Fig. 56). A Navarrese painting shows one uncovered (Fig. 57) and the full bulk can be appreciated. It is interesting that these examples are found in the part of Spain nearest to Italy, where also men wore the roundlet.

Caul

Useful for holding long hair in place was the caul, often of net, gold or silk, fitting the head closely. Sometimes it covered the ears. The sculptor Forment shows himself in one of plain net (Fig. 58), narrowly bound at the edge and strengthened with a wider band farther back, under a half cap. A tormentor (Fig. 59) wears a caul of gold thread worked into a series of vivid stripes in macramé technique. The fullness is drawn together at front under a round button. A Portuguese example of

Fiber headgear

52 MAN—PALM-LEAF BONNET 1495, from misericord by Master Andrés and Master Nicolás (Nájera. Monastery of Santa María la Real)

53 PILGRIM—PALM-LEAF BONNET 1496–1499, from figure of St. James the Great, main retable, by Gil de Siloe (Burgos. Monastery of Miraflores)

54 TOWNSMAN—STRAW HALF CAP 1498–1499, from figure of bystander in *Jesus Bearing the Cross* by Felipe Vigarny (Burgos. Cathedral, Trasaltar)

Roundlet

55 COURTIER 1526, from figure of king's entourage in *St. Mary Magdalene Preaching*, retable of St. Mary Magdalene, by Pere Mates (Gerona. Cathedral, Tesoro)

56 TOWNSMAN 1526, from figure of bystander in *Jesus Preaching*, retable of St. Mary Magdalene, by Pere Mates (Gerona. Cathedral, Tesoro)

57 EXECUTIONER ca. 1530, from *The Beheading of St. John the Baptist*, retable of St. John the Baptist, by Juan del Bosque (Pamplona. University, Chapel)

Caul

58 SCULPTOR 1509–1515, from self-portrait, predella of main retable, by Damián Forment (Zaragoza. Cathedral of El Pilar)

59 TORMENTOR ca. 1520, from *St. Felix in Prison*, retable of St. Felix, by Joan de Burgunya (Gerona. Church of San Félix, Sala de Museo)

60 HALBERDIERS ca. 1521, from *Entrance of the Catholic Kings into Granada*, main retable, by Felipe Vigarny (Granada. Royal Chapel)

61   1506   **62**   1515–1525

Draped headdress

61 HORSEMEN 1506, from *Reed-spear Tournament at Valladolid* (Écaussines. Château de la Follie, Collection of Comte Charles-Albert de Lichtervelde)

62 HORSEMAN 1515–1525, from bullfight scene, staircase ramp (Salamanca. University)

netting (1526–1550), finished at the edge with a handsomely figured band, fits lower over the brow (*Jesus Nailed to the Cross.* Setúbal, Museu Municipal). Prince Juan had silk nets called *garvines* to wear at night. Cauls were made also of woven textiles. Vigarny gives such headdresses to halberdiers (Fig. 60): a green caul striped in red; a red, slashed, showing green puffs in the openings. Here also the material is gathered at front under a round medallion. In another such example, green with narrower cream-colored stripes (1525–1529), the medallion is jeweled. Saint Teresa's father's inventory (1507) lists three *cofias,* probably cauls, of fine linen *(holanda),* black worked in gold, and another, also of linen, embroidered in red and blue silk.[71] When a minor official asks permission to enter the establishment of La Lozana Andaluza, she gives orders to change the sheets, take his wig, and give him an *escofia*.[72] The Constable of Bourbon in Spain (1525) wore under a small black silk *chapeo* a gold *escofia* that did not allow a single hair to show.[73] A late mention is the record of five black silk *escofias* in the inventory of the great warrior, García de Paredes, drawn up at Bologna in 1533.[74]

Draped headdress

The turban frequently appears in such scenes as the *Epiphany* and the *Slaughter of the Innocents,* but I have not found it depicted in portraits or in secular woodcuts. However, forms of it certainly were worn at one time by Spaniards, as Vital's description of 1517 indicates. When Charles V was on the way to Valladolid, he was met in the road by the old Marquis of Villena, wearing a *toque* like the Saracens' and resembling one of the Wise Men from the East. Such a headdress was all of linen, 20 to 24 aunes long in Vital's estimate, and wound about the head so as to leave two ends, each an aune long, free at the sides for wiping the face. This *toque,* he says, had been worn in Castilla, but when he was there it had fallen into disuse except among elderly men who hated to give up their old customs. He saw it also on several countrymen.[75] The description fits the headdress worn, with two plumes added, by a horseman prepared to fight bulls (Fig. 62). It is wound about the head and two ends float beside it. Such drapery would seem to constitute the traveling headdress *(toca de camino)* which Baeza recorded: for making two such *tocas* 5 varas of linen at 220 maravedis were supplied (1486); their hem-finishings or pipings *(vivos)* cost 108 ½. Similar linen drapery with a Moorish name, *alhareme,* was worn in the reed-spear tournament (1424),[76] and with a draped headdress the players are seen (Fig. 61) in that celebrated in honor of Phelipe el Hermoso; a back view shows two streamers hanging. Reed-spear tilters of 1538 (Fig. 9) wear their drapery sometimes wound about the base of a tall, conical crown. A Christian inventory (1503) describes an *alhareme* as of linen 14 ¼ varas long and ⅔ vara wide, with narrow worked edge-bands *(orillas)* of white silk.[77] For the Prince 9 varas of Asturian linen, very fine, were provided (1489) to make an *alhareme* for the road. Another draped headdress known as *almaizar* appears in Christian inventories. Alvaro de Zúñiga (1468) had one 3 varas and a little more long; at the ends were gold cross-stitches *(cruces)* and macramé fringes *(rapacejos)* in black, brown, and tawny with little knots of gold. Recorded at the Royal Chapel, Granada, was a "very good" Moorish *almaizar* of white taffeta, 6 varas or more in length; woven with silk and gold, each end bore 12 lines of Moorish letters in gold.[78] The length of the *almaizar* could be 10 varas and more. Draped headdresses were used by women also.

Body Garments

Jerkin

The knee-length jerkin, worn over doublet or armor, under gown or cape, was a distinctive garment of our period. Spaniards termed the garment *sayo;* related to it were *sayete, sayón, sayuelo.* For this discussion *sayo* will be translated "jerkin", while the variants will be used in their Spanish form. *Sayete* and *sayuelo* imply something diminished from the norm, sleeveless perhaps (Fig. 66, 68) or with a shorter skirt (Fig. 67), while *sayón* is augmentative. The term *sayo* lingered on, though Alcega's patterns for it (1580) show the skirt of one as practically a peplum.[79]

Pedro Girón in 1537 described "the oldest jerkins remembered in Spain" as having been "entire, of four quarters with no joining *(trenzadura)* at the middle. And because they were narrow from the waistline downward, they were opened, and pieces of cloth called *jirones* (gussets or gores) were set in. These pieces began a little above the waistline, and there they were very narrow and pointed; lower down they widened. Of these triangles there were three or four in each garment. The jerkins were long, the sleeves very narrow; the body was high enough to cover almost all of the [doublet] collar at front, but at back two or three fingers' length of it remained outside." This statement corresponds

to the neckline of the white jerkin in Figure 10; Italian paintings of the fifteenth century, middle and later, show a similar neckline or one even more pointed at back.

"Afterward, jerkins with *jirones* inserted fell into disuse, and it became the style to wear them joined *(tranzados).* From the waistline upward they were fitted to the body *(justos al cuerpo);* from the waistline downward they were all of *nesgas* (gores) five or six fingers wide, sewed one to another because they made the skirt wider than had the *jirones*."[80] The final sentence suggests that *jirón* might mean "large gusset" and *nesga* "gore". A *sayon gironnat* (1490) was made of twenty-four long gores, twelve of black velvet and twelve of violet cloth of gold with frizzed nap.[81] A Spanish miniature (Fig. 77) records such gores in many colors, consecutively yellow, rose, dark blue, pink, green, bright red, dark blue, rose, green, and blue.

The development described by Girón can be illustrated. A page (Fig. 63) wears a jerkin with the fronts laid in folds that run continuously from shoulders to hem, indicating no seam at the waistline. A Magus (Fig. 10) shows continuous folds down the center back in a jerkin of white silk brocade. The neck, finished with heavy gold braid, dips to expose a V-shape of red doublet, probably of velvet, which reappears at the wrist. The jerkin of his companion Magus, green and hanging to below the knees, is hemmed with ermine. At the neck front, above long vertical folds, a heavy gold chain conceals all but the standing collar of another red doublet, also with red sleeves.

When a body fits smoothly and fold lines appear only in the skirt (Fig. 64), we may infer that the two parts have been cut separately and joined at the waistline. When the lines occur evenly all about the skirt (Figs. 66, 68, 71), the rounded folds between them may perhaps be called "cartridge pleats". There would seem to be a relation between the jerkin skirt and the military skirt called "bases", which also was set in cartridge pleats (Fig. 65). Of the latter there is at The Metropolitan Museum of Art (New York) an early sixteenth-century example of blue and metallic brocade, which is pieced horizontally but not gored. Padded with compacted flax and lined with heavy blue linen, it is ⅜ to ½ inch thick. The thickness gives roundness to the pleats which are held evenly in place with two strong narrow tapes, sewed inside horizontally at one third and two thirds, respectively, the height of the skirt.

63   1490's   **64**   ca. 1516   **65**   1508–1528

66   ca. 1497   **67**   1526   **68**   ca. 1530

69   ca. 1500–1510   **70**   ca. 1520   **71**   1531

The tape is run over a pleat edge and stitched through there, making a pinch ¼ or ⅜ inch deep, and then it is turned back and continued to the next pleat edge. I have found no mention of padding material in Spanish accounts of the jerkin. Perhaps a velvet lining gave enough support to keep the pleats rounded; certainly a fur lining would give that effect. Also, seams of the many gores indicated by Girón would help to set the pleats.

Jerkins could be of handsome material. An official on horseback (Fig. 69) has one of large-figured, black and gold brocaded velvet with body panel and foresleeves of plain, crimson velvet; the green at his neck belongs to the doublet. A man of high rank (Fig. 70) appears in brocaded silk patterned with a sweeping design of linear character. The low square neckline, the sleeve wrists, and the skirt hem are bordered with a dark fabric, possibly matched in tone by the narrow belt. Baltasar (Fig. 71) in

an *Epiphany* wears a Hispano-Moresque weave, yellow striped with kufic letters in green or red and finished at front and hem with a narrow red band.

Attendants had woolen jerkins, but those for Prince Juan were generally of silk, 12 in 1493, 11 each in 1494 and 1495. The most expensive material used was a brocade of black, drawn gold *(oro tirado)* priced at 35 doblas (12,775 maravedis) the vara; 4⅛ varas were required. "Drawn gold" refers to the thread of which the brocade was woven—gold wire. Crimson figured velvet *(altibajo)* at 3,000 maravedis was, in comparison, modestly priced. A lesser crimson velvet *(terciopelo)* could be had for 2,250–2,500, crimson satin *(aceituní)* for 2,270–2,700, crimson silk for 1,200–1,450. The other satin *(raso)* in crimson cost 1,200; in tawny, mulberry, or green, half as much. Of woolens, both London red cloth and Florentine black were priced at 1,300 maravedis. Green cloth from Valencia for hunting clothes— jerkin, cape, and hood—cost only 347 the vara. Cheap black cloth *(paño de brunete)* at 186 went into jerkins and other garments for the Bragança princes (1495), probably to be used in mourning.

Linings for Prince Juan's jerkins were handsome, of velvet, lamb, or ermine (see Furs). In those days furs were used not so much for display as for comfort in the cold stone rooms of winter. A mulberry velvet jerkin of the Prince (Fig. 100) betrays a fur lining by the fringe of gray hairs projecting at the edges.

This garment must have opened at front, though artists do not always make the fact obvious. Fronts could meet from the throat downward—collarless (Figs. 64, 70), with a small rolled collar, with a flat collar—or they could be turned back in revers (Figs. 72, 75, 80). They could also be cut to expose the chest with curved edges making a large U (Fig. 73), or with straight edges making a V (Fig. 74).

Sleeves were a vehicle of change. They could be long; a pair belonging to a *sayón* of 1490 reached to the ground "in the Spanish mode".[82] A long sleeve might be opened vertically near the top (Fig. 75) to let the arm and the doublet sleeve through, leaving a long tube to hang empty, or it might be cut up from the hem to above the elbow (Figs. 76, 77), so that when a man walked or rode, his sleeves must have flowed out like wings behind him. A generous sleeve with a tight wrist (Fig. 4) might carry one or two long vertical cuts, exposing the doublet sleeve through the middle. Open at the wrist, a sleeve might vary there from wide (Fig. 72) to very wide. Narrow sleeves mentioned by

Jerkin and Bases

63 PAGE—EARLY-TYPE JERKIN 1490's, from figure of page on tomb of Martín Vázquez de Arce (Sigüenza. Cathedral)

64 KING—JERKIN ca. 1516, from figure of King-Saint Sigismund by Juan Gascó (Barcelona. Guerin Collection)

65 DUKE—BASES 1508–1528, from effigy of Juan de Aragón, 1st duke of Luna, Genoese-Neapolitan School (Montserrat. Monastery)

Sleeveless jerkin, *Sayete, Sayuelo*

66 PAGE ca. 1497, from *Miracle of St. Narcissus*, retable of St. Narcissus, by the St. Narcissus Master (Valencia. Cathedral)

67 FOOTMAN 1526, from figure of Sosia in *Tragicomedia de Calisto y Melibea*. Toledo, 1526. XIII aucto (London. The British Library)

68 NOBLEMAN ca. 1530, from figure of Saint in *St. Julian after Killing His Parents*, main retable, by the Ororbia Master (Ororbia. Parish Church)

Jerkin material

69 OFFICIAL—VELVET PLAIN OR BROCADED ca. 1500–1510, from figure of Roman prefect in *St. Margaret Keeping Sheep*, retable of St. Margaret, by the Paredes Master (Paredes de Nava. Church of Santa Eulalia)

70 COURTIER—BROCADED SILK ca. 1520, from figure of St. Sebastian in *St. Martial and St. Sebastian* by Juan Gascó (Barcelona. Museo Diocesano)

71 KING—HISPANO-MORESQUE SILK 1531, from figure of Magus in *Epiphany* by Fernando Yáñez de la Almedina (Cuenca. Cathedral)

72   1499

73   ca. 1530

74   1531–1536

75   1489–1495

76   ca. 1496

77   1515

78   1496

79   1518

80   1527

Girón ran a fair course (Figs. 78–80). In the most popular style a full top-puff was combined with a snug foresleeve (Figs. 64, 69, 81–83). The last example (Fig. 83) shows an early use of the shoulder-armscye trim *(brahón)*, possibly of the loops illustrated in Figures 108–110.

Jerkins without sleeves were at least once (1517) called "Flemish" *(senza maniche, alla fiamenga)*.[83] A young page (Fig. 66) wears such a jerkin, red with black bands, over an apricot-colored doublet. The sleeveless jerkin of red, black, and gold brocade (Fig. 68), worn by a noble patron, lets through elaborate doublet sleeves of crimson velvet panes. A footman (Fig. 67) appears in a sleeveless *sayete* or *sayuelo* short enough to reveal upperstocks.

Of slashing in Spanish jerkins, early examples consist of two cuts *(cuchilladas)* in the long tight sleeves worn by young men (Figs. 78, 84). Later, a foresleeve would be divided into sections and cut vertically (Figs. 85, 86). Slashing flourished at Na-

ples by the time of the Great Captain. There, the bodies of a jerkin and a cloak matched in brown were cut to reveal a lining of tawny damask. By 1517 this feature had been fully developed. At Charles's entrance into Valladolid he wore a rich jerkin bipartite in his colors, yellow, white, and red. One side of drawn gold *(or trect)* and the other half of cloth of silver, both were "cut in great slashes through which one could see the [lining of] crimson satin. Slashes in the cloth of gold were tied with love knots of silver thread, those in the silver with gold. There must have been a hundred slashes and more in the jerkin, all so well set out that one could not have arranged them better."[84] In more subtle ostentation metallic cloth served as the lining to be glimpsed only through tiny slashes in the satin covering, white over gold, crimson over silver.

Of all the jerkin trimmings detailed in *Questiõ de amor*—a historical novel laid in the Spanish-dominated society of Naples (1508–1512)[85]—and in Vital's chronicle of Charles's early days in Spain (1517–1518), painters have recorded only the most elementary—bands (called "guards" in England) of contrasting fabric applied sometimes in groups of three (Fig. 87, black on yellow), sometimes singly or in pairs (Fig. 66, black on red). Baeza (1493) assigns three half-vara lengths of black velvet to be used for trimming three jerkins in black damask, mulberry satin, or mulberry silk. Besides bordering edges, bands could lie across each other forming squares, or in short lengths parallel like hatchings. In 1537 Charles V discouraged such trimming by allowing on the outside of a man's garment only one band *(faja)* up to 4 fingers wide, or from two to four narrow strips *(tiras* or *ribetones)* that totaled the same width.[86]

A spectacular form of elaboration already mentioned was to make the garment bipartite *(a mitades)* of contrasting fabrics. In 1495 Prince Juan had such a jerkin, one half *(medio sayo)* cut from a vara of London red cloth and the other from 1⅓ vara of yellow from Rouen. The yellow or crimson satins allowed for trimming (⅔ vara each) doubtless were cut into bands and applied on the opposite colors, as in a case at Naples where, on a jerkin of white velvet and black satin, bands of the materials were counterchanged. A jerkin could also be put together in quarters *(cuarteado, a cuartos)* or be cut from materials joined in squares like a checkerboard *(a escaques)*. The most complicated example at Naples was both bipartite and checkered, the squares on one side of rich brocade

---

Jerkin front

72 KNIGHT 1499, from *How Oliveros Departed Alone* in *La historia delos nobles caualleros oliueros de castilla y artus dalgarbe*. Burgos, 1499. sig.a⁷ (The Hispanic Society of America)

73 NOBLEMAN ca. 1530, from statue of St. Julian, main retable (Ororbia. Parish Church)

74 KING 1531–1536, from figure of young Magus in *Epiphany* by Juan Rodríguez and Lucas Giraldo (Avila. Cathedral, Trascoro)

Long, slit jerkin sleeve

75 KING 1489–1495, from figure of Fernando V, king of Castilla and Aragón, in *Surrender of Castil de Ferro*, choir stall, by Master Rodrigo (Toledo. Cathedral)

76 KING ca. 1496, from figure of Magus in *Epiphany*, scenes of the Nativity, by Alonso de Sedano (Burgos. Cathedral, Museo Diocesano)

77 ARMORED KNIGHT 1515, from miniature in *Fundación del Mayorazgo del Marqués de Villena*. v⁰fxvi (Madrid. Museo Lázaro Galdiano)

Narrow jerkin sleeve

78 YOUTH 1496, from Aesop. *Libro del ysopo*. Burgos, 1496. fXLI (Paris. Bibliothèque Nationale)

79 COURTIER-HUNTSMAN 1518, from figure of St. Hubert in panel of St. Mark by Vasco de la Zarza (Avila. Cathedral, Trasaltar)

80 PAGE 1527, from *La cronica del rey don Rodrigo* by Pedro del Corral. Valladolid, 1527. Title-cut (The Hispanic Society of America)

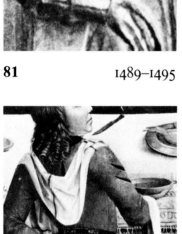

81   1489–1495

82   ca. 1515

83   ca. 1530–1540

84   1496–1497

85   ca. 1525–1530

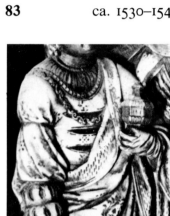

86   1520–1534

87   ca. 1520

88   ca. 1520

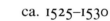

89   1540–1550

and crimson satin, those on the other of brocaded satin and crimson velvet. At Bologna (1529) the Emperor's pages had jerkins of yellow velvet striped with bands of mulberry, the left sleeve checkered in those colors.

The simplest kind of stitched ornament was appliqué. At Naples the bipartite, checkered jerkin just mentioned had crosses of Jerusalem—cut from the fabrics and decorated with silver cord—counterchanged on the squares. Among Charles V's contemporaries (1517–1518) cloth of gold or of silver in the shape of leaves and scrolls or of dragons was applied to crimson satin or velvet. Netting also might be listed under appliqué. Netting of silver cord, with small silver doorjambs *(batientes)* attached at the knots, spread over the yellow satin half of a Naples jerkin, the other half being of white satin.

Full-topped jerkin sleeve

81 PAGE 1489–1495, from *Siege of Loja,* choir stall, by Master Rodrigo (Toledo. Cathedral)

82 PAGE ca. 1515, from memorial to Alonso II de Fonseca (Salamanca. Casa de las Muertes, Façade)

83 PAGE? ca. 1530–1540, from figure of youth with angel, main retable, attributed to Juan and Pedro Gascó (San Esteban de Bas. Parish Church)

Slashed jerkin sleeve

84 PAGE—NARROW SLEEVE 1496–1497, detail from *The Marriage at Cana* by Master of the Retable of the Reyes Católicos (Washington, D.C. National Gallery of Art, Samuel H. Kress Collection)

85 ARMY COMMANDER'S SON—FULL-TOP SLEEVE ca. 1525–1530, from statue of St. Martin from Cacabelos (The Hispanic Society of America)

86 KING—SECTIONED SLEEVE 1520–1534, from figure of Magus in *Epiphany* (Huesca. Cathedral, Chapel of El Sacramento)

Jerkin trimming

87 GENTLEMAN—VELVET BANDS ca. 1520, from figure of bystander in *St. Felix Preaching,* retable of St. Felix, by Joan de Burgunya (Gerona. Church of San Félix, Sala de Museo)

88 KNIGHT COMMANDER—JEWELED BANDS ca. 1520, from effigy of Comendador Cristóbal de Santisteban, destroyed, formerly at Convent of San Francisco, Valladolid; drawing by Valentín Carderera y Solano (The Hispanic Society of America)

89 EMPEROR—EMBROIDERY 1540–1550, from water color of jerkin in *Inventario iluminado de . . . la Armería de Carlos V* (Madrid. Armería Nacional)

The embroideries challenge imagination. On a crimson satin jerkin at Naples, a grapevine with runners, leaves, and grapes, ripe or unripe, was worked in relief with drawn-gold or silver thread and colored silks. Other motifs were a gold eagle with fire issuing from it set on crimson satin, and a bull poised above burning logs of gold in high relief on black velvet. Place was found also for the mottoes which were so important. One jerkin announced in letters of gold or scarlet on a white band:

> Happiness has not deserted me,
> I left its company.[87]

The motifs in Charles V's jerkin (Fig. 89) are leaf-and-flower scrolls of heavy gold scaled to the size of the crimson skirt panels and to smaller panels in the body. A curious detail is the fact that the front panel is not centered.

Some Spanish nobles blazoned their jerkins with precious stones, as is indicated in a now-lost effigy (Fig. 88). Diamonds, rubies, emeralds, balas rubies, and pearls were set along front openings of a cloth-of-gold jerkin worn by the Duke of Alba (1518).

For ultimate extravagance take the small repoussé motifs, mostly of silver but sometimes of gold, in a multiplicity of designs—dragon, medallion in antique style, crescent moon, thistle leaf, pomegranate, chain, wheat sheaf—that were sewn on jerkins and in larger size on horse caparisons. After a tournament the tiltyard must have been strewn with precious bits. The only possible illustration I have found is that of a lance rest *(ristre)* in relief repeated on the long gown of Juan II (Fig. 258). Such ornaments, however, have a lengthy history. Gold reliefs were lavishly used by pre-Christian Scythians. A Swiss convent preserves a fragment of red velvet from a medieval queen's gown that still carries over 1,300 such pieces in silver—deer, unicorns, triangles, flowers, leaves, grape clusters, disks, etc.—each pierced generally with three or more holes at the rim through which it is sewn with red thread to the velvet. Animal figures are caught over the legs. Henry VIII, celebrating the birth of a son (January 1st, 1511), invited court ladies to pick off the golden letters and devices that ornamented his dress and that of his courtiers. He was overheard by common people who rushed in and plucked to such effect that the King was reduced to doublet and hose. A London shipmaster sold the beaten-gold letters he had snatched for 3 pounds, 14 shillings 8 pence.[88]

A telling description of the Spanish use of decora-

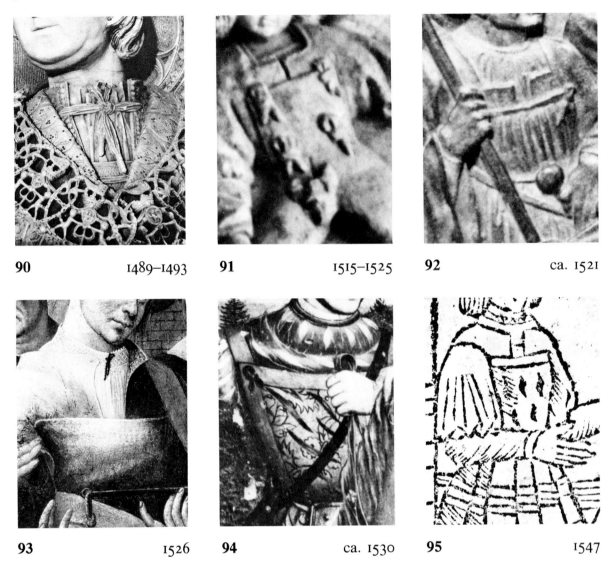

90   1489–1493   **91**   1515–1525   **92**   ca. 1521

93   1526   **94**   ca. 1530   **95**   1547

Stomacher

90 KING 1489–1493, from effigy of Juan II, king of Castilla, by Gil de Siloe (Burgos. Monastery of Miraflores)

91 PAGE 1515–1525, from bullfight scene, staircase ramp (Salamanca. University)

92 HALBERDIER ca. 1521, from *Entrance of the Catholic Kings into Granada,* main retable, by Felipe Vigarny (Granada. Royal Chapel)

93 COURTIER 1526, from figure of king's entourage in *St. Eligius Weighs a Saddle* by Pedro Nunyes (Barcelona. Museo de Arte de Cataluña)

94 NOBLEMAN ON HORSEBACK ca. 1530, from figure of Saint in *St. Julian Hunting,* main retable, by the Ororbia Master (Ororbia. Parish Church)

95 SERVANT 1547, from scene of Aesop carrying fowls in *Libro del sabio y clarissimo fabulador ysopo.* Toledo, 1547. *f* VIII (The Hispanic Society of America)

tive letters was "newly printed" in 1542: "Until today [Lisandro] you serve and celebrate [Roselia] with a thousand reed-spear games, and tournaments, with magnificent clothes on your person and various liveries on your servants over which you spread letters of passion, all the clothes bearing the name of your lady in letters both embroidered and *chapadas* (cut from thin sheets of precious metal). Even on the horse trappings and on the crest of your helmet you take pleasure in inscribing her name."[89]

The use of letters as costume decoration must have been stimulated by if not derived from Muslims, among whom inscriptions often were woven into textiles.

Stomacher

That the stomacher existed in Spain there can be no doubt; illustrations reveal it. But comparatively little evidence appears in the texts. English in this respect is precise with "stomacher" and "placard"; French is vague with *pièce,* anatomically exact with *pièce d'estomac.* For the Spanish term *puerta* I am indebted to Carmen Bernis, who discovered it in Antonio de Torquemada's satirical colloquies, first published in 1553. Speaking of clothes worn "not long ago", he says that jerkins, "low-necked like women's chemises, had a very small *puerta* in front of the breasts, secured with four ribbons or points."[90] A document of 1505 gives its length as one-half vara and its greatest width as a long quarter vara.[91]

The points are shown with amusing emphasis in a stone relief (Fig. 91). Through paired eyelets the ties were passed forward through the stomacher and knotted in a single loop. This method of attachment is used in all cases where the detail is clearly rendered. Figure 91 and other reliefs of the same series are the only examples yet encountered that show points at the lower corners.

Stomachers generally appear smooth and flat, as in the effigy of Juan II where the accessory (Fig. 90) is seen only as a triangle of crosshatching with pearled edge, used over the doublet and under the cloak. Gathered stomachers were in vogue in France under Charles VIII (1470–1498), and a Spanish example—green tied with a gilt-agleted red lace over a green jerkin—is worn by a halberdier (Fig. 92).

As an area of concentrated embellishment, the stomacher riveted attention. That worn by the young Charles V for his entry into Valladolid (1517) is described by the complacent Vital: "The *pièce* in front of the breast carried two score slashes tied, like the others [of its jerkin], some with gold thread, others with silver. This piece was enriched with many fine, large balas rubies, so beautiful that their value is beyond my computation. And it was a rich and noble thing to see those stones shine against the sun. Because of their reverberation, beauty, and clarity, they dazzled the eyes beholding them. Of that beauty and of the number of those great balases I can well speak, since I had charge of them for several days in my wardrobe chests containing all the King's clothes." Later, in a tournament, Charles V wore a stomacher of crimson satin striped with a vertical ray of gold and trimmed with disks *(rondz),* a hand's breadth wide, of knotted silver and sky-blue silk embroidery. "Not a disk but was tied on with cords and aglets, more than a hundred of them. This I know, because at the command of the King himself I had them made."[92] In another tournament (February 1518) Spanish nobles were not far behind. With a cloth-of-gold jerkin the Duke of Nájera wore a stomacher laden with precious stones estimated to be worth great sums. The Marquis of Aguilar had his trimmed with pearls as well as with gem stones.

Cloth of gold is suggested in the greenish-yellow stomacher (Fig. 93) of a dashing courtier accompanying a king. Here no ties are visible. A second handsome example is that worn by a horseman (Fig. 94), black and gold brocade cut with diagonal slashes, bordered with a band of plain material, and tied on with black laces. The stomacher is recorded in *Aesop.* A servant has it plain in a woodcut of the 1521 Sevilla edition, but in the 1547 of Toledo the servant's figure is reversed (Fig. 95), the sleeve-puff is larger, and the stomacher is slashed vertically with small cuts. Two sets of narrow, horizontal bands, as in 1521, persist on the jerkin skirt. The slashed stomacher is worn by men of higher category also in woodcuts of both editions.

Examples illustrated hardly suggest the gorgeous pieces worn by the young Charles and his entourage.

Doublet

The doublet (*jubón* from the Arabic *ýubba*), a neck-to-waist garment linked to the hose, was fated to develop into an independent piece that eventually became the waistcoat *(chupa).* In our period, pages and soldiers normally appeared in doublet and hose. To wear such attire in public was unusual for a gentleman, but King Ferrante of Naples found excuses to remove a jerkin in order to display his good figure. In moments of stress anyone might so appear. During the sack of Rome the Portuguese ambassador was taken in doublet and hose *(en cuerpo)* and led off to prison. The Great Captain in doublet and hose would lead his soldiers in an assault. Only in scenes of action is the doublet completely revealed.

Doublets played a part in the battle of Pavia. Charles V's general, Marquis of Pescara, wishing to convey cash to his German fighters, ordered two pairs of doublets made of fustian. One pair, padded with three thousand escudos, he entrusted to a couple of peasants who were bidden to set up a shop

96   1505

97   1506

98   1526

99   ca. 1475–1480

100   ca. 1485

101   ca. 1496

102   1489–1495

103   1507

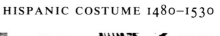

104   ca. 1530

in the French camp. Two soldiers received the other doublets. The soldiers went into the camp and ordered coats *(casacas, casaquillas)* made by a tailor. Just before collecting the finished garments, they called at the peasants' shop and exchanged their doublets for those padded with escudos. The money reached Pescara's Germans, and he won the battle. François I having been less considerate of his mercenaries, they let him be captured (Fig. 7) and stripped to his doublet.[93]

Well-fitted, padded, buttoned or laced down the front, pierced with holes along the lower edge to receive points from the hose, the doublet might carry a short skirt. Standards of fit and finish were high; doublet makers *(jubeteros)* formed a special branch of the tailoring trade. At Granada in the 1540's, an aspirant had to pass two years as apprentice and two as workman under a master before presuming to apply for guild membership, a matter entailing two or three days of acute questioning and convincing demonstration. So demanding was the craft that thirty years of practice would not ensure that a master understood it completely.[94] Every human frame was different.

For doublet makers at Sevilla (1522) ordinances were drawn up. Silks, woolens, and fustian were the materials. Brocade was to be cut lengthwise of the goods, the design right side up in collar and sleeves as well as in the body. So expensive a fabric required three linings, one of linen colored like the brocade, another of coarse canvas, and a third of white linen. Cotton was the stuff for padding, not wool or goat's hair *(borra)* or any other thing. The client who preferred fewer layers of linen and less cotton should be humored. Doublets of minor silks received only two linings, the canvas and one linen in the body, the white linen and the fabric-colored one in the sleeves. Bad canvas and old linen were unacceptable. As examination pieces for guild entrance a *jubetero* had to make a satisfactory doublet in the French style (with wide sleeves) and another in the Castilian. Fustian doublets could be produced for the ready-to-wear trade as well as to order;[95] at Granada such garments might be padded with wool. There the rules demanded also a reinforcement of tailor's canvas *(entretela)* in sections where eyelets for laces were to be made[96] (For laces or points see Figs. 224–235).

A document of 1512 describes a doublet of white linen *(holanda)* and cotton as quilted *(colchado)*.[97] In Vives's *Diálogos* (1538) a lad being dressed is asked whether he will wear a simple doublet or a quilted. He chooses the simple because in it, when he plays ball, he can move faster.[98] Ordinances of 1566 speak of doublets as being *estofados*,[99] that is, with backstitching round designs in cotton forming reliefs. Alcega (1580) suggests that, in cutting satin for a doublet to be backstitched, three fingers be added to the length, because the stitchers *(pespuntaderas)* would take up the length as they sewed; the width they reduced very little.[100]

By using old materials, washed, dyed, or turned, doublet makers could be guilty of deception, making buyers believe their garments to be new. At Sevilla (1522) old-clothes men were not allowed immediately to rip up or dye things they had bought, they could only mend them. Victims of robbery who came looking for their clothes would not recognize them if they had been altered. Secondhand garments

---

Parti-colored doublet

96 SOLDIER—PLAIN AND STRIPED FABRICS 1505, from figure of soldier, German woodcut of 1505, in Livius, Titus. *Las quatorze decadas.* Çaragoça, 1520. *f*CXI (The Hispanic Society of America)

97 ATTENDANT—LARGE CHECKS 1506, from *Reed-spear Tournament at Valladolid* (Écaussines. Château de la Follie, Collection of Comte Charles-Albert de Lichtervelde)

98 SERVANT—SMALLER CHECKS 1526, from figure of Tristan in *Tragicomedia de Calisto y Melibea.* Toledo, 1526. XIV aucto (London. The British Library)

Doublet collar

99 COURTIERS ca. 1475–1480, from *Banquet of Herod,* retable of St. John the Baptist, by Pedro García de Benabarre (Barcelona. Museo de Arte de Cataluña)

100 PRINCE ca. 1485, from figure of Juan, prince of Asturias, in *The Virgin of Mercy with the Catholic Kings* by the Milá Master (Burgos. Convent of Las Huelgas)

101 KING ca. 1496, from figure of Magus in *Epiphany,* scenes of the Nativity, by Alonso de Sedano (Burgos. Cathedral, Museo Diocesano)

Doublet with low neckline

102 PAGE 1489–1495, from *Siege of Alcora,* choir stall, by Master Rodrigo (Toledo. Cathedral)

103 EXECUTIONER 1507, from *The Beheading of St. John the Baptist,* retable of St. John the Baptist, by Juan Gascó, destroyed (formerly Sant Joan Galí. Parish Church)

104 FLAGELLATOR ca. 1530, from *The Flagellation of Jesus,* main retable, by the Ororbia Master (Ororbia. Parish Church)

105   1510–1530   **106**   1520–1530   **107**   1525–1529

108   ca. 1510   **109**   ca. 1520–1530   **110**   1526–1550

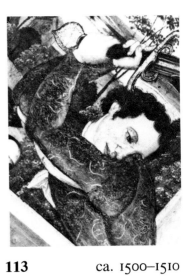

111   1489–1495   **112**   1497   **113**   ca. 1500–1510

had to hang at a shop door for three days, and the dealer had to declare to the authorities how long he had owned them. He could not unmake them until eight days had passed.[101]

Fabrics used in doublets for Prince Juan in his fifteenth year are named in Baeza's accounts (1493): satin in mulberry color; silk in blue, crimson, mulberry, or black; brocaded satin in mulberry, white, tawny, or green; brocaded velvet in tawny, black, or green. Black velvet is cited for trimming, and crimson brocaded velvet "rich and wide" for sleeves and collar. Contrast was employed in color (white body with mulberry-colored sleeves, both of brocaded satin) or in fabric (silk body and velvet sleeves, both black, or brocaded satin body and brocaded velvet sleeves, both tawny or green). Where

Doublet with square or round neckline

105 SWORDSMAN 1510–1530, from *Presentation of the Head of St. John the Baptist* by the Astorga Master (Chicago. Art Institute)

106 COURTIER 1520–1530, from *Investiture of a Knight of Santiago,* retable of St. James, attributed to Cristóvão de Figueiredo (Lisboa. Museu Nacional de Arte Antiga)

107 KING 1525–1529, from figure of crowned saint, choir stall, by Andrés de Nájera and Guillén de Holanda (Valladolid. Museo Nacional de Escultura)

Doublet neckline with slashed trim

108 ARCHDUKE ca. 1510, detail of portrait of Charles V, emperor of the Holy Roman Empire as archduke of Austria (Edinburgh. The National Gallery of Scotland)

109 SPEARSMAN ca. 1520–1530, from *St. Vincent on the Rack,* retable of St. Vincent, by Juan Gascó (Vich. Museu Episcopal)

110 PAGE 1526–1550, from *Epiphany,* retable of Setúbal (Setúbal. Museu Municipal)

Narrow doublet sleeve

111 KING 1489–1495, from figure of Fernando V, king of Castilla and Aragón, in *Surrender of Castil de Ferro,* choir stall, by Master Rodrigo (Toledo. Cathedral)

112 MAN 1497, from *[Man with a Beam in his Eye]* in Gulielmus Parisiensis. *Postilla super epistolas et evangelia.* Sevilla, 1497. *f*68 (Sevilla. University, Library)

113 EXECUTIONER ca. 1500–1510, from *The Martyrdom of St. Margaret,* retable of St. Margaret, by the Paredes Master (Paredes de Nava. Church of Santa Eulalia)

materials differed, the richer in color or weave went into the sleeves. The body of these doublets requiring only ½ to ⅔ vara, it seems unlikely that they had much of a skirt. Two-thirds or ¾ vara were allowed for sleeves.

For hot weather, doublets were made of thinner materials. A sailor drowned at sea (1530) left on board two old linen ones worth but 93 maravedis for both.[102]

Like the jerkin, a doublet could be parti-colored. In a German woodcut of 1505 circulated in Spain in 1520 (Fig. 96), the front panel is divided between plain material and striped. Half crimson and half gray-green is the doublet of a spearsman (Fig. 109). At the May meeting with Henry VIII (1520) the young Emperor's was half of silver brocade and half of silver or gold in alternate stripes. A doublet of large irregular squares in black or white (Fig. 97) is worn by a footman carrying reed-spears in a tournament attended by Phelipe el Hermoso. Charles V in July 1520 had one of gold brocade checkered with silver brocade and another of gold and silver lamé put together in triangles.[103] Doublet sleeves with checkered puff and foresleeve striped diagonally enliven the sleeveless jerkin of Tristan, Calisto's footman (Fig. 98).

Complaining that competition in dress was ruining the country, officials in 1523 persuaded their sovereign to renew the decrees against the use of elaborate materials. Artisans were forbidden to wear any silk at all, except in doublet and headgear.[104]

Fashion changes focused on neckline and sleeve. In the decade before our period and even earlier, the doublet had a collar that stood high at back, hugging the occiput. At front the collar-ends, cut on a downward slant, remained apart, as in Figure 99; one man's collar is of red brocade edged with black, the other's of plain materials in cool red or blue with rose-red facing. The same Girón who described the jerkin (1537) says, "Formerly men in Spain wore doublets with high collars made in this fashion. [The collar] began with a point almost at the end of the doublet in the middle of the back, and from there it widened upward until it covered all the nape *(pescuezo)* and part of the head. . . . Near the shoulders it commenced to diminish on each side until it came to nothing on both sides near the chin." Such a back point is conveniently illustrated in a painting (Fig. 127), but apparently it had been lost before Alcega's tailoring book came out.

"The collar was lined with canvas and paste, mak-

114   ca. 1490–1500   **115**   ca. 1530   **116**   ca. 1535

117   1511–1517   **118**   ca. 1530–1540   **119**   1532

120   ca. 1520   **121**   1526   **122**   1536–1538

ing it very thick and hard and strong. It rose up, and its top appeared above other garments. Knights and noble people wore this collar in velvet."[105] Others, like the Prince, had collar and half sleeves of brocade. The hard, high collar was a protection: King Fernando might have been decapitated (1492) had not his doublet collar deflected a sudden dagger thrust.[106] In 1522 an ordinance prohibited the use of paste in collars, allowing only canvas and cloth stitched (bastados) with thread,[107] but by that time collar stiffness must have ceased to be important.

In the wash and wave of fashion the collar decreased in height. Figure 100 shows Prince Juan's, of black and gold brocade, open and shallow. Later, it increased in circumference, standing out from the neck in a wide circle, the ends well separated at front (Fig. 101). From this stage it was but a step to leave off the collar altogether. When a close, standing collar next appears, it will be as part of the shirt.

Slashed or paned doublet sleeve top

114 CRIMINAL ca. 1490–1500, from *St. John the Evangelist and the Poisoned Cup*, retable of the two St. Johns, by the St. Nicholas Master (Bilbao. Museo de Bellas Artes)

115 FLAGELLATOR ca. 1530, from *The Flagellation of Jesus*, main retable, by the Ororbia Master (Ororbia. Parish Church)

116 EXECUTIONER ca. 1535, from *The Martyrdom of St. Agnes* by Vicente Masip (Madrid. Museo del Prado)

Slashed or paned foresleeve

117 ATTENDANT 1511–1517, from *St. Paul Journeying to Damascus*, main retable, by Damián Forment (Zaragoza. Church of San Pablo)

118 TORMENTOR ca. 1530–1540, from *The Crowning with Thorns* attributed to Juan Correa de Vivar (Cádiz. Cathedral)

119 EMPEROR 1532, from portrait of Charles V, emperor of the Holy Roman Empire, by Jakob Seisenegger (Wien. Kunsthistorisches Museum)

Sleeve in puffs slashed or paned

120 LANSQUENET ca. 1520, from *The Nobleman Gothard Finding St. Roch*, retable from Corbillos, attributed to Juan Rodríguez de Solís (León. Cathedral, Museo)

121 *NOUVEAU RICHE* 1526, from figure of Calisto in *Tragicomedia de Calisto y Melibea*. Toledo, 1526. XX aucto (London. The British Library)

122 ATTENDANT 1536–1538, from *Epiphany*, main retable, by Gabriel Joly (Teruel. Cathedral)

If we may trust the pictures (Figs. 2, 32), Phelipe el Hermoso brought with him to the Peninsula the collarless neckline. This line had been foreshadowed in Spain by a low-necked shirt over which the doublet front (Fig. 102) was cut away almost to the waistline, as in the jerkin of Figure 73. In low-necked doublets later, the front is filled with a similarly shaped panel. One such panel (Fig. 103), darker than the rest of the doublet, is bordered with a lighter band. The German woodcut (Fig. 96) suggests buttons at the top corners of the doublet panel, as though it were a stomacher. Calisto's squire (Fig. 123) has the panel cut in vertical slashes across the top. In a late version of the fashion (Fig. 104) the whole doublet is of brocade gold, rose, and black.

Doublets could be cut higher with a square or a rounded neckline visible above the stomacher but still lower than the shirt. In a squared example worn by a swordsman (Fig. 105) who follows Salome to the chamber of Herodias, the fronts are laced together, a holdover from the fifteenth century. Cut lower but still square is the doublet of a Portuguese courtier (Fig. 106), yellow as is his stomacher and trimmed with bands brown or gold. The rounded neckline (Fig. 107) appears in a Spanish relief of a royal saint.

A characteristic neckline trim at this period consisted of a band slashed across at intervals and stayed apparently at top and bottom to a narrower band, so that through the middle the slashed fabric puffed outward, forming loops. Such a trim adorns the neck of a black doublet worn by the boy Charles (Fig. 108) and can be seen on the later crimson and green one of a spearsman (Fig. 109). In a Portuguese picture (Fig. 110) such slashing is repeated in a wider band above the waistline.

The slashed band, doubled upon itself, made a series of tabs that could be used to adorn a neckline (Fig. 18), as well as for insertion at armscye (Fig. 116) or wrist (Fig. 119). These tabs foretell the piccadills which in time would form the familiar shoulder trim called *brahón*.

That all gentlemen were not eager to expose the Adam's apple is suggested by the fact that in two portraits of Charles V—by Joos van Cleve (1520's) at The Hague and by Titian (1530's) at Vienna—a modest standing collar is provided for the imperial doublet. Seisenegger (Fig. 13) obscures with a leather jacket (cuera) the body of the doublet, which probably matched the foresleeves (Fig. 119).

The doublet sleeve, Girón describes as very narrow and opened in the lower part for five or six

123   1514

124   ca. 1530   **125**   ca. 1540

126   1493   **127**   ca. 1505–1510   **128**   ca. 1520

fingers' breadth. There eyelets were made, which some laced with one ribbon. Others put a ribbon into each pair of eyelets, thus using many ribbons with their knots and bows. The ends soon remained hanging, which was deemed the best arrangement. Some gentlemen had foresleeves or half sleeves *(medias mangas)* of brocade, like the collar, while others had only tips of three or four fingers' breadth at the bottom of the foresleeve. And few who had collar and foresleeves of silk or brocade did not have a fabric of poorer quality in the rest of the doublet.[108] Torquemada reveals further hidden economies. "Not long ago in Spain"—he published in 1553—"people dressed so plainly that a lord having an income of ten million did not wear what a squire with a capital of five hundred ducats puts

on today. . . . He who had a doublet was not doing poorly. . . , They wore jerkins without sleeves in order that those [of the doublet] might appear, and some wore only sleeves with a false collar of velvet visible above the jerkin. And others did not put in more than sleeve-ends *(puntas)* four or five inches deep, which for gala effect they pulled outside the jerkin sleeves so that they might be seen."[109]

There is evidence of a simple, moderate sleeve for the doublet (Fig. 112), but tight-fitting ones are likely to be open at the back seam, as Girón describes, releasing a part of the shirt sleeve. A king on horseback has added room for his elbow (Fig. 111), while an executioner's sleeve (Fig. 113) is opened slightly higher. To my knowledge the earliest illustration of such a relation between an outer and an

Sectioned doublet sleeve

123 SQUIRE 1514, from figure of Sempronio in *Tragicomedia de Calisto y Melibea*. Valēcia, 1514. II auto (Madrid. Biblioteca Nacional)

124 FLAGELLATOR ca. 1530, from *The Flagellation of Jesus,* main retable, by the Ororbia Master (Ororbia. Parish Church)

125 KING ca. 1540, from figure of Magus in *Epiphany* (Budapest. Collection of Professor Odön Farago in 1922)

Doublet or Paltock

126 FARMER TYING SHEAF 1493, from *June* in Li, Andrés de. *Reportorio de los tiempos.* Burgos, 1493. sig.d[6] (The Hispanic Society of America)

127 TORMENTOR WITH ROPE ca. 1505–1510, from *The Death of St. Vincent,* retable of St. Vincent (Barcelona. Museo de Arte de Cataluña)

128 EXECUTIONER ca. 1520, from *The Martyrdom of St. Hermengild,* retable of the Martyrs, attributed to Juan Ramírez (Granada. Museo Provincial de Bellas Artes, Palacio de Carlos V, Alhambra)

---

inner sleeve is that in a painting of 1445 by Giovanni di Paolo,[110] which suggests that the fashion originated in Italy. This style, which earned comment from a clothes-conscious cleric (1477)—"the shirt sleeves much pulled out"[111]—served to lend interest to the doublet sleeve (Figs. 141–143), as well as to exploit the beauty of the inner one. For Spanish women the feature was fully developed (see Figs. 427, 453).

The sleeve with a large puff *(musequí)* above the elbow and a fitted foresleeve, seen often in jerkins (Figs. 81–83), was favored for the doublet also. Italians were using it in the mid-fifteenth century. An early Spanish example of plain material (Fig. 114) shows the puff small and cut with slashes. Larger puffs without ornament occur in a beige garment (Fig. 127), in one of scarlet with tan upper sleeves (Fig. 128), and in the parti-colored one (Fig. 109). In a puff of 1530 (Fig. 115) the slashes are so long that they almost divide the rose, gold, and black brocade into the panes that were the next development. The crimson panes of St. Julian's doublet sleeves, contrasting conspicuously with his jerkin of red, black, and gold brocade (Fig. 68), are divided into three puffs. In the last example (Fig. 116) panes of plain yellow fabric over a blue lining are sectioned into puffs. Through slashes in the blue jacket the yellow body of the doublet can be seen.

The foresleeve or half sleeve, usually matching the collar, could contrast with the doublet. The left-

hand man in Figure 99 has brocaded foresleeves as well as collar with his plain red doublet. Unusually long foresleeves, extended in a point over the hand (Fig. 117), are decorated with short slashes. In another type (Fig. 118) a foresleeve of panes, banded into two sections, is combined with a well-slashed upper sleeve. Charles V's foresleeve (Fig. 119) is made up of white satin panes stitched with gold thread vertically and sewed horizontally to the lining to make the five puffed sections that are visible. Foresleeves could be closed with small buttons (Fig. 128) or lacing (Fig. 127) and trimmed at the wrist with doubled tabs (Fig. 116).

Another elaborate sleeve is that puffed *(follada)* in sections from shoulder to wrist, which can be seen in full glory in the white doublet of a lansquenet (Fig. 120). Of continuous, narrow panes, the six puffs are secured to the sleeve lining with narrow bands of the fabric. The wrist is finished with a double band. Calisto dies in a similar doublet with slashed body and paned sleeves of three puffs (Fig. 121). The four puffs of an attendant to a Magus (Fig. 122) seem to be rendered as slashed rather than paned, and only stitching between them is suggested.

Puffs might be combined with fitted sections. Calisto's squire (Fig. 123) wears sleeves with a slashed puff each at shoulder and elbow separated by a fitted section, all above a fitted foresleeve. In the crimson velvet doublet of a flagellator (Fig. 124) the shoulder puff is paned over a dark lining, the elbow one over white. A late example reverses the sectional order (Fig. 125). The shoulder part is plain except for an edging of scallops. There follow a slashed puff, a plain elbow section, two slashed puffs, and last a row of tabs.

Paltock

A garment similar to the doublet, or indeed a form of doublet, must have been the paltock *(paletoque),* which for Prince Juan (1493–1495) required only 1½ or 1⅓ varas of material with perhaps more for the lining—mulberry velvet lined with mulberry satin, white brocaded satin with crimson velvet, rich brocaded black velvet with crimson satin. In Aragón (1499) a paltock of *grana* had a stomacher of black velvet.[112] Lazarillo reveals that the garment carried laces; his clerical master used a paltock lace for tying on a key.[113] A French "doublet in the form of a *palletot"* (1536) was furnished all over with cords of gold and silk tagged with gold aglets. The English paltock served for

129   ca. 1498

130   1524

131   1537

132   ca. 1520

133   ca. 1520–1530

134   1520–1534

135   1524

136   ca. 1530–1535

137   1537

trussing up hose. Norris illustrates it as a sleeveless, waist-length garment, open in a wide, deep V from shoulders to waistline and provided with holes for lacing to both hose and stomacher.[114]

The Spanish Academy dictionary (1737, 1970) states that the paltock had no sleeves, but Baeza paid for white, brocaded-satin turnbacks (vueltas) on the sleeves of a crimson satin paltock for Prince Juan (1495), and a sleeved paltock of reddish woolen (grana encarnada) is listed in an inventory (1512). Queen Isabel sent to her embroiderer paltock sleeves of crimson cebtí to be used on a chasuble, probably as a base for stitchery.[115] In 1505 paltock sleeves of tawny, brocaded satin measured about $\frac{2}{3}$ vara long by $\frac{5}{12}$ vara wide.[116]

It seems likely that the skirtless doublets illus-

Shirt neckline, low

129 ARCHDUKE ca. 1498, from portrait of Phelipe el Hermoso, king of Spain as archduke of Austria, by the Master of the Magdalen Legend, 1515–1530 (Windsor Castle)

130 FLAGELLATOR 1524, from *The Flagellation of Jesus*, retable group, by Damián Forment (Zaragoza. Church of Santa María Magdalena, Chapel of El Cristo)

131 PHYSICIAN 1537, from statue of St. Damian, retable of St. Cosmas and St. Damian, by Gabriel Joly and Juan de Salas (Teruel. Church of San Pedro)

Shirt neckline at throat

132 EMPEROR ca. 1520, from portrait of Charles V, emperor of the Holy Roman Empire (Kettering. Boughton House, Collection of the Duke of Buccleuch)

133 OFFICIAL ca. 1520–1530, from figure of Pilate in *Jesus before Pilate*, predella of main retable, attributed to the Egea Master (Uncastillo. Church of San Martín)

134 SCULPTOR 1520–1534, from self-portrait, main retable, by Damián Forment (Huesca. Cathedral)

Neckband of fulled material

135 ARCHDUKE 1524, from portrait of Ferdinand I, emperor of the Holy Roman Empire as archduke of Austria, attributed to Lucas van Leyden (Firenze. Galleria degli Uffizi)

136 EMPEROR ca. 1530–1535, from portrait of Charles V, emperor of the Holy Roman Empire, by Monogrammist "IR" (New York. The Cooper Hewitt Museum of Decorative Arts and Design, Smithsonian Institution)

137 EMPEROR 1537, from medal of Charles V by Hans Reinhart the Elder (The Hispanic Society of America)

---

trated in Figures 126–128, all of which have sleeves, are actually paltocks. They show clearly eyelets for laces used in trussing up hose. A farmer's laces (Fig. 126) strain while he works, but a tormentor, who wears a beige garment (Fig. 127), has loosed his gold-agleted yellow laces and lets them hang. Vermilion lined with gray, an executioner's garment (Fig. 128) has eyelets worked in black for his gold-agleted white laces, which are entirely disconnected from the paltock and hang from the top of his hose (Fig. 166).

Shirt

The shirt (camisa from the Latin camisia) is an old garment. For its discussion we may begin with a prelate in Valladolid threatening to excommunicate men who wore fancy shirts. There was some doubt, especially among women, as to whether the prelate had the authority to go so far,[117] but Fernando de Talavera (1477) agreed that people of their time sinned by taking sensual delight in the softness of fine cloth or silk, and by going to excess in the matter of costly linens such as hollands and sheer Bretons. To Talavera the third manner of sinning was to seek a thousand modes and novelties in garments and costumes. "Beginning with the males: sometimes they wear long shirts (camisones) a little coarse (bastillos), sometimes very delicate, contrary to the real purpose (invención) of the shirt, which was for sleeping, or at most for preserving modesty, or because formerly no one used sheets. . . . Sometimes they wear short ones, sometimes long, sometimes lace-trimmed, sometimes pleated. Sometimes their neckbands (cabezones), like those of women's chemises, are expensively embroidered."[118]

In the fifteenth century the shirt was glimpsed as a narrow panel between the doublet fronts, under slender lacings or a ribbon tie. The effigy of Juan II (Fig. 90) suggests a full shirt front compressed under the doublet-tie into soft, irregular pleats of elaborately embroidered fabric. At the turn of the century a notable change takes place: from a vertical panel, the visible portion of the shirt becomes a shallow horizontal zone, low enough sometimes to reveal the collarbones, and a neckband consistently appears. A complete shirt can be illustrated in the figure of an earnest flagellator (Fig. 130). The low neckline is finished with a band, and the sleeves are of moderate width; the shirt length would seem to reach the knees.

Shirts as well as doublets figured in the battle

138   1531   **139**   ca. 1530   **140**   ca. 1539

141   ca. 1475–1480   **142**   1488–1495   **143**   1489–1493

144   ca. 1519   **145**   ca. 1530   **146**   ca. 1530

of Pavia (1525), fought in February snow. At a council of war Charles V's commander, the Marquis of Pescara, issued an order: "Tonight at nine o'clock . . . everyone armed, and with a shirt over his armor or clothing, shall sally forth to where the squadrons are made up. Any who have more shirts than they need, be pleased to give them to those Germans (lansquenets) who have none. The rest with sheets and tent awnings *(tiendas),* and if there are not enough of these, with two sheets of paper . . . will make short cloaks or hoods *(sambenitillos)* to whiten themselves in order that they may be known."[119] This device was helpful because lansquenets were fighting on both sides of the battle.

A homely note comes from the observant Vives who has listened in on a man dressing.

"Boy, bring me a clean shirt, this one I have worn for six days. Hey, catch that flea jumping there! . . .

"I don't want this shirt with the collar quilted

Shirt collar

138 KING 1531, from portrait of Ferdinand I, emperor of the Holy Roman Empire as king of the Romans, by Barthel Beham (New York. Prints Division, The New York Public Library, Astor, Lenox and Tilden Foundations)

139 GENTLEMAN ca. 1530, from portrait, entitled *Gabriel de Salamanca,* by Jan Gossaert (formerly Private Collection, New York)

140 YOUNG PRINCE ca. 1539, from portrait medallion of Felipe II, king of Spain as prince of Asturias (The Hispanic Society of America)

Shirt sleeve confined or pulled out

141 GENTLEMAN ca. 1475–1480, from *Banquet of Herod,* retable of St. John the Baptist, by Pedro García de Benabarre (Barcelona. Museo de Arte de Cataluña)

142 YOUNG DANDY 1488–1495, from tomb of Pedro Martínez Gadea (Burgos. Cathedral, Cloister)

143 INFANTE 1489–1493, from effigy of Infante Alfonso by Gil de Siloe (Burgos. Monastery of Miraflores)

Folds or frill at sleeve wrist

144 EMPEROR ca. 1519, from portrait of Charles V, emperor of the Holy Roman Empire, by Bernhard Strigel (Roma. Galleria Borghese)

145 KNIGHT OF SANTIAGO ca. 1530, from portrait (Barcelona. Palacio Real Menor, Jesuitas)

146 GENTLEMAN ca. 1530, from portrait, entitled *Gabriel de Salamanca,* by Jan Gossaert (formerly Private Collection, New York)

(colchado) but that other with the plain one, because such creases at this time—what are they but nests and lurking places of lice and fleas?"[120]

Though finding no proof that Queen Isabel spun the linen for her husband's shirts, her eulogizer Clemencín was convinced that she did spin or embroider in moments of relaxation.[121] Baeza's accounts show that she paid for shirts for Prince Juan, for the refugee sons of Bragança, for the King, for nine Englishmen who had been imprisoned by the Moors, for a man who swept out her ladies' quarters, etc. In 1493 ten shirts for the Prince required 31 varas of fine holland *(holanda delgada),* at 265 maravedis the vara, and 7 ounces of fine white silk twist, at 126 maravedis the ounce, for sewing them, a total cost of 9097 for the ten. Holland at 150 sufficed for the dependent Braganças in 1487. Later, 3 varas at 190, the silk used, and the work of embroidering and sewing brought the price to 690 each for six Bragança shirts (1493). For an attendant *(contino)* of the Queen (1497) "half holland" was supplied. The Queen commanded that three or four dozen shirts be always available in her son's wardrobe. They were to be sewn and washed in the presence of the chamberlain's wife.[122]

We have seen a neckband in the costume of a page (Fig. 102), whose low-cut doublet reveals a full-gathered shirt front. A good example is in a shirt of Phelipe el Hermoso (Fig. 129), exposed by a low-placed stomacher. Exquisite pleats, fixed in place with several rows of white stitching, hold the body fullness flat to the neckline, which is finished with a galloon, probably of gold. The shirt has slid down the Archduke's right shoulder, leaving it bare and seductive as a girl's.

In a relief portrait Charles V wears a handsome shirt (Fig. 23), low at the neck where the body fullness is gathered into a band shaped to lie flat. Edged with a tiny frill, the band is embroidered in contiguous lozenges, each with a dot at center. In the similar neckline of a young Magus (Fig. 74) the pattern on the band consists of triangles and lozenges separated by vertically paired dots. From the textual references to pearls, gold, and precious stones adorning neckbands, one may suppose these motifs to suggest jewels rather than embroidery. A late example of the low neckline supplied for a physician-saint (Fig. 131) is without ornament except for the frill edging the very narrow band.

With a square-cut doublet the shirt neckline likewise could be square, as seen in Figures 105 and 106, but the round line showed the more interesting

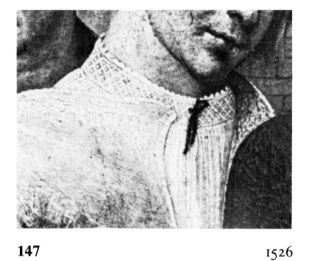

147   1526

148   1538–1539

149   1522–1549

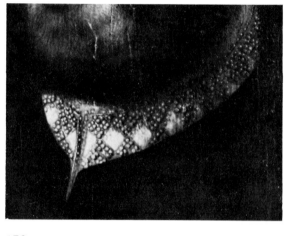

150   ca. 1530

151   ca. 1526–1530

152   ca. 1530

development. It could rise to the throat, and from there the neckband could continue into a standing collar.

A neckband just covering the collarbones (Fig. 132) seems to be of linen embroidered in leafy scrolls and edged with a narrow frill. That of a sculptor (Fig. 134), which has a narrow frill, carries a simple design of lozenges. That provided for Pilate's shirt (Fig. 133) also is embroidered.

The neckline went higher: at the first tournament held in Valladolid (1517) Charles V wore a shirt gathered into a high collar *(hault collet)*.[123] Illustrative evidence comes later. In a shirt of 1524 (Fig. 135) a low collar consists of the shirt fullness gathered to fit closely and held erect with shirring. A portrait of Ferdinand I (ca. 1530) by Barthel Beham (Wien. Kunsthistorisches Museum) indicates at the neckline a casing and cord for gathering in the fullness, which rises to a modest height, held in at the top possibly with another casing and cord. The fullness could be stitched into a high collar (Fig. 136) and then released in a frill. In the shirt of Charles V's portrait (ca. 1532) by Christoph Amberger (Berlin-Dahlem. Gemäldegalerie) two narrow bands embroidered in scrolls confine the shirt fullness—one at the throat, the other higher on the neck—above which the fullness, visible between them, escapes in a frill. The same arrangement occurs in a medal (Fig. 137) where the artist has recorded two points for closing the collar at front.

Embroidered shirt collar or neckband

147 COURTIER—GEOMETRIC DESIGN 1526, from figure of king's entourage in *St. Eligius Weighs a Saddle* by Pedro Nunyes (Barcelona. Museo de Arte de Cataluña)

148 COURTIER—GEOMETRIC DESIGN 1538–1539, from *Banquet of Herod*, retable of St. John the Baptist, by Gregório Lopes (Tomar. Church of São João Baptista)

149 KING—SCROLLS 1522–1549, from figure of St. Sigismund in *St. Vincent and St. Sigismund* by Pedro Gascó (Vich. Museu Episcopal)

150 KNIGHT OF SANTIAGO—PEARLS ca. 1530, from portrait (Barcelona. Palacio Real Menor, Jesuitas)

151 EMPEROR—GOLD AND PEARLS ca. 1526–1530, from portrait of Charles V, emperor of the Holy Roman Empire (Chantilly. Musée Condé)

152 GENTLEMAN—GOLD AND BLACK EMBROIDERY ca. 1530, from portrait, entitled *Gabriel de Salamanca*, by Jan Gossaert (formerly Private Collection, New York)

A straight, upstanding neckband is apparent in the 1530's. Plain and shallow, one edged with a frill (Fig. 138) is open at front and tied with a tasseled cord. A higher band (Fig. 139), worked with gold and black and tied with two cords, is finished along the top with a gold-edged strip that is slightly full but not really ruffled. A neckband of the youthful Felipe, Charles V's son (Fig. 140), appears to be jeweled along the lower portion, while the upper edge bears a well-developed frill. This is the frill that developed into the huge ruff of the late sixteenth century.

Illustrations of handsomely embroidered collars are available. Geometric designs in relief were worked in white, producing a simple lattice as in Figure 147 or overlapping squares as in a Portuguese example (Fig. 148). An inventory of 1503 describes the neckband of a fine holland shirt as "embroidered with white thread in little comfits *(confiticos)*",[124] a motif used also on coverlets. In the province of Zamora (1926) men's shirts with a standing collar embroidered in geometric designs provided striking illustration of the persistence of a style which, having begun in sixteenth-century court circles, could four hundred years later be found in an isolated village.

Charles V's high collar of 1517 was "very handsomely worked, quilted *(estofée [estofado])*[125] and enriched with pearls and precious stones". On the neckband of a king-saint (Fig. 149) the leafy scrolls stand in relief as though they had been stuffed with cotton *(estofado)*, like the patterns of a quilt (Plasencia. Private Collection) said to have been used by Charles V at Yuste. In another richly decorated collar (Fig. 151) the white of the linen, except for the frill, is almost obscured with large pearls and heavy gold stitchery. This collar has been described as belonging to the doublet, but since the doublet carries a transverse band while the collar opens at front, it seems more likely that it belongs to the shirt. The black outline stitchery of Figure 152 encloses areas of gold, patterning birds, florets, scrolls, and the armillary sphere that is associated with Manuel I of Portugal. In Figure 150 the collar is embroidered with seed pearls applied over color, possibly gold.

Phelipe el Hermoso (1499) owned four shirts from Spain. One with narrow sleeves was embroidered round the neck with blue silk and gold and trimmed from the neck down *(en avalant)* with 45 gold bands. Another with narrow sleeves was open at front and back. Wristbands, neckband, and all the seams were

153   1519

154   ca. 1520

155   ca. 1530

156   1515–1525

157   ca. 1520–1530

158   1535

159   ca. 1490–1500

160   1526

161   1531–1536

covered with gold; there were 26 bands or outlines *(trasces)* of gold and also gold aglets.[126] The inventory of 1503 includes a shirt of white silk trimmed at neckband, wrists, and hem with galloons or fringes *(franjas)* of gold and silver. This shirt has also ten strips *(tiras)* of spun gold together with ornaments of silver gilt applied on the body and three on each sleeve; sleeve-ends and hem were cut with battlemented edges *(almenadas)*.[127] Embroidered bands for a shirt body appear in Figure 139 as black geometric motifs about knots of gold on puffs pulled out through slashes in the doublet.

Shirt sleeves, which have been described as being narrow, as of medium width, as trimmed with gold galloon, are visible only in the puffs or pull-outs that escape through openings in the doublet sleeve. In one case (Fig. 141) the fullness is contained between red and gold brocade sleeve-edges with pairs

---

Long hose

153 HALBERDIER—STRIPED HOSE 1519, from *Amadís de Gaula.* [Roma?] 1519. Title-cut (The Hispanic Society of America)

154 ARCHER—PLAIN HOSE ca. 1520, from *The Martyrdom of St. Sebastian,* retable of the Martyrs, attributed to Juan Ramírez (Granada. Museo Provincial de Bellas Artes, Palacio de Carlos V, Alhambra)

155 FLAGELLATOR—PARTI-COLORED HOSE ca. 1530, from *The Flagellation of Jesus,* main retable, by the Ororbia Master (Ororbia. Parish Church)

Long hose plain or slashed

156 DRUMMER—HOSE WITH MARTINGALE? 1515–1525, from staircase ramp (Salamanca. University)

157 SPEARSMAN—SLASHED HOSE ca. 1520–1530, from *St. Vincent on the Rack,* retable of St. Vincent, by Juan Gascó (Vich. Museu Episcopal)

158 SOLDIER—SLASHED HOSE 1535, from *The Capture of Tunis,* tapestry IX in the *Conquest of Tunis* series, designed by Jan Cornelisz Vermeyen (Madrid. Royal Palace)

Embroidered hose

159 TOWNSMAN ca. 1490–1500, from figure of man poking fire in *St. Dominic and the Albigenses* by Pedro Berruguete (Madrid. Museo del Prado)

Crossed garter

160 SQUIRE 1526, from figure of Sempronio in *Tragicomedia de Calisto y Melibea.* Toledo, 1526. XII aucto (London. The British Library)

161 KING 1531–1536, from figure of young Magus in *Epiphany* by Juan Rodríguez and Lucas Giraldo (Avila. Cathedral, Trascoro)

---

of black cords or narrow ribbons, apparently sewed fast. A young dandy proclaims his flamboyance by having his shirt sleeves wide enough to be pulled out in extravagant puffs (Fig. 142), defined by agleted laces at the back edges of his cuffed doublet sleeves; the shirt can be seen also through ovoid slashes above the cuffs. Slashes over Infante Alfonso's shirt sleeves (Fig. 143) are bordered with narrow braid, while the open back, heavily decorated at the edges, reveals moderate pull-outs between agleted laces.

Plainly dressed men showed only an edge of white shirt sleeve at the wrist, but in exalted circles the wrist received attention. Phelipe's shirt sleeve was long enough to end in soft folds, an arrangement worn by Charles V as late as 1519 (Fig. 144). However, in a Vermeyen portrait of the same time (formerly Chester. Private Collection), the young Emperor's wrist fullness is gathered into a tight narrow band, plain and frill-less. The Chantilly portrait shows a narrow pearl-trimmed wristband in sympathy with the embroidered neckband (Fig. 151), together with a frill as deep as the sharply pleated one in Figure 214. For a knight of Santiago the wristband matches the collar with seed pearls (Fig. 145); a shallow frill frames the hand. A larger frill, softly pleated (Fig. 146), is embroidered with the black stitchery mentioned above, which resembles the "black work or Spanish work" popular in England at this time.

Leg Coverings

Hose

Developed first by northern peoples, hose in the Middle Ages became longer and longer, covering each leg to the crotch. Eventually the two pieces were extended to the waist and joined, except that the tops at front were left separate for convenience. The opening was covered with a pouch placed just above the crotch and fastened on with buttons or points.

It is at this stage that our period opens, with long hose *(calzas enteras)* extended from waistline to foot, sometimes including a sole and fitting so tightly that a front patch was really needed. As has been mentioned, hose were supported by being laced to the doublet-hem. They were made of cloth and lined. The ideal demanded that they fit perfectly; in pictures they generally appear without a wrinkle. Trade rules for Sevillian hose makers in 1522 required their materials to be preshrunk: "In hose that are fashioned of whatever manner, of whatever cloth or grogram . . . such cloth shall have been completely submerged and soaked. [Hose] shall be cut according to the nap *(al pelo)* and on the bias *(al sesgo).* Those of serge *(estameña)* shall be cut along the thread and wale *(a su hilo y cordón derecho).* Linings also must have been wet completely, and they must be well provided with two thicknesses of hempen canvas *(cañamazo doblado)."*[128] To achieve a perfect fit over so complicated a section of the human frame required skill of high degree. For guild entrance at Sevilla an applicant had to present three types of hose: in the Castilian style, with a whole foot *(peal entero),* and with a martingale.

Prince Juan had two pairs of new hose each month. His chamberlain every morning helped him to draw them on and to truss them up. Those he took off at night, valets cleaned the next day. [Vives speaks of shaking hose to remove dust and then of brushing to clean them.] The chamberlain was instructed always to keep on hand thin red and fine black cloths for the Prince's hose. For young men's use Celestina approved hose of *grana.*[129] Oliveros wore red hose with green velvet shoes *(alcorques).* Other colors and materials are mentioned: light green; rose, mulberry or white in grogram; white frieze. Weiditz illustrates light gray, lavender, blue, and green. Leather hose are listed among a Mendoza's effects in 1530.[130] A man shooting an arrow at Saint Sebastian wears glove-fitting hose (Fig. 154) of brick red with dark gray or black points. A flagellator (Fig. 155) has one leg striped brown and beige, while the other is plain blue. Of men's white hose found in the wardrobe of a Catalan castle (1523), one pair was banded with yellow cloth and blue satin, another with the yellow cloth only.[131] In the striped hose worn by a young halberdier (Fig. 153) can be distinguished the pieces joined over the instep.

Charles V had his German fifers and drummers at a tournament in Valladolid (1518) wear hose of scarlet varied with yellow and white—bands of cloth of gold, of silver, or of crimson velvet, pinked and slashed in the lansquenet fashion. His "gentlemen lackeys" wore scarlet overlaid with gold and silver tissue *(toile).*[132] Attendants to Isabel de Portugal on her wedding journey into Spain (1526) had hose of *grana* combined with brocade.[133] The Marquis

of Astorga provided embroidered hose for his gentlemen on foot during the imperial coronation (1530).[134] A pair of an earlier generation are wine red embroidered in gold (Fig. 159).

Slashes in hose could be patterned geometrically, as in Figure 157, where the right leg is gray-green over cream at top and gray below, the left crimson over green at top and yellowish red below. Occasionally the accent is on puffs of lining material (Fig. 158) pulled out through the slashes.

It has been stated that from the fifteenth century long hose, clear to the waist, were knitted, and those illustrated in Figure 154 fit so smoothly that one might judge them so made, except that the long line of a seam is faintly visible on the right leg. In the 1528 inventory of a marquis at Zafra (Badajoz), knit hose *(calzas de aguja)* are mentioned, two pairs red and two white.[135] Unfortunately the material is not indicated, but one would like to think them early examples of the long silk hose, possibly knitted, that became so great a luxury abroad. "King Henry the eight, did weare only cloath hose, or hose cut out of ell broade Taffety, or that by great chaunce, there came a payre of Spanish silke stockings from Spain[.] King Edward the sixt, had a payre of Long spanish silke stockings sent him for a great present."[136] In Alcega's tailoring book approved for printing in 1579, no hose are represented, either because at that time knitted hose had taken over or perhaps because the hose makers' trade was separate from the tailors'.

Martingale

Untying and retying the points that united hose and doublet must have been a tedious business, and there were situations when time was of the essence. To take care of such occasions the martingale was in common use by 1522 at Sevilla. It was something added to the hose: *"Las calzas llevan m[art]ingala,"* says Martín de Salinas,[137] ambassador to Charles V's brother Ferdinand. Judging by the piece of horse harness called "martingale" in both English and French, one might suppose it to have been a sort of belt, round the waist and between the legs.[138] Pisetsky describes *calze a la martingala* as laced to the belt and opened at back.[139] The point was that the whole thing, hose and martingale, responded to a single button or lace. An old captain (1568) would have himself attended by two pages at arms, one of the sword to tie and untie his martingale lace, another of the lance to present a urinal.[140]

With a martingale, Brantôme says, the matter could be attended to in no time at all.[141] When Salinas was at Savignano, Italy (1536), he went about like other men in doublet and hose to prove himself a warrior, though he found it inconvenient, perhaps embarrassing, that the martingale could not be concealed.[142] It seems possible that a drummer carved in the Salamanca staircase (Fig. 156) wears hose with a martingale: the narrow front flap bears little relation to the broad patch of the codpiece, but may well be connected with a strap between the legs.

Garter

It was always important that a courtier's hose fit smoothly. In the thirteenth century a Provençal poet noted that a knight wore his hose so fine and tight-fitting "that you would say they had been born with him."[143] The garter (*liga,* or *cenojil* derived from *hinojo,* the word for "knee") was a help in that direction. Early examples in our period are the narrow black garters of a page (Fig. 162), which bind brown-tan netherstocks; the darker brown-tan upperstocks are trimmed with black bands. The man spearing Saint Vincent (Fig. 157) has tied a garter under the knee of his yellowish-red netherstock. Sempronio, sending Celestina to death on the point of his sword, wears upperstocks cross-gartered (Fig. 160). High relief bands about the knees of a Magus (Fig. 161) may or may not indicate cross-gartering, but it is difficult to associate them with any other function. The bands or rolls are slashed diagonally and embroidered with florets between the slashes.

Wide ribbons also were used. Barely visible below the violet and black jerkin of a Catalan horseman (Fig. 247), a bow and an end of wide green ribbon, fringed with gold, suggest a garter over hose striped green and vermilion. Wide ribbon, ending in a knot and a tassel (Fig. 163), garters the slashed hose of a lansquenet in Portugal, and another wide ribbon, the slashed hose of a swordsman beside him. A later use of such garters, fringed, appears in the engraving of a Spanish dragoon (Fig. 164).

Breech-hose

Hose are old in Spain; the name, *calzas,* is derived from the Latin *calceus* (shoe). What is new in our period is the addition of a breech section (*braga,* derived in both form and name from the *braca* of North Europeans) to the tops of hose, forming a single garment, breech-hose *(calzas bragas).* In this development apparently the first step was merely to define the breech sections *(coxales).* A man throwing stones at Saint Stephen (Fig. 165) wears rust-colored hose, seamed at back, the breech sections marked out with narrow bands of black; his laces, only a few of which engage the doublet, are black with gold aglets. In the gray hose of a tormentor the breech section (Fig. 127) is squared off with wider bands, probably of black velvet. In a later example, the breech section above green hose (Fig. 166) is of lavender material bordered with narrow black bands and cut with long slashes that reveal blue underneath. The *Diario ferrarese* made allusion to *calze a braga* in 1495 and 1501,[144] and Carmen Bernis has found *calzas bragas* listed in important men's inventories of 1508 and 1516.[145] Actual breeches without hose, owned by Charles V (Fig. 167), have empty holes in the legs, doubtless for laces to support stockings; they and the breeches could be sewed together also.

Although clearly the Emperor and other courtiers wore garments of this type, their upper hose generally were covered with a jerkin skirt and thus did not often come into view except for reasons of vanity, as in the case of King Ferrante at Naples, or in situations of violent action when the jerkin was left off. Thus it is that the men who model these garments are usually soldiers, flagellators, or executioners. The Marquis of Pescara fought in the battle of Pavia armored only with a sallet, being clad for the rest in a shirt rich with gold and pearls, a crimson doublet, and hose of *grana.*[146] Calisto dies in doublet and hose (Fig. 121). An influence popularizing such exposure must have been the lansquenet (Fig. 5) who boldly revealed his entire figure. Duke Heinrich the Pious of Saxony, as has been mentioned, had himself so portrayed in 1514. The Count of Saldaña at Charles V's coronation (1530) wore under his gown of cloth of gold, lined with pine marten, only cloth-of-gold doublet and hose "in the fashion of Guadalajara", though his peers were faithful to the jerkin.[147] For his full-length portrait in 1532 (Fig. 13) the Emperor also left off the jerkin, while Henry VIII in 1537 was still appearing in its pleated skirt.

Upperstocks

Breech-hose developed into upper- and netherstocks. Upperstocks, for which the word *muslos* appears in 1534,[148] crept towards the knee. A lans-

162   ca. 1497

163   1522–1530

164   1577

165   ca. 1520

166   ca. 1520

167   1540–1550

168   ca. 1520

169   ca. 1530

170   ca. 1530

quenet has them rather long of white material (Fig. 168) slashed in patterns of large crescents and varied slits. For an executioner (Fig. 169) the two legs are treated differently. On one a composite band is wound about the thigh, while on the other is a proper stock cut with long slashes; both legs carry a double, slashed band above the knee. Another executioner (Fig. 170) wears the stocks low on his hips, from which they cannot slide further because they are laced to the doublet. Long slashes ease the thighs and short ones, the knees.

Slashed stocks could be reinforced with horizon-

Narrow or wide garter

162 PAGE—NARROW GARTERS ca. 1497, from *Miracle of St. Narcissus,* retable of St. Narcissus, by the St. Narcissus Master (Valencia. Cathedral)

163 LANSQUENET AND SWORDSMAN—WIDE GARTERS 1522–1530, from *Emperor Heraclius with the Holy Cross,* by Cristóvão de Figueiredo (Coimbra. Museu Machado de Castro)

164 DRAGOON—WIDE GARTERS 1577, from *Dress of a Spanish Dragoon* (Ferentarij) in [Bruyn, Abraham de] *Omnium pene Europae . . . gentivm habitvs.* [Antwerpiae, ca. 1581] pl. 39 (The Hispanic Society of America)

Breech-hose (Calzas bragas)

165 STONE THROWER—BANDED BREECH SECTION ca. 1520, from *The Martyrdom of St. Stephen,* retable of the Martyrs, attributed to Juan Ramírez (Granada. Museo Provincial de Bellas Artes, Palacio de Carlos V, Alhambra)

166 EXECUTIONER—SLASHED BREECH SECTION ca. 1520, from *The Martyrdom of St. Hermengild,* retable of the Martyrs, attributed to Juan Ramírez (Granada. Museo Provincial de Bellas Artes, Palacio de Carlos V, Alhambra)

167 EMPEROR—BREECHES WITHOUT HOSE 1540–1550, from *Inventario iluminado de . . . la Armería de Carlos V* (Madrid. Armería Nacional)

Slashed upperstocks

168 LANSQUENET ca. 1520, from *The Nobleman Gothard Finding St. Roch,* retable from Corbillos, attributed to Juan Rodríguez de Solís (León. Cathedral, Museo)

169 EXECUTIONER ca. 1530, from *The Beheading of St. John the Baptist,* retable of St. John the Baptist, by Juan del Bosque (Pamplona. University, Chapel)

170 EXECUTIONER ca. 1530, from *The Martyrdom of St. Tiburtius* in [Vega, Pedro de la] *Flos sanctorum.* Sevilla, 1569. *fcccxxxj* (The Hispanic Society of America)

---

tal bands. An executioner of Saint John the Baptist has slashed, crimson and gold material with plain bands of gold (Fig. 171); blue laces hang down at the waist because he has left off his doublet. The Emperor's upperstocks (Fig. 172) match the sleeves of his doublet in vertical panes of white satin stitched with gold, first along the length and then four times, crosswise, to the lining. They end in bands of warm gray matching the netherstocks. Sculptured upperstocks (Fig. 173) show longer panes; only two horizontal bands run across them.

In an early example with no confining bands (Fig. 174) the panes are rendered as lying close together, separated only by long lines. Here also the laces are free, but they hang from the short doublet. In the upperstocks of a flagellator (Fig. 175) slashes open long spaces; the legs are finished with thick bands like those of Charles V's garment. A regent's upperstocks (Fig. 176) have panes quite separate, except that they are confined at top and bottom. Of cream-colored satin decorated with gold braid, they stand over a puffed lining of cream satin. At the lower edge, the confining band, also trimmed with braid, is almost covered by the cream-colored netherstocks.

Stockings

When did the *braga* become independent of the *calza?* Cunnington says that with Englishmen it was in the 1570's.[149] It cannot have occurred in Spanish courtly wear during our period, because in 1549 upperstocks of yellow velvet, lined with yellow satin, and stockings *(medias)* knit of silk constituted the *calzas* of knights attending Prince Felipe of Spain.[150] The term *medias* is a shortened form of *medias calzas.* A mariner who was washed overboard on the way to the West Indies in 1530 left behind new white *medias calzas* which sold at auction for 44 maravedis on arrival in the New World. He left also a pair of old breeches called *calzones* as well as wide drawers or breeches *(zaragüelles),* a pair in canvas and another of linen, that could have been worn with the *medias.*[151] *Zaragüelles* and *calzones* of such as the mariner probably were not complicated with slashes and lining.

Codpiece

The codpiece *(bragueta,* diminutive of *braga),* which served to bridge the gap between the upper sections of tight hose, began as a simple "cod" or

171 ca. 1521

172 1532

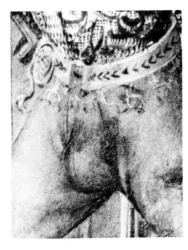

173 1536-1544

174 1516

175 ca. 1535-1545

176 1550

177 ca. 1500

178 1507

179 1532

bag which might be secured in place with a single button (Fig. 177). It widened so that two buttons were required (Fig. 178) or a pair of laces (Fig. 226). The lansquenet with his flair for exaggeration developed it to an extravagant extent, even trimming it with bows, but Spaniards seem to have been more restrained. Charles V's codpiece (Fig. 179), though decorated with gold stitchery, is of modest size, hardly large enough to accommodate the orange that Panurge stowed away in his,[152] but quite able to contain a letter. The Bishop of Málaga, entrusted by Queen Juana with a letter to her father, carried it in his codpiece until Phelipe searched him and found it there.[153] However, Hermosilla writing in 1573 when this peculiar feature was still flourishing, does say that a Spanish page stuffed a roast partridge, stolen, into his codpiece, leaving a telltale leg of the bird outside.[154]

Only in Italy have I found record of women com-plaining about this masculine detail. There in 1553, when lords and masters were charging that feminine skirts were immodest because they were short enough to reveal the feet, ladies had the spirit to retort that the fashion of the codpiece was much more "dishonest". Indeed, they could no longer look at it![155]

The Armería Nacional at Madrid has examples of the codpiece handsomely wrought in mail and steel to be used by knights fighting on foot.

Footgear

MANY TYPES OF MEN'S footgear are mentioned:

shoe *(zapato)*
buskin *(borceguí)*
boot *(bota)*
slipper *(servilla)*
hemp-soled slipper *(alpargata)*
mule *(chinela)*
pantofle *(pantuflo)*
cork-soled shoe *(alcorque)*
wooden-soled shoe *(galocha)*
sabot *(zueco)*

Materials used in the making include:

ass hide, calfskin, chamois, cowhide, deerskin, goatskin, horse hide, sheepskin, felt, hare pelts, *grana*, silk, velvet, cork, rope or straw, gold thread, hemp thread, linen thread.

Shoe sizes were reckoned in points *(puntos);* from three to eleven (Navarra), from four to fifteen (Castilla).[156]

In 1495 Queen Isabel's treasurer paid 13,465 maravedis for footgear supplied to Prince Juan, afterward to become the perquisite of his chamberlain: shoes, 14 pairs; buskins, 94; boots, 2; slippers, 11; pantofles, 6; cork-soled shoes, 22.

Shoe

Pointed shoes could be found in 1499 and even in 1529 (Fig. 307), but the new look was broad. James Laver notes the appearance of the very broad shoe in Germany: drawings representing Nürnberg butchers demonstrate that in 1492 shoes were still pointed; in 1493 they were less pointed, in 1494 they

Upperstocks with panes banded

171 EXECUTIONER ca. 1521, from *The Beheading of St. John the Baptist,* main retable, by Felipe Vigarny (Granada. Royal Chapel)

172 EMPEROR 1532, from portrait of Charles V, emperor of the Holy Roman Empire, by Jakob Seisenegger (Wien. Kunsthistorisches Museum)

173 ATTENDANT 1536–1544, from *Pilate Washing His Hands,* choir stall, by Cornelis de Holanda and others (Avila. Cathedral)

Upperstocks with long panes

174 EXECUTIONER 1516, from *The Beheading of St. John the Baptist* by Francisco de Colonia (Burgos. Cathedral, Puerta de la Pellejería)

175 FLAGELLATOR ca. 1535–1545, from *The Flagellation of Jesus* attributed to Guillén Doncel (León. Museo de San Marcos)

176 REGENT 1550, from portrait of Maximilian II, emperor of the Holy Roman Empire when regent of Spain, by Antonio Moro (Madrid. Museo del Prado)

Codpiece

177 SCOURGER ca. 1500, from *The Scourging of St. Marina,* main retable, by the Palanquinos Master (Mayorga. Church of Santa Marina)

178 EXECUTIONER 1507, from *The Beheading of St. John the Baptist,* retable of St. John the Baptist, by Juan Gascó, destroyed (formerly Sant Joan Galí. Parish Church)

179 EMPEROR 1532, from portrait of Charles V, emperor of the Holy Roman Empire, by Jakob Seisenegger (Wien. Kunsthistorisches Museum)

180   1498–ca. 1503

181   ca. 1520

182   ca. 1530

183   1514

184   1511–1517

185   ca. 1520

186   1490's

187   1525–1529

188   1529

189   ca. 1520–1530

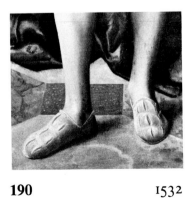

190   1532

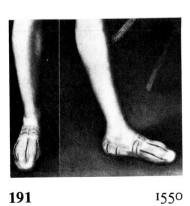

191   1550

were broad.[157] With a translation of Ptolemy's *Geography*, written in 1485, is included a miniature showing broad-toed shoes.[158] Whether the style came from France or Germany or from the court of Maximilian, as Laver suggests, it soon made its way into Spain. Blunt-toed shoes were carved in choir stalls executed at the turn of the century (Fig. 180), the vamp cut low and a strap provided for security. An extreme example of this type (Fig. 181) is worn by a bearded hidalgo with long hair and a handsome, fur-collared gown. The style continued at least until about 1530 (Fig. 182).

Kelly and Schwabe apply the term "duck-bill" to splayed shoes with rounded toe and "bear's-paw" to those with square toe.[159] Of the latter kind an early example in Spain would seem to be the pair worn by Calisto's squire (Fig. 183), which are held on with a strap. Sometimes this toe was slashed (Fig. 184). Saint Martin in a statue (1520–1530) at the Hispanic Society wears the square toe, unslashed, combined with a long vamp. The sole of a low-cut black shoe, also without slashes (Fig. 185), can be seen on an executioner raising his foot to bring his axe down with greater force. A late example of the slashed toe is worn by a Magus in a retable by Forment dated 1539–1540 (Santo Domingo de la Calzada (Logroño). Cathedral).

Shoes reflecting the natural form of the foot continued to be worn. A type with ankle-high uppers, found in the 1480's, prevailed for forty years, the toe varying with fashion. One pair worn by a page with wrinkled hose (Fig. 186) is laced at the sides and ended with a blunt toe. In another (Fig. 10), a tongue from the center front is folded forward upon the upper. Still other shoes splay out to a broad toe (Fig. 187), while some of the period (Fig. 188) return to a fair point and carry multiple slashes.

A lower-cut type displays an affinity for slashes, midway of the vamp for an official (Fig. 189). Charles V's shoes (Fig. 190), warm gray in color, carrying repeated slashes and crossbands, resemble in treatment his paned sleeves and upperstocks (Figs. 119, 172). In cream-colored shoes of 1550 (Fig. 191) the crossbands are omitted and the slash-edges are finished with overcast stitching. Brian Reade interprets this pair as "satin-covered".[160] Their long-slashed vamps and short-slashed quarters present a style that continued into the nineties.

Rules for the shoemakers' guild at Sevilla, published in 1527, make it clear that the goatskin called *cordobán* was the most highly prized leather in the trade. Footgear of ass or horse hide was to be rejected with threat of fines should it be offered. Goatskin had to be of superior quality—strong *(de cabeza)*, heavy, and true *(fiel)*. A shoemaker was instructed to combine with it no fragment of any other leather except the cowhide *(suela)* required for sole and welt *(vira)*. Soles had to be cut from the center back *(cerrada)* or from the shoulder of a hide, never from the flanks which "cannot be good". Each shoe truly of goatskin was to have the sole tinted with a band of color.

Shoe with broad toe

180 PAGE 1498—ca. 1503, from figure in choir-stall border by Master Rodrigo (Ciudad Rodrigo. Cathedral)

181 GENTLEMAN ca. 1520, from figure of bystander in *The Beheading of a Bishop,* end panel of earlier silver-gilt casket (Bañolas. Parish Church)

182 FLAGELLATOR ca. 1530, from *The Flagellation of Jesus,* main retable, by the Ororbia Master (Ororbia. Parish Church)

Shoe with square toe

183 SQUIRE 1514, from figure of Sempronio in *Tragicomedia de Calisto y Melibea.* Valēcia, 1514. II auto (Madrid. Biblioteca Nacional)

184 ATTENDANT 1511–1517, from *St. Paul Journeying to Damascus,* main retable, by Damián Forment (Zaragoza. Church of San Pablo)

185 EXECUTIONER ca. 1520, from *The Martyrdom of St. Hermengild,* retable of the Martyrs, attributed to Juan Ramírez (Granada. Museo Provincial de Bellas Artes, Palacio de Carlos V, Alhambra)

Ankle-high shoe

186 PAGE 1490's, from tomb of Martín Vázquez de Arce (Sigüenza. Cathedral)

187 KING 1525–1529, from figure of crowned saint, choir stall, by Andrés de Nájera and Guillén de Holanda (Valladolid. Museo Nacional de Escultura)

188 CONQUISTADOR 1529, from *Don Hernán Cortés* in Weiditz, Christoph. *Das Trachtenbuch. f77* (Nürnberg. Germanisches Nationalmuseum)

Slashed shoe

189 OFFICIAL ca. 1520–1530, from figure of Pilate in *Jesus before Pilate,* predella of main retable, attributed to the Egea Master (Uncastillo. Church of San Martín)

190 EMPEROR 1532, from portrait of Charles V, emperor of the Holy Roman Empire, by Jakob Seisenegger (Wien. Kunsthistorisches Museum)

191 REGENT 1550, from portrait of Maximilian II, emperor of the Holy Roman Empire when regent of Spain, by Antonio Moro (Madrid. Museo del Prado)

192   ca. 1510

193   ca. 1510–1530

194   ca. 1535–1540

195   1508

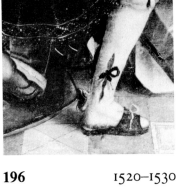

196   1520–1530

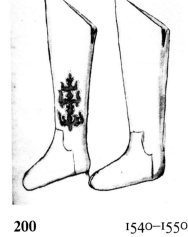

197   1531

198   ca. 1500–1510

199   ca. 1530

200   1540–1550

White shoes put together with leather thongs should be of deerskin, of cowhide, or of the chamois buck, not the doe. When leather thongs were not available for sewing them, a guild official would grant approval to use twine of hackled and cleaned hemp *(cerro de cáñamo)*, heavy and well rubbed with wax and pitch *(cerapez)*, which made it strong and durable. Such shoes had linings "in the usual places", a leather chape and a stiffener *(contrahorte)* inside, and outside a piece called *barreta* (which at the present time is placed inside to cover the sewing and protect the foot from dampness).

Two kinds of sheepskin, *badana* and the softer type known as *baldrés* suitable for gloves, were less valued for shoes. When *badana* was used, it was expected to be black and not white, have been tanned with grease and tallow, be strong and true, and be sewed with leather thongs or with hempen twine. Popular colors may be deduced from a rule prohibiting shoemakers from using *badanas* dyed red, yellow, tawny, blue, green, silver, or brown, because dyeing desiccated a sheepskin unless it had been tanned with grease and tallow, the presence of which was not tolerated by the colors listed.[161] In 1508 at Sevilla a pilot received for shipment to Santo Domingo in America a cask containing 400 pairs of *cordobán* and *badana* shoes "in all colors". Colonists of Hispaniola (1503) were forbidden to import shoes on their own account, that trade being one of the monopolies of the crown.[162]

No shoes or women's slippers could be resoled unless they had been brought to the mender for that purpose. This restriction was intended to prevent menders from resoling used shoes in their stock with pieces of old, rotten leather, or of painted-leather wall hangings *(guadamaciles)*, that would fall to pieces the day the shoes were bought. In this whole bundle of rules the only reference to style is the statement that goatskin shoes might be sharp-pointed *(agudos)* or blunt *(romos)*.[163] The latter term suggests the duck-bill or the bear's-paw toe.

Buskin

192 GENTLEMAN ca. 1510, from figure of bystander in *Foundation of the Church at Mont St. Michel*, main retable, by the Sinobas Master (Haza. Church of San Miguel)

193 BUSKIN STYLE ca. 1510–1530, from emblem of Guild of Shoemakers carved at later date (Barcelona. Cathedral, outer wall)

194 EMPEROR ca. 1535–1540, from portrait of Charles V, emperor of the Holy Roman Empire, by Cornelis Anthonisz (Amsterdam. Rijksprentenkabinet)

Boot

195 NOBLEMAN 1508, from figure of St. Julian, retable center, by Juan Gascó (Vich. Finca del Pradell, Collection of Ramón d'Abadal i de Vinyals)

196 KNIGHT 1520–1530, from *Investiture of a Knight of Santiago*, retable of St. James, attributed to Cristóvão de Figueiredo (Lisboa. Museu Nacional de Arte Antiga)

197 KING 1531, from figure of Magus in *Epiphany* by Fernando Yáñez de la Almedina (Cuenca. Cathedral)

198 EXECUTIONER ca. 1500–1510, from *The Martyrdom of St. Margaret*, retable of St. Margaret, by the Paredes Master (Paredes de Nava. Church of Santa Eulalia)

199 FLAGELLATOR ca. 1530, from *The Flagellation of Jesus* (Valladolid. Museo Nacional de Escultura)

200 EMPEROR—BOOTS 1540–1550, from *Inventario iluminado de . . . la Armería de Carlos V* (Madrid. Armería Nacional)

Buskin

"Hose I wear and even buskins of the light kind you mention, in order to flee better than another," says Pármeno as he waits for Calisto to meet with Melibea.[164] Light and flexible this shoe must have been—"Of him who is easy in his opinions so that he can be swayed by anyone, it is said that he can be turned like a buskin"[165]—and perishable—in July 1482 three dozen skins for buskins were supplied to King Fernando and the same number in the next September and December.[166]

Available descriptions of the buskin *(borceguí)* or half boot, none so early as our period, agree that it extended above the ankle, had a thin sole *(soletilla)*, and closed with laces of cord or leather. The term *borceguí*, well known in Spain in the fifteenth century, in an older form *boszeguí* may have been the source for "buskin", which came into use in England during the early sixteenth century for a foot covering "usually softer [than the boot] . . . made of Spanish leather or velvet, and sometimes lined with fur—lamb or coney".[167] White hare pelts lined a few for the Prince (1493, 1495). In hot weather, Salinas discovered (1536), the coolest thing to do was to wear buskins without hose.[168]

A buskin corresponding to the descriptions appears in a relief (Fig. 193) set into the outer wall of Barcelona Cathedral to mark the Chapel of San

Marcos belonging to the shoemakers' guild. Accompanying scrolls and leafage may date from the time when a new retable was installed (1692), but the buskin decoration, a double row of slashes or loops, resembles a neck trim used on early sixteenth-century doublets (Figs. 108–110). Similar bands of loops or slashes trim buskins worn with the jerkin shown in Figure 68. The stone relief shows a moderately pointed toe, a thin sole, and a seam across the instep; a single leather thong is laced down the side. An example in wood relief (1497–1503) bears large incised fleurs-de-lis matching those in the wearer's jerkin (Ciudad Rodrigo. Cathedral, choir stall). Talavera in his famous *Tractado* speaks of buskins in a thousand colors, trimmed with bands or made without them, some very wide, others very narrow and tight on the feet,[169] as must have been Prince Juan's despite the Queen's admonition to have them made easy because of his tender age. Two valets held the Prince's chair while the shoemaker pulled on his buskins in the morning. Red, white, and yellow were the skins provided for King Fernando. For Moorish horsemen silvered buskins are mentioned in a ballad.[170]

A turned-down cuff at the top (Fig. 192) was characteristic from the period of King Fernando in the *Siege of Cantoria* (Toledo. Cathedral, choir stall) until the time of his grandson (Fig. 194). The cuff could contrast with the leg: a crimson buskin with a white cuff is worn by an official dressed in brocade (Fig. 69).

About 1522 at Sevilla buskin makers were buying Cordovan and Moroccan leathers, goatskin and sheepskin, but sheepskin they were allowed to use only on special order. A *borceguinero* aspiring to become a master had to make three types of buskin: one plain *(llano),* another with a lacing *(de lazo),* and a third completely laced *(de todo lazo).* They were not to be pieced on the outside. Toledo in 1533 demanded that buskins be sewed with good linen thread.[171]

A book on horsemanship (1600) reports that white buskins go with any trappings save those of mourning, if the white is good and the flesh side *(carnaza)* is turned outward. The "date-colored" *(datilado)* type of Barbary also suits any trappings. A buskin foot must fit tightly, because it looks better and is readier for whatever may happen. The entrance and the instep should be wide, because this is becoming to a foot in the stirrup. The calf must be tight in order not to slide down. It should be closed to the top and not rise above the knee.[172] The buskins

that María Eugenia de Beer etched for a *rejoneador* (1643) extend up two thirds of the leg; they are accompanied with low shoes. Her author says that buskins opened on the inside with a ribbon and buttoned on the outside, but that a rider dressed for a gala affair would have them sewed on.[173]

With the buskin was worn other footgear from mules (Fig. 192) to boots. When Prince Juan met his bride Margarita de Austria (1496), he wore buskins and pantofles. Phelipe el Hermoso after death (1506) was dressed in buskins and shoes. The Duke of Béjar, accompanying the Infanta Catalina on her bridal journey to Portugal in January 1525, rode with boots covering two pairs of buskins.

Boot

The boot must have been in less common use or much sturdier than the buskin: Prince Juan in 1495 received only 2 pairs of *botas* against 94 of buskins. Painters often show boots light in color, sometimes white. Those of a Magus in a painting (ca. 1496) by Alonso de Sedano (Burgos. Cathedral), probably white and reaching to above the knees, reveal the characteristic instep seam, a narrow arch beginning high, running down with straight sides for several centimeters, at the ankle bone curving toward the heel, and then taking a sharp turn downward. Between two parallel lines defining the seam runs a line of small dots. In a somewhat puzzling example of footgear (Fig. 195) the dark-brown leg sections are probably boots, and the black foot sections, mules. Through slashes at knee, side, and toe, red color can be seen, arguing for red hose. The very long boot-slash is tied with four pairs of black laces ending in gold aglets.

The boots of a Portuguese knight dressed in olive-green velvet are more elaborate. Worn over yellow hose (Fig. 196), they are white lined with yellow. Short slashes ease the knee. Edges of a slash at the side are tied togther with a lace of black dotted with gold and finished with gold aglets. The instep seam is faintly visible. There are other Portuguese illustrations of these impressive white boots.

A silk-clad Magus (Fig. 71) wears handsome boots of beige-tan embroidered in deeper tan (Fig. 197). In the design, the arch of the instep seam, defined with parallel lines, dictates the arrangement of anthemia or palmettes and scrolls. The seam stitching can be detected behind the parallel lines on the Magus's left boot. Long slashes at the knee reveal dark brown hose. Also on the effigy (Segovia. Hospital de Viejos) of Pedro López de Medina, who died in 1518, the boots are enriched with embroidery across the front, and similar decoration is recorded for those of Charles V in an engraved portrait (1548) by Lucas Cranach the Younger (Madrid. Biblioteca Nacional).

Just how such long boots were kept in place and unwrinkled is not clear. In the next period they seem to depend on garters from above, as in the portrait (copy) of Charles V by Pantoja (Madrid. Museo del Prado).

High boots could appear with the top turned down or folded into a cuff. Those of Figure 198, yellow, are drawn over green hose. The ankle fits rather loosely and prepares one for tops slipped down above a mass of folds as worn by a flagellator (Fig. 199), by King Herod, Saint Roch, a Magus, etc. Of those in a final illustration (Fig. 200), white embroidered with gold, only the front could reach the knee. A short slit appears in the top toward the back, and the instep seam is plainly rendered.

An ordinance issued at Toledo in 1533 prescribes that the maker of boots "of whatever quality shall fashion them carefully and [see] that they are lined at the toes *(puntas)* and from the middle upward, and that they have their stiffeners *(contrahortes)*, and their reinforcing strips *(barretas)*, and their stopping piece *(chapeta)* at the closing." The sentence clearest in meaning now is that insisting on two soles, "the first one *(primera)* of suitable hide *(corambre)* and that over it *(la de encima)* of loin or back leather *(lomo)*, each of the same size as its mate and sewed with hempen thread."[174]

Mule

Overshoes, mule and pantofle, were made without quarters but with toes responsive to change in fashion. In the leather-soled mule *(chinela)* the toe at different times was broad and rounded (Fig. 201), narrower and square (Fig. 202), or shaped to the foot (Fig. 203). Jorge Manrique (before 1479) refers to a woman's,[175] while Palencia (1490) evidently is thinking of the man's, when he suggests that *chinelas* were shoes to wear when preparing to ride or going to the field, alike for both feet *(q̃ fazẽ a amboz pies)*.[176] A description of 1552 states that the *chinela* was of goatskin, without cork.[177] Covarrubias says it might have two or three soles of leather but no heel piece or quarter *(talón)*. According to him, it was easy to put on and to take off and was worn over the buskin by horsemen. He

states that there was no distinction between right and left and that the *chinela* had a blunt toe *(punta roma)*.[178]

Alcorque

The cork-soled *alcorque* also was an overshoe. In an old story translated from the Arabic (1253), a king, departing hastily before the arrival of a husband, leaves on the bed where he has been sitting his *arcorcoles*(diminutive of *alcorques*).[179] The term *alcorque* is from the Arabic *qúrq*, which made its way into northern Europe as "cork or *kork*." In the England of 1463-1464 "corke" meant "cork shoe"; bottle stoppers came later. Oliver Asín traces the industry of making cork footgear from Hispano-Romans through Spanish Muslims who gave it "an extraordinary impulse".[180] For Prince Juan (1493, 1494, 1495) ¼ vara of velvet, mulberry colored, crimson, or black, was allowed for a pair of *alcorques;* sometimes a bonnet would be cut from the same material. A *pragmática* of 1515 forbade artisans and farmers to use silk for their cork-soled shoes.[181]

Pantofle

Alcorque must have been a general term. Percyvall translates it as "pantofle", and under the heading *alcorque* Covarrubias proceeds to speak of chopines. Specifically, a mule with cork sole was the *pantuflo*, which was well known in Europe, the name having cognates in at least six other languages. Now that the neat ascription to the Greek *pantophellos* has been abandoned, its origin is deemed uncertain. At Toledo (1533) shoemakers who produced pantofles of cordovan were required to put on surrounds *(cercos)* that were strong, not cut from thin flank leather *(hijada)*, to use corks that had been well scraped *(ruñados)* and scorched *(quemados)*, together with soles of leather from the back *(lomo)* of the animal, and to sew them well with hempen thread.[182] Francesillo de Zúñiga made fun of men who used many layers of cork: "There are persons who don't appear to be men without their pantofles." Apparently he was complaining of the platforms worn by the Duke of Alba and his brother, giving them an advantage over other dignitaries.[183]

There is a Valencian account (1487) of the city's paying for two pairs of pantofles in black long-piled velvet *(velludo)* lined with *grana* for King Fernando.[184] Pantofles were worn by Prince Juan's

201   1525–1529   **202**   1539–1543   **203**   1557

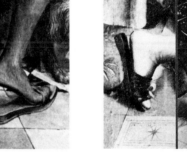
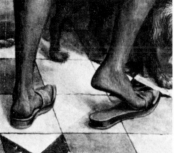

204   1467–1481   **205**   1496–1497   **206**   1520–1530

207   1494–1499   **208**   1529   **209**   1568

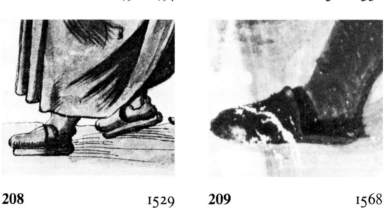

valets, except that while serving him they left them off, together with bonnet and sword. They set pantofles lined with *grana* beside his bed at night, and when he went hunting they carried extra shoes, buskins, and pantofles for him in a red bag, the next day cleaning those that had been used. Riding to meet his bride in 1497, the Prince wore pantofles of crimson velvet over red buskins.[185] A courtier preparing to dance would lay off his cape and step out of his pantofles.[186] Nobles attending the young Charles V at Valladolid in 1518 walked in rain and mud to the Church of San Pablo, ruining their pantofles and scarlet hose.

In 1524 at Granada two types of pantofle were known, "half" and "entire", for each of which was prescribed an insole of goatskin lined, or of calfskin unlined.[187] Pantofles in illustrations likewise are of two kinds. Early examples, secured only with a band behind the toes, may be of the "half" type; one pair (Fig. 204) is worn over a buskin or a loose-fitting boot. In an engraving of 1488, *The Virgin of the Rosary* (The Hispanic Society of America), a kneeling knight of Cologne, booted, has placed on the floor his cap and his pantofles, in which the narrow bands seem to stand exaggeratedly tall. The engraver presumably was from Valencia, which

Mule

201 GENTLEMAN 1525–1529, from figure of saint, choir stall, by Andrés de Nájera and Guillén de Holanda (Valladolid. Museo Nacional de Escultura)

202 KING 1539–1543, from figure of Solomon, choir stall, by Felipe Vigarny (Toledo. Cathedral)

203 MARQUIS 1557, from kneeling effigy of Juan de Rojas, 1st marquis of Pozas, by Francisco Giralte and Manuel Alvarez (Palencia. Church of San Pablo)

Half pantofle

204 CENTURION'S SON 1467–1481, from figure of St. Lupercio, choir stall (León. Cathedral)

205 PAGE 1496–1497, detail from *The Marriage at Cana* by Master of the Retable of the Reyes Católicos (Washington, D.C. National Gallery of Art, Samuel H. Kress Collection)

206 KNIGHT 1520–1530, from *Investiture of a Knight of Santiago,* retable of St. James, attributed to Cristóvão de Figueiredo (Lisboa. Museu Nacional de Arte Antiga)

Entire pantofle

207 GENTLEMAN 1494–1499, from figure of bystander in *Investiture of St. Thomas Aquinas,* main retable, by Pedro Berruguete (Avila. Church of Santo Tomás)

208 CLERIC 1529, from *Thus Go Rich Prelates in the Kingdom of Toledo* in Weiditz, Christoph. *Das Trachtenbuch. f17* (Nürnberg. Germanisches Nationalmuseum)

209 ELDERLY HIDALGO 1568, from miniature of Foli del Burgo Canaus and Family in Philip II. *Carta ejecutoria.* Granada, 1568 (The Hispanic Society of America)

---

long was famous for its production of cork-soled footgear.

The page serving at a wedding feast (Fig. 205) has kept on his banded pantofles, which are brown, over wine-red hose. In those worn by a Portuguese knight (Fig. 206) the band is deeper, so deep as almost to constitute a vamp, and divided into two parts which are laced together. The upper is crimson velvet edged with black; the ties are yellow with gilt aglets. Bright crimson is the insole, brown the outsole, the sole edge black. These pantofles are worn over white boots.

The "entire" pantofle must be that with a complete vamp, as in Figure 207. This pair—open at the toe, light in color, and without shoes—belongs to a courtier in a handsome brocade gown attending a ceremony at Naples, a very Spanish city in the time of the painter Berruguete. In closed-toe pantofles, black over black shoes (Fig. 208), a Spanish cleric walks along, wearing a broad-brimmed hat and having his long skirt carried by a page. Forty years later black pantofles still appear (Fig. 209). They are worn over thin-soled black shoes and black stockings by an old-fashioned gentleman who has his beard cut square (Fig. 25).

Slipper

Servillas, the slippers of which the Prince had eleven new pairs in 1495, have not been identified in illustrations. An ordinance of 1518 allowed them to be made of sheepskin *(badana* or *baldrés)* and required them to be well sewn and with insoles *(plantillas)* of the same material,[188] so they must have been soft. In 1552 they are described as being used within buskins.[189]

Hempen-soled sandals *(alpargatas)* and wooden-soled shoes *(zuecos)* were seldom if ever listed in inventories.

Accessories

Glove

> Hat, galoshes, gloves,
> The gallant should wear,
> Sing well and compose
> In couplets and rhymes.[190]

Luis Milán is more explicit, defining his courtier as "son of the mode . . . friend of cleanliness and foe of unpleasantness . . . habitually decent and clean, well dressed, with good gloves *(guantes)* so tanned as to give off no offensive odor."[191]

Gloves cover the praying hands (Fig. 210) of Infante Alfonso, brother of Queen Isabel, as he kneels in effigy. The finger stalls fit snugly; over the third finger of one hand a ring is worn. Hand proper and wrist hang loose, a single button or jewel marking the outer edge. Gloves must have been perishable, as they were supplied in such quantity. Queen Isabel's treasurer provided the Bragança princes (1490's) with two or four dozen pairs at a time, priced at about 20 maravedis each. Prince Juan's gloves could be more expensive; two dozen pairs from Ocaña in the province of Toledo (1493) cost 730 maravedis. In the same year, 1,095 were paid for only three pairs. The largest order was from a

210   1489–1493

211   1490

212   1508

213   ca. 1530

214   ca. 1532

215   1508

216   1520–1530

217   ca. 1530–1540

Madrid glover (1495), one hundred pairs for 2,500 maravedis. The Prince's gloves of otter *(nutria)* lined with Rumanian lambskin cost 465 maravedis a pair. Otter gloves were worn by the Duke of Béjar and the Count of Feria also. Gloves of 1533 were lined with velveteen *(pana)*.[192] Of embroidered gloves, said to have been popular, I have found only one record and that early (1468): a yellow pair, lined throughout *(doblados todos)* and embroidered with silk in a design of hearts. The same inventory lists a pair of moth-eaten woolen gloves.[193]

A king's glove (Fig. 211) fits better through the hand and ends in a moderate gauntlet. In the striped glove of a young man (Fig. 212) the softly draped gauntlet hangs at one side in a long point, which carries a bead and a thin tassel. Such a point was favored at this time.

After his coronation at Bologna the Emperor appears in the most elaborate gloves (Fig. 214) illustrated for the period—the hand and all the fingerstalls slashed in rows. Slits were made to reveal the brilliance of a fine jewel, like the Emperor's ring on his bare hand. Lacking a gauntlet, the gloves are pinked or scalloped at the wrist. Gabriel de

Salamanca crushes his gloves (Fig. 213), leaving visible a soft, scallop-edged gauntlet from which extends a plain-edged, pointed tab. The flexible, asymmetrical gauntlet, inherited from the Middle Ages, was to give way to a straight cuff, and later to a stiff gauntlet larger and of even depth.

In the sixteenth century gloves were made at small towns, Ocaña (Toledo) and Guadalupe (Cáceres), as well as at capital cities. Those of Ocaña, believed to keep hands white and soft, were extremely popular. Ocaña made shipments to all parts of Spain and even to the best dealers in Rome.[194] At Guadalupe glove makers had to compete with monastery scribes for the available supply of kidskins; according to law, townspeople could buy none until the monastery scriptorium had been supplied. From the Prior of Guadalupe in 1576 King Sebastião of Portugal was happy to receive six dozen pairs of gloves.[195] At Sevilla makers were commanded to use kid and lambskins softened and whitened with a dressing of alum, flour, and eggs.[196] Long famous for the tanning of fine leathers, Spain exported gloves to England, until the 1580's saw the industry developed there. For perfect gloves, it was said at one time, Spain should have tanned the skins, France have cut the pieces, and England have done the sewing.[197] During Charles V's first visit to England (1520), when a banquet was followed by dancing, "the ball throughout was 'the Gloves of Spain' "[198] which suggests the title of a song.

Scented gloves are mentioned frequently. In the famous "Accounts of the Great Captain", supposed to have been drawn up to justify his expenditures, is a fantastic entry of 10,000 ducats spent for perfumed gloves "to preserve troops from the bad odor of enemy corpses lying on the field of battle".[199] Substances used for perfuming gloves in Spain were ambergris, civet, and musk. Antonio de Guevara, a courtier prelate, spoke with a mother (1529) who boasted that whoever took her daughter to wife would get a girl who knew how to perfume a husband's gloves. But Guevara's candidate was a blacksmith, always covered with charcoal dust, and telling him that his wife would perfume his gloves with civet would be to offer him a public insult. The prelate approved sprinkling a shirt with rose water, permitted sprinkling a handkerchief with clover water, praised the sprinkling of pillows with orange-blossom water. But paying 6 ducats (2,250 maravedis) for a pair of perfumed gloves, he absolutely cursed. "Nobody buys gloves for 3 reales (63 maravedis) or more from necessity but for reasons of

---

Glove

210 INFANTE 1489–1493, from effigy of Infante Alfonso by Gil de Siloe (Burgos. Monastery of Miraflores)

211 KING 1490, from figure of Magus in *Epiphany*, retable from Enviny, by Pere Espalargues (The Hispanic Society of America)

212 NOBLEMAN 1508, from figure of St. Julian, retable center, by Juan Gascó (Vich. Finca del Pradell, Collection of Ramón d'Abadal i de Vinyals)

213 GENTLEMAN ca. 1530, from portrait, entitled *Gabriel de Salamanca*, by Jan Gossaert (formerly Private Collection, New York)

214 EMPEROR ca. 1532, from portrait of Charles V, emperor of the Holy Roman Empire, by Christoph Amberger (Berlin-Dahlem. Gemäldegalerie)

Tassel

215 NOBLEMAN 1508, from figure of St. Julian, retable center, by Juan Gascó (Vich. Finca del Pradell, Collection of Ramón d'Abadal i de Vinyals)

216 SWORDSMAN 1520–1530, from figure of bystander in *The Wedding of the Virgin*, retable, by the Master of O Paraíso (Lisboa. Museu Nacional de Arte Antiga)

217 COUNT ca. 1530–1540, from portrait of Alonso Felipe de Aragón y de Gurrea, count of Ribagorza; later 16th-century copy by Roland de Mois (Madrid. Palace of the Duke of Villahermosa)

fussiness or frivolity."[200] Secular courtiers took a different view: perfumed gloves, 40 pairs worth upwards of 200 ducats, were offered as the appointed prize at a tournament (Valladolid, 1523), in which Charles V took part.[201]

Spanish gloves had the reputation of retaining their scent. That a glover's shop was a treat to the nose, Don Quijote implies in suggesting the odor shed by his Dulcinea: "Didn't you sense [Sancho] . . . an aromatic fragrance, something good—I don't know what, I can't give it a name—I might say a fume, an emanation, as if you were in the shop of some good glover?"[202] By 1723 the sophisticated French could no longer endure the strong perfumes of Spanish gloves, and the fashion for these once popular imports was practically dead in France.[203]

King Ferrante of Naples, who liked to reveal his fine figure, disliked his hands and hardly ever took off his gloves.[204] Other monarchs responded to an occasion. When Charles V swore to the rights of Valencia (1528), he removed bonnet and gloves, placed his hands on the missal brought to him, and kissed it.[205] That gloves were not worn for dancing is borne out by the fact that they fail to appear among the luxurious details listed in *Questiõ de amor*.

Fernández de Oviedo describes a bit of form that had crystallized about this accessory. "Who would not think, if king or prince were to drop a glove, that true civility would have one pick it up, kiss and return it? That would indeed be correct if you and the king were alone. But if others were present, especially persons superior to you in rank, you would be committing a grave error. If you happen to be standing nearest, you may with due reverence stoop to pick it up. Then, making a slight bow and kissing the glove, hand it to the principal dignitary present, and he, not you, after making his bow, will hand the glove to the prince or the king. This is the custom kept by the royal house of Castilla where I was brought up, and this is how I saw it done."[206]

Tassel

For a certain period the dagger carried by gentlemen was accompanied by a large tassel *(borla)* attached to the dagger sheath or to the strap from the belt which supported it. A young man wears a green silk tassel with a small, plain head (Fig. 215). Charles V has one with a white skirt and an elaborate head of filigree gold (Fig. 13). The dagger tassel in a portrait of the Count of Ribagorza (Fig. 217) is of black silk covered with gold netting that ends in fringe. A more elaborate example hangs from the sword belt of a Portuguese (Fig. 216). Greenish brown, its long core is overhung with eight or ten smaller tassels and topped by a head in two tiers.

Purse

Until pockets were sewed into clothes, probably not before 1550, gentlemen carried small necessities in a purse attached to or pendent from the belt. When both pocket and purse were lacking, the codpiece could serve, or a sleeve. Beltrán de la Cueva, on a journey with Queen Isabel, was able to accommodate her at a barren place in the road with a handsome mirror, pins, and anything else she required for mending her coiffure by pulling them out of his sleeve.[207]

Of the many types of purse three are illustrated here. The first, shaped like an envelope and attached to the belt, appears early in small size. That in a portrait (Madrid. Museo del Prado) of the Marquis of Santillana, who died in 1458, or of his son is adorned with pearls set in vertical lines. King Fernando's purse, like that of his son in the same group (Fig. 100), is even smaller, the flap secured with a narrow strap and buckle. The King's is plain black matching his belt, while Juan's appears to be embroidered. Saint Julian's somewhat larger purse (Fig. 218), black under white lattice work, also matches the belt. His fellow falconers in other countries carried similar pouches. A large envelope bag in cream color (Fig. 221) is trimmed with black cords, buttons, and tassels and is worn by a man in an orange-colored gown who stands listening to the Master's talk at Simon's table.

Examples of the long purse have been found in illustrations of characters sometimes identified as Jewish high priests. The simpler bag (Fig. 219) is carried by a band with rounded end, which fastens over the belt with button and buttonhole. Pearls outline the band and wire circles the button, jeweled at center. The pouch itself is worked with a design of overlapping leaves which suggests tooled leather. Three balls or rosettes finish the bottom. An engaging detail is the small key in plain sight, hanging on a ribbon. A similar bag apparently of leather, scored vertically and adorned with large pearls scattered singly, is worn in a vulnerable position, at center back, by a man in *The Entombment* by Juan de Flandes (Palencia. Cathedral). The green purse of another "high priest" (Fig. 222) is made with iron fittings. From a horizontal bar depends an oval frame enclosing a panel of green material, shirred at the top and disposed of less smoothly at the bottom. The frame must support the pouch itself, which, also shirred, is adorned with tassels. The whole hangs by a metal loop from a gilded belt. This kind of purse with its full, rounded bottom calls up the French term, *bourse à cul de vilain*.

Of the third type, an actual example in metal and leather (Fig. 220) fortunately exists. A divided metal loop supports a short horizontal bar with two descending verticals, to which are attached the voluted ends of a horizontal, oval frame. Two other volutes at the bottom of the frame may form part of the fastening. Vertically scored leather fills the frame, which is hinged at the sides. A crease in the leather between the hinges suggests the many foldings it has endured when the purse was opened. The lower section, evidently cut on straight lines, is fulled to the oval frame and thereby is drawn into a pleasing curve. A purse of Maximilian II, regent and later emperor (Fig. 223), reveals the luxury this type attained just before it succumbed to the hidden pocket. The frame, hanging from the leather belt by an ornate motif and a plainer loop, is of gold, while the green fabric, probably velvet, is richly embroidered in a design of gold lines, silver scrolls, and pink flowers.

During our period several words were used to signify "purse"—*bolsa, escarcela, garniel*—but it is difficult to identify the word with the object. *Bolsa* would seem to have been the general term, straight from the Latin *bursa*; it appears in accounts and inventories recorded by men who had little talent for description. In 1487 Prince Juan received a *bolsa* of green *cebtí* trimmed with tassels, a garnet, and gold. The Braganças (1490) each had a *bolsa* of *grana* associated with a belt of gold thread ending in a gilded iron point or points *(rejos)* and costing 3,370 maravedis. That fat and furious warrior, García de Paredes, left behind (1533) several *bolsas:* a new one of black velvet; one of white satin, embroidered and adorned with six silver-gilt Agni Dei; three purses of silk, one black, two brown; and one of tawny leather for keeping documents.[208] Manuel the Fortunate of Portugal owned eight *bolsas* when he departed this life (1521). One of black velvet had the opening *(bocal)* of gold enameled in black and a small gold key for closing it. Another of crimson

velvet sewn with seed pearls was made on frames *(ferros)* of enameled gold; the ring or swivel *(tornel)* by which it hung also was of gold.[209] At Sevilla *bolsas* were produced by the point maker *(agujetero)*. Those sold to a silk merchant had to be of kidskin *(cabrito)* and be lined with kidskin.[210]

As Puiggarí describes it, the *escarcela* featured a guard or lid doubled back *(dobladiza)*.[211] The French *escarcelle* could be made with an iron frame "which sometimes attained the proportions of a work of art".[212] The Duke of Milan (1488) requited the gift of a falcon with a handsome Spanish *escarcela*, together with a very handsome belt fittingly embroidered.[213] It was into an *escarcela* that the chamberlain put the cash that Prince Juan required for each day. Pilgrims carried the *escarcela*. Covarrubias traces the word from the tinder *(yesca)* used with flint for making a light—*yesca, iesquero* (a little pocket attached to a belt), thus *iescarcela, escarcela*—but the Spanish Academy derives it from the Italian *scarsèlla*, which is tentatively taken from *scarso* meaning "short of money".

In the estate of a marquis (1528) four ducats was the appraised value of a *garniel* of black velvet embroidered with drawn-gold thread, the crosspiece *(travesaño)* worked in silver thread.[214] The present-day definition of *garniel* is "belt, with pouches of leather or sheepskin attached, for keeping money".

A large *gipsière* of Morocco leather "trimmed with silk in the Spanish manner and with three tassels of white silk" was listed in the inventory of Phelipe el Hermoso (1509).[215] Puiggarí interprets the word as *gibecera*,[216] which is ignored by the Spanish Academy. Both *gipsière* and *gibecera* must be adaptations of the French term *gibecière*, which, according to Larousse, was used in the Middle Ages for a sacklike purse without iron frames *(ferrures)*. A fourteenth-century example is rectangular, richly embroidered, and hung with tassels on three sides.[217]

Fastener

Men's garments were secured with several types of fastener. A dialogue between two friends and a male servant (1538) mentions four.

"*Bellio.* Well, for my part, I pay more attention to convenience in clothes than to how well they look. Those hooks *(corchetes)* and their eyes *(hembras)* are loose; you knave, you always unfasten them without watching what you do.

"*Maluenda.* I find it preferable to use buttons

218   1508

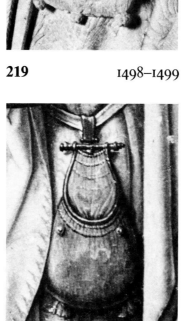

219   1498–1499

220   ca. 1550

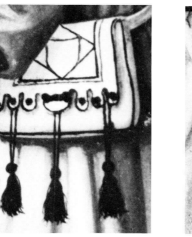

221   1526

222   ca. 1510

223   1550

224   1493

225   ca. 1520

226   ca. 1520–1530

and buttonholes; they look better and are less trou-
blesome in dressing and undressing.

"*Bellio.* Not everyone thinks the same in such
matters. . . . These points have lost their aglets!
This trimming band is ripped off and torn—see that
they mend it! And take care also that no ugly stitching shows.

"*Gomecillo.* That would require a full hour and
a half.

"*Bellio.* Then fasten it with a pin, so it doesn't
dangle."[218]

As described by Covarrubias, the hook is "a clasp
of iron wire consisting of male and female [parts].
It was called *corchete* because of the small, curved
(corbado) hook of the male which catches in the
female."[219] Leloir says that hooks and eyes go back
to remote antiquity, having from earliest times the
form that is used today.[220]

Purse

218 NOBLEMAN 1508, from figure of St. Julian, retable
center, by Juan Gascó (Vich. Finca del Pradell, Collection of Ramón d'Abadal i de Vinyals)

219 DIGNITARY 1498–1499, from figure in decorative
framework beside *Jesus Bearing the Cross* (Burgos.
Cathedral, Trasaltar)

220 GENTLEMAN—LEATHER PURSE WITH METAL
FRAME ca. 1550 (Barcelona. Capmany Collection)

221 TOWNSMAN 1526, from figure of bystander in *Jesus
in the House of Simon*, retable of St. Mary Magdalene, by Pere Mates (Gerona. Cathedral, Tesoro)

222 DIGNITARY ca. 1510, from figure of bystander in
Ecce Homo, main retable, by Juan de Flandes (Palencia. Cathedral)

223 REGENT 1550, from portrait of Maximilian II, emperor of the Holy Roman Empire when regent of
Spain, by Antonio Moro (Madrid. Museo del Prado)

Leather point

224 FARMER—DOUBLET AND HOSE 1493, from *June*
in Li, Andrés de. *Reportorio de los tiempos.* Burgos,
1493. sig.d⁶ (The Hispanic Society of America)

225 EXECUTIONER—DOUBLET AND BREECH-HOSE ca.
1520, from *The Martyrdom of St. Hermengild*, retable
of the Martyrs, attributed to Juan Ramírez (Granada. Museo Provincial de Bellas Artes, Palacio de
Carlos V, Alhambra)

226 SCOURGER—CODPIECE ca. 1520–1530, from *St.
Vincent on the Rack*, retable of St. Vincent, by Juan
Gascó (Vich. Museu Episcopal)

Point or lace

Conspicuous fasteners in our period are points
or laces *(agujetas)* tipped with aglets *(clavos, cabos,*
or *herretes)*. Prince Juan's chamberlain helped him
every morning to truss his points, obviously a task
not easily done alone. In a morning dialogue (1538)
a youth speaks with the maidservant.

"*Emanuel.* Give me the leather points.

"*Beatriz.* They are broken. Take the silk ones,
as your tutor directed. Next, do you wish the
breeches and hose? It is hot.

"*Emanuel.* Not at all. Give me the drawers
(calzoncillos). Truss me up, for heaven's sake.

"*Beatriz.* How now? Are your arms made of hay
or butter?

"*Emanuel.* No, but they are sewed on with fine
thread. Ugh, what points you give me, tagless and
broken.

"*Beatriz.* Remember, gaming with dice yesterday,
you lost the whole ones."[221]

Leather points had other uses as well. When the
rebel Boabdil was captured at Lucena (1483), the
Christian alcaide, ignorant of his prisoner's status,
took a deerskin point and tied together the thumbs
of the unfortunate Prince, who thus on a pack animal was conveyed to the alcaide's castle.[222] Baeza's
cuentas record one payment of 10 maravedis each
dozen for five dozen kidskin points furnished to
the Bragança princes (1493). Ordinances published
in 1527 lay down rules for makers at Sevilla: "All
the points for half arming *(medio armar)* shall be
[cut] from good kidskins or good lambskins. Both
for buckling *(abrochar)* and for trussing *(atacar)*
they shall be well made, well tagged *(clavadas)* and
polished *(limadas),* point and head. Those of kidskin
shall be entirely of kidskin and not of lambskin
almost like it *(a vueltas)*. . . . If peradventure a
master should wish to make points with old aglets
(de clavo pasado) and should receive an order to
do so, he shall make them of good kidskins pierced
with a short-bladed awl *(punzón de corta pieza),*
pierced also with a slender awl that passes from
side to side and with its aglet that passes from both
sides. And the aglet must not be weak."[223]

An essential use of points was to lace hose or
breeches to the doublet. A later ordinance (1546)
sets forth requirements that must always have been
necessary. In order that the breeches waistband
(pretina) should not rip under strain, it was to be
interlined with two layers of canvas before eyelets

227   1489–1493

228   1515–1525

229   1520–1525

230   ca. 1498

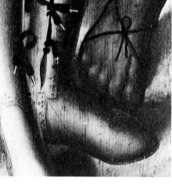

231   1503–1506

232   ca. 1510–1520

233   ca. 1498

234   ca. 1519

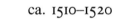

235   ca. 1554

(ojetes) were worked to receive points. Doublets (1541) were interlined for the same reason.[224] A farmer reaping grain (Fig. 224) kept his laces taut, while a courtier living in a village might enjoy slacking his: "If a doublet oppresses him, he loosens the points," says Guevara.[225] An executioner, like a farmer, probably would use leather points. For violent action, those at the waistline (Fig. 225) could be untied, while those at the codpiece (Fig. 226) were left secure.

Officials were concerned with the quality of fabric laces also. At Granada (1541) no ribbons, braids, or cords except of silk, silk and linen *(media seda de hilado)*, ferret *(hiladillo)*, or something else related to silk were to be tagged for points. Those of silk or ferret (1527) were to be well tagged with aglets of solid brass *(latón gordo)*, beaten smooth and polished. Every aglet was to be so firmly attached to its ribbon that it would not fly off, on pain of 200 maravedis fine to the maker (1541). A craftsman standing for examination to enter the trade had to tag, under observation, six dozen wide-ribbon points—two dozen with the aglets beaten and polished, two with them perforated and tagged, and two *grafiladas,* that is, with the aglet surface milled.[226]

A mariner might use points of white linen thread (1530), but for Queen Isabel's menfolk yards and yards of silk ribbon, wide or narrow, black or in colors, were paid for by Baeza—60, 80, 160 varas at a time—for making points. In another account 9 dozen had been tagged from 80 varas of ribbon,[227] giving a possible length for each point of about 24 inches. Wide-ribboned points or laces can easily be illustrated. That closing the neck of King Juan's doublet (Fig. 227) might well have measured 24 inches, but others seem shorter. The very wide points at the upper corners of a stomacher (Fig. 228) are no exaggeration when compared to three that close the outer edges of King Manuel's gown sleeve, in his kneeling effigy of 1517 (Belém. Monastery, Portal), and the single one at the ermined edges of another Portuguese sleeve (Fig. 229).

Points of narrow ribbon also can be illustrated. One ties together the edges of a divided bonnet brim (Fig. 230). Others close the slit in high leather boots above the anklebone (Fig. 231). A point of gold cord (Fig. 232) on a level with the ermine collar secures a gown of black and gold brocade. The cord runs through two golden rings, which may illustrate the *ojales* that are listed among buttons and aglets in Queen Juana's inventory: 126 *ojales* of gold, enameled, each with three little loops or handles *(asicas),*[228] presumably for sewing it on a garment. Through similar rings is threaded the lace of King Juan's doublet (Fig. 227).

Point of wide ribbon

227 KING—DOUBLET 1489–1493, from effigy of Juan II by Gil de Siloe (Burgos. Monastery of Miraflores)

228 HORSEMAN—STOMACHER 1515–1525, from bull-fight scene, staircase ramp (Salamanca. University)

229 PRINCE—GOWN SLEEVE 1520–1525, from *The Meeting of Prince Conan and St. Auta,* retable of St. Auta, by the St. Auta Master (Lisboa. Museu Nacional de Arte Antiga)

Point of narrow ribbon or cord

230 ARCHDUKE—BONNET ca. 1498, from portrait of Phelipe el Hermoso, king of Castilla as archduke of Austria (Paris. Musée National du Louvre)

231 KING—BOOTS 1503–1506, from figure of Magus in *Epiphany,* retable of the cathedral of Viseu (Viseu. Museu Grão Vasco)

232 KNIGHT—GOWN ca. 1510–1520, from *Warrior Saint* attributed to the Visitation Master (Chicago. Art Institute)

Aglet

233 ARCHDUKE—BONNET ca. 1498, from portrait of Phelipe el Hermoso, king of Castilla as archduke of Austria (The Hispanic Society of America)

234 EMPEROR—HAT ca. 1519, from portrait of Charles V, emperor of the Holy Roman Empire, by Bernhard Strigel (Roma. Galleria Borghese)

235 PRINCE—GOWN SLEEVE ca. 1554, from portrait of Felipe II, king of Spain as prince of Asturias, by Titian and Workshop (Firenze. Palazzo Pitti, Galleria Palatina)

Aglet

The aglet of this period was short, half or a third as long as those used by women in the 1560's, by which time few if any men were wearing them. Those described in detail are always of gold. In 1493 Baeza paid for 21 pairs, "plain [except that] some are cleft *(rajados)*", and 4 other pairs enameled. For Prince Juan (1492) three pairs, ¼ ounce of 21-carat gold on gold braid, cost 486 maravedis a pair. Twenty aglets at a ducat each (375 mrs.) were made for him in 1495, and in the same year 51 pairs costing only 1 real (31 mrs.) for two pairs. Points with aglets of gold were used on a Spanish shirt belonging to Phelipe el Hermoso (1499).[229]

A tournament at Valladolid (1517) saw Charles V wearing a jerkin of cloth of gold and of silver slashed over gold-striped satin, the slashes tied with points of rich cord carrying aglets *(éguillons)* of gold enameled in red, white, or yellow, his colors.[230] One hundred tagged cords secured crimson satin disks on a stomacher of his.

Aglets could serve as decoration, independent of use. On a bonnet (Fig. 233), sets of two points knotted closely and their four plain aglets adorn the upturned brim. In large hats worn by Charles V, the brim may carry on the under side a wide ribbon tied across at intervals with tagged laces. The Strigel portrait shows aglets (Fig. 234) square in section and elaborately fashioned. Their use continues on hats and bonnets of the 1530's. In a late example of such trimming, paired aglets (Fig. 235) have alighted on the sleeves of a gown worn by Felipe II.

Moorish Garments

DURING THE RUGGED YEARS of the Reconquest, Christian magnates of the rude north seized when they could on the smooth, silken comforts of the Muslim south. The usurper Ordoño the Bad, supported by bands of Gallegans but thrown out of his kingdom, took the petitioner's trail to Córdoba with twenty of his followers. For his audience with the Caliph at Al-Zahrâ (962) he wore a tunic and a cloak of white brocade "of Christian manufacture". Afterward he was presented with a tunic and a burnoose of gold tissue constituting a "robe of honor", which in Oriental usage meant something of the Caliph's own wearing. Every one of Ordoño's followers, counts and others, received a costume befitting his station.[231] Dozy says that Ordoño died at Córdoba,[232] but some of his followers must have reached home in distant Galicia with their exotic souvenirs.

Among Spaniards of succeeding centuries there were relaxed characters, such as Pedro I and Enrique IV of Castilla, who borrowed heavily from the rival culture. That Martín I and Alfonso V of Aragón also wore Moorish clothes is proved by their inventories. Among other classes of Peninsular society the draped headdress would seem to have been the principal item adopted (see Figs. 61, 62). Doublets, jerkins, gowns called "Moorish" in Baeza's accounts were so termed probably not because of their fashion, but because of their rich decoration of gold thread and silk, used in edgings, braids, and embroidery.

Four garments distinctly Moorish in origin were popular among Christians of our period—the *quezote*, the *aljuba* or *marlota*, the *capellar*, and the *albornoz* (burnoose).

Quezote

Girón says, "In summer some men wore *quezotes* which in name and fashion must have been taken from the Moors. They were jerkins of coarser or finer linen. Some had the front and the lower hem embroidered; others were striped *(gayado)* with handwork, and some had linen hoods. I do not remember having seen or heard of important people wearing this garment."[233] Nevertheless, Prince Juan almost yearly (1485-1489) had two or three *quezotes* of fine linen, requiring 2½ to 3½ varas each. They were adorned with passementerie edgings or fringes *(caireles),* sometimes of red and white silk, once of red silk and gold. Other *quezotes* are recorded as bearing insertions *(randas)* and fringes *(franjas)* of gold and silk. Linen generally was white.

Carmen Bernis has identified as a *quezote* the rather long, white garment of a Magus,[234] worn under a sleeveless jerkin of brocade and over a velvet-sleeved doublet (Fig. 238). Fullness at the neck is gathered into a narrow binding. In the illustration the vertical lines appear to be caused by fine pleats rather than by embroidered stripes *(gayas)*.

Aljuba

Pietro Martire d'Anghiera writing from Egypt (1501-1502) equates the Granadine term *algiubba* with the Spanish *marlota*.[235] By the term *aljuba* were listed parti-colored garments matched with caparisons for Prince Juan (1495), one set of inexpensive satins, blue and yellow, another of crimson *aceituní* and white *cebtí*. At the same time he had a *marlota*-and-caparison set embroidered with 88 ounces of silver (11 marks). A ninth-century visitor to Spain had seen Arabs there using *djobbas* as springtime wear,[236] and warm-weather materials were still mentioned for *aljubas* in the sixteenth century—thin striped silk *(zarzahan,* 1503) and white linen *(lienzo blanco,* 1509). In *Questió de amor* (1508-

1512) noble gentlemen wear *aljubas* of white brocade and red satin for tilting in a reed-spear tournament.

Marlota

For engaging in such a tournament or the bull-fight, Spanish gentlemen provided themselves generally with a *marlota,* worn in place of a jerkin, and a *capellar* or a burnoose which were forms of the cape. The *marlota* is most often mentioned—a loose garment hanging from the shoulders and permitting action, in contrast with the jerkin which drew in about the waist. Carmen Bernis has found three *marlotas* listed in an inventory (1456) of the Count of Plasencia,[237] thus prolonging the period, 1480–1680, set by Robert Ricard[238] for this Hispano-Moresque garment. Furnished with sleeves, it opened down the front and reached generally to the knees or a little below; one of ground length is recorded as a shroud.

Ricard suggests that the *marlota* may have had a hood, but none appears in the diagram (Fig. 240) or figures in the text of Alcega: "For this *marlota* in silk it will be necessary to take five sixths of a vara for the left sleeve, which will go without any shaping *(proporción)* whatever. The silk that remains will be doubled, half the varas being placed upon the other half, according to nap and design *(a pelo y labor)* should the material be damask. From our left hand comes the front, and later the back of this *marlota* will be cut, head to foot with the front. And from the sides come the back and front piecings *(cuchillos). . . .* The collar *(cabezón)* of this *marlota* comes from against the sleeve wrist, below the skirt-foot at the back."[239] Alcega's garment would be 1½ varas in length. Each piecing was to be cut so that its design would match the direction of that in the body, front or back.

The fullness of the *marlota* skirt could be increased with gores. An inventory of 1503 lists a sleeved *marlota* of camlet shaped with *jirones.* In *Questiõ de amor* a horseman wears one gored *(nesgada)* of tawny-colored satin and black *aceituní.* Parti-colored *marlotas* had long been favored. A Bragança prince (1493) received crimson *aceituní* and brocade for such a garment. In 1495 Prince Juan gave to his chamberlain 3½ varas of turquoise *cebtí* for half a *marlota.* One of both black and white materials sewn with gold thread is recorded as turning the Marquis of Villafranca into a Moor.[240]

Again referring to the wardrobe of Prince Juan,

6 varas of crimson brocade of rich pile and broad width, costing 10,585 maravedis the vara, were supplied when he was fifteen (1493) to make him a *marlota* and also sleeves and collar for a doublet. The *marlota* lining, 7½ varas of blue *ceti,* brought the cost of the materials to 68,610 maravedis. The next year 5¾ varas of brocade, woven of "white drawn gold" for the total price of 73,456, made him another *marlota* and matching doublet sleeves. Also in 1494 a *marlota* drawn from the royal wardrobe was lined for the Prince with 7⅙ varas of crimson satin from Venice at 1300 maravedis the vara.

At Valladolid (1518), when "young princes and noble gentlemen" of Castilla fought on horseback with reed-spears to entertain the young Charles V, all were "accoutered in the Moorish fashion", which implies *marlotas.* "And I assure you," writes Charles's aide-de-chambre, "that in several, cloth of gold or of silver was not spared, and it was so slashed that it could not possibly serve any useful purpose, unless one were to melt and burn it to extract the metal."[241]

Rich trimmings were lavished on rich materials. A *marlota* of white brocaded satin for Prince Juan (1494) was adorned with strips *(tiras)* of crimson *cebtí,* besides being embroidered with 26½ ounces of gold bugle beads *(cañutillos)* together with 6 ounces of edging gold *(oro de orilla)* for the said embroidery. To another of his were added 30 fringes *(flecos)* of *oro de orilla.* For a Bragança (1494), 9½ ounces of silver thread were required for buttons and trimming on a *marlota* of crimson, brocaded satin. Sleeves received special attention. In the crimson, brocaded velvet *marlota* for the Prince (1493) mentioned above, the sleeves were garnished with gold trimming and embroidery stitched with silk; on these sleeves and a burnoose were lavished a total of 26⅜ ounces of spun gold *(oro hilado)* and 2 ounces of silk.

After Granada had been won and the subsequent Morisco rebellion had been crushed (1570), the tradition of the Moors' grace and luxury moved their former foes to write innumerable ballads setting forth brilliant pictures of the late wars and festivals. In one such ballad, sleeves and gores of a Morisco *marlota* in mulberry carry a thousand blue roundels in groups of thirteen.[242] Another describes the beautiful Galiana embroidering for her valient Sarrazino the right sleeve of the *marlota* he is to wear when tilting with reed-spears. With seed pearls and fine pearls she enamels the sleeve between raised designs of gold and bows of silver. Then over the entire

236   ca. 1483

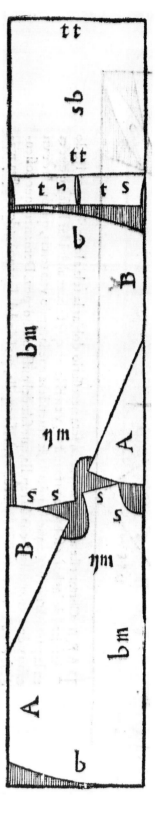

237   ca. 1496–1497

238 ca. 1470–1480   **239**   1577   **240**   1580

surface she sews emeralds and rubies until the sleeve is worth 4,000 doblas (1,460,000 mrs.). It must have been tied into the armscye, because Sarrazino can pledge it at a ring tourney, and when he loses, the rich sleeve is laid before the portrait of his rival's lady.[243]

The ballads give special significance to the color of the garment: black for mourning, white for innocence, yellow for hopeless love, green for good hope, dark green for dead hope. Orange indicates firmness; a happy lover does not need to hope. Tawny is the hue for sadness, mulberry for loving. Combined colors tell a story: a tawny *marlota* sprinkled with mulberry flowers shows that between grief and joy, hope has flowered again. Light green and mulberry betoken firm friendship; sapphires and emeralds publish jealousy dead and hope alive.[244]

At Madrid there still exists what is considered a *marlota* of the late fifteenth century (Fig. 236). After the Moorish Prince Boabdil was captured at Lucena (1483), his *marlota* and other trophies were displayed in a monastery within the jurisdiction of the victors, the Fernández de Córdoba family. The story is, though doubt has been expressed, that the *marlota* remained for centuries in the possession of that family; by 1907 it had been presented to the Museo de Artillería (now Museo del Ejército)

___

Marlota

236 MOORISH PRINCE—*MARLOTA* ca. 1483 (Madrid. Museo del Ejército)

237 KING ca. 1496–1497, from figure of Magus in *Epiphany* by Bartolomé Bermejo (Granada. Royal Chapel, Museo)

239 *REJONEADOR* 1577, from *How Spaniards Equip Themselves to Chase Bulls* in Bruyn, Abraham de. *Diversarvm gentivm armatvra eqvestris.* [Coloniae, 1577] pl.37 (London. Victoria & Albert Museum; Crown Copyright)

240 PATTERN 1580, from Alcega, Juan de. *Libro de geometria, pratica, y traça.* Madrid, 1589. *f*51; first published in 1580 (The Hispanic Society of America)

Capellar

237 KING ca. 1496–1497, from figure of Magus in *Epiphany* by Bartolomé Bermejo (Granada. Royal Chapel, Museo)

Quezote

238 KING ca. 1470–1480, from figure of Magus in *Epiphany* by Fernando Gallego (Barcelona. Museo de Arte de Cataluña)

at Madrid.[245] The *marlota* is of cut, voided satin velvet in crimson and beige with a design of wreaths, pomegranates, and flowers enclosed within large leaf forms, which are carefully matched in the two fronts. Each cut in one piece, fronts and back flare out from the armscye as in the Alcega pattern (Fig. 240). Neck, fronts, sleeves, and hem are edged with narrow braid, probably of gold. Still attached to this braid along the hem, but separated from it down the fronts, is a wider braid of geometric openwork. A vertical slit, long enough to admit a hand and edged with braid or stitchery, appears in each side front near the waistline. Three half frogs remain on the right front.

Carmen Bernis recognizes another *marlota* of our period in a garment worn by Baltasar, the black Magus (Fig. 237).[246] Of plain green material, the *marlota* evidently hangs from the shoulders; below the waistline it is bound with a sash of yellow silk striped with red, white, and black. There is no other decoration, fronts and sleeves being finished with a simple, turned-back fold.

A *rejoneador* of the late sixteenth century (Fig. 239) has combined with the traditional *marlota* the neck and wrist ruffs of his period. The garment closes at front with frogs, and wide scroll-patterned bands decorate the full skirt down the center and the side fronts and along the hem. The hanging tube sleeve looks strange without a matching sleeve top to support it (see Figs. 252–254).

Capellar

In bright vermilion a hooded cloak *(capellar)* contrasts vividly with the dark-green *marlota* worn beneath (Fig. 237). The overgarment is open down the front, except for a brief closing with tasseled gold cording at the neck. Its hood, edged like the fronts with gold stitchery or narrow braid, extends through turban and crown to end in a generous tassel. A handsome gold fringe hangs from the hem. In the ballads *marlota* and *capellar* are contrasted in color: a red and silver taffeta with a mulberry cloth of gold; a mulberry *marlota* with a yellow *capellar;* a red *marlota,* slashed over a green lining, with a brown silk *capellar,* which is lined with cloth of silver; a parti-colored red and blue with a yellow.[247] Later, Covarrubias speaks of the two garments as "livery" worn in reed-spear tournaments.[248]

A garment very like the *capellar* was included in the uniform of Spanish cavalrymen in the Mo-

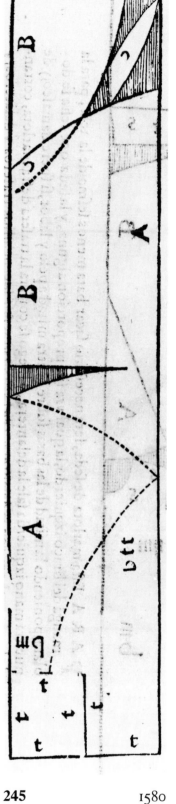

241   1448–1483   **242**   1448–1483

243   ca. 1521   **244**   ca. 1530   **245**   1580

rocco of 1929—a hooded cape of blue cloth with a patch of green joining the fronts over the chest. For a special occasion a mounted Moorish corporal appeared in two such capes, a white and a salmon pink, both of fine woolen.

Burnoose

The burnoose *(albornoz),* a hooded cape also worn with the *marlota,* seems in our period to have been closed from hem to chest. Moors had to pull up their burnooses to get at their weapons. A prisoner taken at the siege of Málaga (1487) persuaded his captors that he would reveal to King Fernando how to conquer the city. Thereupon he was given his burnoose and a cutlass and brought to the tent where a nobleman and a lady were playing tables *(tablas),* a kind of backgammon. Mistaking them for the King and the Queen, he raised his burnoose ostensibly to receive a jar of water; instead, he snatched out his cutlass to hack at the players. They lived, but he was cut in pieces.[249]

A noble Spanish poet (1490) left behind a black burnoose, a white one worked with gold and green, and another of unknown color with green, grayish brown *(pardillo),* and gold.[250] Prince Juan (1493) had one of crimson satin adorned with fringes or galloons, buttons, and other ornaments of spun-gold thread *(oro hilado),* which was made by winding strips of gold or silver-gilt foil over a silk core. For a Bragança burnoose (1494) requiring 6 varas of crimson satin, 7½ ounces of gold thread at 365 maravedis the ounce were supplied; the making cost 1,500. In the next century a marquis's black burnoose (1528) carried black silk trimmings, macramé *rapacejos* and passementerie *caireles* that were fringes or edgings.[251]

Carmen Bernis has identified this garment also in illustrations of Magi.[252] The earlier (Fig. 241)

shows a yellow burnoose lined with scarlet; a hood is suggested at the back. Black stitchery bordering the skirt-hem is repeated along the band of Arabic or pseudo-Arabic letters (Fig. 242) that runs down from the shoulder. The long undergarment is blue-green. A Moor in line for baptism (Fig. 243) wears a plain burnoose which seems to be hooded. In the rose-red one of another Magus (Fig. 244) a hood is clearly indicated; the generous neck opening is closed with a brooch. Simple stitching follows the burnoose edges, while from the hem hangs a hardly visible fringe. Here the undergarment, which may be a *marlota,* is yellow or gold figured with red and blue.

A pattern for a burnoose to be worn at the tourney of reed-spears (Fig. 245) is given by Alcega. "In order to cut this burnoose from silk it will be necessary to double the material down the width, placing half the varas over the other half. In the fold at our left hand, made by doubling the silk, taking away a square of material one-third vara by one-third leaves the hood *(capilla)* projecting from the burnoose. With the back sewn, the hood is made."[253]

In an illustration of the tournament (Fig. 9) the outer garment is draped about the body, leaving the right arm free, and it is thus that Helene Dihle has arranged a burnoose made to one third the size of Alcega's pattern. The hood lies at one side like a collar.[254]

Burnooses of the ballads are quite as rich as *capellares.* Abenumeya wears over a tawny *marlota* worked with mulberry flowers a straw-colored burnoose embroidered with columns. Audalla presents himself in a rose-colored burnoose embroidered with white roses and a white *marlota* also bearing roses. Zelizardo arranges a reed-spear tournament in order to display his burnoose of blue worked with gold and frosted *(escarchada)* silver and adorned with golden arrows, each bearing the legend, "No defense suffices."[255]

In a prose tale the good Malique Alabez, mounted on a dapple-gray horse, rides in a bullfight. When his turn comes, he leaps from his mount with his burnoose of fine silk in the left hand, and, as the bull lowers his head, throws the garment across his eyes. With the right hand he seizes the bull's right horn and stops him. Gripping both horns, Alabez goes up and down with the jumping bull until, with a final twist, he throws him to the ground. Then, picking up the burnoose, he rejoins the lackeys holding his horse and vaults into the saddle.[256]

Burnoose

241, 242 KING 1448–1483, from figure of Magus in *Epiphany,* retable of Alloza, attributed to Jaime Huguet (Zaragoza. Museo Provincial)

243 MOOR ca. 1521, from *Baptism of Moorish Men,* main retable, by Felipe Vigarny (Granada. Royal Chapel)

244 KING ca. 1530, from figure of Magus in *Epiphany,* main retable, by the Ororbia Master (Ororbia. Parish Church)

245 PATTERN 1580, from Alcega, Juan de. *Libro de geometria, pratica, y traça.* Madrid, 1589. v°f 51; first published in 1580 (The Hispanic Society of America)

246   1493

247   ca. 1512

248   1527

249   1495

250   ca. 1510–1520

251   ca. 1525–1530

252   ca. 1530

253   ca. 1535–1540

254   1552

Outer Garments

Gown

Over doublet, hose, and jerkin were worn different garments, of which the most characteristic of our period was perhaps the gown *(ropa)*—knee-length, hanging free from the shoulders, sleeved and collared, faced and lined with contrasting material, most luxuriously with fur. Its generous dimensions (Fig. 13) produced the almost square silhouette favored by gentlemen of this ebullient age. Occasionally the collar, large or small, extends no farther than to the front edges of the gown (Figs. 249, 250), but generally a broad collar is joined to wide facings (Figs. 246, 247) which appear to narrow going downward.

A large, simple sleeve, as in a gown of 1493 (Fig.

Gown with wide sleeves

246 SON OF A DUKE 1493, from figure of Leriano in [San Pedro, Diego de] *Carcel de amor* [*Lo carcer d'amor.* Barchelona, 1493] sig.bj (London. The British Library)

247 HORSEMAN ca. 1512, from *Catelonia* in *The Triumph of Maximilian.* pl. 48 (Madrid. Biblioteca Nacional, Sección de Manuscritos)

248 TOWNSMAN 1527, from figure of listener in *St. Ildephonsus Preaching*, altar of the Descent of the Virgin, by Felipe Vigarny (Toledo. Cathedral)

Gown with columnar sleeves

249 SWORDSMAN 1495, from choir stall by Master Andrés and Master Nicolás (Nájera. Monastery of Santa María la Real)

250 KNIGHT ca. 1510–1520, from *Warrior Saint* attributed to the Visitation Master (Chicago. Art Institute)

251 OFFICIAL ca. 1525–1530, from figure of St. Abdon or St. Sennen, retable of three saints (Barcelona. Masriera Collection)

Gown with puff-topped sleeves

252 NOBLEMAN ca. 1530, from figure of Saint in *St. Julian Supervising the Construction of His Hospital*, main retable, by the Ororbia Master (Ororbia. Parish Church)

253 EMPEROR ca. 1535–1540, from portrait of Charles V, emperor of the Holy Roman Empire, by Cornelis Anthonisz (Amsterdam. Rijksprentenkabinet)

254 NAVIGATOR 1552, from Medina, Pedro de. *Regimiẽto de navegaciõ.* Sevilla, 1563. v°fxxxv (The Hispanic Society of America)

246), widens toward the wrist where a fold is turned back. A transverse cut in such a sleeve has been observed in a gown of crimson and gold brocade (Fig. 247). This type, without the cut, later is found on a somewhat longer garment (Fig. 248). Another style of sleeve, a cylinder set in plain at the shoulder (Figs. 249–251), hangs almost to the gown hem or below it. In front of the elbow an opening allows the doublet or jerkin-sleeved forearm to come through—a short vertical cut (Fig. 249) or a longer one as in a gown of black and gold brocade lined with ermine (Fig. 250). The warrior saint's right gown sleeve has been pushed to the shoulder, so that his arm comes out of the wrist opening instead of through the slit. In a sleeve with both vertical and transverse cuts (Fig. 251) the edges of the vertical cuts are drawn together with agleted ties. In France, according to Joan Evans, the fashion of slitting to free the arms was credited to a Spanish origin.[257]

A characteristic sleeve, which flourished far beyond our period, presents at the top the large puff *(musequí)*, which previously has been seen in the jerkin (Fig. 83) and the doublet (Fig. 115). An early example belongs to Juan de Aragón (Fig. 297). The puff might be plain as in Figure 252, where a crimson gown sleeve lets through a black velvet jerkin foresleeve, or be elaborated into panes (Fig. 253). In the medal of Charles V (1537), of which a detail is shown in Figure 137, the panes are edged with pearls and joined at intervals with small clasps or short-agleted ties. The woodcut of a navigator (Fig. 254) makes the slit and the hanging tube clearly visible. This gown with puffed and hanging sleeves, worn all over Europe in the sixteenth century, Carmen Bernis identifies with the *ropa francesa* mentioned in Spanish documents.[258] Felipe II and his nobles carried it with them to damp and foggy England for the marriage to Mary Tudor.

From his mother's wardrobe *(cámara)* Prince Juan received used *ropas* to be relined or otherwise altered for his wear, but gowns for which new materials were provided him bore the augmentative label of *ropón.* The fabrics were rich, the linings warm, sometimes exceeding in cost that of the outer material. In 1493 and 1494 certain *ropones* for the Prince required the following:

6 varas of mulberry satin at 600 mrs. the vara	3,600	
3¼ varas of red cloth (grana colorada) at 1,700 for lining	5,525	9,125
5½ varas of crimson velvet at 2,500	13,750	
3 varas of red serge (grana colorada de estameña) at 1,875 for lining	5,625	19,375
5½ varas of black damask at 600	3,300	
2½ varas of red London cloth (grana colorada de Londres) at 1,150 for lining	2,875	6,175

The *grana* specified for linings—either native or from London—must have been twice as wide as satin, damask, or velvet because half as much yardage was needed. Widths indicated by Alcega are ⅔ vara for silks, 2 varas for woolens. Furs also were used for lining *ropones*.

The handsomest example of the *ropa* is that portrayed for Charles V (Fig. 13), which corresponds closely to the description of his apparel when at Bologna for the imperial coronation—"*veste franzese di tela de argent fodrata di cibellini*".[259] In the portrait, cloth of silver shimmers in soft folds over the bulk of the sable lining, and sable makes he deep collar and the broad facings. Below the sleeve puffs, which are trimmed with bands of gold network, an opening is provided for the forearm and the doublet foresleeve. Titian, in his version of the subject, patterns the silver cloth more conspicuously and repeats the gold network at the end of the hanging tubular sleeve.

There is abundant textual evidence on men's gowns of the early sixteenth century. One source is *Questiõ de amor*, the novel laid at Naples. France defeated and the Great Captain gone home (1507), Naples was an outpost of Spain, where an elegant society took its pleasure in contests of love, in tournaments of reed-spears, in dancing or hunting. Hispanicized Italians and Italianized Spaniards lived a dream of luxurious harmony, unaware that their enviable bubble would burst with the French victory at Ravenna (1512). The author, blessed with total recall, describes the clothes worn by his peers. A knight favors the same colors as his lady, perhaps adding a third. Belisena, a duchess's daughter, uses red and white; her suitor Flamiano, red, white, and gold or yellow. At a tournament velvets are worn as well as silks. The viceroy has a gown all crimson, of velvet lined with satin. Fabricano, who has been identified with Fabricio Colonna, appears in mul-

berry figured velvet *(altibajo)* lined with white satin; the Duke of Altamira, in tawny velvet banded with wide and narrow galloons of checkered gold.[260]

Ornaments applied on satin trimming bands refer to the wearer's motto. A tawny-lined white gown of the Marquis of Pescara carries, on tawny bands, quill pens in gold relief, reinforcing his plaint:

> My passion cannot be
> Written
> Because it cannot be borne.[261]

The red trimming bands of a prior's blue gown, lined in red satin, carry gold lanterns keyed to this sentiment:

> The fire that consumes the soul
> Though covered
> Is revealed by grief.[262]

Goldsmiths must have worked incessantly to respond to the rhymed mottoes with an adequate supply of small golden clues: yokes, young crescent moons, wings, medallions showing different faces, seals for closing letters, mallow plants, candlesticks without candles, eyeglasses *(anteojos)*, Arabic numerals for 1,000. The last belong to the Prior of Mariana whose motto proclaims:

> The tale of my troubles
> Can be numbered in thousands.[263]

Embroidered motifs include bunches of golden bells, hands making the sign of good fortune, broken oars, open sepulchers in high relief. Brown lined with mulberry is enlivened with "insults" *(improperios)* embroidered on mulberry trimming bands. Black satin is quilted in waves with stitches of gold thread. Palm-Sunday leaves, "because they are said to protect against lightning", decorate a gown of black, drawn gold.

Gowns in cloth of gold or of silver were displayed at a tournament given for Charles V (Valladolid, 1518). The young King and his brother Ferdinand had them of drawn gold lined with sable. Even these costly fabrics were enriched with trimming. The Constable's gown of precious metal was covered with black velvet cut *(décopé)* in an openwork pattern of half lozenges, each solid area bearing a plaque of beaten gold. The Duke of Arcos had cloth of silver lined with cloth of gold *frisé* (with frizzed nap) and covered with delicate *(tenuet)* velvet cut in points which carried floral motifs of beaten gold. Estimated as worth more than 6,000 ducats, the Marquis of Astorga's gown of cloth of silver, lined with crimson satin, was laden at openings *(fents)* and edges with beaten-gold motifs resembling goads *(aguillons)*, interlaced like a trellis. In another gown, cloth of gold *frisé* was strewn with gold plaques and precious stones, and lined with speckled ermine. Pedro Girón had cloth of drawn gold on which were applied chevrons of silver tissue interlaced and laden with roses and pomegranates of fine gold. The Viceroy of Murcia's son wore cloth of silver cut out in half lozenges over gray velvet; the collar and the fronts bore gold motifs of pomegranate trees and pomegranates so thickly set as to touch one another.[264]

At Charles V's coronation (Bologna, 1530) noblemen who carried the imperial insignia wore crimson gowns lined with ermine. Other gowns repeated the rich fabrics of other years. A notable trimming was that of contrasting strips of material—two of cloth of silver on brocaded velvet *(pelo)*, one of black or of red velvet on cloth of gold—the kind of trimming used on jerkins.

Valencia was another scene of luxurious costume displays. When Queen Germana married the Duke of Calabria (1526), she was vicereine of Valencia. Charles V conferred equal honor on him, and as viceroys they reigned together there for ten years. In a region where the Duke had long been imprisoned, he finally could organize the entertainments dreamed of by a Renaissance prince. His enthusiasms were for book collecting and hunting. In an estate on the Turia River, once the pleasure ground of a Moorish king, the Viceroys enjoyed a garden well planted with trees, furnished with ponds and aqueducts, and it may have been in that delicious place that guests were invited to hunt deer and wild boar.

One spring day hunters and their wives came in matching gowns, mostly of velvet elaborately embroidered. The Duke of Calabria and Queen Germana wore crimson velvet stitched with gold thread in a pattern of genista plants with large expensive, Oriental pearls for seeds. Another couple had mulberry velvet trimmed with passementerie of gold and silver and worked with buttonholes or loops *(ojales)*, each enclosing an eye. Two velvet gowns, lined with cloth of gold, were adorned with medallions and with metallic embroidery of spirals or quills; medallions on the husband's gown bore facing profiles of himself and his wife. Pedro Mascó and Castellana Bellvis had red velvet embroidered in a design of apple trees, leaves green and fruit red, with gold letters hanging from them. Another

couple wore blue velvet enriched with raised work in gold and silver and with embroidered nightingales, "birds that sing and are happy only in the spring."

Hunt ended, the company rode off to dine at Liria,[265] on the skirts of a hill dominating a wide valley.

Long gown

Before leaving Flanders, Charles V chose suitable persons to rule the country from those of "the long gown" as well as from the nobility. This act reflects the Burgundian custom of calling the young and elegant "men of the short gown" and dignitaries of the church, law, or letters "men of the long gown".[266] In Spain the floor-length gown was worn by royalty and high nobility and by officialdom as well. Between the long gown *(ropa larga)*, the state gown *(ropa de estado)*, and the trailing gown *(ropa rozagante)* it is difficult to make a distinction.

In 1494 a *ropa larga* for Prince Juan required 13 varas of crimson velvet, over twice as much as was needed for a *ropón*. Lined with ermine, 730 skins, and costing 71,900 mrs., it must have been an important garment trailing on the floor, like the *ropa rozagante* or the *ropa de estado*. Long gowns occasionally were black. The Constable of Castilla, "an old and honest prince", entering a town with Charles V on the way to Valladolid (1517), wore a long gown of black satin slashed over cloth of gold. Charles in the same year chose one of black satin to wear at services conducted over his father's body while he visited his mother at Tordesillas. But crimson was often seen. In a tournament at Valladolid (1518) the Duke of Béjar's dress again drew comment—this time a long gown of crimson velvet lined with cloth of silver. Abundantly slashed, the velvet nevertheless was laden with columns or towers of gold estimated at 8,000 ducats. "I handled one," says Vital, "that could well have been worth more than ten ducats."[267] The columns had been ordered as a compliment to Charles V, whose device included the Pillars of Hercules.

A long gown of rich brown brocade with beige fur collar (Fig. 257) is slit to above the knee. The right sleeve, open at front to reveal a dark brown doublet sleeve, hangs in a tube almost to the gown hem. The left sleeve tube is grasped in the right hand of the royal wearer, as he watches the weighing of a saddle.

Painters seemed to have evaded the task of repre-

255   1489–1493   **256**   1499   **257**   1526

258   1489–1493   **259**   1489–1493   **260**   1500–1505

261   1489–1493   **262**   1489–1493

senting intricately ornamented materials, but sculptors manfully faced up to the problem in two royal effigies and one other. In the alabaster figure of Prince Juan's grandfather (Fig. 255), the style of the long gown is simple—a turn-back collar deeper at back, fronts hanging straight, skirt flaring over the feet, moderate sleeves set in smooth at the armscyes. Each sleeve is slit from a point below the shoulder to another well above the wrist hem, which is turned back in a double fold. It is the fabric that is so astonishingly rich, the surface calling for applied pearls and embroidery in relief rather than for any form of weaving. The allover pattern (Fig. 258) consists of circles tangent at four points and separated by quadrilaterals, some of which enclose a lance rest or socket *(ristre)*, suitable emblem for a king who "jousted well" and was "very happy" at jousting festivals.[268] In the original it probably was wrought in gold or silver. Each circle is surrounded with a cord to which on the outside are addorsed small triangles. Inside the cord runs a series of cusps, each framing three small cusps, over a ground of small florets. Raised above the florets

Long gown

255 KING 1489–1493, from effigy of Juan II, king of Castilla, by Gil de Siloe (Burgos. Monastery of Miraflores)

256 KING 1499, from *Messengers Come from the Kings of Ireland, Declaring War* in *La historia delos nobles caualleros oliueros de castilla y artus dalgarbe.* Burgos, 1499. v°sig.dij (The Hispanic Society of America)

257 KING 1526, from figure of Clotaire II, king of France, in *St. Eligius Weighs a Saddle* by Pedro Nunyes (Barcelona. Museo de Arte de Cataluña)

Long-gown fabric

258 KING—DESIGN OF CIRCLES 1489–1493, from effigy of Juan II by Gil de Siloe (Burgos. Monastery of Miraflores)

259 INFANTE—DIAPER DESIGNS 1489–1493, from effigy of Infante Alfonso by Gil de Siloe (Burgos. Monastery of Miraflores)

260 YOUNG KNIGHT—CIRCLES AND JEWELED BORDER 1500–1505, from effigy of Juan de Padilla, School of Gil de Siloe (Burgos. Museo Arqueológico Provincial)

Long-gown lining and jeweled band

261 KING—SLEEVE 1489–1493, from effigy of Juan II by Gil de Siloe (Burgos. Monastery of Miraflores)

262 INFANTE—SLEEVE 1489–1493, from effigy of Infante Alfonso by Gil de Siloe (Burgos. Monastery of Miraflores)

are the six or more petals of a flower enclosing a circlet, twisted or pearled, about a round center.

A complex band—stripes of pearls, Gothic leaves, twisted rope of four pearls alternating with two longer beads, galloon set with jewels, and then more pearls—finishes each side of the gown front. The sleeve banding, less complex (Fig. 261), begins at the outer edge with a line of pearls, continues with a narrow galloon, twisted about a line of smaller pearls, to a wider galloon set with jewels and bordered at each side with a twisted cord and a line of tiny pearls. A narrow band of seed pearls set with jewels brings one to the inner side, which is finished with pearls of moderate size.

The long gown on the effigy of Queen Isabel's brother Alfonso, wrought at the same time as their father's, is patterned with large diaper designs of four leaf-shapes, outlined with narrow, pearled bands and centered on a circle or a quadrilateral (Fig. 259). Within each leaf-shape on a background of couched gold threads *(punto de oro llano)* is placed a serrate leaf; inasmuch as the top portion turns over upon itself, the actual leaf may have been of sheet gold or silver. A mounted jewel in a cusped setting occupies the center of each circle, and a disk with pearls that of each quadrilateral. The Infante's sleeves are folded back to show the lining and the doublet sleeve (Fig. 262). Sleeve linings of both effigies suggest cut voided velvet, the incised motifs forming the pattern, hatched portions the background.

In another long gown of this period, that for the effigy of young Juan de Padilla who was ambushed and slain by Moors (1491), the use of large pearls, or of gold beads like those "marking the decade of a rosary", is so excessive that the effect is that of popcorn-stitch crochet. The overall design (Fig. 260) again consists of tangent circles. Bounded with an openwork border of tiny spheres and small balusters, each circle contains a pattern of four large cabochons and four smaller alternated about a circlet of twisted cord or wire that surrounds a round center in a cusped setting. The materials appear to be pearls and seed pearls upon a background of heavy, couched gold threads. A wide band set with massive jewels and edged with large pearls finishes each front, the sleeve opening, and a back slit, while fringe hangs from the gown hem.

An extreme example of the state gown was worn in January 1461 by Constable Miguel Lucas de Iranzo for his wedding at Jaén. Of crimson-mulberry, long-piled velvet *(carmesí velludo morado)* lined

263   ca. 1520   **264**   1526   **265**   1525–1529

266   1491   **267**   1516   **268**   1527

with sable, it was very long, "too long", and four pages walked behind the bridegroom's horse to carry the train on their shoulders. Eight gentlemen performing a masquerade dance *(momería)* at Naples came in state gowns of brocade lined with damask or satin, one of white brocade lined with reddish satin.[269]

At a supper given in honor of Juan's and Margarita's wedding (Burgos, 1497) the most expensively clad guest was the Duke of Béjar in a trailing gown trimmed with gold ornaments besides pearls and precious stones. While Isabel and Fernando at Toledo (May 1502) were content to dine in woolen, their handsome son-in-law wore a trailing gown of brocaded satin lined with crimson satin. In a miniature of the period (Fig. 2) his long gown of strikingly patterned fabric is lined with ermine. For King Fernando's entry into Naples (1506) the Great Captain got him into something more regal than his Toledo woolen—a trailing gown of crimson velvet lined with crimson satin. The Captain himself wore one of crimson satin lined with handsome brocade; open at the sides, it revealed a jerkin of hammered gold.

Neapolitan nobles attending the ceremonies wore trailing gowns of brocade lined with silver damask. On the Spanish official scene, six councilmen greeting Juana and Phelipe upon their entry into Toledo (1502) wore such gowns of blue velvet lined with yellow satin. City officials and other dignitaries meeting Charles V as he came into Sevilla for his wedding (1526) had them of crimson satin. Moderately trailing gowns are illustrated in woodcuts. In that of Figure 256 the sleeves are long and simple, widening toward the wrist.

Cloak

In English, "cloak" is the general term for outer garments "commonly longer than a cape". Many a *capa* reached to the ankle, and those known to be of this length we shall call by the Spanish term, for which the English equivalent is given as "cloak or mantle". A knee-length example will be called "cape", even though Webster describes this garment as "usually not reaching below the hips". In translation, when the length cannot be determined, *capa* will appear in the English cognate. Really short capes (*bohemio* and *ferreruelo*) came into fashion after our period.

Mantle

The cape is an ancient garment; it must have existed as soon as skins or furs were sewn together. By the sixteenth century in Spain it had developed many forms, of which the simplest, it would seem, was the mantle *(manto)* of the military religious orders. The effigy of Alvaro de Luna (Toledo. Cathedral), dating from 1489, shows a long mantle open from neck to foot down the center front. On another effigy (Fig. 263) the top fullness is gathered into a casing at the neck, where the mantle closes with a knot of heavy cording slipped up over long, heavy cords, each finished with a tassel. The sword-cross of Santiago, here cut in relief on the armor, would have been applied in red on a white mantle. Associated with ceremony, the mantle was worn hanging straight, or with the sides pulled up and back over the shoulders.

Capa

Also open down the front, a *capa* could be put on in various ways. The rich and ostentatious Calisto (Fig. 264) has the left side of his *capa* swept across the front and thrust high at the right; the fingers of his left hand appear at his throat, securing the drapery. Another gentleman (Fig. 265) lets the

---

Mantle

263 KNIGHT OF SANTIAGO ca. 1520, from effigy of Rodrigo de Cárdenas from Ocaña (The Hispanic Society of America)

Capa

264 *NOUVEAU RICHE* 1526, from figure of Calisto in *Tragicomedia de Calisto y Melibea.* Toledo, 1526. XII aucto (London. The British Library)

265 GENTLEMAN 1525–1529, from figure of saint, choir stall, by Andrés de Nájera and Guillén de Holanda (Valladolid. Museo Nacional de Escultura)

Capa **with arm-slits**

266 PAGE 1491, from San Pedro, Diego de. *Tractado de amores de arnalte y lucēda.* Burgos, 1491. [facsim.: Madrid, 1952] Title-cut (The Hispanic Society of America)

267 GENTLEMAN 1516, from figure of bystander in *The Beheading of St. John the Baptist* by Francisco de Colonia (Burgos. Cathedral, Puerta de la Pellejería)

Capa lombarda

268 GENTLEMAN 1527, from figure of bystander in *La Piedad* (Sevilla. Cathedral, Chapel of Santa Cruz)

269   1496–1497   **270**   ca. 1500–1520   **271**   ca. 1525–1530

272   1529   **273**   ca. 1530–1540   **274**   ca. 1540

left side of his *capa* hang straight, while the right is drawn across the front to fall over his left arm. These *capas* are trimmed along the edge, Calisto's with two bands of silk or velvet, the gentleman's with an embroidered band, a continuous wavy stem carrying small dots that suggest flowers.

Lazarillo's master took good care of his cape. Removing it, he asked whether Lazarillo's hands were clean; then the two of them shook the garment briskly and folded it. The master, having blown the dust off a stone bench, placed the folded cape upon it for the night. In the morning he shook all his clothes and put them on, the outer cape-end sometimes over a shoulder and sometimes over an arm.[270] When Juan Fernández, in Luis Milán's *Cortesano,* came without a cape to play *pelota,* the fact was noted. And when he went to the eleven o'clock Mass in the main church, the Mass of the lazy, without a cape and with his jerkin unfastened, it was so grave a sin that only the Bishop of Fez would absolve him.[271]

Wool is the material most often mentioned for capes, though there are exceptions in silk. Prince Juan in 1493 and 1494 was provided with from 4 to 5 varas for a cape. Black Florentine cloth was used for four, of which only one was trimmed and that with edge-strips *(ribetes)* of velvet. A red cape of *grana* was more generously treated with expensive crimson velvet. In *Questiõ de amor,* also, the

capes generally are of wool. A prior's of yellow cloth carries interlaced ciphers of blue velvet and red satin. On another of yellow cloth strips of white satin and of red are twisted *(antorchadas)* about each other in orders of three. The hero and a cardinal attend a masked party wearing capes of black frieze, which are latticed with narrow gold galloons set over white "eyelashes" *(pestañas),* bands so-called because, according to Covarrubias, an edge might be pinked *(picado).* In the lattice openings silver butterflies are mounted with wings spread.[272] Charles V, after an attack of quartan fever, wore constantly a black frieze cape which he did not exchange for a gayer one, even when the news came that François I had been captured in Italy (1525).[273] During a tournament in the Plaza de San Francisco at Sevilla, after the Emperor's wedding (1526), Juan Alonso de Guzmán wore a cape of frieze adorned with large seed pearls in a band eight inches wide where dolphins were represented, locked by the tails.[274]

That there was a Spanish style of cape was recognized by Charles V's Flemings at Valladolid (1517, 1518). At a tournament the young King wore a "very rich" Spanish cape in which cloth of gold was applied in a cordlike design of knots and interlacings over gold cloth *frisé;* its lining of crimson satin was slashed and stitched with gold in the Italian fashion. The King wore his cape so skillfully arranged that spectators could see the workmanship inside as well as out. Later, the Marquis of Aguilar had a Spanish cape of cloth of gold covered with delicate *(tenuet)* satin, slashed; between the slashes lay great lozenges of gold worked into a design of ermines. This cape was lined with cloth of silver.[275] A Castilian cape is mentioned in 1528, trimmed with velvet. At the coronation in Bologna (1530) Manrique de Toledo wore one of black cloth of gold trimmed with two bands of cloth of silver embroidered with gold thread.[276]

Capas were sometimes slit to provide openings *(maneras)* for the hands *(manos)* and arms. Examples are those of a busy page (Fig. 266) carrying letters for his master and of a young swordsman (Fig. 267). In a fur-lined *capa* of gold and crimson (Fig. 298) the slits run to near the shoulders, letting through the rather wide sleeves of a black jerkin. *Maneras* have been cut also in the cape, black or brown with gold trim, worn by a warrior saint (Fig. 270). In a choir-stall relief of 1521 (Santo Domingo de la Calzada (Logroño). Cathedral) and on a statue of Saint Julian (Fig. 73) the cape shows an opening

Cape with collar

269 GENTLEMAN 1496–1497, detail of bridegroom from *The Marriage at Cana* by Master of the Retable of the Reyes Católicos (Washington, D.C. National Gallery of Art, Samuel H. Kress Collection)

270 KNIGHT ca. 1500–1520, from central figure, *Warrior Saint,* in retable by the Girard, or Gualba, Master (Montserrat. Monastery, Sala Gótica)

271 ARMY COMMANDER'S SON ca. 1525–1530, from figure of St. Martin from Cacabelos (The Hispanic Society of America)

Hooded cape

272 TOWNSMAN 1529, from figure of escort in *Thus in Cataluña One Conducts Noblewomen When They Mourn* in Weiditz, Christoph. *Das Trachtenbuch.* *f*44 (Nürnberg. Germanisches Nationalmuseum)

273 GENTLEMAN ca. 1530–1540, from figure of bystander in *Martyrdom* (Valladolid. Museo Nacional de Escultura)

274 REJA MAKER ca. 1540, from effigy of Cristóbal de Andino (Burgos. Church of San Cosme and San Damián)

275   ca. 1470–1480   **276**   ca. 1510   **277**   1531–1536

278   ca. 1470–1480   **279**   1497   **280**   1499

for the right arm only. Inventories mention capes with sleeves. The black satin cape of a marquis (1528) had both sleeves and half sleeves.[277] A *capa* of gold brocade, which has been called "Lombard", shows a long panel falling over the arm (Fig. 268).

Cape collars were flat early in the period. A bridegroom (Figs. 11, 269) wears one of ermine on his crimson garment, which is secured with chains, one bearing pendants. Saint Roch appearing with a lansquenet (Fig. 5) has a deeper, plain one on his *capa,* while a warrior saint's collar (Fig. 270) is large enough to be called "capelet". A prince's collar (Fig. 298) is faced with the same fur that lines his *capa.* Later on, a cape collar could be full with ample folds. That copied for a statue of Saint Martin (Fig. 271) seems to have been cut circular, while one belonging to the Archduke Ferdinand (Fig. 138), had been cut on the thread and gathered into the neckband of the cape. Saint Martin's cape is red patterned with gold as in a brocade, edged with a band of plain gold which is bordered with narrow, thicker bands suggesting velvet.

Benedetto Varchi, writing in Italy (1529), speaks of capes "in the Spanish style, that is, with a hood at back".[278] Pedro Girón (1537) describes the Castilian cape as open at front and having at back a closed hood;[279] of this type illustrations are available. The suggestion of a hood appears at the neck

---

Closed *capuz*

275 TOWNSMAN ca. 1470–1480, from figure of bystander in *Adoration of the Relics of St. Ildephonsus,* retable of St. Ildephonsus, by Fernando Gallego (Zamora. Cathedral, Chapel of San Ildefonso)

276 DIGNITARY ca. 1510, from figure of bystander in *Ecce Homo,* main retable, by Juan de Flandes (Palencia. Cathedral)

277 MERCHANT OR EXPLORER 1531–1536, from figure of worshiper in *The Virgin of the Navigators* by Alejo Fernández (Sevilla. Alcázar)

Capuz open at sides

278 KING ca. 1470–1480, from figure of Magus in *Epiphany* by Fernando Gallego (Barcelona. Museo de Arte de Cataluña)

279 MAJORDOMO 1497, from *[Rich Man and Majordomo]* in Gulielmus Parisiensis. *Postilla super epistolas et evangelia.* Sevilla, 1497. *f*74 (Sevilla. University, Library)

280 KING 1499, from *Artus Conquers the King who Holds Oliveros Imprisoned* in *La historia delos nobles caualleros oliueros de castilla y artus dalgarbe.* Burgos, 1499. sig.fiiij (The Hispanic Society of America)

of an earlier cape (Fig. 87) of crimson with dark red bands, which is worn over a gold-colored doublet banded in black. Attendant on a noble Catalan lady in mourning, the escort wears a black cape (Fig. 272) with a hood hanging not quite to his waistline. A later cape (Fig. 273) has a larger hood which at top covers the wearer's neck. The front view of a hooded cape (Fig. 274) shows a chain connecting the two fronts across the chest. As the cape shortened after mid-century, the hood grew even longer.

Tailors at Sevilla (1522) were required to know how to cut both *capas gallegas* and *capas lombardas.*[280] For Dom Jaime de Bragança (1490) a Gallegan cape needed 3¾ varas of *contray mayor,* a Flemish fabric named for Courtrai, and ⅓ of black velvet for *ribetes.* An inventory of 1516 specifies "a short, black Gallegan cape with strips of damask".[281] Lombard *capas* could be handsome, as in Figure 268. Town officials at Valladolid, during Fernando's and Germana's reception there (1509), had them in crimson lined with marten or other precious materials.[282] Lombard *capas* of *grana* and velvet appear in an inventory of 1512; one had sleeves trimmed with bands of velvet and buttons and at the chest a cord *(torzal),*[283] perhaps with a slide like that in Figure 263. For the reception of Charles V at Valencia (1528), magistrates were issued Lombard *capas* of velvet or of black silk, each according to his category.[284] Charles V took over the Milanesado, including Lombardy, in 1535, but before that event Lombard merchants evidently had made their presence felt in the Peninsula, as well as in France and Germany.

Capuz

The *capuz* also was a cloak or cape, generally with a hood. Girón says that closed *capuces* were like Castilian *capas,* except that they were closed at front.[285] Carmen Bernis has found an illustration of one hanging down all round in a retable by Fernando Gallego (Arcenillas (Zamora). Parish Church),[286] but generally the closed *capuz* is shown with the sides draped over the shoulders to free the arms, as it is worn by a townsman (Fig. 275) taking part in the adoration of relics. A disagreeable-looking character at the court of Pilate (Fig. 276) has the *capuz* in bright red edged with braid or embroidery in sharp triangles, which suggest gold or possibly olive-green silk. This example covers a garment of white brocade or damask, edged and doubtless lined with tan fur; other details are a gold belt, a greenish purse with iron frame, green or greenish-blue hose, and brown shoes.[287] A later *capuz* (Fig. 277) also is red, but banded with black velvet at the edge and on the hood.

The garment could be open at the sides, perhaps for use indoors. When Margarita de Austria arrived from Flanders (1497), Prince Juan met her near Santander, riding on a cold April day in a closed *capuz* of mulberry-colored *grana,* which was trimmed inside with a three-inch band of matching satin. After they had entered lodgings, he changed into a crimson velvet one open at the sides and carrying a hood which was cleft to the middle.[288] When Charles V came to Sevilla for his wedding (1526), men from surrounding towns and villages, dressed in yellow hoods and *capuces,* armed with shields and lances, and mounted on horses, were appointed to appear with officials meeting him outside the city.[289] A Sevillian ordinance forbade old-clothes men to take material from old *capuces* in order to sell it. Nevertheless, an alcalde found that their main business was to make jerkins and skirts from *capuces* and other garments, and that their street would be ruined if the business were abolished.[290]

In illustrations, the open *capuz* is slit at the side from hem to shoulder. A Magus (Fig. 278) has it in red with a jewel hanging from a chain at the bottom of the neck opening. In woodcuts the men who wear this garment are Nicodemus and the clever steward who forgave his lord's debtors (Fig. 279); his *capuz* buttons at the neck and carries a trimming band at the edges. A king wears it with a rather deep collar (Fig. 280). No hood is evident in these examples.

Queen Isabel's treasurer provided woolens to make *capuces* and occasionally velvet to trim them—for royal huntsmen, for English and French captives retaken from the Moors, for servants, as well as for the Prince. Three to 5½ varas were required. A sweeper of the women's apartments was issued local cloth *(paño de la tierra),* huntsmen received red, green, or black material, a secretary was given *contray.* Prince Juan had black or mulberry Florentine cloth at 1300 or 1400 maravedis the vara, red *grana* at 1800. Silk fabrics also were used for him—mulberry velvet, expensive crimson *aceituní* lined with white *cebtí.* The amplitude of the *capuz* is suggested by the fact that inside it Prince Juan's servant of the basin could hide the silver chamber pot, when he carried it to his master.[291]

In *Questiõ de amor, capuces* are richly trimmed— one of black velvet, lined with white satin, is garnished all over with mulberry taffeta *pestañas.* A prior's of mulberry velvet is checkered like a chess board with squares of red satin. Another, half of black velvet and half of white satin, is lined with the same fabrics, white within the black, black within the white. Still another of grayish brown *(pardillo)* is slashed over a lining of tawny damask.[292]

Escuba

Further outer garments—*escuba, tabardo, gabán, loba*—King Fernando (1515) wished to prevent every one not royal from wearing in precious fabrics.[293] At Sevilla (1522) a tailor being examined had to know how to cut an *escuba,* which in inventories is described as being of blue satin lined with *aceituní* or of brownish-gray velvet lined with black fur (1516), or of damask (1528).[294] But illustrations of it have not been found, and the word *escuba* in this century is appropriated for a liqueur.

Tabard

The tabard, known well over Europe, generally was open at the sides. The Spanish *tabardo* had distinctive features. Pedro Girón describes it as being closed like a *capuz* and with a closed hood at back, but with arm openings at the sides and just behind them long, narrow sleeves, as long as the *tabardo* itself.[295] Such sleeves were sometimes called "wings" *(alas).* It was worn in woolen *contray* or in an English fabric *(londres)* by servants, huntsmen, and the Bragança princes. For each of 25 huntsmen (1495), Prince Juan required one vara of red London cloth for sleeves and 7 varas of green for the body, which implies a certain amplitude. His own *tabardos* in 1495 were more expensive, of green velvet (15⅞ varas), of black Florentine cloth (5¾ varas) trimmed with "double" black velvet, of black damask (12 varas) trimmed with black velvet. For one of 1494 the trimming was completed with gold ribbon. A ballad of about 1500 lists the sandals, bare legs, tow-cloth shirts, and raincoats of rustics in contrast with the bow-tied shoes, good cloth hose, embroidered shirts of fine linen, and *capuces* or *tabardos* enjoyed by gentlemen.[296]

The best illustration of a *tabardo* yet found is that in a scene of the Inquisition where, complete with side opening, long sleeve, and hood (Fig. 281), it is worn in red by a clerk. For appearing on the same platform as the Emperor (1522), when a general pardon was issued after the *comunero* uprising, the Duke of Béjar, chief justice of Castilla, put on a knee-length *tabardo* of shag *(frisado)* with sleeves to the floor.[297] There was considerable variation in the garment. A count's black damask one of 1468 had no hood,[298] while Girón says that in later times the *tabardo* could be without sleeves. His remark that "even today [1537] some people still wear it,"[299] indicates that the *tabardo* then was nearing its end. It does not appear in Alcega.

Gabán

The cloak called *gabán* makes few appearances in silk during our period, except in the wardrobe of Prince Juan when he was between the ages of ten and sixteen. There often it was lined with the same or a contrasting fabric—mulberry velvet with mulberry brocaded satin, crimson *cebtí* with crimson velvet, green velvet with green *cebtí*. The Prince's most expensive *gabán* (1493) was of crimson *ceti* (almost 10 varas at 1,450 maravedis) lined with black brocaded satin (about 8 varas at 5,035 mrs.). One of black cloth with a lining of crimson *cebtí* (1490) was adorned with embroidery—10 ounces of drawn-gold thread *(oro tirado)* and 4½ ounces of edging gold *(oro de orilla)* worked on black *cebtí*. Carmen Bernis has found the *gabán* listed in inventories (1508, 1512),[300] but the literary record associates it mainly with shepherds. Juan de Valdés, friend of Erasmus writing at Naples about 1535, reports, "*Gavan* and *balandran* [are words] we left off using years ago."[301] A closed cloak with sleeves and hood, the *gabán* persisted into Covarrubias's time as the habit of shepherds and villagers, worn also by country people and travellers. City people, he comments, used it as a house coat,[302] which may have been its service in our period, inasmuch as the *gabán* does not figure in available descriptions of important occasions.

Capote

The *capote,* Guevara mentions as being worn in heavy rain. Covarrubias describes it as differing from the cape in having several types of hood—round and with a collar, itself serving as a collar, or with long bands *(chías).*[303]

Loba

The *loba,* a long sleeveless garment, could be of rich colored materials or of black from dear to cheap. The name is thought to derive from the Greek *lope* (leather cloak), and *lobas* of black leather, one lined with cloth, appear in an inventory (1503).[304] Girón (1537) details features of the garment, except the length: ". . . completely closed and without a hood, but with a little collar a finger more or less in height, an opening three or four fingers long in front, and *maneras* open at the sides for taking out the arms. Some persons use these *lobas* open all the way down the front."[305]

King Fernando's example (Fig. 283) stresses the columnar silhouette. At the baptism of Infante Ferdinand (Alcalá de Henares, March 1503), the Marquis of Villena wore over a woolen jerkin a *loba* of fine mulberry cloth and with it a mulberry velvet cap or hood *(caperuza).*[306] The 1503 inventory mentions a *loba* of silvered *(plateado)* damask lined with black cloth. Prince Juan had two that were crimson—one of them (1494) requiring 10⅓ varas of figured velvet *(altibajo),* plus 2 of crimson satin to carry embroidery—and another (1495) of tawny Rouen cloth trimmed with double black velvet; but mainly they were black, of satin or damask if not of woolen cloth. For Good Friday (1495) he had a *loba* and a cap *(capirote)* of shag *(frisado).* The hopeless suitor in *Questiõ de amor,* mourning his friend's dead mistress, refuses to put on a handsome *loba* of shag slashed so many times that the black damask lining shows through, even though the slashes are tied with skeins of black silk thread. His garment carries a motto:

> Clearly my sorrow discovers
> My sadness and another's.[307]

A *loba* of cheap black cloth was worn for mourning. The Bragança princes had it in shag (1493) for the death of the brother of a lady-in-waiting to Queen Isabel, in more expensive cloth (1494) for that of the King of Naples. Rules for mourning dress were issued in 1502: No one should wear coarse frieze *(jerga)* for anyone's death, no matter whose. For that of royal persons, or of their children, male mourners should wear *lobas* of sheared cloth *(paño tundido),* closed at the sides, with a train *(falda)* and a cap *(capirote).* For mourning grandees, prelates, titled persons, and others of like rank, the *loba*

281   ca. 1491–1498   **282**   1499   **283**   1492–1495

284   ca. 1479   **285**   1489–1495   **286**   1494–1499

287   ca. 1480   **288**   ca. 1521   **289**   1499

should be closed at the sides but not be extended into a train. In the case of lesser persons, the *loba* should have arm openings and be long enough only to reach the floor, not to drag.[308] Thus the presence of a train and complete closure were tributes to rank in the deceased. Most of the *lobas* worn in the funeral procession of Phelipe el Hermoso (Fig. 304) seem to be closed, but their trains are modest indeed. At Sevilla a new mourning *loba* with cap could be rented at five maravedis the day; an old one at three.[309]

In Girón's time the *loba* already was the garb of scholars—physicians, academics with the degree of doctor, students, and clerics. Their material could

be fine cloth, but their colors were mulberry, gray, or other hues considered decorous.[310]

Balandrán

A long outer garment still to be mentioned enters into Talavera's protest against men who went too far for his taste, either in showing off or perhaps only in trying to keep warm: "I say [it is] too much . . . when some one wears at the same time doublet, jerkin, and *balandrán* or *zamarro* and *capapuz (capuz?)*."[311] In illustrations identified by Carmen Bernis[312] the *balandrán* as in Figure 282 opens down the front, the sleeves are long and generous, the wide skirt hangs to the floor. Here it shows a confining belt.

To young princes Baeza furnished inexpensive woolens for only a few *balandranes*—3½ varas of black *contray mayor* (1492), 3¾ of brown London cloth (1493), and 5¼ varas of mulberry Rouen cloth (1495). A Portuguese ambassador in India (1515) used one of scarlet *(grão)*.[313] The elderly Duke of Béjar, on the road in January 1525 with a Spanish bride for Portugal, had a little cape, rather like an abbot's mozzetta, on his *balandrán*.[314] In February 1530, during Charles V's coronation at Bologna, a poet saw two handsome examples worn by marquises—one of red velvet lined with "very fine, rich" cloth of gold, the other of "very costly gold".[315]

Patterns in the Alcega book[316] present the *balandrán* as markedly changed from the form shown in Figure 282. It has become as short as the hip-length cape *(ferreruelo)* which it resembles, except that it has two fronts attached to the cape at the shoulders and under the arms, and also a hood. It was in the longer form undoubtedly that the *balandrán* continued to be used by scholars. Though Covarrubias apparently does not admit the term in his *Tesoro*, Carmen Bernis finds it used in connection with men of letters in pragmatics of 1537, 1611, and 1623, unavailable here.[317]

Various outer garments

281 CLERK—*TABARDO* ca. 1491–1498, from *Auto de Fe Presided over by St. Dominic* by Pedro Berruguete (Madrid. Museo del Prado)

282 KNIGHT—*BALANDRÁN* 1499, from *Artus Meets the White Knight* in *La historia delos nobles caualleros oliueros de castilla y artus dalgarbe*. Burgos, 1499. sig.fij (The Hispanic Society of America)

283 KING—*LOBA* 1492–1495, from *Their Royal Highnesses Don Fernando and Doña Isabel and the Royal Infanta Doña Juana* in Marcuello, Pedro. *Devocionario de la Reyna d.ª Juana, á quien llamaron la Loca. vºf* 30 (Chantilly. Musée Condé)

Jornea

284 PAGE ca. 1479, from figure in tomb of Iñigo López de Mendoza, 1st count of Tendilla (Guadalajara. Church of San Ginés)

285 KING 1489–1495, from figure of Fernando el Católico in *Entrance into Gurarca [Huércal]*, choir stall, by Master Rodrigo (Toledo. Cathedral)

286 SON OF A COUNT 1494–1499, from figure of Saint in *Investiture of St. Thomas Aquinas*, main retable, by Pedro Berruguete (Avila. Church of Santo Tomás)

Cota de armas

287 HERALD ca. 1480, from sketch of transept for Church of San Juan de los Reyes, Toledo, by Juan Guas (Madrid. Museo del Prado)

288 HERALD ca. 1521, from main retable by Felipe Vigarny (Granada. Royal Chapel)

Badge of recognition

289 MESSENGER 1499, from *Messengers Come from the Kings of Ireland, Declaring War* in *La historia delos nobles caualleros oliueros de castilla y artus dalgarbe*. Burgos, 1499. vºsig.dij (The Hispanic Society of America)

Bernia

A cloak of shaggy woolen material, originally from Ireland *(Hibernia)*, was used in Spain with the name of *bernia*. A luxurious one of fine *aznal* (?) was brought from Sevilla (1489) for Prince Juan. An old white one worn by a seaman is recorded (1530).[318] The *bernia* is described in a series of jokes related by the buffoon of Charles V: "The Emperor many times joined with the grandees who were present, discussing what should be done to fatten up Don Alonso de Fonseca, archbishop of Santiago, . . . to prevent the Marquis of Los Vélez, when he talked, from squeaking like a new mountain cart, and to kill the Marquis's son's tutor because he had a *bernia* that had been new in the days of King Juan [the Emperor's great-grandfather]. Tawny-colored, made with two arm openings, and trimmed with hoops *(verdugos)* of green satin, the *bernia* was girdled with sword straps of the olden time."[319]

Jornea

A short outer garment of sandwich-board style was the *jornea,* which as *giornea* had been popular with Italian military since the mid-fifteenth century. Of hip length and open at the sides, it seems in Spanish examples to have had no sleeves. An early one is that of a page (Fig. 284), the body crossed with diagonal bands and the edge decorated with Roman letters in sharp-cut relief, A C I M I . . . N A . . . , a sculptured record rarely found of this literal trimming so often mentioned in texts. A *jornea* bordered with a pearled band is worn by King Fernando on horseback (Fig. 285). A young noble about to exchange secular dress for religious attends the ceremony in a *jornea* of red and gold brocade (Fig. 286), edged with white fur and confined with a belt. The sleeves of his green doublet end in a long red cuff. The hose also are red.

A pragmatic of 1499 allows that "for the honor of the cavalry and of the persons who belong to it *(que la siguen)* we permit those who ride with long stirrups *(a la brida)* to wear their *jorneas* and short gowns above the knee, of silk and ornamented with metal relief designs *(chapería),* as they wish, over armor and not in any other manner."[320] King Fernando (Fig. 285) rides with a long stirrup, but he does not seem to be in armor.

The Segovian inventory of 1503 records three *jorneas* of red *(colorado)* taffeta lined with reddish *(encarnado)* linen and adorned with the arms of Castilla and León within a border of caldrons. In the same inventory an old *jornea,* quartered of red or crimson velvet, is described as adorned with gold-letter inscriptions that once included castles and lions. A *jornea* of mulberry velvet (1528) was embroidered with gold.[321]

Cota de armas

Such descriptions bring the *jornea* very near to the emblazoned *cota de armas,* also short and open at the sides but carrying sleeve panels over the upper arms. This garment once was worn by the armored knight, but as foot soldiers rose in the world they ventured to pluck him off his mount by hooking halberd or partisan into his *cota.* Knights learned to discard it, and by the middle of the sixteenth century the *cota de armas* had become the exclusive wear of heralds or kings-of-arms.[322] Heralds in *cotas* with royal arms omitting the emblem of the pomegranate, not yet earned by the conquest of Granada (1492), were drawn by Queen Isabel's architect (Fig. 287).[323] On a *cota de armas* paid for by Baeza (1493) certain pieces embroidered with pomegranate designs were enlarged, requiring 5 ounces of gold thread at 330 maravedis the ounce and 1½ ounces of silk at 95 for the stitching. The embroiderers worked 16 days at 65 per day. A tailor, who put the *cota* together for 120 maravedis, lined it with 4 varas of red taffeta and added one vara of red and gold fringe.

Kings-of-arms in the funeral cortege of Phelipe el Hermoso (Fig. 304) wear brilliant escutcheons, which include the pomegranate. In a later *cota* (Fig. 288) Spanish quarterings cover the surface down to the fringed edges. A chronicler says, "It is a very old and much used custom among princes that while kings-of-arms are wearing their *cotas,* they may pass safely through any and all lands, even those very foreign." Nevertheless, Charles V's king-of-arms bearing a message to François I (1528) was refused permission to enter Paris in his *cota.* He declared that such treatment was an insult to him and an injury to the Emperor, and that he would not stir unless he could put it on, or at least until he knew that the French king himself had forbidden his wearing it. From the palace came word that he would run great risk if he went out displaying conspicuous emblems; they might rouse the populace. He replied that since he could not perform his duties, he wished to return to the Emperor. After another reference to the palace, he was allowed in his *cota de armas* to enter Paris and proceed to his lodgings.[324]

Badge of recognition

A single quartering could be used for the badge of recognition which also served to identify heralds and messengers.[325] A mounted herald of the 1460's, wearing a wind-blown *jornea,* carries the badge on the right side of his chest (Avila. Palace of the Marqués de las Navas, relief over portal). A king's messenger, whose short cloak is cut with short sleeves (Fig. 289), has the insigne on his left side.

Furs

SPAIN COULD BE WINTRY in its season, and Johannes Dantiscus, Polish ambassador to Charles V, missed the furs he had left behind to the mercy of Polish moths, while he wore Spanish sheep fells dearer than fox at home. He found the cold of Granada and Valladolid more penetrating than that of Poland; nevertheless, after enduring the infernal fires of a Spanish summer, he was glad to see winter come again.[326]

Furriers at the great fair of Medina del Campo took stations on the plaza. Their trade was considered one of the base, despicable occupations, which is understandable if it be true that "pelts of the furs shown in medieval and later pictures were certainly stiff smelly and very apt to split."[327] It is hard to believe that Spaniards who were famous for the excellence of their leathers should not have been equally skilled in dressing furs. These are listed in Spanish accounts and inventories, not as separate pieces of apparel, but as decorative borders or purfles *(perfiles)* or, more often, under the head of linings *(aforros, enforros)*. In fact, it is claimed that fur coats did not appear in the world until after the middle of the nineteenth century.[328]

Sheep fell

Least expensive pelt-lined wear of our period was the *zamarro* made of fine, soft sheep fells; its name developed from the Arabic *çammor* (fur cloak). An inventory of 1503 speaks of black, aborted lambs as a source of fells,[329] and Covarrubias (1611) carries on in the same vein, defining the *zamarro* as "garment of the fells of lambs or of those unborn *(abortos)* which are fine and have a soft, short fleece. These are the coats of gentle people. Other [coats] are called *zamarras,* the proper habit of shepherds; they have large fells, although clipped."[330] In the *zamarro* the fleece counted as lining, being worn inside. When it appeared otherwise, the fact was noted: "He had a squire very old, with an old *zamarro,* the fleece outside."[331]

King Fernando was happy to receive a gift of *zamarros* from the Monastery of Guadalupe (Cáceres). In a letter written at Alcalá de Henares (1485), he says that they arrived at a very good time (December).[332] For some seasons *zamarros,* costing from 620 to 750 maravedis each, were given to two royal guards (1492–1494, 1496). That the gar-

ment was considered village wear is suggested later: "Not small, but great, is the freedom of the village . . . if it is cold, one puts on a *zamarro.*"[333] When King Sebastião of Portugal visited Guadalupe at Christmas time in 1576, the present he valued most was a *zamarro,* beautifully made.[334]

Lamb

Become fashionable in Burgundy during the second half of the fifteenth century, lamb developed into an article of luxury. As Gay's *Glossaire* (v. 1, p. 11) cites *agneau de Navarre* (1498) and *de Roumanie* (1497), it seems reasonable to assume that the *peñas navarriscas* and the *peñas de Rumanía* that figure in Baeza's accounts actually were lamb. For the Portuguese princes (1493), two black velvet *ropones* were lined with 5¼ dozen black Navarrese skins at 2 florins the dozen, or 44⅙ maravedis each skin. For Prince Juan in the same year, an expensive, mulberry brocaded-velvet jerkin was lined with 4 dozen Navarrese skins at 156¼ maravedis each. A black cloth *ropón* of the Prince (1494) was lined with 4¾ dozen black Rumanian skins at 5 doblas the dozen, or 152½₂ maravedis each skin. Rumanian skins were used also for lining a pair of the Prince's gloves made of otter (1495). One is inclined to see some kind of lamb in the tightly curled fur of the long gown worn by a young Magus (Fig. 292). It obviously makes the collar and lines the whole garment, being revealed at the sleeve wrists and in the skirt clear to the floor. A similarly curled fur composes the hat with upturned brim (Fig. 293) that is represented for an infante's kneeling effigy. The brim carries a bow of ribbon and a jewel. Also of lamb must be the wavy-fur collar and lining of the gown worn by a kneeling older Magus (Fig. 294).

Squirrel

Squirrel, which had been popular in earlier centuries (stained-glass windows at Chartres picture furriers selling linings of Siberian squirrel), had lost favor even before our period, and only a few mentions of it have been found. One hundred fifty-eight *esquiroles* (Catalan and Aragonese term for the native squirrel, *ardilla*), at 35 maravedis the skin, lined a black satin *ropón* for Prince Juan in 1493. Not

290   ca. 1475–1485   **291**   ca. 1520   **292**   1531–1536

293   1489–1493   **294**   1537–1540

rendered in the tidy medieval idiom, but repeating a shield-shaped form that can represent no other fur, squirrel appears in an Aragonese picture of a saint (Fig. 291), whom tradition places as a high official of Persia. Wearing a gown that lies in folds on the floor, he strikes a pose similar to that of a monarch with squirrel-lined gown in a German woodcut of 1505, reprinted at Zaragoza to adorn an edition of Livy's *Decadas* (1520). The saint's squirrel is plainly visible as a lining and also as collar, facings, and sleeve edges.

Rabbit

Rabbit was a useful fur. In 1489 Prince Juan had 44 skins, at 120 maravedis each, to line a *loba* of black cloth, and 24, at 70 each, lined a jerkin for one of the Portuguese princes. A crimson satin gown *(ropón)* of Prince Juan (1494) required 50 skins, at 124 each, for the lining. Rabbit was sometimes imported from England.[335] The skins exported from the Peninsula were considered by a Frenchman inferior to those of his own country.[336]

Cat

Catskin served as trim as well as lining. For Prince Juan in 1493 five catskins *(gatos)*, at 155 maravedis each, were cut into wide purfles for trimming a *ropón* of mulberry satin *(aceituní)* lined with rose-red woolen *(grana rosada)*. Of light-colored fur that could be cat or rabbit, bands, wider at neck and hem than at the sides, edge the red and gold brocade

Fur lining and facing

290 DUKE—ERMINE ca. 1475–1485, from portrait of Alonso de Aragón, 1st duke of Villahermosa; later 16th-century copy by Roland de Mois (Madrid. Palace of the Duke of Villahermosa)

291 OFFICIAL—SQUIRREL ca. 1520, from figure of Saint in *St. Abdon and St. Sennen* by the Javierre Master (Tarrasa. Museo Municipal de Arte)

292 KING—LAMB 1531–1536, from figure of young Magus in *Epiphany* by Juan Rodríguez and Lucas Giraldo (Avila. Cathedral, Trascoro)

Fur hat and collar

293 INFANTE—LAMB 1489–1493, from effigy of Infante Alfonso by Gil de Siloe (Burgos. Monastery of Miraflores)

294 KING—LAMB 1537–1540, from figure of Magus in *Epiphany*, main retable, by Damián Forment (Santo Domingo de la Calzada. Cathedral)

garment of a young lad (Fig. 286). For lining two black satin *ropones*, the Portuguese princes (1495) were allowed 93 catskins *(gatos de lomos)* at 104 maravedis each.

Lynx

Lynx became popular in the sixteenth century. An excellent rendering is that by Miguel Sithium in his portrait of a knight in handsome brocade (Fig. 299). The fur evidently makes a collar at the back, besides facings at front and a lining visible along edges of the divided sleeve. In the gown worn by Juan de Aragón, nephew of King Fernando (Fig. 297), the fur, if not wolf, may be lynx. Grayish spotted with darker tone, it forms a collar and generous facings, appearing as well at slits in the sleeves—both upper puff and hanging tube—and at the hem, as though it lined the whole garment. The long aglets in the sleeve betray the copyist of the 1560's, being too large for the period of Juan de Aragón.

Ermine

Most luxurious furs were ermine and sable, state wear for kings, princes, and nobles. An ordinance of 1493 speaks of ermines *(peñas veras)*, Siberian squirrels *(grises)*, and martens or sables *(maças, martas ?)* being brought to Sevilla by sea.[337] Sables *(martas cebellinas)* and ermines probably originated in Russia or the Near East. The Spanish term *armiño* is derived from "Armenia", and until late in the seventeenth century ermine was known to the French as *rat d'Arménie*. In *Viaje de Turquía*, the mid-sixteenth-century author states that at Constantinople (which received furs from Astrakhan by way of the Caspian and the Black Sea) sables and martens were more common than lamb fells *(corderunas)* in Spain.[338] From Constantinople furs were shipped to markets at Genoa and Venice, and from the latter, according to Covarrubias, ermines were imported into the Peninsula. In the tenth century Spain had exported beaver and sable. Muslim Zaragoza was noted as a center for dressing furs, the Spanish winter being ruder than that in other parts of the Muslim West.[339]

Ermines were purchased in Spain by the *timbre* (also *tynbre* or *timble*), a term unnoticed in this sense by the Spanish Academy dictionary, though it was current in Europe to signify "a package containing 40 skins (i.e. half-skins, 20 pair) of ermine, sable, marten, and the like." As described for the Russian trade, "The pelts . . . were sewn together

295   ca. 1483–1485   **296**   1494–1499   **297**   ca. 1516

298   ca. 1520   **299**   ca. 1515–1516

in pairs and packed in bundles, usually of forty, flat between two boards,"[340] whence the name "timber". Paz y Mélia uses the Latin *quadragenas*, borrowed no doubt from the Polish ambassador's text, to express 40's of sables in the time of Charles V.[341]

On Prince Juan's account (1494), of the 71,900 maravedis spent for a long gown of crimson velvet, 40,150 went for 730 ermines and 2,500 to the furrier for work on the lining. In the same year 213 ermines, also at 55, were required to line a jerkin for the Prince of black uncut, long-piled velvet *(velludo vellotado)*. When Charles V arrived in Spain (1517), his hosts appeared with linings of ermine or sable, and of leopard or genet as well, in their gowns of cloth of gold or of silver, of crimson velvet or satin. At Aachen for his first coronation (1520), Charles V wore a gold brocade mantle lined with ermine, and the same fur was used in his cloth-of-gold mantle with long train on the great day of the Bologna coronation (1530). Four nobles who carried the imperial insignia had crimson gowns lined with ermine.

The long gown, ermine lined, is illustrated in a portrait (Fig. 290), copied doubtless from an earlier version, of King Fernando's illegitimate brother, first duke of Villahermosa. The black gown, of velvet probably, against which the spotted lining makes vivid contrast, is open to reveal a generous panel

---

Fur trimming and facing

295 ATTENDANT—BROWN FUR ca. 1483–1485, from *The Beheading of St. John the Baptist*, retable of St. John the Baptist, by Pedro Berruguete (Santa María del Campo. Parish Church)

296 GENTLEMAN—ERMINE 1494–1499, from figure of bystander in *Investiture of St. Thomas Aquinas*, main retable, by Pedro Berruguete (Avila. Church of Santo Tomás)

297 DUKE—LYNX (OR WOLF) ca. 1516, from portrait of Juan de Aragón, 1st duke of Luna; later 16th-century copy by Roland de Mois (Madrid. Palace of the Duke of Villahermosa)

Fur lining, facing, and collar

298 PRINCE—SABLE (OR MARTEN) ca. 1520, from figure of Saint in *Martyrdom of St. Hermengild*, retable of the Martyrs, attributed to Juan Ramírez (Granada. Museo Provincial de Bellas Artes, Palacio de Carlos V, Alhambra)

299 KNIGHT—LYNX ca. 1515–1516, from portrait of a knight of the Order of Calatrava by Miguel Sithium (Washington, D.C. National Gallery of Art, Andrew W. Mellon Collection)

of fur at each side front. A diagonal slit at the side, in which ermine is seen also, is hardly explicable unless it belongs to a hanging sleeve tube, as in Figure 254.

Sable

As for sables, Charles V and his brother Ferdinand wore gowns of drawn gold lined with that fur at a tournament in Valladolid (1518). During a visit to England (1520), the young Emperor's long gown, half of cloth of silver, half of alternate strips of gold or silver cloth, also was lined with sables. Back in Spain (1527) he received a gift of sables from Russian envoys and responded to their courtesy with bags of cash: 1,000 ducats to him who presented two timbers, 700 to another who had given two, and 300 to an interpreter, giver of one timber. This recompense varied from 12½ to 7½ ducats per skin, something above the price at which such furs for the Empress were valued later.

At Bologna (1530) the Emperor was reported wearing cloth of silver and sables, as in the gown portrayed by Seisenegger (Fig. 13). The handsome, dark brown skins which obviously line the gown become visible in a broad collar at back and in generous facings at front. No one apparently presumed to reveal the cost of the Emperor's clothes at Bologna, but 1,800 ducats (675,000 maravedis) was estimated for the *martas* lining a gown worn by the Marquis of Villena—brocaded velvet banded with cloth of silver and touched with gold.[342] At such a price the *martas* could only be sables *(martas cebellinas)*; in the 1490's "common martens" had been worth but a tenth as much. A long cape of gold and crimson brocade for a prince-saint (Fig. 298) suggests similar luxury with its lining of brown fur which is seen in the farthest reaches of the hem, as well as in front facings and a large collar at back. The winged cape of gold brocade, tentatively called *capa lombarda* by Carmen Bernis,[343] is richly furred (Fig. 268) with edge bandings, front facings, and large, rounded collar probably of sable. The same fur may line, as well as edge, the blue velvet jerkin of a palace attendant (Fig. 295).

By the end of the century the fur trade had fallen off considerably, as people more and more used plush for their linings.[344] Portraits (copies) by Bartolomé González (Madrid. Museo del Prado, on deposit or in storage) show Karl, archduke of Styria (d. 1590) wearing a cloak with conventional marten or sable, while his young son Leopold proudly displays a lining of red plush.

III WOMEN AND THEIR DRESS OCCASIONS

300 PRINCESS AND ATTENDANTS   ca. 1483–1485

Salome in Herod's Palace, detail of *The Beheading of Saint John the Baptist*, retable
of Saint John the Baptist, by Pedro Berruguete (Santa María del Campo. Parish
Church)

301 LADY IN AN ARMY CAMP 1489–1495

Detail of *Sally of Moors during the Siege of Málaga,* choir stall, by Master Rodrigo (Toledo. Cathedral)

302 DAMSEL AND COMPANIONS ON A DAIS   ca. 1490–1500

High Priest Conversing with the Virgin, main retable, by Pedro Berruguete (Paredes de Nava. Church of Santa Eulalia)

303 QUEEN RECEIVING AN AUTHOR 1492–1495

Her Royal Highness Doña Isabel, Queen of Castilla and Aragón, in Marcuello, Pedro. *Devocionario de la Reyna d.ª Juana, à quien llamaron la Loca vº f*54 (Chantilly. Musée Condé)

304 ROYAL FUNERAL PROCESSION 1506

Funeral Procession of Phelipe el Hermoso from the Casa del Cordón, Burgos (Écaussines. Château de la Follie, Collection of Comte Charles-Albert de Lichtervelde)

305 QUEEN ca. 1521

Isabel I, Queen of Castilla and Aragón, by Felipe Vigarny (Granada. Royal Chapel, Museo)

306 WOMAN OF SEVILLA 1529

In This Manner Women Go about the Kingdom of Marcilia in Sevilla, the City of 50,000 Houses in Weiditz, Christoph. *Das Trachtenbuch. f*60 (Nürnberg. Germanisches Nationalmuseum)

307 Lady and Escort Walking 1529

Thus Go Rich Women in Barcelona. . . . These Are the Maids in Weiditz, Christoph. *Das Trachtenbuch. f71–72* (Nürnberg. Germanisches Nationalmuseum)

308 MARCHIONESS-COUNTESS ON MULEBACK ca. 1530

Mencía de Mendoza, Marchioness of El Cenete, detail of *Count Hendrik III of Nassau and His Three Wives*, tapestry cartoon, by Bernart van Orley (München. Staatliche Graphische Sammlung)

309 KING AND QUEEN ca. 1531

François I and Éléonore d'Autriche, King and Queen of France, French School (Hampton Court Palace)

Women and
Their Dress Occasions

THE IDEAL DAY of a great Spanish lady in our period was set forth by the Hieronymite prior, Fernando de Talavera. His own tastes were simple, which intensified the clarity of his vision as he focused on the weakness for luxurious dress of his fellow Christians, including the Queen. For a Countess of Benavente—possibly before he reluctantly consented about 1474 to serve as confessor to Queen Isabel—the Prior laid out the program of a fourteen-hour day.

In winter the Countess was to rise at eight, say a few prayers and attend Mass, during which time no one—secretary, page, maid, relative, or duenna—was to break in upon her thoughts, unless it was absolutely necessary. Her next duty was to hear the cases of those who asked for justice, beginning with the poor. She would then inspect the establishment to see what her women were doing. If all was clean and in order, she might visit her little children and then the sick, were there any such. It would now be almost noon. Returned to her dais *(estrado)*, she would eat dinner, remembering to share it with the poor.[345] On the brocaded cushions of a dais, noble ladies—feet crossed and knees spread wide—sat like Chinese idols, as Spaniards would remark when they saw such idols in the Orient.[346] Covered with rich rugs, a dais could be warmed by a stove underneath, burning straw where wood was scarce.[347] While ladies sewed or embroidered (Fig. 302), an older gentlewoman sometimes read aloud to them.

After dinner, the table cleared away, a half hour of recreation followed—improving conversation, music, or reading, which would be the best—and then a half-hour nap. In summer, having risen earlier, the Countess would sleep longer. At three she was to take up needlework. The Prior recommended making passementerie for church textiles, mending sheets and blankets for hospitals, sewing shirts for the poor. At five she should again hear those who had suits to bring and then spend a while with the majordomo, who was in charge of what she owned and what she owed. As exercise was good for her health, she should walk through the house again, casting a watchful eye over her maids. After another visit to her little children and another half hour in the oratory, she should have supper at seven or at least by eight. She might enjoy more recreation until ten when she should go to bed, having said her prayers on her knees.[348] It is notable that no time was alloted to be spent with the Count, her husband.

The actual life of a high-born lady might not run so smooth a course, especially if her husband had been taken prisoner by the Moors and held for ransom. A Countess of

133

Castañeda—possibly Beatriz de Velasco, childless wife of the third Count—traveled from place to place begging with tears for money from all her husband's friends and kinsmen, until after almost two years she succeeded in raising the enormous sum required to free him. Furthermore, she carried it safely to Granada.[349]

Conspicuous personae of the time were the members of the royal family. Fernando and Isabel had four daughters who became queens and a granddaughter who rose to be empress. Juana la Loca also mothered queens, two of whom, Leonor and Catalina, appear in this book. Fernando's second wife, Germaine de Foix, ten years younger than Juana, was known in Spain as Queen Germana. A prominent heiress, Mencía de Mendoza (Fig. 308), who descended from an acquisitive and munificent cardinal, was bestowed by the Emperor on a Flemish count.

Occasions when noble ladies and their clothes were on display were church ceremonies, weddings, tournaments, royal receptions for ambassadors, and entrances into towns.

We shall begin the presentation of such displays with Queen Isabel on her way to church at Sevilla (August 1478) to offer her month-old son to the Lord, surely the proudest and happiest moment of her life. Generally she appeared with ranks of ladies, but here she had only one attendant. Musicians led the way and then came Fernando, bearing his share of the glory in a gold-trimmed hat and a long gown of gold-ornamented brocade. He rode a dapple-gray jennet harnessed with gold-trimmed black velvet, and Isabel followed on a white trotter *(trotón)* with long trappings of gold and silver. She sat in a heavily gilded saddle, wearing a dress *(brial)* of brocade embroidered with many pearls and seed pearls. The Constable of Castilla and a count held the bridle, while beside her walked the Governor of Andalucía and one of the powerful Fonsecas. The Prince was carried in the arms of his nurse who rode a mule with a velvet-covered packsaddle. Grandees of the realm walked to the cathedral, where the royal mother dismounted to present a gold offering.

It is appropriate that Queen Isabel should make her appearance here in the saddle. The court had no settled home, and her duties carried her across plains, over mountains and rivers, into far corners of the realm. In the midst of this travel, she gave birth to her five children, no two in the same city. On long trips she might be carried in a litter *(andas),* borne by men or between two mules hitched tandem, but on important occasions her people had full view of their Queen on horseback. In a relief at Toledo (Fig. 480), which shows her riding with Fernando at the capture of Moclín (Granada), she sits sidewise on her mount, a hoop skirt somehow disposed about her and a small dog on her lap. The type of saddle suggested was called *angarillas* and consisted of a scissors chair secured over a packsaddle. A board hung at one side to support the feet.[350] In another type called *silla,* a woman rode sidewise also, one foot in a stirrup. The Infanta Juana in her ninth year (1488) had a *silla* with two gilded stirrups, suggesting that a young girl might ride astride. Ladies also sat on the croup behind a male rider. Steps *(tablas de cabalgar)* were carried to help them mount. Those for the Queen's pampered daughter Isabel (1490) were of wood with gilded hinges. The steps were encrusted with 156 ounces of silver and 75 ducats worth of gilding, besides more gold in enamels and coats of arms, to a total value of almost 135,000 maravedis. On cross-country trips important people were accompanied by hundreds of pack animals bearing equipment and supplies, the owners identified by their heraldic symbols on the packcloths *(reposteros).*

A clear description of Isabel and her court in residence at Medina del Campo (Valladolid) was made by a Frenchman with a Portuguese name in the service of England—Roger Machado, who had an eye for detail and the fortitude to record it.[351] He was in Spain as king-of-arms with ambassadors whom Henry VII had sent to treat for the marriage of the two-year-old Prince of Wales, Arthur, and the youngest Infanta, Catalina, a year older. The party arrived at Medina on March 12th, 1489.

Two days later they were summoned to the royal palace, which faced the town plaza. It was seven in the evening, and a great number of torch bearers lighted their way. Isabel and Fernando were found seated in a great hall, probably on the *estrado,* under a cloth-of-gold canopy bearing the arms of Castilla and Aragón. The King wore cloth of gold lined with fine sables; the Queen had a dress of the same fabric in the national style. Its golden sheen gleamed through great slashes in a black velvet capelet *(manteline),* which was further adorned with a heavy, broken line of gold bars, each a finger long, half a finger wide, and set with precious stones—"a thing so rich no man ever has seen the equal." In her necklace of gold roses, enameled white and red, every rose carried a large gem. At each side of her bosom two ribbons blazed with big diamonds, pearls, balases, rubies, and other gems of great value, a hundred or more. Her cloak, a short one *(demy manteau),* hung from the left shoulder; of fine crimson satin lined with ermine, "It was good to see and very glossy." Except for a *coiffe de pleasaunce,* which may have been the headdress shown in Figures 314–319, her head was bare. Machado estimated the clothes and jewels displayed by Isabel that evening to have been worth 200,000 gold crowns *(escus),* a fair dowry for a princess. The calculating Henry must have gloated when he heard this report of the portable wealth behind his future daughter-in-law.

Fernando had great nobles as his attendants, the Queen thirty-seven ladies and maidens of high rank, all richly attired in the national mode. Before this assemblage even Machado quailed: "Their dresses of cloth of gold or other rich fabrics, it would take me too long to describe."

The next day, when the ambassadors returned for a reply to their proposals, Fernando wore a gown of crimson velvet lined with sables and a gold collar of good price. Isabel appeared again in cloth of gold with a *manteline* of black velvet bearing a band of beaten gold strewn with gem-set roses, red and white, of beaten gold. Her necklace carried large balases and carbuncles of great value. After their business was finished, the ambassadors wished to pay their respects to the royal children. Fernando immediately sent the Constable of Castilla to fetch Prince Juan and Infanta Isabel. The Prince, aged eleven, came in a gown *(robe)* of rich, figured crimson velvet lined with ermine, and a hat "black in the French style" with a long, hanging end *(cornette)* of purple, very narrow and slashed like the branch of a tree. The eighteen-year-old Infanta, entering with four maidens, wore a kirtle *(cettelle)* of cloth of gold with a great train coming out from under it of green velvet, very rich. Her cap was of net in gold and black, garnished with pearls and precious stones.

Outside the palace, for a joust at which many lances were broken, viewing stands as in Figure 9 had been erected to accommodate spectators. The ambassadors were seated there early so that they might enjoy the pageantry of the royal entrance. First, on good mounts, came grandees, most of them dressed in the French style "as nearly as they could". After them appeared four sergeants-at-arms, and then the heralds, English and Spanish. The Prince was next, wearing a cloth-of-gold gown and a hood *(chaperon)* of black velvet "in the old style"; at his neck lay a rich ornament *(huchure)* garnished with great balases and other gems. The King's sword, carried by a gentleman on a good jennet, preceded the King himself, who rode a noble charger, its harness decorated with goldwork. Fernando's cloth-of-gold gown was lined and bordered with ermine; the large collar was "turned down in the German mode".

The Queen arrived on a handsome mule, its harness studded with pearls and precious stones. Over her cloth-of-gold dress she had a velvet *mantellyne* worked all in lozenges, black or crimson, each one carrying a large pearl *(margaritte)* and [with] every *margaritte* a balas of beechnut size. Her necklace was laden with gems. On her coif was a jewel estimated at 12,000 *escus*—two balases the size of pigeon's eggs with a large pearl *(perle)* at the end of each. The value of the Queen's clothes and ornaments that day, "No one could accurately judge." She was escorted by the Cardinal of Castilla. After them rode Infanta Isabel likewise wearing cloth of gold and a rich necklace, succeeded by thirty-six ladies and maidens of high rank, all clad in cloth of gold, not in one livery but in dresses of different designs, "so rich and beautiful that it was marvelous to see." Dismounted, Isabel and Fernando, the Prince, and the Infanta came up and sat near where the ambassadors had been placed.

After the tournament, the sovereigns returned to the palace, taking the Englishmen with them. In the great hall, on a dais before a velvet hanging embroidered with the arms of Castilla and Aragón and the royal motto, *TANTO MONTA,* the royal family sat down, the Prince at the King's right and the Infanta at the Queen's left; the Cardinal was seated beside her. The ambassadors were placed a little lower on a bench at the King's right, grandees at the other side of the Queen. Musicians appeared and there was dancing by the jousters and the court ladies; at ten, by the Prince and the Infanta. Then attendant ladies withdrew; a table was placed on the dais, water brought for the royal hands. The Prince rose and held the towel for the King and the Queen. Water was provided also for the Prince and the Infanta and for the ambassadors, who were seated near her at the corner of the table. After a banquet, rich, abundant, and varied, handsomely served with silver vessels, the ambassadors were commanded to retire. It was one o'clock before they got to bed.

A bullfight in their honor is dismissed with few words. More attention is paid to the reed-spear tournament which pleased them. This time three of the Infantas joined the Kings and the Prince in the stands. The Englishmen were happy to see that the Queen had with her their little Princess of Wales. Fernando wore a gown of black cloth with open sleeves, the left bordered with large balases and great pearls as was traditional for the reed-spear tournament. The Queen's costume illustrates a favorite color combination of the period, green and red. Her dress, of green satin richly figured with embroidery in lozenges, was finished at the top with a necklace-like border two fingers wide of large gems and great pearls. The crimson velvet sleeves, which hung to the ground, carried a popular kind of trimming: letters of beaten gold a quarter vara high (about 7½ inches), forming the motto *TANTO MONTA*. Each letter was garnished with large pearls, "the richest thing I have ever seen." The Prince's tunic, which reached only to the hips, also bore the motto.

Machado noted that the Queen's ladies wore a different dress at every entertainment, but he did not even try to record "the richness of the changes". On March twenty-seventh, the marriage agreement having been attested, the Kings left Medina del Campo. "God knows that they departed in great pomp," Fernando and Juan riding together, the Queen and her daughters following with a troop of their ladies and damsels. The ambassadors accompanied them two bowshots out of town, where the King commanded them to return. They kissed his hands, the Queen's, the Prince's, and the Infantas', and took their leave of the Cardinal. The next day at Medina they received the presents appointed for them by the King—horses, silks, silver—and four days later they set out for Portugal. On the way they lodged at Plasencia with Don Francisco de Zúñiga, uncle of a duke. They dined and supped alone in their chambers, because Don Francisco wished to eat with his wife, and it was not the custom for wives to dine with strangers.

A royal marriage at this period involved betrothal ceremonies besides the actual wedding. The first marriage of the family was that of Infanta Isabel to the Prince of Portugal, Afonso, three years younger. The betrothal, after which she would be called "Princess of Portugal", took place by proxy April 18th, 1490, at Sevilla. There Fernando and Isabel, having captured Baza and Almería the previous December, received so great a welcome that they had to remind the Sevillians not to spend too much on this reception: the wedding had to be paid for and the rest of the Moorish war. Isabel had pawned her jewels on behalf of the Baza siege. The betrothal was formalized on April eighteenth "with writing and rings" in the person of a Portuguese ambassador. In the ensuing two weeks the royal parents lavished great sums on music, dress, hospitality, and entertainment in honor of their first-born. It was expensive for guests also, grandees from all Spain and even from Sicily. By day tournaments were held in a field between the dockyards and the Guadalquivir; silk fabric made the barrier. Fifty stands at each side had been erected and hung with tapestries of silk and cloth of gold. Into the boxes mounted the bride, the Queen dressed in cloth of gold, great ladies and young girls—seventy clad in brocades, gold ornaments, expensive pearls and precious stones—the Prince, prelates of the realm, and lords not entering the contests. At night the company assembled at the Alcázar, ladies—even the least important preceded by eight or nine torches—riding there on mules richly harnessed.[352]

The wedding was to be celebrated in November at Lisbon. But with plague coming on, the scene was transferred to Evora, where also the plague arrived. By physicians' advice the people and the Portuguese court vacated the city for two weeks, leaving behind prudent and dependable guards. From the region round about, the King ordered in countless cattle to sleep within the city at night. After the two weeks the cattle were taken away, and the city was considered clean, all the streets and houses fumigated. Before the King came back, they were whitewashed. "And with these great efforts and mainly by God's mercy, many prayers and alms having been devoted to Him at the same time, the city was made completely sound."[353] Everything ready for the coming of the Princess, King João II sent word to the Catholic Kings, and the bride set out from Córdoba. Wishing to demonstrate to their cousins and neighbors not only the largeness of their souls but also the prosperity of their dominions, the royal parents gave their daughter, in addition to the usual dowry in gold, 1,000 *marcos* of silver (2,077,000 maravedis) and 500 of gold (12,125,000 mrs.), jewelry, luxurious fabrics, and clothes. There were twenty coats of brocade, four of cloth of gold, half a dozen of silk, and beautiful linen wear including fifty chemises, all of which, together with other things for the Princess's personal use, was estimated at 20,000 gold florins (5,300,000 mrs.).[354]

As they departed, the Princess and her nine ladies were accompanied by Cardinal Mendoza and many grandees. Fifteen hundred mounts and pack animals carried the assemblage and their possessions including beds, each marked with the name of its owner. They left Constantina (Sevilla) on November 11th, 1490, crossed the Guadiana at Badajoz, and met the Portuguese on a bridge over the frontier river Caia. There Dom Manuel, twenty-one-year-old duke of Beja and cousin-brother-in-law to João II, received the Princess from the hand of the Cardinal and took her rein to lead her into Portugal. Many Spaniards now turned back, but others went on with the great company of Portuguese, who spread a canopy over the Princess as she rode and welcomed her with festivities.

She arrived at Estremoz on the twenty-third. King João and the Prince, impatient to meet her, came on the same evening. When the Princess knew that they were expected, she could not eat but rose from the table, changed her dress, and had her chambers put in order. She awaited them above a stairway, dropping to her knees when they came to the top and striving to kiss the King's hands, which he courteously refused to permit, raising her gently. Then he gave place to the Prince and, kneeling, the young pair embraced. The Prince at her right hand, his father at her left, they went to sit on an *estrado* richly decorated, where the King expressed his happiness and pleasure at her coming. The marriage ceremony was celebrated that evening, after which the King and the Prince returned to the Duke's house where they were lodged.

The next day they hurried on to Evora, while the Princess and the Duke traveled more slowly to the Monastery of Nossa Senhora do Espinheiro outside the city. It was rumored that here, before her splendid entrance into Evora, the Prince and the Princess came together, which shocked a good many people because it was within the house of Our Lady. That same night a piece of battlement fell from the church wall near the chamber where they were lying.

At Evora the wedding festivities continued for thirty days, twice as long as those at Sevilla, whose celebrations the Portuguese did their best to outshine. Through it all the Princess remained a spectator on display, wearing handsome dresses and magnificent jewels, saying nothing thought worthy of record yet proving herself a woman "of much skill and great esteem". Within eight months the resplendent future had faded: her Prince fell from a horse and died. The country went into mourning, the people wearing cheap, coarse white cloth, royalty appearing in black. There was not enough coarse material *(burel)* to make the apparel needed, and working people could sell the *burel* covers off their beds at the price of fine cloth. Men sheared their hair and their honored beards, women scratched their faces to bleeding. The Princess had her cherished tresses cut. As reported in Spain, she did not undress and for forty days ate no bread, only drank a little soup. For three months she did not go to bed. She wore sackcloth *(jerga)* and drew a mantle *(manto)* over her head, so that no one should see her face. When King João II and the Queen had a bed placed for her, she would use it only on condition that it had no sheets. The windows of her chamber being closed, it was lit by one candle. Most of the time she wept, and she always had a fever.[355] Finally she put a black hood *(vaso)* on her shorn head and went back to her family in Spain.

The astonishing return of Columbus (March 1493) apparently bred no occasions that required new clothes. But ambassadors continued to arrive. When the Queen's confessor, Talavera, got the report of her entertainment of the French at Barcelona, he fired a protest all the way from Granada, where he had become the first archbishop.

"I do not condemn the gifts and the favors, though to be good and proper they should be moderate. Nor the hours of supping and lunching at Your Highnesses' table and with Your Highnesses . . . nor the expense of coats *(ropas)* and new dresses *(vestiduras)*, although whosoever overdid it does not escape blame. But what in my view offended God . . . was the dances, especially by one who should not have danced. . . . And furthermore, the license of French knights mingling with Castilian ladies at supper, and each one taking whomsoever he would by the rein. . . . Oh, how inspired the French will be by Castilian decorum and gravity! . . . And what shall I say of the bullfights, which indisputably are a spectacle condemned? . . . God knows how open I keep my eyes to watch the ground your chopines tread."[356]

The Queen replied from Zaragoza on her way to Castilla. "I should not wish to appear to excuse myself. But because it seems to me that they reported more than actually happened, I will tell what took place. . . . If they said there that I danced, I did not; it did not even enter my thought. . . . Neither I nor my ladies had new costumes, nor even new dresses. Everything I wore there I had worn [before]. . . . I had only one dress made of silk with three *marcos* (24 oz.) of gold, the plainest I could. . . . As for taking the reins of the ladies, I did not know it was done until I read your letter. . . . Having the French sup at table is a very common thing; they do it continually (and will not take the example from here). Each time the principal dignitaries eat with the Kings here, the others eat at tables in the hall of ladies and knights . . . never the ladies alone. . . . The men's clothes were very costly. I did not order it, but hindered it all I could and admonished them not to do it. As for the bulls . . . that is not a question for me alone."[357]

Not long after this spirited exchange Fernando and Isabel issued a pragmatic, the first of a long, futile series, prohibiting indulgence in costly fabrics.

"Our subjects and native-born have forgotten all respect and exceeded all rule in their gowns *(ropas)* and suits of clothes *(trajes)*, and also in their trimmings *(guarniciones)* and horse trappings *(jaeces)* . . . with the result that, in order to satisfy their appetites and conceit, many squander their revenues, while others sell, pawn, and consume their capital and inheritances and revenues . . . in order to buy brocades, cloths of drawn

gold, and embroideries of gold and silver for their own wear and even to adorn their
horses and mules. . . . There is another universal damage to all our kingdoms in that
commonly these brocades and cloths of drawn gold are brought hither by foreigners,
who take out of our kingdoms the gold and silver they obtain by their sales. . . . Therefore,
we prohibit and command that in this present year [1494] . . . and in the two following
. . . no one shall presume to bring in or to introduce into these our kingdoms from
outside [woolen] cloths *(paños)* or any pieces whatsoever of brocade, satin, or velvet *(pelo)*
or gold or silver cloth, or cloth of drawn gold. That clothes made thereof, or embroideries
of gold and silver . . . they shall not venture to sell or to exchange: neither embroiderer,
nor tailor, nor doublet maker, nor trimming maker, nor saddler, nor anyone else whosoever
shall presume to cut or sew or make any of the aforesaid articles from new cloth."[358]

These commandments apparently did not apply to the royal family. The Queen's
expense accounts for 1494–1496 show any number of purchases for Juana, who was to be
married, of satins, velvets, and brocades; none of cloth of gold appears, though she and
her ladies conspicuously displayed it. Noticeable entries are those of fur for linings: sable,
squirrel, marten, rabbit, and some kind of cat *(gato).*

In the marriage arrangements of Juan and Margarita and of Juana and Phelipe, dowries,
for parental convenience, had been omitted. However, Margarita's father, the Emperor
Maximilian, stipulated for her a court of sixty Flemish ladies to be supported by the
Spaniards, and the Catholic Kings responded with a Spanish quota for their daughter to
be maintained in Flanders. Isabel went with Juana to Laredo on the Cantabrian coast to
see her off (August 16th, 1496) in a fleet of 120 ships with 15,000 men intended to make
a firm impression of Spanish power and, perhaps, to launch an attack on France. After
a storm which blew them over to England, the Genoese carrack entrusted with much of
Juana's trousseau and the wardrobes of many of her ladies went aground, losing most of
the clothes. When she came ashore (September 8th), Phelipe el Hermoso was still in Austria
with his father, but the people of Antwerp welcomed their young Archduchess with joy.
Enough of her apparel had been saved to make a favorable impression. "This very illustrious
and virtuous lady, aged [sixteen], of beautiful carriage and gracious manner, the most
richly adorned that ever was seen in the Archduke's country, was mounted on a mule
after the manner of Spain, her head uncovered. She was followed by sixteen noble ladies
and a matron, all dressed in cloth of gold and mounted in the same manner. . . . This
very excellent lady was habited in cloth of gold encrusted with jewels so precious and
rich that one could not estimate their value."[359]

Because of the bad relations with France no word of Juana's departure could go
overland from Spain, and only after her arrival in Flanders was a message sent to Phelipe.
When he finally reached Lierre where Juana awaited him (October 19th), he had come
in post haste and insisted on being married that night. The nuptial Mass took place the
next day.

Also in Flanders Margarita had been betrothed to Prince Juan at Malines (November
5th, 1495) with the Spanish ambassador acting as proxy, a sagacious man but inclined to
parsimony. A compatriot provided him with a gown of costly brocade woven with gold
loops in three heights *(brocado de tres altos),* and on the day of the ceremony told him

that he must be sure he was well dressed throughout, for he would have to strip to doublet and hose before playing the part of bridegroom by laying one leg beside the Princess as she waited in the betrothal bed. He said that he was, but at the moment of truth his hose were seen to be in such a state that his shirt stuck out behind.[360]

Margarita expected to go to Spain with the ships that had brought Juana, but months went by without a favorable wind. Meanwhile, soldiers and sailors of the fleet persisted in dying from hunger and the Flemish cold, until by February (1497) only 6,000 remained to make the voyage home. After enduring terrible weather and making a forced call at Southampton, Margarita's ship with three or four others arrived (March 6th) at Santander, where she dispatched a message to the court at Burgos. As soon as possible the Constable and other grandees came to meet her, having sent ahead 120 mules carrying plate and tapestries for the journey. Isabel and Fernando had commanded the district to be well supplied with provisions. Four days were required for unloading her boxes from the ship, and nine for the trip overland.[361]

At her meeting with the King and the Prince, their musicians with trumpets and bugles, pipes and flutes blew a fanfare so loud that one could almost hear God thunder. Margarita, in the saddle as were her hosts, wore a French dress (saya) of cloth of gold with a long skirt tight at the waistline, gold earrings and a French hood (chapiron). Her belt was a golden chain thick as the little finger. At Burgos, where they arrived with great ceremony, the royal wish was conveyed that the easy manners she had learned in France and Flanders should be replaced with the gravity and formality (autoridad) of Spain. But she was to keep the 100 attendants she had brought, and they were to serve her according to their custom.

The wedding on April third occasioned the most brilliant season of the reign, Spanish grandees having come from all over the kingdoms and ambassadors from Christian states of Europe. Isabel and Fernando looked forward to a golden future for an established dynasty—until the Prince died. Margarita's eagerly awaited child proved to be a daughter still-born, and her attendants, dissatisfied in Spain, persuaded her to leave. She did not go empty-handed. Her father's and her brother's ambassadors (September 28th, 1499) signed a receipt running to 20½ whole sheets (de pliego entero) for valuables delivered to them on her behalf at Granada—horse trappings, clothes, and jewels. Fernando's benevolence ended there. Margarita had to borrow money from Spanish merchants to pay for the journey home. Her father Maximilian now being at peace with France, she could avoid the sea and travel overland. Flemish nobles came to join her at Bordeaux, and others at Paris. When Phelipe met her outside Ghent (March 5th, 1500), she was wearing a Spanish type of headdress (tocado) and a long mantle (manto) and traveling in a two-horse litter covered with black velvet. He kissed her through a window. She remembered kindly her life in Spain and reappeared in tocado and manto for the christening of her nephew Charles (March 7th, 1500). For her betrothal with the proxy of Duke Philibert II of Savoy (November 28th, 1501) she wore to the ceremonial bed, after banquet and dance, a dress or coat (robe) of gold cloth over gold cloth made in the Spanish style and lined with crimson satin, the skirt slit (fendue).[362]

Prince Juan and his child removed from the board, the royal inheritance passed to his eldest sister Isabel, who had gone back to Portugal. King Manuel I, formerly duke of Beja, needed a queen and wanted Princess Isabel, whom he had escorted to her first marriage. After much persuasion she agreed to accept him, and the wedding was fixed for the autumn of 1497. The Princess and her parents with their entourage set out in mid-September for the border town of Valencia de Alcántara (Cáceres). Manuel came to Castello de Vide on the Portuguese side, whither he had summoned prelates, lords, and hidalgos to appear, each in the best state he could show.

Suddenly, Fernando was called to the bedside of Prince Juan at Salamanca, from which he wrote that the eager Manuel should not await his return but go at once for the bride with the smallest possible number of attendants. Manuel crossed into Spain in early October and received the Princess in marriage just about when Isabel the Catholic learned of her son's death, which she concealed from all but her son-in-law. Withholding the sad news from his bride, Manuel took her to Castello de Vide, where celebrations prepared for the wedding were carried out so as not to waste the money the Portuguese had spent. He did not inform her until they reached Evora, where obsequies were held and the court went into mourning.

In December the young Queen, now pregnant, and Manuel received the news of Princess Margarita's unfortunate accouchement and the urgent request of Fernando and Isabel that they come to Spain to be sworn in as heirs. At Toledo (April 1498) the luster of the ceremonies was somewhat dimmed by the prevalence of mourning dress, still worn by both Portuguese and Spaniards, but the mourners had ways of enhancing it. When visiting courtiers were to be presented to the older Queen, a Portuguese assisted because he knew what honors each personage had won and what courtesies and favors were owed him—"a dangerous debt to pay in all nations and most dangerous in the case of the Portuguese".[363] Having completed the Castilian installation in less than a month at Toledo, the royal party went to Aragón, where three months were spent at Zaragoza wrangling with nobles unwilling to accept a woman as heir. The younger Isabel became impatient: "Why does Your Highness wish so to temporize with them?" she said in council to her father. "It would be better to leave Aragón and come back to conquer it anew, and then make and impose what laws you will."[364] When her son Miguel was born, the matter was settled: they had a male heir. She died in childbirth (August 24th, 1498), and Manuel returned alone to Portugal, leaving the tiny Prince with his grandmother. Before two years had passed the child died at Granada, and Manuel ceased to resist marriage with the Infanta María. The Catholic Kings sent her into Portugal (October 1500) without fanfare but with a dowry of 200,000 gold doblas, payable in three installments, and an annual income of four and a half *contos* (4,500,000 maravedis) based on rents from Sevilla. Of María's nine children six became kings, prelates, or scholars; one daughter married the Duke of Savoy and another, the Emperor Charles V.

Ever since the English mission to Spain recorded by Machado (1489), negotiations, or rather hagglings, had been going on over the marriage settlement of Infanta Catalina, future Princess of Wales. Henry VII and Fernando were matched in their regard for lucre. The English expected the Catholic Kings to send the Princess to London in a decent manner and at their own expense—suitably dressed, possessed of as many jewels as became her position, and furnished with a dowry of 200,000 crowns. Her parents held out for 100,000 Castilian gold ducats or 100,000 gold florins of Aragón, from which they proposed to deduct the value of their daughter's ornaments and clothes. Henry was unwilling to accept the deduction. They countered that his refusal broke with custom: husbands furnished their wives' clothes; provided that the cost could be applied toward the dowry, they would buy any number of dresses and ornaments. It was finally agreed that the plate, clothes, and ornaments that Catalina brought with her should enter into her marriage portion, which was to total 200,000 escudos.

Isabel and Fernando wished to send with their daughter a permanent entourage of 150 persons, but Henry VII and his Council desired her to bring the smallest possible number of Spanish servants; she would have loyal English attendants. Guests of high rank who would come only for the wedding and then return to Spain would, to any number, be gladly entertained with the greatest hospitality. The detailed list of Catalina's household comprises 55 persons.[365] When she set out from Granada (May 21st, 1501), her retinue included duenna, majordomo, confessor, chamberlain, steward, butler, marshal, equerries, maids of honor, laundresses, pages, cooks, and bakers. They sailed from La Coruña on August seventeenth, driven by storm ran back to Laredo (Santander), and after another departure reached Plymouth on October second. Catalina would henceforth be known as "Catherine of Aragon".

It was the custom for a Spanish bride of high birth to have no communication with her new family until the day of the wedding. Henry VII refused to accept this rule as applying to a sovereign father-in-law and overbore her escort to have Catherine presented for his inspection (early November 1501).[366] Greeting her in English to which she replied in Spanish, he saw a charming, poised, healthy girl with thick russet-gold hair. He was pleased with his daughter-in-law.

At Catherine's entrance into London, young Prince Henry at her right and the Roman legate at her left, she rode a great mule with handsome Spanish trappings. Her bright hair, confined in a coif of carnation red, hung long over her shoulders. The coif was fastened at the middle of her head upward, so that her hair could be seen from the middle down. Over the coif a little hat was tied on with a golden lace. Four Spanish ladies on mules paired with four English ladies on palfreys rode behind her. The saddle of the first Spaniard was an *angarillas,* which was likened to a folding stool with four staves crossing, two by two. According to English usage, Catherine's countrywomen were mounted on the wrong side, so that the pairs of ladies rode back to back in the procession. For the marriage ceremony at St. Paul's (November 14th, 1501) both bride and bridegroom wore white satin. Certain details of Catherine's dress marked "the straunge dyv'sitie of rayement of the countreth of Hispayne".[367] Her coif or rather veil on that day, of white silk bordered with an inch-and-a-half band of gold, pearls, and precious stones, covered much of her face and also of her body down to the waistline: "her gowne very large, bothe the slevys and also the body, with many plights, moch litche unto menys clothyng: And after the same forme the remen⁻nt of the ladies of Hispayne were arayed."[368] Their skirts carried hoops in the Spanish style.

Arthur died on the Welsh border (April 2nd, 1502) and Catherine was moved back to London, where her widow's household exclusively of Spaniards became "a miniature court in exile, reproducing on a tiny scale all the ordered ceremony, all the gradations of precedence, all the intrigue"[369] and rivalry of Toledo or Granada. The contest over her dowry intensified, and this girl, only sixteen, had to bear all the blows directed at each other by two kings. Fernando and Isabel did not complete the payment of her dowry and sent no money, because Henry should maintain her. He would not settle her widow's dower upon her until the marriage portion had been fully paid and, meanwhile, conferred on her only a slender income, enough to feed her household, which allowance he stopped more than once. The clothes that had occasioned so much argument began to wear out. Under her duenna's supervision Catherine sewed new hems on her dresses. Ladies in waiting renewed theirs by turning them inside out. Her courtiers were threadbare. In 1506 she wrote Fernando that she had nothing for chemises and had sold bracelets to get a dress of black velvet. Since leaving Spain she had acquired only two new costumes (widow's weeds?) and had nothing left but some dresses of brocade.[370]

A contract pledging Catherine's marriage to Prince Henry as soon as he should become fifteen years old had been signed (June 23rd, 1503), but that birthday passed in 1506 without effecting a change in her status. Isabel was dead, and Fernando forwarded nothing but excuses for not sending the rest of the dowry. Catherine could not pay her servants or replace old liveries and tattered hangings. They lacked money even for food; she had to sell gold and silver plate. Her ladies wished above all else to return home, and a new ambassador who had brought her dowry money to England quarreled with Henry VII. Catherine's only hope lay in the Prince.

When the father died (April 21st, 1509), the son moved. Six weeks after the old King was buried, Henry VIII and Catherine were quietly married, he almost eighteen, she twenty-three. They were crowned on Midsummer Day. Wearing white satin, she rode to Westminster in a litter of cloth of gold carried by two white palfreys.

Even before Catherine left Spain, Fernando and Isabel had realized that their laboriously established dominions were going to Juana, the second daughter. As soon as their Portuguese grandson died (July 20th, 1500), they sent by swift mail (11 days) summoning Juana and her husband to replace little Miguel and become Prince and Princess of Asturias. Trouble had already found the dowerless Archduchess in Flanders: Phelipe kept her isolated in her palace; she could not pay her household. But by the time they set out for Spain (November 4th, 1501), she had given birth to three children, the second fortunately a son, Charles, duke of Luxemburg.

Contrary to the wishes of the Catholic Kings, Phelipe let himself be persuaded to go through France, where he owed allegiance as count of Flanders. For a regal ceremony at Blois (December 8th) he and Juana were expected to accept money for an offering in token of his vassalage, but she refused the trap to her sovereignty and rejected the money. Thereafter, she and her ladies appeared in Spanish dress. As they entered Fuenterrabía (Guipúzcoa), the young heirs were met by Spanish noblemen with large retinues. The rules had been relaxed so that those who had been authorized to wear silk doublets might have silk jerkins and have them in colors. Beyond the village where Phelipe had been bedded with the measles, they were greeted by 120 of the King's falconers, dressed in green with one gray sleeve. A league outside Toledo, the King himself appeared with grandees and the town notables, who carried above the royal trio—Juana riding at Fernando's left and Phelipe at his right—a cloth-of-gold canopy bearing the arms of both lines.

Queen Isabel, they found dressed in black wool and seated in a chair in a large hall, accompanied by high-born ladies wearing rich jewels and crimson velvet furred with ermine or other skins. As she greeted the Princes at the door, they knelt to kiss her hands. (Where the Kings wished to take residence, proprietors were obliged to vacate half a palace with its furnishings.) The guest chambers were hung with cloth of gold and rich embroideries. For the ceremony of recognition (May 22nd) Phelipe wore a trailing gown of brocaded satin lined with crimson satin; Juana had a Spanish dress of crimson velvet.

Fernando gave a supper which lasted two or three hours, and there one of the most beautiful girls was observed flirting with three gentlemen at once. To one bareheaded and on his knees she talked a good hour and a half, to a second a quarter hour, and to the third an hour. While speaking with one, she ogled another and kept her hand on the shoulder of the third. Her justification was, "We take pleasure in treating them thus before we are married, for afterward they shut us up in chamber or castle. Thus we are well avenged for the time when we have to marry them."[371]

The Aragonese made no difficulty about recognizing Phelipe and Juana; for the ceremony at Zaragoza (October 27th), where he wore Flemish dress and she Castilian, they gave him a chair but seated her on a cushion. The Princes returned separately to Castilla. Juana again was pregnant, and her parents implored Phelipe to remain until her child should be born, or at least until Christmas. Unmoved, he departed on December twenty-second, and despite Spanish friction with the French he again traveled overland. Juana was desolated. No distraction relieved her despair, not even the offer of gold and jewels. After her fourth child, Ferdinand, had safely arrived (March 10th, 1503), she made every effort to escape and join her husband, but, hindered by her mother's design and finally by the weather, she could not sail until May of the next year. Her Spanish lady attendants remained behind.

The Princess landed after an easy voyage of nine days, but not to find felicity: the Prince had grown strange. The Spanish court heard that Juana had attacked a blond-haired mistress of his and that then Phelipe attacked his wife.[372] Queen Isabel, already ill, failed and died (November 26th, 1504). Her body was taken to Granada for burial, a tedious journey through December rain, floods, and mud.

Fernando, renouncing his claim to the Castilian crown, sent for the heirs, and Phelipe readied a fleet which finally sailed despite the season (January 8th, 1506). They had fair weather until "the great gale that the sailors had smelled came roaring out of the southwest."[373] The royal ship lost a mast; fire broke out in the forecastle. Phelipe had himself sewn into a wineskin which then, inflated and marked on the back "El rey don Phelipe", was planted before a religious image. If the sea was to be their tomb, Juana also would go into it labeled, but more subtly: she put on fine clothes and jewels. When a collection was taken as a vow to the Virgin of Guadalupe, she searched among her ducats for a half piece and remarked that a king had never died of drowning.[374] They rode out the storm, made an English port, and Henry VII invited the unexpected guests to Windsor. Phelipe enjoyed the festivities, but Juana stayed there only a night or two and saw her sister Catherine for a very short time. Henry VII, widowed, found the Archduchess-Queen desirable.

Ships repaired, the company sailed for La Coruña, where they arrived April twenty-sixth. Juana had left behind her Flemish attendants, bringing only two ladies and some Spanish slaves. After Phelipe and Fernando had conferred, the Queen and her King-Consort traveled eastward towards Valladolid. A secondary source says that when she met with representatives of the Castilian cities, they asked her whether she did not wish to dress in the Spanish mode and to take into her service noble ladies and damsels of the country, to which she replied that she did intend to wear Spanish clothes but that the matter of court ladies was her own affair, not that of representatives.[375] During Phelipe's illness at Burgos she watched faithfully at his bedside. After his death, Flemings embalmed the body and bound it with bands of waxed linen sewed fast; then it was placed in a lead coffin within a wooden box. The funeral procession (Fig. 304) passed from the Casa del Cordón, where the King had died, to the Monastery of Miraflores, where the coffin was deposited. Juana put on mourning, and hers may be one of the dark-veiled figures toward the left; another may represent her faithful companion, Doña María de Ulloa. It is difficult to explain the conspicuous dress of the girl who wears crosses of Burgundy on her skirt (Fig. 466). The Queen would not sign documents, insisting that all decisions be left to her father, and an urgent call was sent to Fernando at Naples.

King Phelipe had willed that his body should be buried at Granada beside that of Queen Isabel, and Juana prepared to take it there. No one dared oppose her for the sake of the child she was carrying. The coffin, covered with a regal gold and silk brocade, was placed on a cart drawn by four horses and accompanied by two friars, the famous letter writer Anghiera, three bishops, their servants, and almost a hundred soldiers. Doña María de Ulloa was the only other lady. Setting out on December 20th, 1506, they traveled by torchlight towards Valladolid for two nights and on the third came to Torquemada (Palencia). Juana would travel only after dark because a widow should not make conspicuous entrances into towns. The Office of the Dead was performed each day, and soldiers mounted guard over the coffin. At Torquemada her sixth child, Catalina, was born (January 14th, 1507).

Despite the presence of the plague, the Queen would not move until May first, and then only two leagues to Hornillos de Cerrato, a town of perhaps twenty-eight huts *(cabañas)* on higher ground. She was fairly comfortable in a house, but her attendants had to find lodging where they could, some in tents. Most of the court was accommodated at Palencia. When news came that Fernando had disembarked at Valencia (July 20th, 1507), Juana would have gone to the Aragonese frontier, but by letter he dissuaded her and they met at Tórtoles de Esgueva (Burgos). The next week they moved to the well-supplied Santa María del Campo, Fernando departing at dawn and Juana following after dark with her five-year-old son Ferdinand and the baby Catalina. After this taste of small-town hospitality, the King would have taken his daughter into Burgos, but she rebelled at reentering the city where she had lost Phelipe and stopped at Arcos (October 9th, 1507). Fernando left her there and went about urgent business in the country until February 1509, when with "patience, praises, and threats" he succeeded in conveying her to a palace at Tordesillas (Valladolid) and the coffin to a church cloister, where she could see it from a window.

During her journeys with the coffin Juana was never more than three or four days' travel from Burgos, until this move which was the last. "We suppose that there she will pass the rest of her life, content in her Saturnian solitude," wrote Anghiera.[376] "Content" is hardly the word for a woman betrayed by husband, father, and son. The type of protest that was to become familiar at Tordesillas had surfaced earlier. After Fernando took Infante Ferdinand away from her (July 1508), she refused to change her chemise or to wash her face. She slept on the floor and ate from plates on the floor. When at Arcos the King came for her, the clothes she was wearing "were such as it is impossible to endure, such as one should not even write about. . . . But the Queen showed pleasure in obeying her father and busied herself at once with casting off clothes that were an offense to her royal dignity and health."[377]

At Tordesillas, where the dour Aragonese majordomo appointed by Fernando said that he ruled the palace as though it were a convent, there were murmurs against his severity. Serving the Queen were, among others, the traditional royal bodyguards, *monteros de Espinosa,* a physician, a confessor, and Doña María de Ulloa, keeper of the wardrobe. In 1510 Fernando designated "twelve noble ladies who should look out for the Queen and dress her, even if it were against her will," but she could not bear them in her sight.[378] The visit of Charles and Leonor (1517) found their mother wearing a dress of cheap gray cloth, while their little sister Catalina, now almost eleven, looked like the daughter of a simple gentleman in her plain dress and a leather coat *(chamarré de cuir)* worth about 2 ducats. She had a white coif on her head and her hair, which hung in a braid, was wrapped, which suggests the style shown in Figures 314–319. Early the next year Charles had the Infanta kidnapped and brought to Valladolid, where she was given a dress of violet satin embroidered with gold and a lady to carry her train. But the Queen's suffering at this loss was so intense that Catalina was sent back to Tordesillas, and she remained there until her departure (1524) for marriage in Portugal.

The Tordesillas governor appointed by Cisneros, regent after Fernando's death, was a more sympathetic character: he cut a window so that the Infanta could see children of the town playing and watch horses being led to the river. He allowed Doña Juana to appear in public, and she dressed suitably. Charles replaced him (March 15th, 1518) with the Marquis of Denia, made governor of the town as well as of the palace. His charge was to keep the Queen isolated, to report whether she had eaten, whether she had consented to go to bed, whether she had wished to dress. The Marquis established a veritable court of 200 persons in the conventional categories, which was maintained by his heirs until the Queen died (April 12th, 1555). While his wife and daughters enjoyed free use of the palace, Doña Juana was sequestered in a chamber lit only with candles. With this situation contrasts unbelievably the regal tale of her possessions. The inventory of 259 folios, covering the years 1509–1555,[379] includes jewelry, church books, and vestments, horse and mule trappings, and all the furnishings of a palatial establishment, besides clothes. Thirty-three French coats are listed. In Flanders Juana may have dressed in that fashion customarily, but, as has been noted, she had clothes of Spanish style to wear when occasion demanded. Of over 200 chemises, seven are noted as Castilian, eight as French, and four as German.

As for young Queen Germana, when her clothes are described, the style is that of her native France. She brought in the custom of dining sumptuously, whereas Spaniards, even their kings, were used to moderation. At one banquet for her (1511), 3,000 maravedis were spent just for radishes. Many people died from overeating, says a historian of Charles V.[380] Though plump and a little lame, she journeyed faithfully with the aging King. On a trip from Toledo to Córdoba flaming heat rose from the fields; some of the travelers cried that they were being burnt like heretics. The sky emptied itself, and the whole company had to take shelter in a village of seven thatched huts. Covers of the beds they carried were swimming in water. They enjoyed no better protection than did the oxen, all of them having to force their way into the King's own shelter, their clothes dripping. Even at the end of the day's journey they were still squeezing out drops. "From this . . . you can see more or less what one has to suffer at court."[381]

The estate settled on Germana by Fernando and her appointment by Charles V to the viceroyalty of Valencia were enjoyed by her subsequent husbands: a needy German and the penniless Duke of Calabria, son of the dethroned king of Naples.

In the Naples of *Questiõ de amor,* where the Great Captain had departed (1507) and a Spanish viceroy ruled over a brilliant and elegant society dominated by Spanish tastes, women made half the cast. Though "the inexorable scythe of death", the French victory at Ravenna (1512), waited in the wings, noble ladies devoted themselves to lively pleasures. For riding in a hunt, to which she had invited high-born guests, a duchess appeared as usual in black. Her daughter Belisena wore a dress *(saya)* of white satin with many bands *(fajas)* of reddish brocade placed over pinked-edged borders *(pestañas)* of crimson. Other dresses reflected masculine usages: a princess's daughter had mulberry velvet quartered with tawny brocade, and for a countess's daughter mulberry velvet had been slashed over reddish satin. The ladies assembled at the home of the duchess, and gentlemen joined them there so that they might ride off together. The trappings of Belisena's palfrey were of crimson velvet trimmed with galloons *(franjas)* and fringes *(floques, flecos)* black, white, and reddish, besides a motto: "The three run an equal chance/Of happiness."[382] After the hunt the ladies moved on to baths not far from Naples to spend the month of April.

At a reed-spear tournament after Easter, ladies as usual were accommodated in a great stand (see Fig. 9) which had been set up and hung with tapestries in a plain between Naples and the sea. Following the event they withdrew to a princess's home. Supper was served at a long table, ladies seated at one side and gentlemen opposite them, a merry time. Then the men went away to put on their best clothes; they returned to dance. At the end of the evening many gentlemen sent their handsome garments to the musicians *(ministriles)* and jesters *(aldabaranes)* who had entertained them.[383]

A "royal" tournament was initiated by two Spaniards who wished by jousting to publish their grief at the state of their love affairs. Prizes were offered to those taking part in the action. Of the ladies attending, the most handsomely dressed would receive a diamond worth a hundred ducats. Forty days were allowed for preparing clothes worthy of the occasion. The ladies' judges would be three widows, all dressed in black, headed by the Queen of Naples. The Queen's black velvet, it must be confessed, was relieved with many pieces of gold, precious stones, and pearls on her cap and on her sleeves. Dresses competing for the prize were even more elaborate than those seen at the hunt. Belisena wore, over white satin brocade, black satin deeply slashed, the cut edges tied together with cords of red silk and gold. Tawny velvet of the lady Ysiana was checkered with brown brocade as for a game. Porsisana had a dress of white satin covered with a lattice *(celosía)* of gold galloons *(fresos, frisos)* mounted on *pestañas* of tawny taffeta. Who won the prize is not reported, for the author "changes his style" as he comes to the grievous battle of Ravenna, where the greater number of his lords and knights were killed or taken prisoner.[384]

Back in Spain with young King Charles and his elder sister Leonor beginning their travels (September 1517), a chronicler describes the tall headdresses, painful to wear, of Asturian women he saw, details the cloth-of-gold dress and the lavish jewelry of a young hostess at San Vicente de la Barquera, but fails to notice the Infanta's costume until the last day of October at Becerril de Campos, just north of Palencia. There the Constable of Castilla and the Bishop of Palencia had arrived to welcome the young guests, and they made a formal entrance into the town. Charles, preceded by the sword of justice, rode with the Bishop at his right hand and the Constable at his left. Next came Leonor, wearing a cloth-of-gold coat lined? *(plaine)* with crimson satin and having at her left hand the Constable's eldest son.[385]

Leonor was of marriageable age. After her father's death Manuel of Portugal had made overtures to her grandfather, Emperor Maximilian, proposing his son João as a match for her, but Queen Maria having died, Manuel now decided to take Leonor himself. The people of Portugal were far from enthusiastic about another marriage for their King. They already had eight royal heirs, the country was small, and how would they provide for more heirs from a young wife?[386] The Italian Anghiera admired the Infanta, "the most graceful and beautiful of nymphs", and sympathized heartily when it was arranged for her to marry "an old man who in gigantic steps is making his way to the tomb." Leonor wept until her "venders" persuaded her that it was better to marry a king than a prince.[387] The Duke of Alba and other grandees brought her on her bridal journey (November 1518). When she crossed the Sever River into Portugal, the Duke of Bragança with 2,000 knights was there to receive her. Alba asked whether he had the consent of King Manuel to take charge of the Queen's person, and the Duke showed a document signed by the King. It was read aloud and handed to Alba, who thereupon took the end of a golden chain hanging from Leonor's arm and placed it in the hand of Bragança. Thus she was transferred. At Crato, King Manuel and Prince João met her and the wedding took place. At Almeirim she was greeted by other cousins, now become her stepchildren.[388]

Only forty-nine years old at the time of this marriage, King Manuel has been described as very clean in his personal habits, gallant, extremely well dressed, wearing something new almost every day.[389] When he suddenly died three years later, Leonor was inconsolable. Attendants could hardly drag her from his burial place; she wanted to keep him company to the end of her life. Finally she was removed and settled in the royal palace to live thenceforth as a saintly and honest widow,[390] at the age of twenty-three. But Leonor was again eminently marriageable. The country would have had the new King take her and keep the dowry, but João III refused to marry his father's wife. "God came to the rescue" in the form of letters from the Emperor asking leave for his sister to return to Spain; he had his own design for her future. The widowed Queen lingered on, hoping to take with her from Portugal her small daughter Maria, but the Portuguese, for reasons of property, refused to release the child,[391] and Queen Leonor finally had to go alone (May 1523).

Before he died, Manuel had asked Prince João not to take a wife himself until he had found a husband for his sister, Infanta Isabel. The preferred bridegroom, the Emperor, had other things on his mind at the moment, and King João III completed arrangements for his own marriage to Charles V's youngest sister Catalina, desirable because she would have been brought up with clothes and customs similar to those of the Portuguese. The King sent to Spain an ambassador so richly and expensively accoutered that he almost obscured the memory of all previous ambassadors. With him went more than a hundred horsemen, of whom many were relatives and friends, dressed in the Castilian mode of mourning instead of in the long gowns *(lobas compridas)* the Portuguese were still wearing for the death of King Manuel. The dowry was agreed upon in July 1524: 200,000 gold doblas, three payments in three years, from which would be deducted the value of the gold, silver, and jewels that the Spanish Infanta might bring with her. The Emperor would provide her with clothes and furnishings suitable to her rank; the King would settle on her a third of the dowry.[392] As Queen Juana could not believe that Catalina had reached marriageable age, the Infanta left Tordesillas without saying goodbye to her mother.[393]

Her cortege, headed by a bishop and a duke and handsomely dressed, was met at the border (February 14th, 1525) by two brothers of King João, the Duke of Bragança, and their train. Catalina traveled in a litter *(andas)* slung between two handsome mules *(acémilas),* which were harnessed with velvet trappings. The litter, covered with black velvet and trimmed *(atrocelado)* with twisted cords of white silk, was lined with crimson taffeta elaborately embroidered. The King himself had prescribed the ceremony of her reception. When his young Queen crossed the River Caia, his horsemen were to dismount and kiss the royal hand, each personage introduced by a Portuguese hidalgo. Bragança in his turn was to get down, but Catalina was to command him to remount, and from horseback he was to make his salutation; the King's brothers would follow suit. Most of the Spanish nobles then turned back to Badajoz, while the Portuguese accompanied their Queen to Crato and the wedding. According to a servitor of the King's aunt Leonor, "Few queens, they say, have come to Portugal with their persons so well endowed: she brings many dresses and many rich necklaces of gold and precious stones given her by the Emperor, who has turned over to her all the jewels of the Queen his mother."[394]

In a royal Portuguese wedding scene (Fig. 12), the bride wears an olive-green dress trimmed with black and gold bands and topped with a black yoke or partlet. At the neck a narrow frill finishes the white chemise. Headdress, pendant, and girdle are of gold set with pearls, rubies, and diamonds. The groom in crimson jerkin and cloak, yellow boots, and black shoes places his right hand over the bride's right, while the prelate, his left hand laid on the groom's hand, blesses with his right. They seem to stand in the crossing before the chancel in a simple Gothic interior.[395]

As for Infanta Isabel, not every Portuguese was entranced with the idea of marrying her to the Emperor. Some felt that a great deal of money would be involved, that it would be better to invest their treasure at home than to surrender it to create power abroad. But when the Emperor sent two ambassadors to Portugal (October 1525), they had no trouble in coming to a satisfactory settlement, a dowry of 900,000 gold doblas. True, the Portuguese pared it down somewhat by various deductions: the 23,066 doblas of rents in Spain that the Infanta had inherited from her mother; the 165,232 doblas and 16 maravedis—the Portuguese figured closely—that the Emperor still owed on his sister Catalina's dowry; plus 51,369 doblas and 315 maravedis of the cash that he had borrowed at the time of the Comuneros' uprising. For his part Charles's deputies promised that he would settle 300,000 gold doblas on his bride, besides paying annually 50,000 doblas for the support of her person and her household.[396] On November first, the Infanta and the Emperor were betrothed, one of his ambassadors serving as proxy. Since the principals were first cousins, and they had as well a common great-great-great-grandfather in John of Gaunt, time was required to obtain a proper dispensation for their marriage, and Isabel did not leave Portugal until the next year.

Meanwhile, Queen Leonor was "on deposit", as it were, in the European marriage market. Charles V promised her first to his useful ally, the Duke of Bourbon, but in a settlement with France that move was canceled, and she was pledged to the Duke's mortal enemy, François I. Naturally and not without reason, the Duke's advocate advised against the marriage: the King's love affairs would keep her always jealous, he had a communicable disease, his mother would treat her like a kitchen maid. But Leonor would not dispute the will of her brother. François, captured in Italy (February 24th, 1525) and brought to Spain (June 1525), bore himself admirably as a prisoner and won all hearts with his courtesy and affability.[397] In the fortress at Madrid he was betrothed to Queen Leonor (January 20th, 1526), General de Lannoy who had taken his sword at Pavia serving as her proxy, and a week later she was pledged at Torrijos (Toledo) to his proxy, Monsieur de Brion.

François was freed to meet his bride at Illescas (Toledo), where Doña Leonor was accompanied by Queen Germana. The King and the Emperor arrived on February 17th, 1526. Dismounted at their inn, each held his hat and waited for the other to enter first. Finally the Emperor went ahead (as usual). After eating, they proceeded on foot to the lodging of the Queens and walked up to the gallery where the royal ladies were standing. Charles took off his hat and bowed deeply to his sister, who bowed deeply in return. He did the same with Germana. Meanwhile, the King of France stood two or three paces aside, his hat on his head. When the Emperor and the Queens turned toward the King, he removed his hat and bowed deeply to his betrothed, and she to him. Leonor knelt and begged his hand to kiss it, but he said, "I shall give you nothing but the lips," and embracing, kissed her on the cheek. All the gentlemen present gave a shout of joy. François bowed to Germana and she bowed in return. The four royal figures passed into a drawing room, where they stayed a while. Their ladies and gentlemen danced.[398] Leonor, having ceased to mourn the good King Manuel, wore a coat *(ropa)* of grayish-brown velvet elaborately slashed over cloth of gold. Her hair was bound in the Grecian manner with fillets of gold and precious stones.[399]

Charles V and François I, traveling in the same litter, came back to call on the Queens the next day, and then the King departed for his own dominions, accompanied by a great number of Spaniards. After appointing the Constable of Castilla to accompany Leonor to France, the Emperor was free to attend his wedding. Leonor followed François as far as Vitoria but waited four years to be summoned to her place as his queen.

Meanwhile, in early January 1526, the Duke of Calabria, the Archbishop of Toledo, and the Duke of Béjar, together with their retainers, had left Toledo for Portugal, empowered by Charles V to receive his bride and bring her into Spain. From Badajoz they sent word to João III of their arrival; on January thirtieth Isabel de Portugal, accompanied by the flower of Portuguese nobility, departed from Almeirim expecting to go to Toledo.[400] Her brothers, Infantes Luís and Fernando, were to leave her at the border, while the Marquis of Vila Real as ambassador would continue the whole way. In his train the Marquis had forty pack animals, the packcloths *(reposteiros)* quartered black and white and embroidered with his device, a winged animal. The pack that contained his traveling bed was easily distinguishable by its cover of crimson velvet banded with cloth of gold. He had also twenty-four halberdiers dressed in his colors and twenty-four valets *(moços da câmara)* on horseback.

From Elvas the Empress traveled in an open two-horse litter of gold-looped brocade lined with crimson satin. She was attended by eight footmen *(moços da estribeira)* in brocade jackets and red hose, eight others in black velvet jackets and white hose, three pages in cloth of gold, and by trumpeters, shawm players, and drummers besides. The Infantes rode one at each side of the litter. Before it went a king-of-arms, a herald, and four mace bearers. Near at hand were a courier *(aposentador)*, carrying the mounting steps *(tábuas)* the Empress would use, and a mule harnessed with a scissors saddle *(andilhas)* of silver, a crimson velvet saddle cloth, and trappings of cloth of silver on tawny velvet. There was also a whitish pony with gold and silver-trimmed velvet trappings and a yellow velvet saddle cloth. On the way masked horsemen, arriving in groups, rode up to the litter, bowed and took their leave, shouting compliments to the bride and her ladies.

At the border, the River Caia (February 7th), the Empress descended from her litter and mounted the mule to receive the Spanish dignitaries, each preceded by lesser lords and attendants. Her own train was even greater, and with difficulty a circle was cleared about the royal bride so that the Spaniards could be invited to cross the bridge. First came Béjar's thirteen musicians at full blast, and his eighteen pages, mounted. Next the twenty-one musicians of the Archbishop, and then his black velvet litter surrounded with twenty-four lackeys and five mules. Calabria had brought eight or ten pages on performing horses. After the lesser nobles had gone over, the principals—Calabria in the middle and the Archbishop at the right riding mules, Béjar at the left on a chestnut jennet—crossed the bridge and dismounted to kiss the hand of the Empress.

Silence established and Spaniards remounted, a secretary read aloud the power of attorney sent by the Emperor, to which Infante Luís responded by taking his sister's reins and saying, "In the name of the King of Portugal, my lord and brother, I deliver to Your Excellency the Empress, my lady, as wife, as she is, of his Caesarean Majesty, the Emperor." Hat in hand, the Duke of Calabria took the reins and in the name of the Emperor accepted delivery of the Empress. Then all the drums and the trumpets sounded, and for a quarter of an hour Calabria's pages made their horses leap and caracole about the bride, after which the Infantes took leave of the Spaniards and of their sister and the Marquis of Vila Real.

With Calabria and Vila Real at her right and the Archbishop and Béjar at her left, the Empress continued to Badajoz, to be received at the Guadiana Bridge by town officials. She stayed in the city a week, uncertain whither to proceed since no direction had come from Charles V because of his involvement with François I. At last word arrived that she should go to Sevilla, but by short stages, in order that the Emperor might catch up with her on the road. Thus a journey that could have been accomplished in five or six days required over three weeks, a state of things little to the taste of Vila Real, whose King had promised to pay all the Empress's expenses until she met her husband and for a fortnight after. Fortunately, at Llerena (Badajoz) a further message instructed the company to dally no longer but to push on to Sevilla, where the Empress alone would accept the reception prepared for the bridal pair. In the Sierra Morena news was received of the birth of João III's and Catalina's first son, and at the next stop Isabel received all who wished to congratulate her on the happy event. Portuguese and Spaniards put on their best clothes. Isabel's dress was so becoming and she looked so radiant that the Marquis of Vila Real begged her to wear the same costume for her meeting with the Emperor. Through roads deep in mud after heavy rains, she reached Sevilla on March third.

Officials, guildsmen, ecclesiastics, townsmen, merchants, nobles, the Sevillians flocked outside the city to greet their Empress. At the Macarena gate she stepped from her litter to mount the white horse and ride under a canopy of brocade woven with three sizes of gold loops (de tres altos) and embroidered with her arms and the Emperor's in gold, precious stones, seed pearls, and very large pearls. This canopy, which cost 3,000 ducats, was carried on twenty silver poles. The Empress wore white satin slashed over cloth of gold and a bonnet of white satin trimmed with white plumes, precious stones, and pearls of great value. As she began to move through the streets, she sent an officer to request the Sevillian ladies to take off their hats because she wished to see their faces. On Sunday, dressed in black velvet, she left her quarters in the Alcázar to visit other sections of the old palace. Charles arrived (March 10th) and the wedding took place, but it was rather an anticlimax, only an "improvised" affair. The Polish ambassador commented somewhat sourly, "The Emperor's marriage was celebrated . . . with little expense and without inviting the ambassadors, because of its being Lent and because of the mourning for the death of the Queen of Denmark, sister of the Emperor."[401]

A Briton credits Isabel with taking for her motto Cesare Borgia's *Aut Caesar, aut nihil* (Caesar or nothing), which would seem to indicate ambition. She had also self-control. In heavy labor with her first child, she said, "I will die, but I will not scream."[402] During the thirteen years of the marriage, Charles V spent much of the time abroad. The Empress is reported (1532) to have taken her meals, silent, alone, dining on cold food and watered wine, with many eyes upon her. Her table was attended in the Portuguese style by three

ladies on their knees, one to carve and two to serve the dishes brought in by men. Other
ladies stood near, accompanied by gallants with whom they talked and laughed, sometimes
so loudly that the Empress noticed the noise. This report was made by a bishop who
had to bless her table at dinner and supper, whereby his own meals were uncomfortably
delayed.[403]

After giving birth to a lifeless son, the Empress died at Toledo on May 1st, 1539.
For the journey to her tomb at Granada, the body, embalmed with bitumen, myrrh,
aloes, and other substances, was wrapped and placed in a tight-fitting coffin of lead within
a second of tin plate. Vacant spaces were stuffed with wads of cotton scented with musk
and other perfumes. A two-horse litter carried the body out of the city. Beyond the Bridge
of Alcántara, it was loaded on the backs of two saddled mules, the best the Empress
had, which could hardly carry the burden. Having accomplished two difficult leagues,
the funeral party sent back to Toledo, imploring the Emperor to let the coffins be opened,
presumably to lighten the weight, but, obedient to the Empress's explicit wish, he refused
the request.[404] After two weeks of travel over plain and mountain, the coffins were opened
at Granada to identify the remains. Their appalling state occasioned the famous conversion
of Francisco de Borja.

The story of Queen Germana must be picked up in the happier days of the Empress's
wedding. Before the imperial couple left Sevilla (May 18th, 1526), Charles V rewarded
the Duke of Calabria for faithful service. He was the Neapolitan Fernando de Aragón
whom King Fernando had shut up in the Castle of Játiva and whom Charles V had
forgotten there until 1523. Now the Emperor married him to Queen Germana, who is
reported to have been in love with him during two marriages and two widowhoods. The
Polish ambassador commented on this event also: the Duke, "forced by penury, has fallen
into marriage with this fat old woman. . . . Truly now he dines on gold and silver who
once used earthenware."[405] Germana and the Duke were not yet forty, and they had
time to enjoy Valencia where they served as viceroys. About their court and for the
gratification of lady readers of Castiglione, Luis Milán wrote his *Libro intitulado El Cortesano,* which describes their pleasures and their handsome clothes.

Queen Leonor did not spend her years of waiting at Vitoria; in 1527 she served as
godmother to Prince Felipe at Valladolid. But her course ran less than smoothly. At the
same time that François was writing affectionate, husbandly letters to her, he was maneuver-
ing to marry an English princess. Furthermore, with her high expectations and all the
waiting, Leonor fell into debt and had to appeal to the Emperor to advance part of her
dowry. François finally prevailed upon his nobles to make up their share of the 2,000,000
gold *écus* needed to settle his obligations and ransom his sons, who had been prisoners
in Spain ever since he returned to France. On pack mules his grand master brought 1,200,000
écus worth of gold to Bayonne. Henry VIII's ambassador arrived to present claims for
sums loaned to Maximilian and Charles V, now charged to France, and to return jewels
that had been pledged. By agreement with the Spaniards, the gold and other valuables
were rowed to a pontoon in the middle of the River Bidasoa, between France and Spain,
the French princes were conveyed thither, and the exchange was made (July 1st, 1530).[406]
Now Leonor could join her husband. She crossed the Bidasoa and in a litter traveled

310 KING AND QUEEN AT TABLE   ca. 1470–1480

Banquet of Herod, retable of Saint John the Baptist, by Pedro García de Benabarre (Barcelona. Museo de Arte de Cataluña)

311 ROYAL FAMILY   ca. 1490

Figures of Fernando V, king of Castilla and Aragón, Juan, prince of Asturias, Isabel I, queen of Castilla and Aragón, and Infanta Isabel, princess of Portugal, in *The Virgin of the Catholic Kings* (Madrid. Museo del Prado)

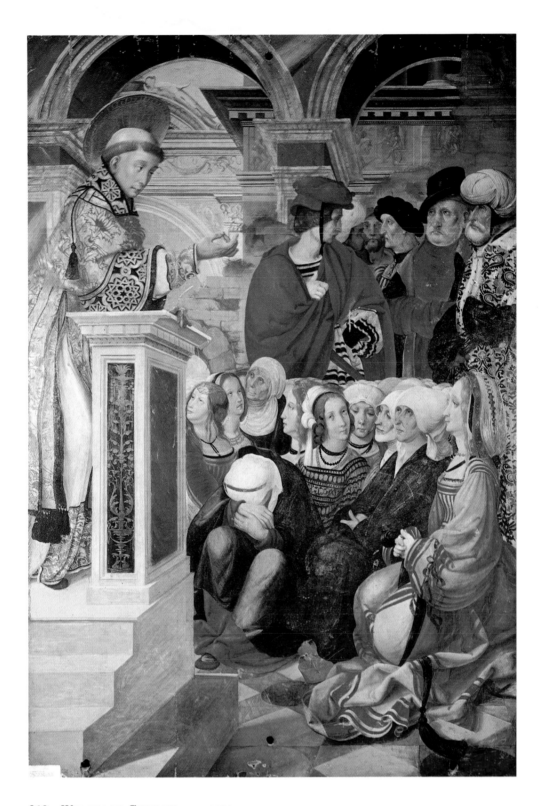

312 Women in Church ca. 1520

Saint Felix Preaching, retable of Saint Felix, by Joan de Burgunya (Gerona. Church of San Félix, Sala de Museo)

313 EMPRESS 1526–1539

Isabel de Portugal, Empress of the Holy Roman Empire; North-Italian
copy of lost work by Titian (Wien. Kunsthistorisches Museum)

with her stepsons to St. Jean de Luz. From Mont de Marsan she was summoned to meet François I at the Abbey of Capsieux, a small nunnery with only four or five spare rooms where her train could not follow her. She arrived at nine in the evening, the King after midnight; they were married at once. In France she was known as Éléonore d'Autriche.

At her first entrance into a French city (Bordeaux, July 13th, 1530), "The said queen . . . , dressed in the Spanish style, had on her head a coif or crispine of cloth of gold *frisé,* shaped in butterflies. Her hair, wound with ribbons, hung down behind to her heels. She had a bonnet of crimson velvet covered with jewels [and trimmed with] a white feather arranged *(tendue)* like one the King was wearing that day. At each ear hung a gem big as a nut. Her dress of crimson velvet was lined with white taffeta. From its sleeves, covered with embroidery in gold and silver, white taffeta was puffed out instead of the chemise. Her coat was of white satin, covered all round with [motifs of] beaten silver and a great many precious stones." Later at Angoulême the Queen wore a French costume but kept her Spanish headdress.[407]

Max von Boehn says that Éléonore was upbraided in France for introducing foreign fashions into that country and for having tempted François, by her bad example, to array himself also in the garb of Spain.[408] Thus was foreshadowed the influence that later was to spread Spanish styles throughout Europe.

In dresses of the period the style begins with a moderately cut neck, but soon the line drops low; sometimes it is rounded. The square neck is later filled in by the chemise or with a yoke or partlet. Sleeves at first fit snugly, opened at back to free small puffs of the chemise, but the openings lengthen, and chemise sleeves grow extravagantly. Skirts, long and simple, meet the bodice at the natural waistline or a little below. A distinctive feature of the period is the system of hoops applied to the outside of a skirt and covered sometimes with a contrasting fabric, making a decorative series of raised bands. Shoes are seldom visible except the tall chopines which were put on for walking abroad.

Ladies moving about are described in *El crotalón,* which at mid-century finds Spanish society in a state of upheaval, persons of negligible birth and fortune wishing to rise in the world and to share the pleasures of gentlemen. "Virgins, as well as wives, widows, and spinsters, all alike, live very free and undisciplined *(disolutas)* in their glance, gait, and swing. In the street they walk with a singular step, head uncovered and hair unconfined, exposing masses of indecorous locks. They carry the neck very high and affected *(estirado)* and wink at all whom they encounter, making lascivious movements with their bodies."[409] This comment follows not unexpectedly upon the earlier account of a girl's behaviour at Toledo.

A different impression, perhaps of ladies higher born, is derived from a mechanical doll of about the same time, which "serves to supplement our imagination. . . . A combination of stateliness and grace characterizes its movement. The feet move slowly, the figure seems to float. The skirt disguises the shape of the body completely. In contrast, the hands and head are in free and elegant motion. The head describes exquisite curves to the music produced by the sensitive delicate hands. . . . Agreed, there is no natural expression of the body through its dress—but dress and movement together give a picture of dignity and grace that makes these ladies appear as the true counterpart of the men who claimed all freedom and licence for themselves, and who, in spite of their many defeats, remained rulers of the world for decades."[410]

IV WOMEN'S DRESS

314   ca. 1370–1390   **315**   ca. 1447   **316**   ca. 1500

317   ca. 1521   **318**   1524–1527   **319**   1529

Hair Styles

BLONDES LIKE Infanta Isabel (Fig. 311) must have been preferred, because Talavera, the fashion-obsessed friar (1477), thus begins a paragraph on hair: "Married women and those yet unmarried undo themselves, first in tending and bleaching *(azufrar)* their hair, commencing to represent the sulphur *(azufre)* of hell and the live flames of that terrible, smoky fire . . . in which they with [their hair] must burn."[411] Moralists noted also with lively distaste that ladies wore hair not their own. Eximeniç's *Libre deles dones,* published in 1495, tries to frighten fair readers by suggesting that false hair was taken from corpses, which should provoke horror.[412] But, considering how niggardly nature can be, one hardly blames women—faced with a fashion demanding long, thick hair—for resorting to helpful devices from whatever source.

Hanging braid

During fifty years (1480–1530), with forerunners observable a century earlier (Fig. 314) and late devotees into the forties, Spanish ladies keeping high

---

Hanging braid

314 WOMAN ca. 1370–1390, from *Massacre of the Innocents,* retable from Monastery of Suso, San Millán de la Cogolla (Logroño. Museo Provincial de Bellas Artes)

315 SERVANT GIRL ca. 1447, from *The Marriage at Cana,* retable of the Transfiguration, by Bernardo Martorell (Barcelona. Cathedral)

316 PRINCESS ca. 1500, from figure of Salome in *The Beheading of St. John the Baptist,* Hispano-Flemish School (Madrid. Museo del Prado)

317 LADY ca. 1521, from figure of Hispania in *Figürliches Musterbuch für Kunstmaler* by Niklaus Manuel Deutsch (Basel. Kunstmuseum, Kupferstichkabinett)

318 WOMEN 1524–1527, from figures of listeners in *St. Ildephonsus Preaching,* altar of the Descent of the Virgin, by Felipe Vigarny (Toledo. Cathedral)

319 LADY OF HIGH RANK 1529, from *Thus Women in Spain Look from . . . the Front* in Weiditz, Christoph. *Das Trachtenbuch. f57* (Nürnberg. Germanisches Nationalmuseum)

style had their hair dressed in a braid hanging down the back (Fig. 316). Divided by a middle parting, the hair could be brought down in a curve beside the cheek, sometimes even lower than the chin (Fig. 339), before being drawn back to the nape of the neck.

The braid generally was encased in a fabric tube. Whether an actual tube or merely a strip wound or crushed about the braid, the casing *(tranzado)* was joined to a cap *(cofia)* of the same or a different material. For a servant girl pouring water into a wine jar (Fig. 315) the cap is doubled down upon the casing, as though they were joined at the neckline. The cap must have slipped off when the girl removed the head pad on which she had carried the water bucket. This headdress is called *cofia de tranzado* in accounts of Infanta Juana's expenses for 1487 and *cofia con su tranzado* in her royal inventory (1509–1555), which mentions also three separate *tranzados.*[413] The casing without a cap is seen in the back view of Infanta Isabel (Fig. 311). Talavera remarks also that braid-casings were costly and very delicate. Gold net of fairly wide mesh was used for both cap and casing of a lady attending the presentation of Leonor de Portugal to Emperor Frederick III, as depicted by Pintoricchio from 1503 to 1507 (Siena. Duomo, Libreria Piccolimini). The casing, tied with gold bands into seven long, sausagelike sections, runs to a bulbous end well below her knees. Holland at 170 maravedis the vara was specified for Infanta Juana's *cofias de tranzado* when she was eight years old (1487). For Christmas presents to his young daughters at Barcelona (1492), King Fernando sent from Valencia three dolls, which with dresses of *cebtí* and velvet had chemises, underskirts, and braid-casings *(trançats* in Valencian) of holland.[414] The tiny detail of those *trançats* is entrancing to imagine.

Talavera mentions the expensive ribbons of silk or gold with which casings were bound.[415] Often a glimpse of latticed ribbons at the nape of the neck is the only indication of a *tranzado,* as in a portrait of Queen Isabel (Fig. 311), whose braid once was pulled during a royal celebration by a lady impelled to warn her, "Remember, you must die."[416]

Ribbons of the cream-white casing of Infanta Isa-

320   1493

321   ca. 1510–1530

322   1529

323   1496–1502

324   ca. 1510

325   ca. 1520

326   1509–1511

327   ca. 1510

328   ca. 1531–1536

bel (Fig. 311) have been said to be bluish, but I could detect no color in them. White ribbons bearing black Roman letters lattice that of Salome (Fig. 316), recalling the Moorish fondness for weaving texts into textiles. About her braid and casing an agleted lace is tied at the top. Red and white figured ribbons are used for binding in Queen Isabel's kneeling statue of wood (Fig. 305). Queen Éléonore's binding can be found in her portrait at Chantilly (Fig. 370).

Early illustrations of the latticed, covered braid appear in the Sigena retable (Barcelona. Museo de Arte de Cataluña) by Jaime Serra who died ca. 1396, in the retable of Bonifacio Ferrer (Valencia. Museo Provincial), and in another of the fourteenth century (Fig. 314). Such examples should dispose of Herbert Norris's theory that this hair style originated in Italy, a theory probably related to the fact that Beatrice d'Este, as donor, is portrayed (ca. 1495) wearing a long braid-casing bound with latticed bands (Mi-

lano. Pinacoteca di Brera).[417] Rosita Levi Pisetsky, in her authoritative work on costume in Italy, presents her first illustration of the latticed Italian braid *(coazzone)* in a portrait of ca. 1490 and offers two possible sources of the style: the example of Beatrice d'Este and the influence of the Neapolitan Court,[418] then an outpost of Spain. Catherine of Aragon may have worn the braid in England. At her wedding with Henry VIII (1509) she had "her heire hangyng doune to her backe, of a very great length, bewtefull and goodly to behold."[419]

Even at the Field of the Cloth of Gold (1520) she appeared "in the Spanish fashion, with the tress of hair over her shoulders and gown."[420] Éléonore d'Autriche met the French with her hair in this style at Bordeaux in 1530.

The social game at different levels in Spain (ca. 1501) used the braid-casing as a counter of value:

As a hidalgo's wife,
she wore a good long train,
a dress with wavy trimming,
a mulberry-colored tabard,
a *tranzado* of ample size.

The silk merchant's artful daughter
wears on days of pleasure
garments mostly borrowed,
puts on a great *tranzado*
to fool some witless fellow.[421]

The *cofia* could also be longer and flow into the *tranzado* in a more casual manner, as the ribbon binding began at a lower point (Figs. 301, 306, 318). Both cap and low-tied casing of a high-ranking lady (Fig. 319) are elaborately decorated. Beige in color, they are latticed with gilt bands; the cap carries gilt balls. The head portion of the lattice may be intended to represent netting.

·Of about forty *tranzados* listed in Empress Isabel's book of accounts (1529–1538), several types stand out: that formed of pieces of hammered gold, for instance of lozenge shapes alternated with little enameled roses; that of gold thread made into little galloons sewn with 594 pearls; that of mulberry-colored net carrying 46 little gold buckles and aglets without enamel; that in which the two parts are of different materials, the cap of net and the casing of white silk or of cotton *(sinabafo* or *lienzo de Calicut).*[422] We must note the use by Portuguese royalty of these two East Indian textiles: fine hollandlike *sinabafo (sinabafa* in Castilian), imported from Bengal, and Calcutta cloth or calico. Late references to the *tranzado*, with frequent mentions of

Earlock

320 LADY 1493, from *May* in Li, Andrés de. *Reportorio de los tiempos*. Burgos, 1493. sig.d⁵ (The Hispanic Society of America)

321 PRINCESS ca. 1510–1530, from figure of Salome in *Presentation of the Head of St. John the Baptist* by the Astorga Master (Chicago. Art Institute)

322 NOBLEWOMAN 1529, from *In This Manner Noblewomen in Valencia Go to Church When It Is Hot* in Weiditz, Christoph. *Das Trachtenbuch.* *f*89 (Nürnberg. Germanisches Nationalmuseum)

Fabric-bound roll

323 ARCHDUCHESS? 1496–1502, from supposed portrait of Juana la Loca, queen of Spain as archduchess of Austria, by Juan de Flandes (Lugano, Switzerland. Thyssen-Bornemisza Collection)

324 LADY ca. 1510, from figure of St. Mary Magdalene in *Descent from the Cross* by the Becerril Master (Palencia. Palacio Episcopal)

325 LADY ca. 1520, from figure of listener in *St. Felix Preaching*, retable of St. Felix, by Joan de Burgunya (Gerona. Church of San Félix, Sala de Museo)

Braids wound about head

326 ATTENDANT 1509–1511, from *Birth of the Virgin*, main retable, by Damián Forment (Zaragoza. Cathedral of El Pilar)

327 ATTENDANT ca. 1510, from *The Entombment*, main retable, by Juan de Flandes (Palencia. Cathedral)

328 ATTENDANT ca. 1531–1536, from *Birth of the Virgin*, main retable, attributed to Juan Rodríguez and Lucas Giraldo (Avila. Ermita de las Vacas)

329   1499?

330   ca. 1515–1530

331   1521–1538

332   1525–1539

333   1526–1539

334   ca. 1530

335   ca. 1499

336 1925

337   ca. 1500

gold net and pearls, are found in descriptions of weddings among Spanish nobility or royalty in the early 1540's.[423]

Earlock

Cap and braid-casing could be accompanied by earlocks *(mechones)* as described by Talavera: "[The women] make a grand parting, twisting the hair and arranging it to cover the ears, and even leaving some little locks *(mechuelas)* outside."[424] A wood-cut maker draws such a lock crudely but unmistakably (Fig. 320), while failing to understand the *tranzado,* which he begins at the brow. In portraits of Queen Isabel similar to that in Figure 348, the earlock appears as a rather untidy escape, and one cannot say much about it except that it is intentionally there. Salome with straight, pendent locks (Fig. 321) now looks forlorn rather than seductive. The earlock of a Valencian noblewoman (Fig. 322) is

of unusual size. Italian and German examples can be found with the lock waved.

Fabric-bound roll

A distinctive style surfaces a few times in this period—rolls of hair tightly wrapped with ribbon or a scarf. A supposed archduchess (Fig. 323) with a middle parting has her hair drawn tightly to just behind each ear and then bound into a firm roll with a narrow ribbon. Strands of the ribbon pass over her head, and ends dangle at back where the hair is free. A related style (Fig. 324) shows the hair wrapped in two short sections, meeting at the nape of the neck, and long blond tresses hanging. In a slightly later version (Fig. 325) brown hair is wrapped beside the ear with a scarf of cream color crossed with black lines. Around the roll and over the head, the scarf is edged with a narrow black band. One scarf-end hangs down in front. Both ends are visible in the scarf worn by a listener in *Jesus Preaching* (1526), retable of the Magdalene, by Pere Mates (Gerona. Cathedral, Tesoro).

Wound braids

Spanish women wore their hair high also. The simplest fashion was that of braids wound about the head, very handsome when the hair was thick and long (Fig. 326). A *tranzado* as well could be treated thus, as in Figure 327, where a girl's slender, latticed braid is wound over a cap which is shaped with a back seam and *entre-deux. Tranzado*-bound hair wound twice about the head (Fig. 328) explains the coiffure of the harlot Areusa illustrated in the *Tragicomedia* of 1526 (III aucto). Uncovered braids appear again, worn by a lady's attendant, in a painting of ca. 1530, *St. Julian and His Wife* (Ororbia (Navarra). Parish Church).

A further use of braids was to arrange them as decorative side pieces. In an early example (Fig. 329) a heavy braid at each side is drawn forward to encircle the ear, while a jewel marks the top of the brow. A saint's statue at Burgos (Fig. 330) has elaborate braids, which appear to begin at the nape. After a forward curve, each braid passes up over the head, and over a draped headdress also, to descend inside the opposite curve and end below the shoulder. That similar treatment was adapted to court wear is seen in a medal of the Empress's sister (Fig. 331), who married in 1521. At each side a braid

---

Braids in side arrangement

329 LADY 1499? from figure of Melibea in [*Comedia de Calisto y Melibea?* Burgos? 1499?] X auto (The Hispanic Society of America)

330 YOUNG WOMAN OF HIGH RANK ca. 1515–1530, from figure of St. Agnes, retable of the Virgin (Burgos. Church of San Gil, Chapel of La Natividad)

331 DUCHESS 1521–1538, from medal of Beatriz de Portugal, duchess of Savoy (Madrid. Museo Arqueológico Nacional)

Braided and waved side piece

332 EMPRESS 1525–1539, from portrait of Isabel de Portugal, empress of the Holy Roman Empire; copy of a lost work by Titian, 1544–1545 (The Hispanic Society of America)

333 EMPRESS 1526–1539, from statue of Isabel de Portugal by Leone and Pompeo Leoni, 1572 (Madrid. Museo del Prado)

334 QUEEN ca. 1530, from portrait of Éléonore d'Autriche, queen of France, by Joos van Cleve (Hampton Court Palace)

Comb

335 LADY COMBING HER HAIR ca. 1499, from woodcut, after a French original, in Bade, Josse. *Stultiferae naues.* [Burgos?] ca. 1499. sig.a⁵ (The Hispanic Society of America)

336 COMB HOLDER OF COWS' TAILS 1925 (Finisterre. Fisherman's house)

337 WOODEN COMB ca. 1500 (Madrid. Museo Arqueológico Nacional)

appears to come from below to rise, narrowing, along the cheek to the brow, where braiding gives way to crimping; ends meet at the top under a jewel. Below each braid a wavy lock escapes. The back hair must be divided into two tresses of which one can be seen, crimped rather than braided, hanging from the crown to the neck.

This analysis of the Princess Beatriz's coiffure is based partly on what can be seen of the Empress's hair style. In the type of portrait which, for reasons explained later, may be considered as depicting a Portuguese dress (Fig. 332), the Empress has her hair parted in the middle. At each side a front lock is braided from the temple and drawn down to hang along a waved and puffed side piece *(lado de cabellos encrespados)*. Two braids arch over the top of her head, the forward one secured with a jewel. This frontal arrangement appears in a majority of the Empress's portraits, though Jean Mone, who made the bridal relief of the imperial couple, apparently misunderstood the braid, making it a thick, stubby affair which begins at the back, winds forward, and thrusts up a knobby end (Fig. 400). One probably can trust the treatment of the hair in the marble, full-length statue of the Empress (Fig. 333); the sculptors must have had dependable documentation for so complicated an arrangement. Again the front braids seem to end under the waved and puffed side pieces. In the back, two braids beginning at the nape of the neck separate to curve upward. At a point just behind the crown of the head, the left-hand braid can be seen to pass forward under its fellow from the right and then to turn back over it and to curve downward. At ear level it makes a loop, passing again under the right-hand braid and turning sharply upward toward the top of the head, where the two braids meet under a jewel carrying a pendent pearl. The braid-crossing near the top of the head is secured with a gold or silver band curved at the ends, and at the side, where three lengths of braid pass, a similar band holds the two that lie farther forward.

In a minority of the Empress's portraits the front locks have been understood as waved, more or less distinct from the waved side pieces, and thus they generally appear in portraits of Éléonore d'Autriche, more distinct in that at Hampton Court (Fig. 334); in that at The Hague the front locks may actually be braided. The top of the Queen's head is arched with a jeweled band, not braids, and there is reason to believe that she disposed of her back hair in a braid with *tranzado*.

Combing jacket

The dressing of hair, then as now, was probably an important rite, for handsome combs remain and combing capes or jackets *(peinadores)* are listed in inventories. A small one of linen (1503) was enriched at the neckband and between trimming strips *(tiras)* with braids of spun gold and blue silk, and edged all round with narrow galloons which carried pendants of silver gilt. A combing cloak *(mantilla de peinar, 1487)*, probably worn in winter, required three varas of red London cloth.

Comb

Combs of the time were rectangular, the finer and the coarser teeth springing from opposite sides of a middle bar which, as in a wooden comb (Fig. 337), could be carved with small scenes. Many of wood were imported from France, especially from Perpignan. In the royal household a dozen combs at a time were bought for Infanta María (1486). One of ivory (1503), carved with figures down the middle, was kept in a box of tawny leather. A large wooden comb was inlaid with bone, the wood itself being carved into letters and a scene of chess playing. As for Queen Juana, despite her indifference to her person, at least 350 combs were accumulated for her at Tordesillas, 268 of which are specified as of wood and 16 of ivory. Her inventory records also a "hair parter" *(partidor de crencha)* jeweled down the middle with one long carnelian, together with other carnelians and stones of different colors. Combs could be stored in cows' tails hung from a kitchen rack,[425] a custom miraculously preserved almost four hundred years later by a fisherman's family of Galicia—two cows' tails (Fig. 336) bound together within a cylinder of netting and fringe.

The sense of Sight, embarked in the Ship of Fools (Fig. 335), combs her hair in public, and the Comendador Escrivá celebrates finding his lady at the same task in the sun:

> I saw the sun then hide himself,
> envious of that very hair;
> we both suffered at the sight,
> he because he lost his light,
> I to be so far away.
> But certainly I had no dread
> to see him blind so suddenly,
> because he thenceforth would not stay
> forever blind and dead
> like me.[426]

Headgear

Cap

The cap accompanying the braid-casing in the fourteenth-century primitive (Fig. 314) falls over the brow, but in our period it could sometimes cover only the back of the head without visible means of support (Fig. 339). Salome's minute cap, white banded with gold (Fig. 361), is held in place by her roundlet, and Queen Éléonore's (Fig. 370) by her bonnet. In many cases the cap is secured with a narrow band. The Virgin Mary (Fig. 338) wears a jeweled band arranged above her brow and down over the cap, which is edged with embroidery, recalling the fact that Queen Juana had such a cap, probably of holland, embroidered in gold and green. The small white cap stitched with black that is worn by a bride, in *The Marriage at Cana* (Fig. 11), apparently is held in place by a narrow black ribbon, carrying pendent pearls, rubies, and emeralds in gold settings, which lies horizontally over brow and head. Later, over a larger cap, the band could be worn vertically (Fig. 340).

An orange-yellow cap striped in brown (Fig. 341) extends well up over the head but ends abruptly at the neck. A ribbon drawn crosswise holds the hair tightly except for two waved earlocks that escape; the *tranzado* is latticed with brown ribbons. In a cap of the longer, looser sort (Fig. 342) sheer cream-colored material is edged with a band of gold, and the midway pattern probably is gold also. Extending forward from the gold band and suggesting inner caps are a black edge and then a white one next to the blonde hair with its earlock; ribbons of the braid casing are black. A Valencian lady on horseback (Fig. 343) has a beige braid-casing attached to the center of her cap, which rises to the crown of the head. The pleating that frames the face suggests an inner cap.

Caul

Women of Spain as well as men wore the caul, for which there are several terms besides the obvious "little net" (*redecilla*). *Albanega* is defined by Cova-

rrubias as a "certain cap of net, round in form, that women wear on the head to confine the hair." It could be of woven fabric as well; Talavera describes silk *albanegas* as being completely woven.[427] For Infanta Juana (1489) sheer Asturian linen was provided to make two or more *albanegas*. This term the Spanish Academy derives from the Arabic *al-banīqa* meaning "hood" *(capillo)* or "woman's bonnet" *(gorro femenino)*. The net *(garvín),* which Prince Juan drew over his hair at night, was used by women, though *La lozana* makes a point of the fact that in twelve years one woman's hair has not been put into a *garvín* or an *albanega* but only into the *princeta* of green silk, customarily worn at Jaén.[428] On the other hand, when Julio in *El crotalón* wishes to be taken for his sister by Princess Melissa in England, his hair is gathered into a graceful *garvín*. Later, the Princess gives him a gold *redecilla*.[429] A further form of the caul was the *crespina*. Six of gold belonging to Queen Isabel (1487) must have had a slender mesh, for together they weighed but a trifle over four ounces. Vives mentions *crespinas,* along with *trençados (tranzados)* and *cofias,* as luxuries that God will surely strip from women on the final, awful day.[430]

The *cofia,* besides being a linen cap, could be a round "head covering of net" for confining women's hair, according to Covarrubias. There is no doubt as to the fabric when a *cofia* is listed as *de red* (of net). An augmentative also appears: *escofiones* of netting—one of braided hair with a pearl at each knot, others of gold—were worn by noble ladies in 1541.[431] In illustrations the net cap takes different forms. The woodcut of a queen ([San Pedro, Diego de] *Carcel de amor* [*Lo carcer d amor*. Barchelona, 1493] v°sig. E viij) shows netted hair at each side of the face sagging to below the chin. In a similar caul (Fig. 369) the hair hangs even longer and the net carries a tassel at each side. One net cap is round and close-fitting (Fig. 317) and another is hoodlike, lined, edged with pearls, and decorated with a flower form at each intersection of the net

338   ca. 1480

339   1507

340   1509–1511

341   1507–1510

342   ca. 1520

343   1529

344   ca. 1500

345   1520–1530

346   ca. 1535

(Fig. 344); both leave the back hair hanging. A Portuguese caul of gold which has a white lining (Fig. 345) seems to hold the hair inside. The edge galloon, patterned with tangent disks, is enriched with pearls and pink and green enamels, while each intersection of the net, as well as every exposed lozenge of the lining, is marked with a pearl. In a later illustration (Fig. 346), the caul is worn by the daughter whom Leonor de Austria had to leave in Portugal. Heavy meshes bear pearls at the intersections. Here the side pieces of hair have been drawn outside the caul, and each crimped mass is secured with a jewel of tangent ovals and a pendent pearl.

Cauls are mentioned in documents. The Duchess of Alburquerque (1479) had two *redecillas*, one tawny, the other white and brownish gray.[432] Machado (1489) saw the Infanta Isabel wear a coif of gold thread and black silk combined "in the manner of a net" *(reeye, rets)*, all adorned with pearls and

precious stones.[433] The Catholic Kings, parting with their daughter-in-law Margarita (1499), gave her a *redecilla* made of hammered gold, of which certain elements were decorated with black enamel and others varnished with sandarac resin *(grasillado)*.[434] Besides a *cofia* of mulberry silk with 46 pieces of gold and another of white thread carrying 299 gold pieces, Empress Isabel had one of spun-gold thread *(oro hilado)* "sown" with 370 pearls, which was appraised at 740 ducats.[435]

Sheer hood

A headdress worn by matrons—a hood of sheer material extended over the shoulders to back and chest—seems to have been peculiar to Spain. The general term for a headdress of sheer material was *toca,* used also for the material itself. Queen Isabel (Fig. 348) wears over a *cofia de tranzado* a hood of gossamer crimped about the face with an almost invisible binding. Sides hang straight down the cheeks; pointed ends meet over the breast to support a red enameled cross and a gold scallop shell with pearls and emeralds. This arrangement, including a gold jewel, is repeated for a donor's daughter of about 1500–1515 (Burgos. Church of San Gil, Chapel of los Reyes Magos, predella relief). The use of similar sheer ends to carry a jewel persisted well through the sixteenth century, even after large ruffs had become fashionable. Carmen Bernis suggests for this type of hood the term *beatilla.*[436]

In another hood (Fig. 347) the fullness, gathered into a cord, ends just under the chin, and the fronts are fastened together with a button. I cannot distinguish how these fronts end, but in the next example (Fig. 349), also transparent and worn over a *cofia de tranzado,* they hang with square corners over the breast. The cording that confines the fullness ends at the throat, and the fronts come together for a fastening, below which they are hemmed.

A distinct development extended lateral folds down to the bottom of the hood, both front and back. In one example (Fig. 350) we can see that folds are created by strain to the button fastenings, but in others, as in Figure 351, the fronts are joined and folds of fullness run easily across the seam. On the effigy of a great heiress, the Marchioness of Villena, three rosettes of pearls are centered down the front folds. Her hood at back (Fig. 352) is smooth at the top of the head and shaped below with a seam running to the neck. Further fullness is taken care of with diagonal folds; the heavier

Cap accompanying the braid-casing

338 YOUNG LADY ca. 1480, from figure of the Virgin in *Presentation of the Virgin* by the Curiel Master (Chicago. Art Institute)

339 PRINCESS 1507, from figure of Salome in *The Beheading of St. John the Baptist,* retable of St. John the Baptist, by Juan Gascó, destroyed (formerly Sant Joan Galí. Parish Church)

340 ATTENDANT 1509–1511, from *Birth of the Virgin* by Juan de Borgoña (Toledo. Cathedral, Sala Capitular)

Variation in braid-casing cap

341 ATTENDANT 1507–1510, from *Birth of the Virgin,* main-retable shutter, inner side, by Fernando de Llanos (Valencia. Cathedral)

342 LADY ca. 1520, from figure of listener in *St. Felix Preaching,* retable of St. Felix, by Joan de Burgunya (Gerona. Church of San Félix, Sala de Museo)

343 LADY RIDING ON THE CROUP 1529, from *Thus Valencians Ride with Their Wives in Their Parks* in Weiditz, Christoph. *Das Trachtenbuch. f*64 (Nürnberg. Germanisches Nationalmuseum)

Net cap or caul

344 PRINCESS ca. 1500, from figure of Salome in *The Beheading of St. John the Baptist,* retable of Jesus and St. John the Baptist (Vich. Museu Episcopal)

345 PRINCESS 1520–1530, from figure of St. Ursula ? in *Three Saints* (Lisboa. Chapel of Nossa Senhora dos Remédios)

346 PRINCESS ca. 1535, from portrait of Maria de Portugal, daughter of Leonor de Austria (Chantilly. Musée Condé)

347   ca. 1490

348   ca. 1495

349   ca. 1530–1540

350   ca. 1513

351   ca. 1520

352   ca. 1528

353   ca. 1513

354   ca. 1528

355   ca. 1531–1536

crosswise folds belong to the mantle. A late example of this hood (Fig. 358) is dated about 1599.

A hood fitted closely under the chin and closed down the front is set in more regular, transverse folds; its top and sides (Fig. 353) are pleated from front to back, suggesting that the sides are sewn to a plainer back panel, such as exists in a statue of Queen Isabel (Fig. 354). This panel appears to extend over the top of the head and to have its fullness at the neck taken up in vertical folds; the pleated sides of the hood are open to well below the throat. Another sculpture shows the hood (Fig. 355) with pleated sides turned back and pushed behind the shoulders. More regular folds recall a lay sister at Santiago de Compostela (1924) pleating a rochet by a primitive method. The heavily starched garment, still damp, was spread double on a board. When I saw her, she was going over the material by hand, pinch by pinch setting it in tiny, zigzag pleats to be secured with pins. After it was thoroughly dry, she would take out the pins, pull the garment off the board, and separate the layers. The starched pleats would spring back into place and remain fixed for some time.

Sheer hood

347 LADY ca. 1490, from effigy (Covarrubias. Collegiate Church)

348 QUEEN ca. 1495, from portrait of Isabel I, queen of Castilla and Aragón, attributed to Bartolomé Bermejo (Madrid. Royal Palace)

349 LADY ca. 1530–1540, from figure of donor in *St. Apollonia and Donor,* retable predella, by Antonio Vázquez (Valdenebro de los Valles. Parish Church)

Sheer hood with puckered front

350 LADY ca. 1513, from effigy of María de Herrera (Santa María del Campo. Parish Church)

351 LADY ca. 1520, from effigy of Teresa Chacón from Ocaña (The Hispanic Society of America)

352 MARCHIONESS ca. 1528, from effigy of María Portocarrero Enríquez, marchioness of Villena, by Juan Rodríguez and others (Segovia. Monastery of El Parral)

Pleated hood, top and sides

353 MOTHER OF A BISHOP ca. 1513, from effigy of Catalina de Sosa (Sigüenza. Cathedral)

354 QUEEN ca. 1528, from statue of Isabel I, queen of Castilla and Aragón, attributed to Diego de Siloe (Granada. Royal Chapel)

355 NURSE ca. 1531–1536, from *Birth of the Virgin,* main retable, attributed to Juan Rodríguez and Lucas Giraldo (Avila. Ermita de las Vacas)

Veil

Over the hood or without it could be worn a veil, probably cut in a half circle, illustrated in paintings as white (Fig. 356). Front edges generally hang straight and end in squarish corners, about even with the hood edge (Fig. 357). A later example (Fig. 358) shows the veil, which is turned back from the brow in a double fold, shorter than the hood.

Roundlet

The draped roundlet *(rodeo, rodete, rollo)* appeared in the fifteenth century and continued into the sixteenth. It could be taken off without disturbing the drapery, for the fabric was wound, not about the head, but about a roll stuffed with wool or rushes *(juncos).* Folds following the circle of the roll were bound in place with other folded sections. An early example in plain white (Fig. 359) is worn by an Aragonese queen. One covered with striped material (Fig. 362) cannot have been completely adjusted, for a long end hangs to below the waistline. At the crown of the head the space is filled in with dark netting and small pearls. The roundlet often appears in Biblical scenes, worn by mothers of slaughtered innocents. In such an example (Fig. 360) the main folds are secured with narrow jeweled bands, criss-crossed, and a large circular jewel is mounted at each side.

A roundlet covered more smoothly is used by ladies of high rank. That of a princess (Fig. 361) shows gold bands enriched with pearls and green and rose-colored stones. In other examples the cover is of striped material. Stripes in a roundlet for the Empress (Fig. 363) are effected with cords over which a sheer fabric is tightly gathered. Four pearls and a cross of dark stones make the conspicuous jewel.

Juana la Loca's inventory mentions several types of *rodeo.* One is of fine linen, three are listed together with pieces of material *(toca),* one rotted *(pudrido)* was from Valencia. Nine from Sicily were still in their own papers, all bound in one bundle. Thirty-nine from Portugal were termed "bulky" *(groseros).* Isabel de Aragón, who married a duke of El Infantado, had three dozen *rodeos* in her trousseau (1515).[437]

The term *rodete* has been current in the twentieth century to signify the ring-shaped pad for the head over which women carry heavy water jars.

356   ca. 1480   **357**   ca. 1550   **358**   ca. 1599

359   1448

360   1531–1536

361   ca. 1500   **362**   ca. 1480   **363**   1526–1539

Cloth hood

The Flemish hood of black velvet that Juana la Loca wears in portraits and the gable hood used by Queen Catherine in England made no headway among Spanish women. Nevertheless, examples can be found of rich, colored materials in hoodlike head-dresses. One rendered as black (Fig. 364) has the deep, turned-back front edge faced with gold (pumpkin yellow) and edged with a fringe of little balls. The figured gold band next to the face evidently edges a *cofia de tranzado*. In a red hood trimmed with gold (Fig. 365) the front portion is turned back only to the ears, where the direction is reversed and the corners point forward. A band of white and blue lies against the blond hair. Rear fullness hangs in directed folds. A hood of green velvet without turnback (Fig. 366) borders the face with a gold band. The green edge bears lines of stitching.

Veil

356 YOUNG MATRON ca. 1480, from figure of mother in *St. Blaise Curing a Child,* panel from Villalonquejar (Barcelona. Pérez de Olaguer Collection)

357 ATTENDANT ca. 1550, from *Birth of the Virgin* (The Hispanic Society of America)

358 LADY ca. 1599, from effigy of Isabel Valero (Jérica. Museo Municipal)

Roundlet covered with drapery

359 QUEEN 1448, from *María de Aragón and the Five Councillors* by Bernardo Martorell in Marquilles, Jaime. *Comentaris sobre els usatjes de Barcelona.* p. [1] (Barcelona. Museo de Historia de la Ciudad)

362 LADY ca. 1480, from figure of bystander in *St. Blaise Curing a Child,* panel from Villalonquejar (Barcelona. Pérez de Olaguer Collection)

360 WOMAN 1531-1536, from figure of mother in *Slaughter of the Innocents* by Juan Rodríguez and Lucas Giraldo (Avila. Cathedral, Trascoro)

Roundlet with tight cover

361 PRINCESS ca. 1500, from figure of Salome in *The Beheading of St. John the Baptist,* Hispano-Flemish School (Madrid. Museo del Prado)

363 EMPRESS 1526-1539, from portrait of Isabel de Portugal, empress of the Holy Roman Empire, attributed to Guillaume Scrots (Poznań. Muzeum Narodowe)

Mantellina

With that hood Carmen Bernis associates the term *mantellina*.[438] The Empress had *mantellinas* made of woolen—Segovia cloth, *grana, raja*—in black, red, or white, as well as of silk—velvet, satin, taffeta—in tawny, black, red-mulberry, crimson, or double-faced red and mulberry. Trimmings were gold cord or braid, passementerie, or bands of velvet in tawny or black. In more than one such garment the velvet inside is described as *vedijudo,* which suggests a crushed pile. Some *mantellinas* must have been white—a quilted one of holland and three of East Indian cotton *(lienzo de la India),* one of them embroidered with white silk in chain stitch.[439]

The *mantellina* varied in length; Covarrubias describes it as covering "not half the body". In the single entry for it found in Queen Isabel's accounts (1491) Baeza provides, for lining a *mantellina* of crimson brocaded satin, 6¾ varas of white Florentine damask, an amount that seems excessive unless the damask was very narrow. One of the Queen's black velvet *mantellinas* seen by Machado was long enough to reveal through its slashes the gold cloth of her dress. Furthermore, it carried a band *(roye, raie)* composed of bars long as a finger and half as wide, all of gold and each garnished with precious stones—"a thing so rich that never did men see the equal."[440]

Bonnet

The name derives from the Latin *bonetus,* which Du Cange defines as "a certain kind of fabric". In Baeza's records, fewer woolen cloths or silks and more velvets in black, green, or crimson—the latter the most popular—are provided for bonnets, the amount for one varying from ⅙ to ½ vara. A crimson *cebtí* bonnet for Infanta Isabel (1488) was embroidered with ¾ ounce of drawn gold. Of the bonnet's many forms, one has the brim turned up about a rounded crown. A plain bonnet of this type (Fig. 367) is worn over a draped hood that is edged with ball fringe. Probably of velvet, a tall dark-green bonnet (Fig. 368) is broadened with a looped band at each side and is lavishly adorned with pearls and jewels. Another tall one appears on a choir door which presents also a lower type, modestly jeweled (Fig. 369).

A "bonnet with halo brim", as Cunnington terms

364   ca. 1520–1525

365   1526

366   1526

367   1495

368   ca. 1500

369   ca. 1512–1516

370   ca. 1530

371   ca. 1528

372   1529

it, Carmen Bernis calls "gorra". That of Éléonore d'Autriche, wider at the sides (Fig. 370), is black—the edge suggests velvet—and carries jeweled ornaments: an oval brooch with pendent pearl and four motifs consisting of pearls, a mounted gem, and paired gold aglets; to the third of these motifs gold cord has been added. Under the bonnet a pearled band carrying another brooch with pendent pearl doubtless edges the cap of the *tranzado,* which is glimpsed at back. A similar bonnet is worn by Mencía de Mendoza on muleback (Fig. 308). This brim carries along the edge curled tips like those of ostrich feathers (see Fig. 51). Another of Queen Éléonore's bonnets, worn in the portrait with her new husband (Fig. 309), is black with stiff white feathers pointed forward over crown and brim. The narrow, upturned brim is ornamented with pearls, paired

Hood of woolen or velvet

364 LADY ca. 1520–1525, from kneeling figure in *Birth of the Virgin,* retable of the Assumption of the Virgin, attributed to Pedro de Cristo (Granada. Church of San José)

365 LADY 1526, from figure of St. Mary Magdalene in *Jesus Preaching,* retable of St. Mary Magdalene, by Pere Mates (Gerona. Cathedral, Tesoro)

366 LADY 1526, from figure of consort in *St. Mary Magdalene at Marseilles with the Ruler's Wife,* retable of St. Mary Magdalene, by Pere Mates (Gerona. Cathedral, Tesoro)

Bonnet

367 LADY 1495, from figure in choir-partition relief by Master Andrés and Master Nicolás (Nájera. Monastery of Santa María la Real)

368 QUEEN ca. 1500, from figure of Herodias in *The Beheading of St. John the Baptist,* Hispano-Flemish School (Madrid. Museo del Prado)

369 LADY ca. 1512–1516, from figure of Sibilla Africana, choir door (Zamora. Cathedral)

Bonnet with halo brim

370 QUEEN ca. 1530, from portrait of Éléonore d'Autriche, queen of France (Chantilly. Musée Condé)

Brimmed hat

371 MARCHIONESS—*SOMBRERO* ca. 1528, from tomb of María Portocarrero, marchioness of Villena, by Juan Rodríguez and others (Segovia. Monastery of El Parral)

372 WOMAN OF VALENCIA 1529, from *Thus Women in the Kingdom of Valencia Go Walking in the Streets* in Weiditz, Christoph. *Das Trachtenbuch. f109* (Nürnberg. Germanisches Nationalmuseum)

gold aglets, and a gold medallion bearing the letter "F" for François at the center and carrying a large pendent pearl. This time the Queen's *tranzado* cap is of netting.

Hat

For ladies traveling in all weathers, as did those of the court keeping up with the indomitable Queen Isabel, a wider-brimmed hat was a necessity under the Spanish sun. Its name, *sombrero,* indicates its purpose, to give shade *(sombra).* Straw and felt are mentioned as materials for the body; Baeza paid 93 or 99 maravedis for a felt, 186 for a straw. Velvet was used for covering *(aforro por cima)* and satin for lining *(aforro de dentro).* Juana (1488) had a hat, at 81 maravedis, lined with ¾ vara of crimson *cebtí* and covered with ¾ vara of expensive crimson velvet and 6 ounces of gold thread, which, together with the making at 396, brought the total cost to 6,102 maravedis. Some hats required ⅚ vara for a lining. Black silk tassels and buttons also were used for trimming. In Princess Isabel's wedding year (1490), Baeza paid 5,800 maravedis for 58 gold roses and 58 twigs or branches *(troncos)* to be used on a single hat for her. One listed at the Segovia Alcázar (1503) must have belonged to a lady. Of moth-eaten brownish *(pardillo)* wool (felt?) it was decorated with seed pearls: on the crown-top a dove in medium-sized pearls worked on linen, about the crown a diadem of larger pearls, and on the brim wavy lines *(ondas).* The hat ribbon, an inch wide and a vara long, was woven of gold and silver.[441]

From the fact that ¾ or ⅚ vara of fabric was required for a lining, one may deduce that the *sombrero* had a fairly broad brim, and so it appears in illustrations. A marchioness's hat, which in effigy hangs by a cord from the arm of an attendant (Fig. 371), has a low crown and a wide brim adorned with cord and three ornaments, each with a conical center, which strongly resemble one worn at the throat in Barcelona (Fig. 307). Weiditz, who observed women outdoors, illustrates several hats. A Catalan lady riding a mule has a straw-colored crown-cover gathered up to a red tassel at the top center.[442] The rich lady on promenade (Fig. 307) wears a low-crowned hat, black with only a touch of gold trimming. The ribbon hanging to below her chin probably could be tightened. This hat might serve as an illustration of that worn by Catherine of Aragon on her entrance into London (1501): "a litill hatte, fashonnyd like a cardinall's hatte, of a

373   1477   **374**   1493   **375**   ca. 1521

376   1492–1495   **377**   ca. 1510–1520   **378**   ca. 1530

379   1482–1495   **380**   1507–1515   **381**   1526

praty brede, wᵗ a lase of gold . . . to stay hit."[443]
A Valencian lady whose costume is alive with fluttering bows, wears a white hat (Fig. 372) embossed with silver and trimmed with buttons and animated black tassels. This hat is repeated in the Codex Madrazo-Daza which has been dated ca. 1540.[444]

Head scarf

Also worn for traveling was the draped *toca de camino*. In 1493 two of the Queen's ladies received 8 varas of linen at 70 maravedis the vara for two *tocas de camino*. Queen Juana's inventory lists two of white silk and gold. That of Biscayan linen had, besides gold *vivos*, a trimming of macramé *rapacejos* twisted from the linen itself.[445] Other scarves to be wound about the head were the Moorish *alhareme* and *almaizar*. Six varas of very sheer Asturian linen for an *alhareme* cost 200 maravedis the vara (1488). The Segovian inventory (1503) lists several, of which the most interesting is 12 varas long, of yellow linen with blue edge bands *(orillas)* three fingers wide, and a red and white stripe down the middle. An *almaizar* 16 varas long of reddish linen and Tunisian silk *(tunecí)* had green *orillas*.[446]

A lady who asked how she could dress for fleeing the plague in Valencia without being criticized, received the following advice from a knightly friend:

> With a graceful *alhareme*
> discreetly wound about
> that the wind may never burn her,
> especially if she fears
> to be known and stared upon.
> The hat of any color
> whatever for the road,
> garnished for the better
> with tassels of fine gold.[447]

Dress neckline, round

373 QUEEN 1477, from figure of Isabel I, queen of Castilla and Aragón, in *Libro blanco*. Libro 1°, *vᵒf*148 (Sevilla. Cathedral, Archivo)

374 PRINCESS 1493, from figure of Laureola, daughter of the King of Macedonia, in [San Pedro, Diego de] *Carcel de amor* [*Lo carcer d amor*. Barchelona, 1493] *vᵒ*sig.fij (London. The British Library)

375 PRINCESS ca. 1521, from figure of Salome in *The Beheading of St. John the Baptist,* main retable, by Felipe Vigarny (Granada. Royal Chapel)

Dress neckline, square

376 COURT LADY 1492–1495, from figure in *Her Royal Highness, Doña Isabel, Queen of Castilla and Aragón,* in Marcuello, Pedro. *Devocionario de la Reyna d.ᵃ Juana, à quien llamaron la Loca. vᵒf*54 (Chantilly. Musée Condé)

377 QUEEN ca. 1510–1520, from figure of St. Catherine of Alexandria in *The Crucifixion* (Córdoba. Museo Provincial de Bellas Artes)

378 QUEEN ca. 1530, from portrait of Éléonore d'Autriche, queen of France, by Joos van Cleve (Hampton Court Palace)

Dress neckline with filler

379 ATTENDANT 1482–1495, from *Birth of the Virgin,* retable of Cardinal Mendoza, by the Luna Master (Guadalajara. Church of San Ginés)

380 WOMAN 1507–1515, from *Jesus and the Woman of Samaria,* choir stall, by Felipe Vigarny and others (Burgos. Cathedral)

381 ATTENDANT TO A RULER'S WIFE 1526, from *St. Mary Magdalene Preaching,* retable of St. Mary Magdalene, by Pere Mates (Gerona. Cathedral, Tesoro)

Body Garments

WOMEN'S DRESS at this time, like men's, develops from the rigidity and narrowness of the Gothic style to the weight and fullness of the Renaissance. Changes of fashion appear conspicuously in neck and sleeve details.

Dress neckline

The neckline of the period can be cut low. In an early round example (Fig. 373) black and gold lace or passementerie finishes the neck of a yellow dress. Later, a rather wide edge-band carries a trimming of jewels (Figs. 374, 375). A square neckline is worn by a lady attending Queen Isabel (Fig. 376). Though possibly she has a sheer partlet, we can see how deep the cut has gone. Her crimson gown is edged with a narrow gold band. Queen Juana's dress is cut quite as low (Fig. 391), but the breasts are hidden with chemise fullness. The edge-trim is a narrow jeweled band. A saint's low neckline (Fig. 377) seems to be rimmed with fluting. In the last type the low neckline arches at the middle, sinking the corners to sharp angles, as in a familiar portrait (Fig. 378). The finish is a jeweled band carrying along the upper edge a line of small enameled trefoils, light in color.

382   1479–1492

383   ca. 1495

384   1526

385   1518 or 1525

386   1525–1539

387   ca. 1544–1554

388   1526–1539

389   1551

390   ca. 1568

Filler

A higher neckline was often accompanied by a filler of sheer material. The simplest form seems to have been a long piece of fabric arranged in fine folds round the back of the neck, the ends brought forward and down to meet about at the dress neckline before disappearing behind it, leaving a V-shaped decolletage. A plain white filler is found with a jewel-bordered, dark dress (Fig. 379). Another plain one, together with a plain dress, is shown very clearly by a sculptor (Fig. 380). In a later example (Fig. 381) the edges of a white fabric are embroidered in wine red, and the apricot gown is bordered with red, green, narrow green, and red fabric bands. Between chemises and partlets Talavera mentions *corpetes* embroidered with gold or silk and worn

---

Collarless partlet

382 DUCHESS 1479–1492, from portrait of María López de Gurrea, duchess of Luna; later 16th-century copy by Roland de Mois (Madrid. Palace of the Duke of Villahermosa)

383 QUEEN ca. 1495, from portrait of Isabel I, queen of Castilla and Aragón, attributed to Bartolomé Bermejo (Madrid. Royal Palace)

384 SERVING WOMAN 1526, from figure of St. Marcella in *St. Mary Magdalene Preaching,* retable of St. Mary Magdalene, by Pere Mates (Gerona. Cathedral, Tesoro)

Plain partlet with collar

385 QUEEN 1518 or 1525, from figure of Leonor (or of Catalina) de Austria in *The Wedding of Manuel I (or of João III) and a Spanish Infanta* by Garcia Fernandes, 1541 (Lisboa. Museu de São Roque)

386 EMPRESS 1525–1539, from portrait of Isabel de Portugal, empress of the Holy Roman Empire; copy of a lost work by Titian, 1544–1545 (The Hispanic Society of America)

387 LADY ca. 1544–1554, from effigy of Catalina de Alcocer (Sevilla. University, Church)

Elaborate partlet with collar

388 EMPRESS 1526–1539, from portrait of Isabel de Portugal; North-Italian copy of lost work by Titian (Wien. Kunsthistorisches Museum)

389 PRINCESS-QUEEN 1551, from portrait of María de Austria, called queen of Bohemia, by Antonio Moro (Madrid. Museo del Prado)

390 DUCHESS ca. 1568, from double portrait of the 3rd duke of Alba and his duchess (El Castañar. Collection of the Count of Mayalde)

---

in front of the breasts.[448] If *corpetes* were not stomachers, they may have been fillers.

Partlet

The partlet *(gorguera),* which also filled in a low decolletage, was a more developed feature. The English name "partlet", used in the sixteenth century, has been superseded by "chemisette" from the French, but among Spaniards the term *gorguera* has persisted to our own time in the little town of Lagartera (Toledo), where it has signified an oblong of white homespun linen, wide enough to lie on the shoulders and extending down over the bust. A hole at the neck and a slit down the front admit the head. The front is enriched with vertical rows of embroidery and drawnwork. A sixteenth-century partlet cannot have been very different in cut, for its effect was similar—it lay flat over breast and shoulders. In contrast, a chemise generally was full over the bosom, and frequently the fullness was gathered into a band. Sleeves belonged to a chemise but could match a partlet.

Talavera knew the partlet intimately: it was so sheer, so embroidered *(labrada),* and so insertion-trimmed *(randada),* he said, that the whiteness of a lady's skin readily shone through (see Fig. 376); she might better have left her breasts uncovered.[449] Queen Isabel's treasurer paid for holland and linen cambric to be used in partlets, but the most numerous purchases for them were of satin. He mentions also other materials far from transparent: crimson *cebtí* and velvets green or mulberry. One-half or one-third vara was required.

Among the forty-four partlets listed in Isabel de Aragón's trousseau (1515) no fabrics are mentioned. The record is solely of the precious metals used—drawn gold, spun gold, gold cut in pieces, silver cut in pieces, gold strips—and of their weight, which fixes the value of the partlets in appraising the dowry but does not identify their types.[450] For Queen Juana's 155 partlets the fabrics were holland; black taffeta; satin; black, brown *(pardo),* crimson, white, or yellow *ceti;* mulberry, blue, or black silk; crimson or black velvet; cloth of gold and silk; netting of spun gold or silver. Several partlets were lined, one of black *ceti* with marten *(martas).*

Some were richly ornamented. A partlet of holland carried 396 pieces of gold, each stamped with the design of a little scallop shell *(benerica, venera),* besides 8 golden buckles and aglets at the opening. Another of Queen Juana's holland partlets was even heavier with gold. Beside each mesh of its gold netting hung a letter "P", for Phelipe, enameled in rose or in black and white. The fasteners consisted of four beads shaped like little chess rooks *(roquecitas);* at the neckband were small roses enameled in colors. Even with 54 P's missing, this partlet weighed over 20 ounces, including the holland. Other gold ornaments for partlets were wrought as buttons (some set with diamonds or rubies), knots, bows, braids, cords, florets, fleurs-de-lis, thistles, ears of grain, or little tree trunks *(tronquitos).* Pieces of gold applied in stripes *(gayas),* 21 in back and 18 in front, decorated a black taffeta partlet. Several of holland had *gayas* embroidered with gold thread and black silk.[451] On a white partlet belonging to the Empress Isabel's sister Beatriz (1522) 10 *gayas* were worked in chain stitch and 11 in heavy seed pearls.[452]

A netting partlet of the Empress, sold at her auction for 177½ ducats (66,562 maravedis), went to a duchess. The making had cost 30,000 mrs.; the rest was for the netting, taffeta [lining], and 830 pieces of gold—754 small ones on the body of the partlet and 38 larger on the neckband, all made in the form of little bundles *(manojicos,* sheaves?) and enameled in black; on the neckband also were 38 little golden stars. The taffeta and the [netting] thread weighed ⅝ ounce and the gold 12³⁄₁₆ ounces. A partlet of 22-carat gold weighing 25¾ ounces consisted of pieces of enameled filigree with roses and little pedestals *(basitas)* between them.

Though netting was a favored material for the Empress's partlets, some needlework is mentioned. Of eight holland partlets seven were embroidered in gold and one in silver. One *embutido* must have been quilted by stuffing cotton into its designs. The technique called *punto apretado* and used on fine linen may have been the same, since *embutir* means "to fill by pressing" *(apretar).* Another white partlet was figured with drawnwork *(deshilado).* Three white and three of gold [cloth] were shirred *(encarrujadas).* Thin silk *(volante)* was embroidered with white silk, trimmed with gold or silver cords and bugles, or used as lining.[453]

Early examples of the partlet are collarless. The Duchess of Luna, who died in 1492 and whose copied or reconstructed portrait was painted decades later, wears what seems to be a collarless partlet (Fig. 382) of shirred white silk, finished at the front edges with gold galloon. A cord is visible, tying the galloons together. A white partlet of Queen Isabel (Fig. 383) is embroidered in black. In the edge-band a lion alternates with four lapped bars suggesting a castle; at the shoulder seams and vertically down the fronts are worked lines, probably *gayas,* of small leaflike figures.[454] A later example of the collarless partlet (Fig. 384), worn with a blue dress, is covered with red netting.

At a further stage a collar and buttons appear. One plain example of this type (Fig. 385) suggests a partlet of black velvet combined with a dress of olive-green fabric, gold galloon, and black bands. The neckband, unbuttoned, reveals the white collar of a chemise, while three gold buttons close the partlet fronts. In a black velvet one of Empress Isabel (Fig. 386) the collar is slashed vertically, revealing small white puffs which may be of silk, while down the front run even smaller puffs between the jeweled pins or buttons. Another plain partlet with collar and buttons is clearly defined in a bronze effigy (Fig. 387).

Returning for a moment to the dress of the Empress (Fig. 386), one must say that it is unusual to find the slashed band worn at the neck by a lady in Spain, though it can be seen on a dress sleeve in a sculptured panel, *Birth of the Virgin* (Burgos. Church of San Gil). Such a collar was used by men—by Charles V as a boy (Fig. 108), by an observer in the monument to Tostado at Avila (1518), by a spearsman (Fig. 109). It is worn by Prince Conan in the Portuguese retable of Saint Auta, painted about 1520–1525 (Lisboa. Museo Nacional de Arte Antiga),[455] but there it can be found also at a lady's neck, which inclines one to believe that this well-known black dress of the Empress originated in Portugal. When she visited Zaragoza in 1533, her all-black costume was described as *a la portuguesa.*[456]

Two of the Empress's spun-gold and silver partlets are described as "high" *(altas),* that is, probably, with a collar covering the throat. Her striped and collared example in Figure 388 is closed with agleted laces. The partlet with collar continued well into the century. In one of plain, cream-colored fabric (Fig. 389) the high collar is formed of vertical pleats stitched horizontally with gold thread and freed at the top to form an angular frill, white edged with gold. Pendent pearls, matching those in the gauze hood, hang from the lines of stitching. The fronts close invisibly, probably with hooks and loops. In a partlet with heavy netting of silver and pearls over a white foundation (Fig. 390), the collar, partly open, is headed with a white frill. There are matching inner sleeves.

The partlet is carefully detailed in accounts of noble weddings which, like *Questiõ de amor,* must have served as fashion reports to eager readers. At the Sessa wedding (1541), says the anonymous reporter, the ladies were very well turned out for Madrid (that provincial town not yet become the capital); some of them exceeded the bounds of luxury that His Majesty had laid down in 1537. The reporter has heard that officials required certain ladies to surrender their finery, but he thinks it likely that for this time they will be forgiven. The bride of the Duke of Sessa, grandson of the Great Captain, wore a partlet of gold net, as did several of the guests.[457] Hers had a pearl at each knot, making it richer than the collared partlet of the Duchess of Alba (Fig. 390), which seems to have a pearl at every other knot. The ultimate example is that in the Sánchez Coello portrait of Felipe II's queen, Isabel de Valois (Wien. Kunsthistorisches Museum)—strings of pearls with rubies at the knots make the netting, all over a rose-colored lining.

A hint of decline for the partlet at rich, flourishing Sevilla is seen at a wedding there, also in 1541. While the mother of the newly married Countess of Niebla wears a partlet of thin silk embroidered with gold and silk, and several of the guests are loyal to collared partlets of gold netting, the bride herself has chosen a high dress *(saya alta)* of brown velvet, possibly of one fabric from collar to hem.[458]

Chemise

The Duchess of Alburquerque (1479) left behind six daytime chemises thought worthy of mention, but royalty owned them by the dozens or hundreds. Princess Isabel's trousseau (1490) included fifty chemises and forty-two were presented to Margarita de Austria when she left Spain (1499). Queen Juana's inventory lists about 230, four of them not sewn. Thirty-three figure in the trousseau of Isabel de Aragón (1515). Three of hers cost 40 ducats each, two of Princess Isabel 50 each, while one of the Empress was priced at 60.

In contrast with the luxurious silks and velvets recorded for partlets, fabrics for the chemise would be washable. Queen Isabel and Queen Juana each owned a chemise of silk, but texts available here generally refer to linens, some of them imported:

> *cambray,* very fine (1503, Segovia. Alcázar; 1529–1538, Empress Isabel)
> sheer holland at 263½ maravedis the vara (1490, Queen Isabel)
> holland at 230 (1492, Queen Isabel's chemise skirts)
> sheer holland at 220 (1490, Infantas Juana and María)
> holland at 200 (1485, Queen Isabel)
> sheer holland at 170 (1489, Infantas Juana and Catalina)
> holland at 155 (1485, Queen Isabel; Juana's chemise skirts)
> holland at 120 (1489, María's night shifts)
> holland at 100 (1487, chemise bodies and sleeves for La Latina, an attendant, possibly Beatriz Galindo)

For the lesser social orders and also for chemise skirts there were cheaper materials of linen or perhaps of hemp:

> *bretaña* at 28 maravedis (1483, chemise bodies and sleeves for a black slave); at 31 (1487, chemise skirts for La Latina, chemises for a Moor turned Christian); at 40 (1485, chemises for a nurse of the Bragança princes)
> *lienzo* at 24 (1483, chemise skirts for the black slave)
> *naval* at 40 (1485, 1488, 1491, slaves)
> *presilla,* a low grade of *brabante,* at 42 (1490, attendants); at 46 (1490, slaves)
> *anjeo* woven of tow, about 40 (1501, chemise skirts for attendants and a mad woman)

Other washable fabrics were the East Indian cottons worn by Empress Isabel.

For their chemises, Queen Isabel's slaves and attendants received about 4 or 5 varas of linen each. Seven and ⅙ to 9⅓ varas are mentioned for the Queen (1485, 1484), 10½ for Infanta Isabel (1487); for two in her trousseau (1490) 41 varas were allowed. A "large chemise" (1503) measured 1¾ vara in length.

Chemises opened at back or front—sometimes not at all—and closed, at least at the neckband and down the front, with buttons or laces. One of Margarita de Austria's chemises (1499) was fastened with 15 gold buttons, hammered into the form of pearls and secured with loops *(ojales)* also of hammered gold. The neckband of another of hers was tied with 2 black silk braids ending in enameled gold aglets; agleted red laces fasten the gold-embroidered collar in Figure 404. A fantastic use of such laces is described for still another of Margarita's

391   1519–1520

392   ca. 1520–1525

393   1526–1539

394   ca. 1520–1530

chemises, each sleeve, open on each side, being closed with over 70 gold-agleted black silk cords, while a single lace fastened the neckband.[459] In one of Queen Juana's chemises a gold-agleted ribbon was run through 10 little golden rings to close it. Cuffs also were fastened with buttons or laces.

The neck of a chemise was finished with a band *(cabezón)* which, at the end of our period, tends to become a collar. In a low neckline (Fig. 392) the chemise fronts are gathered into a band forming square corners. Worn with a dress, the low, square-necked chemise was often almost out of sight. In that of a duchess (Fig. 410) generous front fullness is stitched into a narrow band, which lies but slightly higher than the bodice line. In Queen Juana's effigy (Fig. 391), carved full thirty years before she died, the chemise front—after forming, above the very low-cut bodice, soft background for the heavy neck-lace—runs into a plain band with a narrow frill, which continues round the neck. A higher neckline varies from round, as in an apricot chemise bearing lines of brown (Fig. 395), or squarish, as in a white one lavishly embroidered with gold at the edge and black below (Fig. 396), to bateau, here edged with a frill above a shirred front (Fig. 397). The neckline rises to the throat (Figs. 398–400) and finally achieves a collar. Figure 399 might be considered a partlet as there is little or no evidence of gathers, but one tends to think of the partlet as bearing vertical lines of decoration. A wood reliquary bust, once (1906) in the Almenas Collection and identified as representing Juana la Loca, shows a chemise front gapping slightly between the fasteners and definite diagonal folds accommodating the fullness, which is gathered to an embroidered band at the throat line.

Low-necked chemise with free sleeves

391 QUEEN 1519–1520, from effigy of Juana la Loca, queen of Spain, by Bartolomé Ordóñez (Granada. Royal Chapel)

392 NURSE ca. 1520–1525, from *Birth of the Virgin*, retable of the Assumption of the Virgin, attributed to Pedro de Cristo (Granada. Church of San José)

High-necked chemise with puffed sleeves

393 EMPRESS 1526–1539, from portrait of Isabel de Portugal, empress of the Holy Roman Empire, by Titian, 1544 (Madrid. Museo del Prado)

394 LADY ca. 1520–1530, from *Castilian Lady* in *Dessins français du XVIe siècle*, Album Ob 23, *f*45 (Paris. Bibliothèque Nationale, Cabinet des Estampes)

A neckband generally was decorated. The nurse's low band (Fig. 392) is worked in black chevrons *(puntas?)*, a queen's (Fig. 305) is studded with red rounds and green lozenges. Other sculptured bands show different patterns: that of a duchess (Fig. 410) matches her cuff bands with dots and delicate tendrils; that of a marchioness (Fig. 455) consists of contiguous squares set diagonally and filled with four petals round a center. Collars give opportunity for further decoration. A queen's (Fig. 401), topped with a narrow frill, suggests cloth of gold embroidered with colored flowers and figures, a man in gray and a lady sketched in dark red. A princess-saint's (Fig. 402) is set with colored lozenges and finished with a wider frill, while a countess's (Fig. 403) evidently carries pearls and jewels.[460] The Empress had neckbands embroidered with seed pearls. Prices are recorded for Isabel de Aragón (1515)— 38 ducats for a chemise neckband weighing 5 ounces and comprising 37 pieces of gold enameled with Arabic characters *(cifras)* in black, and 45 ducats for the same number of pieces a little heavier.

In detailed illustrations, gold and silver threads in geometric design hold the minutely pleated fullness of a low-cut chemise (Fig. 405), while gold stitching stiffens one collar (Fig. 404) and jewels stud another (Fig. 406).

Treatment of the neckband is recorded in documents, notably the inventory of Queen Juana. Gold braid appears, but most of the entries list embroidery in gold. Silver also is mentioned as are silks— red *(grana)*, white, black, blue, brown, mulberry, or red and green—generally combined with a metal thread. Black was the most popular silk floss and red next. Spun-gold thread *(oro hilado)* was made by winding a strip of gold or silver-gilt foil over a silk core. Sevillian embroiderers used 12 ounces of gold thread and 3 of silk on each of two chemises for Princess Isabel in her bridal year (1490).

Stitches mentioned are *real, llano, cadenilla, torcido, crucetica,* and *almorafán. Punto real* (royal stitch) appears more than a score of times, often for neckbands. Recent diagrams show it as beginning with two overlapping loops, in which further loops are worked, continuing in rows of two and producing a long band of loops more or less solid. In fifteenth and sixteenth-century *gorgueras* from Lagartera, *punto real* is used to make raised, concentric curves.[461] The next most frequently mentioned stitch is *cadenilla,* which may be related to what is now *cadeneta* (chain stitch). *Punto llano* has been illustrated as used in couching gold thread, and also

395   1507–1510

396   ca. 1530

397   1530–1535

398   ca. 1496–1497

399   1503–1507

400   1526–1529

401   1522

402   ca. 1530

403   ca. 1535–1545

as a flat satin stitch. The dictionary of the Spanish Academy (1970) defines *punto torcido* as a stitch "whose design is a single line to be covered with silk". *Punto de almorafán,* popular with Queen Juana and indeed with her predecessors since the twelfth century, has been tentatively identified with chain stitch[462] but more recently with the present-day *tejidillo,* a darning stitch worked in linen from the wrong side, always in the same direction by counted threads and therefore in geometric designs, a technique which produces, according to María Angeles González Mena, "a most elegant type of needlework, the most perfect of all the Spanish embroideries."[463]

Absent from Baeza's accounts, but often mentioned in Queen Juana's inventory and indicated in the Empress's *Libro de cuentas,* are the stripes called *gayas,* already found in the partlet. They could appear on the chemise front alone, on both the front and the back—where they might be only *medias gayas*—on the sleeves, and occasionally on

Chemise with intermediate neckline

395 ATTENDANT 1507–1510, from *Birth of the Virgin,* main-retable shutter, inner side, by Fernando de Llanos (Valencia. Cathedral)

396 QUEEN ca. 1530, from figure of Herodias in *Banquet of Herod,* retable of St. John the Baptist, by Juan del Bosque (Pamplona. University, Chapel)

397 QUEEN 1530–1535, from portrait of Éléonore d'Autriche, queen of France (Chantilly. Musée Condé)

Chemise neckline at throat

398 ATTENDANT ca. 1496–1497, from *The Circumcision,* retable of the Catholic Kings (New York. Collection of French and Company)

399 EMPRESS 1503–1507, from figure of Leonor, empress of the Holy Roman Empire, in *Leonor de Portugal Presented to Frederick III,* scenes of the life of Piccolomini, by Bernardino Pintoricchio (Siena. Duomo, Libreria Piccolomini)

400 EMPRESS 1526–1529, from double portrait of Charles V and Isabel de Portugal by Jean Mone (near Bruxelles. Staatsdomein van Gaasbeek)

Chemise with collar

401 QUEEN 1522, from portrait of María de Austria, queen of Hungary, by Hans Krell (München. Alte Pinakothek)

402 PRINCESS ca. 1530, from bust of St. Ursula (formerly Barcelona. Carvajal Collection)

403 COUNTESS ca. 1535–1545, from effigy of Mencía de Mendoza, countess of Haro (Burgos. Cathedral, Chapel of El Condestable)

the neckband. The largest number encountered for a single chemise is 26 for the front, 27 for the back, and 11 each for the sleeves. Although gold and black silk braid is recorded for *gayas,* they must generally have been embroidered on the linen. One set was wrought in a combination of *punto real, torcido,* and *llano* stitches; another in *cadenilla* and *almorafán.* In a polychrome bust the full chemise (Fig. 402) bears designs which apparently run in stripes. Converging *gayas* of gold cord in long ovals, alternated with solid gold dots, decorate the Empress's upper chemise (Fig. 393) and horizontal ones mark the puffs in her sleeves.

Chemises were decorated also with strips of material *(tiras).* The Infanta Isabel (1488) had *tiras* of red silk on one linen chemise and of black silk on another. A white silk chemise (1503) carried 10 *tiras* of spun gold and silver gilt on the body and 3 on each sleeve. The "large chemise" of *cambray* (1503) had 24 narrow *tiras* of spun gold on the body and 4 wider ones of spun gold and silver gilt on each sleeve. For the Queen's chemises (1489), 3½ varas of holland were supplied for *tiras* and at the same time 6 ounces of gold thread and 24½ ounces of black or white silk floss, obviously for embroidering them. A sewing woman (1485) was paid 1,500 maravedis for silk floss and the stitchery on *tiras,* and 1,000 more for making the chemise and other work on it. Over thirty of Queen Juana's chemises are described as having *gayas* on the body and *tiras* on the sleeves, up to 20 on each one, where they could run from shoulder to wrist. Stitches mentioned for *tiras* are little crosses *(crucetas), cadenilla,* and *almorafán.*

Colored ribbons likewise were used for trimming, 15 varas for one chemise (1487). And there were insertions *(randas).* The Duchess of Alburquerque (1479) left a chemise of holland with insertions of crimson, gold, and white.[464] Infanta Isabel's with gold *randas* (1485) cost 16 ducats.

Stripes in the chemise of an attendant (Fig. 407) may consist of applied ribbons, if they are not *tiras* indicated by a painter unwilling to render the detail of embroidery. Fortunately the geometric designs used on chemises can be illustrated. In that of a bride (Fig. 408) the figured stripes are wine red; of the horizontal plain rows near the shoulder, three at the top are blue green, the lower ones wine red. The wider stripes of Salome, which would seem to be in *tejidillo* (Fig. 409), are black.

On occasion embroidery eluded the strict form of stripes. A white *cambray* chemise (1503) was

404   ca. 1520

405   1522

406   ca. 1539

407   ca. 1480

408   1496–1497

409   ca. 1500

410   ca. 1500–1515

411   ca. 1515–1525

412   1529

worked all over *(por toda ella)* with large artichokes in drawnwork; it was joined at the seams with spun-gold thread and further adorned with pendants *(pinjantes)* of silver gilt. The Empress's East Indian cotton chemises were embroidered with white silk, one all over, one with a pattern of stars.

A chemise was likely to show Moorish influence. Besides *camisa,* the term *alcandora,* from the Arabic *al-qandūra,* appears in inventories. A *camisa morisca* (1503) was embroidered, and two *alcandoras moriscas* were trimmed with ribbons. The embroidered chemises of the Empress are described as *moriscas.* We have noted Moorish characters enameled on gold motifs for a neckband of Isabel de Aragón. Carmen Bernis points out that pseudo-Arabic letters form the embroidered motifs on a bride's neckband (Fig. 408), and that chemise trimmings such as colored stripes *(gayas),* ribbons *(listas),* galloons *(orillas),* and passementerie edgings *(caireles)* were used on Moorish garments.[465]

In the "large chemise" (1503), the sleeves were as long as the garment itself, 1 ¾ vara, and ½ vara wide. Illustrations bear out these dimensions. In a nurse's sleeves (Fig. 392), the fullness is tightly gathered at the shoulder and the great length is taken up in transverse folds. The sleeve-end hangs at full width from the wrist. In other instances a portion of the sleeve-end is drawn closely about the wrist, while the rest flows down in curves to spill out of the dress sleeve (Fig. 391), or the whole amount is taken up at the wrist (Fig. 305). The sleeve could also be set in puffs which came to an end above the wrist, leaving the entire width to hang free (Fig. 394), or the puffs could end at the wrist, leaving only a shallow frill (Fig. 393). In a further wrist treatment (Fig. 410) the fullness is held within a cuff formed of two bands, patterned with a running design of dots and tendrils, between cordings alternately slender or heavy; a tiny frill escapes at the edge. A similar cuff (Fig. 411) shows five cordings and a tiny frill while, higher up, the sleeve is again confined within a corded band. Weiditz also records the corded band together with a more generous wrist frill (Fig. 412). Documents frequently mention embroidered cuffs, which can be seen, combined with a frill, in the effigy of a marchioness (Fig. 455).

The Empress had a great number of separate sleeves, of which over forty pairs were of linen or of the Indian cottons, *calicud* and *sinabafo.* One such pair is listed as belonging to a chemise, and others probably were of the same category. Some dimensions are given; from one to three *anchos, paños,* or *piernas* wide and 1¾ or 2 varas long. The few of linen were adorned with Flemish drawnwork, embroidered with silk and gold or accompanied by cuffs *(polainas)* worked in silk and gold. No decoration is recorded for sleeves of *sinabafo.* Those of *calicud*—which in Spain can be a thin silk as well as a cotton—were quilted, trimmed with braid of brown and gold, made with frills *(lechuguillas)* at the wrist.[466] Such frills were forerunners of those which at the neck grew into the great ruff known in Spain by that name.

Because of its folds and gathers the lady's chemise, like the man's shirt at this period, must have been a favorite refuge of fleas. On a winter day at Segovia, in a sunny corridor, Queen Isabel was being

---

Chemise neck trimming

404 LADY—GOLD EMBROIDERY ca. 1520, from figure of Saint in *St. Mary Magdalene and Donor* attributed to Juan Gascó (Vich. Museu Episcopal)

405 QUEEN—GOLD AND SILVER EMBROIDERY 1522, from wedding chemise of María de Austria, queen of Hungary (Budapest. Magyar Nemzeti Múzeum)

406 EMPRESS—JEWEL DECORATION ca. 1539, from portrait medallion of Isabel de Portugal, empress of the Holy Roman Empire (The Hispanic Society of America)

Chemise sleeve trimming

407 ATTENDANT—APPLIED STRIPS OR RIBBONS ca. 1480, from *Birth of the Virgin* by Pedro García de Benabarre (New York. Collection of José Montllor)

408 LADY—EMBROIDERED STRIPES 1496–1497, detail of bride's figure in *The Marriage at Cana* by Master of the Retable of the Reyes Católicos (Washington, D.C. National Gallery of Art, Samuel H. Kress Collection)

409 PRINCESS—WIDER EMBROIDERED STRIPE ca. 1500, from figure of Salome in *The Beheading of St. John the Baptist,* Hispano-Flemish School (Madrid. Museo del Prado)

Chemise cuffs

410 DUCHESS—CORDING AND EMBROIDERED BANDS ca. 1500–1515, from effigy of Mencía Enríquez de Toledo, duchess of Alburquerque (The Hispanic Society of America)

411 DUCHESS—CORDING AND A STUDDED BAND ca. 1515–1525, from effigy of Francisca Manrique de Lara, duchess of Cardona (Cardona. Castle, Church)

412 LADY—CORDED BAND AND A FRILL 1529, from *Thus Women in Spain Look from . . . the Front* in Weiditz, Christoph. *Das Trachtenbuch. f*57 (Nürnberg. Germanisches Nationalmuseum)

413   ca. 1470–1480

414   1507–1510

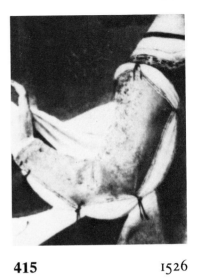

415   1526

416   ca. 1500

417   ca. 1500

418   ca. 1500

419   ca. 1490

420   ca. 1520

421   1524

de-fleaed *(espulgada)* when an important visitor arrived, her confessor Cisneros.[467]

Dress sleeve

Dress sleeves in our period lived a life of their own. Being detachable, they could be sent by ladies to their knights; they could be stolen or given to the poor. In royal accounts they appear as separate items. For Queen Juana are listed over 120 pairs, and for Isabel de Portugal at least 170.[468] We do not know what became of Juana's sleeves. Of the Empress's, a number were given to friends or distributed among her attendants; others were sold at her auction.

Illustrations have been found of the attachment at the armscye. A long closed sleeve is set in with crossed cords (Fig. 413), which figure as a decorative lattice over the fullness of the chemise sleeve. Here the latter makes an escape only at the wrist, its

striped fabric turned back upon the dress sleeve and hung free in a ring of folds. Agleted laces sometimes anchored the sleeve. That this method was used in the 1480's is shown by the figure of Mary Magdalene in a retable of Jesus and the Virgin (Frómista (Palencia). Church of Santa María del Castillo). In a clearer example (Fig. 415), puffs of the chemise sleeve escape between the laces. Dress sleeves were also sewn into the armscye (Fig. 414). In thirteenth-century Portugal they were sewn in at morning and unsewn at night.[469]

One type of dress sleeve was free from the armscye, being only a sleevelet reaching from the wrist to above the elbow. At back it could be open slightly (Fig. 416) or for the whole length (Fig. 417), letting the chemise sleeve escape. Salome wears the sleevelet three times in the same painting, hanging by cords or a lace (Fig. 418) from the shoulder. This sleevelet is dark green edged with a band of pearls and gold stitchery; its bodice is of gold and brown brocade. Two more laces, rose-lavender with gold aglets, tie the sleevelet at back. The chemise sleeve runs out in a long, sharp triangle of black-embroidered white linen (Fig. 316).

In extreme cases a couple of patches of rich fabric tied over the arm sufficed to make a dress sleeve. The open, tubular patches worn by Queen Isabel (Fig. 419)—one above the elbow, the other running up from the wrist—are of green material in charming contrast with the deep purple of her dress and the white of her chemise sleeve. The green patches are trimmed with gold braid, pearls, and green or rose-colored gems cut round, oval, or triangular and mounted in gold settings. Three sets of paired gold cords secure the patch about the upper arm, letting out two puffs of chemise sleeve. The lower section also frees a flow of white. In a later example (Fig. 420) open tubes are crimson except for a middle band of gold. Chemise sleeves, puffed exuberantly at shoulder and elbow, are contained at the wrist. In a sleevelet that appears to comprise closed tubes (Fig. 421), the upper is plain, while the lower is complicated with slashes darkly accented at the edges. The chemise sleeve escapes at shoulder and elbow and provides moderate folds at the wrist.

Carmen Bernis finds no difficulty in identifying sleevelets with the *manguitos* (diminutive of *manga*, sleeve)[470] mentioned in documents. One-half vara of black *cebtí* was required for a pair of *manguitos* for Infanta Isabel (1486), of black velvet for the Queen ⅓ vara (1489), ½ vara (1490). The Infanta had others (1488) of mulberry satin trimmed with

---

Dress sleeve attachment

413 LADY—CROSSED CORDS ca. 1470–1480, from *Revelation to Zacharias of the Conception of St. John the Baptist* (San Mateo. Church of San Mateo, Sacristy)

414 ATTENDANT—STITCHING 1507–1510, from *Birth of the Virgin,* main-retable shutter, inner side, by Fernando de Llanos (Valencia. Cathedral)

415 ATTENDANT—TIED LACES 1526, from *Birth of St. Eligius* by Pedro Nunyes (Barcelona. Museo de Arte de Cataluña)

Sleevelet

416 LADY ca. 1500, from effigy (Valverde de la Vera. Parish Church)

417 ATTENDANT ca. 1500, from *Birth of St. John the Baptist,* Hispano-Flemish School (Madrid. Museo del Prado)

418 PRINCESS ca. 1500, from figure of Salome in *The Beheading of St. John the Baptist,* Hispano-Flemish School (Madrid. Museo del Prado)

Two-part sleevelet

419 QUEEN ca. 1490, from figure of Isabel I, queen of Castilla and Aragón, in *The Virgin of the Catholic Kings* (Madrid. Museo del Prado)

420 LADY ca. 1520, from figure of temptress in *St. Andrew Saving the Virtue of a Bishop* by Joan de Burgunya (Valencia. Cathedral, Museo Diocesano)

421 LADY 1524, from figure of St. Mary Magdalene in *The Crucifixion,* retable of St. Vincent, by León Picardo (Burgos. Cathedral, Museo Diocesano)

422   1479–1492

423   1493

424   1526–1529

425   1456

426   1497–1503

427   1529

428   ca. 1470–1480

429   1497–1503

430   1502

12 ounces of gold motifs. Margarita de Austria was given *manguitos* of crimson velvet trimmed with ornaments of hammered gold, as well as a white pair brocaded with drawn gold. Queen Juana and the Empress had them also.

A closed, entire sleeve can be found at this period, frequently in illustrations of attendants at the birth of the Virgin, though provided also for noble ladies. It may end with a turned-back cuff (Fig. 423), or in a bell shape (Figs. 458, 460). A duchess's sleeve (Fig. 422) is double: an outer part of red velvet, matching the gown, over an inner one of deep-rose satin. In the velvet part, open spaces exposing puffs of the satin seem to be continuous, as though diagonal panes were tied together with the gold-ageleted laces of white silk. The aglets, much longer than

those used in the time of the Duchess (see Figs. 517–519), must be an anachronism introduced by the copyist two generations after her death.[471] She died in 1492, and the sleeve she actually wore probably was slashed in the upper half. Vertical slashes appear in a sleeve of the Empress (Fig. 424). Between narrow, pearled bands that bind it into six sections, slashes permit the chemise sleeve to be drawn out, making each section look like a puff. A frill finishes the wrist.

The dress sleeve shaped to fit with Gothic tightness could be left open at back, presumably to free the movement of the arm as well as to display the beauty of the chemise sleeve. The edges would be joined at intervals with cords or laces, between which the chemise sleeve escaped in white puffs *(papos)*. An early example dated 1456 (Fig. 425) shows the puffs five in number and small in size, paralleling the line of the arm. This type of sleeve having appeared in Italy eleven years earlier, Bernis has it enter Spain by way of the Levante (Valencia).[472] The puffs, generally running down to the wrist, could vary in number and in exuberance, governed by the length of the chemise sleeve. Full puffs of equal length appear (Fig. 426), as well as a long and a short, both meager. I have seen but one example of more than five back-puffs, which still were in use in Weiditz's time with a vermilion sleeve of more generous size (Fig. 427). In these illustrations the wrist is closed, keeping the chemise sleeve in tight bounds.

In another mode, thought to be exclusively Spanish, there was a long opening above the wrist. A gold and black dress sleeve, tied with coral-pink cords or laces to below the elbow (Fig. 428), lets out above the wrist a triangle of white chemise sleeve striped with black *tiras*. That the sleeve could be open to the elbow is shown plainly in Figure 429. Very long chemise sleeves in this style (Fig. 303) hung like inverted sails against the fabric of the dresses. Such an arrangement is worn by Melibea and by the servant with her (Fig. 430).

Some of Queen Juana's silk or velvet sleeves are grouped by color: of 67 pairs, 21 were black (almost entirely of taffeta or *ceti*), 12 crimson (more of velvet than of *ceti*), and 8 yellow (4 of taffeta, 4 of *ceti*). Satin was the preferred material for the Empress's silk sleeves, in several colors. The favorite tone was black, 16 pairs being of satin, 16 of velvet, 3 in both materials, 7 of taffeta, 3 of damask. Of 19 pairs of white sleeves, more were of wool than of any one kind of silk fabric. Crimson came far behind with

Long, entire dress sleeve

422 DUCHESS 1479–1492, from portrait of María López de Gurrea, duchess of Luna; later 16th-century copy by Roland de Mois (Madrid. Palace of the Duke of Villahermosa)

423 QUEEN 1493, from figure of Queen of Macedonia in [San Pedro, Diego de] *Carcel de amor* [*Lo carcer d'amor*. Barcelona, 1493] v°sig.e[8] (London. The British Library)

424 EMPRESS 1526–1529, from double portrait of Charles V and Isabel de Portugal by Jean Mone (near Bruxelles. Staatsdomein van Gaasbeek)

Sleeve with open back secured at intervals

425 LADY 1456, from figure of St. Barbara, retable of the Retailers' Guild, by Jaime Huguet (Barcelona. Museo de Arte de Cataluña)

426 LADY 1497–1503, from figure of wise virgin in *The Wise and the Foolish Virgins*, choir stall, by Master Rodrigo (Plasencia. Cathedral)

427 WOMAN OF BARCELONA 1529, from *Thus Also They Go in Barcelona* in Weiditz, Christoph. *Das Trachtenbuch*. f67 (Nürnberg. Germanisches Nationalmuseum)

Sleeve with long opening above wrist

428 PRINCESS ca. 1470–1480, from figure of Salome in *Banquet of Herod*, retable of St. John the Baptist, by Pedro García de Benabarre (Barcelona. Museo de Arte de Cataluña)

429 WOMAN 1497–1503, from figure of woman soaking her feet, misericord, by Master Rodrigo (Plasencia. Cathedral)

430 LADY AND SERVANT 1502, from figures of Melibea and Lucrecia in *Tragicomedia de Calisto y melibea*. Sevilla, 1502. Title-cut (London. The British Library)

431   1492–1495

432   1503–1507

433   1539–1543

434   1482–1495

435   ca. 1515–1530

436   1526

437   1507–1510

438   ca. 1520

439   1550–1563

only 4 pairs. Brown or mulberry were not too un-common, but yellow or tawny were rare.

The keeper of the Empress's accounts faithfully recorded prices; for her post-mortem auction, values had to be known. Of her silk or velvet sleeves the most expensive pair—knit *(hechas de aguja)* of flesh-colored *(encarnado)* and red *(colorado)* silks, lined with mulberry satin, trimmed with gold *caireles,* embroidered with large seed pearls, and worked at the wrist with gold—was listed at 40 ducats (15,000 maravedis). Others knit of silk and wool, mulberry or red, with wrist bands of white and gold and wrist frills of gold, came to 6 ducats the pair, while very cheap (62 maravedis) were those knit of white wool alone. Sleeves of spun-gold fabric were priced by weight, 16 or 17 ounces at 1½ ducats the ounce.

Of Queen Juana's sleeves about 30 pairs are listed as lined—20 with taffeta, which in 13 cases was

black. Two were lined with martens, one with cloth of gold. Over 40 linings are mentioned for the Empress: 10 of taffeta, 7 of satin, 2 of velvet, 3 of gold or silver cloth, 7 of cotton or linen, 12 of wool, 2 of marten, 1 of muskrat *(almizclera).* There are instances of the same color being used in both sleeve and lining, but generally there was contrast: cloth of silver served as lining for mulberry velvet; cloth of gold for brown velvet; blue taffeta for mulberry satin. Red woolen *(grana)* lined black velvet; frieze *(friseta)* in orange or rose, as well as in reddish, brown, or white, lined black or colored silks.

As to style, there are a few clues in the documents: half, small, small and tight, made with a point *(de punta),* shaped like a wineskin *(borracha).* Cuffs appear with the name of *polainas.* Twenty-five pairs of Queen Juana's sleeves are described as shirred or gathered *(fruncidas).* A few of the Empress's silk or velvet sleeves were quilted *(colchadas)* or slashed *(acuchilladas).* Trimming bands were *tiras* of velvet, or of gold-and-silver cloth, and edge-strips *(ribetes)* of velvet, satin, or taffeta, sometimes at the wrist. *Ruedas* on white velvet sleeves may be explained by the cognate Portuguese *roda* as lace borders. Gold net, cloth of gold or silver, or gold fabric wrought from florins are recorded as forming the lower portions *(cañones,* cf. Portuguese *canhões)* of taffeta or velvet sleeves. Buttons are mentioned. Gold cords, gold bows, and red silk ribbons suggest laces or points. Agleted points are not included in the sleeve inventories; eight twisted aglets *(cabos)* from one pair of Queen Juana's sleeves are listed with the gold ornaments.

The slashing so popular with men appeared in women's clothes, as we have noted in describing a sleeve of the Empress (Fig. 424). Court attendants (Fig. 303) furnish early examples. One sleeve (Fig. 431) matches the dress, which is violet under a tunic of red and gold. Leonor de Portugal, meeting Emperor Frederick III, has a larger number of slashes in the forearm only of a pair (Fig. 432) which are green striped with gold, while the dress is red. The white chemise sleeve, visible through the slashes, hangs in at least three puffs from the open back. Queen Isabel in a kneeling effigy is given open-back sleeves of white, blue, and gold brocade slashed throughout and accompanied by two great puffs (Fig. 305), an arrangement which is found still in obvious favor twenty years later (Fig. 433). In this example the sculptor has recorded the strain on the sleeve fabric where the chemise linen has been pulled through the slashes, as well as the extrav-

Slashing in open-back sleeve

431 COURT LADY 1492–1495, from figure in *Her Royal Highness Doña Isabel, Queen of Castilla and Aragón,* in Marcuello, Pedro. *Devocionario de la Reyna d.ª Juana, à quien llamaron la Loca. vᵒf*54 (Chantilly. Musée Condé)

432 EMPRESS 1503–1507, from figure of Leonor, empress of the Holy Roman Empire, in *Leonor de Portugal Presented to Frederick III,* scenes of the life of Piccolomini, by Bernardino Pintoricchio (Siena. Duomo, Libreria Piccolomini)

433 LADY 1539–1543, from figure of St. Mary Magdalene, choir stall, by Felipe Vigarny (Toledo. Cathedral, Upper Choir)

Cap-sleeve whole or slashed

434 ATTENDANT 1482–1495, from *Birth of the Virgin,* retable of Cardinal Mendoza, by the Luna Master (Guadalajara. Church of San Ginés)

435 YOUNG WOMAN OF HIGH RANK ca. 1515–1530, from figure of St. Agnes, retable of the Virgin (Burgos. Church of San Gil, Chapel of La Natividad)

436 LADY 1526, from figure of singer in Torre, Alfonso de la. *Visió delectable.* Sevilla, 1526. *f*xlj (The Hispanic Society of America)

Cap-sleeve pleated or slashed

437 LADY 1507–1510, from figure in *The Visitation,* main-retable shutter, inner side, by Fernando Yáñez de la Almedina (Valencia. Cathedral)

438 LADY ca. 1520, from figure of St. Barbara attributed to the Becerril Master (Madrid. Museo del Prado)

439 LADY 1550–1563, from figure of St. Mary Magdalene in *Jesus at the House of Simon,* main retable, left wing (Sevilla. Cathedral)

440   ca. 1525–1530

441   1526

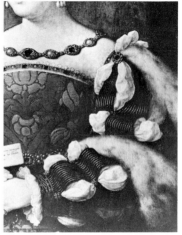

442   ca. 1530

443   1527

444   1529

445   1531

446   ca. 1520

447   ca. 1521

448   1525–1529

agance of two great puffs hanging from the arm. At the wrist a modest frill *(lechuguilla)* of the chemise sleeve projects beyond the jeweled band of the dress sleeve.

A feature of this period is the cap-sleeve reaching halfway to the elbow. Saint Elizabeth in *Birth of St. John* by García de Benabarre (Barcelona. Museo de Arte de Cataluña) wears a plain one of scarlet matching her dress over a white chemise sleeve striped with black *tiras.* Above a widening sleeve of boldly patterned brocade, a rich dark cap (Fig. 434) ends in a band studded with pearls and gems.[473] The cap could be turned up in a cuff (ca. 1480, 1510–1530), be edged with fringe (1493, 1496–1497), or tassels (1515–1525), or tabs (1519). One crenelated at the edge (Fig. 435) is hung with bells above a well-slashed lower sleeve. The cap also could be slashed and trimmed with a row of points (Fig. 436).

Sleeve with panes set in puffs

440 LADY ca. 1525–1530, from figure of St. Barbara in *St. Catherine and St. Barbara,* retable of the Immaculate Conception, by the Pulgar Master (Granada. Church of San José)

441 LADY 1526, from figure of Melibea in *Tragicomedia de Calisto y Melibea.* Toledo, 1526. XIV aucto (London. The British Library)

442 QUEEN ca. 1530, from portrait of Éléonore d'Autriche, queen of France, by Joos van Cleve (Hampton Court Palace)

Sleeve with full top

443 LADY 1527, from figure of Delphic Sibyl on dustguard, retable of the Virgin, by the Alcira Master (Gandía. Church of Los Jesuitas)

444 WOMAN OF SEVILLA 1529, from *In This Manner Women Go About . . . in Sevilla,* in Weiditz, Christoph. *Das Trachtenbuch. f60* (Nürnberg. Germanisches Nationalmuseum)

445 PRINCESS 1531, from figure of Saint in *Martyrdom of St. Ursula* by Master Benito (Palencia. Cathedral)

Long, full sleeve close at wrist

446 LADY ca. 1520, from figure of listener in *St. Felix Preaching,* retable of St. Felix, by Joan de Burgunya (Gerona. Church of San Félix, Sala de Museo)

447 LADY ca. 1521, from figure of Hispania in *Figürliches Musterbuch für Kunstmaler* by Niklaus Manuel Deutsch (Basel. Kunstmuseum, Kupferstichkabinett)

448 QUEEN 1525–1529, from figure of Isabel I, queen of Castilla and Aragón, choir stall, by Andrés de Nájera and Guillén de Holanda (Valladolid. Museo Nacional de Escultura)

A shorter cap-sleeve, finished at the lower edge with a straight band, gave the effect of a puff. Vertical lines in an early example (Fig. 437) appear to represent shadows between box pleats, which are fulled in at the shoulder and also into the finishing band. The plain material is crossed with lines of embroidery. As illustrated in the *Tragicomedia* of 1526 (III aucto), the harlot Areusa wears a full cap-sleeve of plain material gathered in at top and bottom. A cap of gold brocade (Fig. 438) is definitely slashed over the dark, striped material of a long, flowing sleeve. In a later example (Fig. 439) wide slashes run to the top, separating the figured material into panes. The lower edge of this cap-sleeve is finished with scallops and with the looped tabs characteristic of the early sixteenth century.

In the twenties, sleeves could be further segmented. One of rose brocade over a white chemise (Fig. 440) is divided into four disparate sections: a puff of panes, a closed tube, a shorter puff of compressed panes, and a long cuff open at back. The chemise sleeve appears at the wrist, behind the cuff, and in a long "pull-out" below the elbow. Less variety is shown in a sleeve of four almost equal puffs (Fig. 441), which seem to consist entirely of panes. This type leads to that worn by the rich Mencía de Mendoza and the royal Éléonore d'Autriche. Doña Mencía's sleeves (Fig. 308) are of red velvet panes confined with narrow bands of the velvet into four separate puffs. The top one depends from the armscye with chains or laces, between which, as well as from between the panes, escape pull-outs of the chemise sleeves. These fit close at the wrist, except for a narrow frill.

Queen Éléonore's panes (Fig. 442), worn with a dress of brown and gold brocade, are of reddish-brown velvet backstitched in vertical lines. Over cream-colored chemise sleeves the panes are fastened together at intervals with square knots of cord or with pins simulating them; in the Chantilly version of this portrait the fasteners are laces with short aglets (Fig. 519). A frill flows out beyond the wristband, which is stitched in a geometric design. Each sleeve is attached at the shoulder with one or more red-jeweled brooches. The tan fur has been interpreted as forming a large outer sleeve, hung from shoulder and forearm. Panes of similarly stitched black velvet and of gold-corded cream satin are worn by Éléonore's husband, François I, in his portrait attributed to Jean Clouet (Paris. Musée National du Louvre).[474]

Another sleeve of the twenties was like the "demigigot" of the 1890's with full top *(musequí)* and

449   ca. 1500

450   ca. 1520

451   1525–1526

452   1489–1495

453   1517

454   ca. 1543

455   1525

456   1529

457   1538

long, fitted cuff (Fig. 443)—a sleeve used by Italian men as early as 1450 and by Spanish about the time that the Count of Tendilla died (1479; see Fig. 284, also 81–83). Like others, this sleeve could be complicated with panes or slashing. With a crimson dress a Sevillian lady has the sleeve in blue (Fig. 444), long slashes being cut in the full top and short slashes through the long cuff. A further plain example (Fig. 445) matches its dress in red velvet.

Remaining sleeves considered are large. The first type is tight at the wrist. A very large sleeve of gold-yellow fabric banded with rose-red velvet (Fig. 446) is seen to be made in two parts, a short circular

Long sleeve open at wrist

449 LADY   ca. 1500, from figure of donor in *Jesus at the Column* by Alejo Fernández (Córdoba. Museo Provincial de Bellas Artes)

450 PRINCESS   ca. 1520, from figure of Salome in *Salome Dancing before Herod,* attributed to Bartolomé de Castro (Owensboro, Kentucky. Collection of John R. Blewer)

451 LADY   1525–1526, from figure of Saint in *St. Liberata Sentenced to Death by Her Father,* altarpiece of St. Liberata, attributed to Juan de Pereda (Sigüenza. Cathedral)

Long, wide sleeve

452 QUEEN   1489–1495, from figure of Isabel I, queen of Castilla and Aragón, in *Surrender of Moclín,* choir stall, by Master Rodrigo (Toledo. Cathedral)

453 QUEEN   1517, from figure of Maria de Castela, queen of Portugal, by Nicolas Chantarène (Belém. Monastery of Os Jerónimos, Church Portal)

454 QUEEN   ca. 1543, from portrait of María de Portugal, queen of Spain; lithograph in Carderera y Solano, Valentín. *Iconografía española.* Madrid, 1864. v. 2, pl. LXXVI (The Hispanic Society of America)

Sectioned sleeve

455 MARCHIONESS   1525, from effigy of Leonor Manrique de Castro, marchioness of Ayamonte, by Antonio Maria Aprile and others (Santiago de Compostela. Church of San Lorenzo)

456 LADY OF HIGH RANK   1529, from *[Thus Women in Spain Look from Behind]* in Weiditz, Christoph. *Das Trachtenbuch.* f58 (Nürnberg. Germanisches Nationalmuseum)

457 LADY   1538, from figure of spectator in *The Game of Canes* by Jan Cornelisz Vermeyen (Drayton House, Nr. Kettering, Northamptonshire. Collection of L. G. Stopford Sackville)

section, smooth about the wrist, joined to the voluminous upper with black velvet ribbons tied in bows. A sleeve observed by a foreigner (Fig. 447) hangs from the shoulder with narrow bands, probably laces. It is slashed in a strange manner: instead of slits there are curved openings with tongues of fabric hanging over them. The sculptured rendering of a plain sleeve (Fig. 448) shows the great lower fullness gathered into a narrow band which gives it the form of a full wineskin *(borracha).*

Sleeves worked smoothly into the armscye also were worn. Long and flowing, they varied in width from moderate to extravagant. A moderate sleeve of light color (Fig. 449), worn with a dark dress, is trimmed with a band of fur. In another (Fig. 450) all the edges—armscye, wrist, and sleeve back—are bordered with a lustrous band, of satin perhaps. Down the open back the edges are loosely joined with three heavy, tagged laces tied in large bows. The only trim of a later example (Fig. 451) is a turnback at the wrist.

A wide sleeve is worn by Queen Isabel as she rides into Moclín with a little dog on her lap (Fig. 452). In this small sculpture no trimming has been depicted, but in another generous sleeve (Fig. 472) red trimming bands of two widths strikingly adorn the orange-colored fabric. The wide sleeve could be open at back, as in the statue of a queen (Fig. 453), and great puffs of chemise sleeve be drawn out between the fasteners. Here sleeve edges are bordered with a patterned galloon, and the wrist edge is turned back twice to make a double fold. A late appearance of the wide type, closed at back, is recorded by Carderera from a portrait now lost (Fig. 454). He comments on the exaggerated dimensions of the sleeves, probably rose-colored like the gown and garnished with leaves of green silk, which were secured with gold rosettes. The lining also was green,[475] another appearance of the popular red and green combination. This sleeve must be of the type known as *de punta* from its long point hanging near the knees.

In a more elaborate form the wide sleeve could be divided into sections. The effigy of Queen Juana (Fig. 391) suggests eight joined with many ribbons across four lengthwise divisions and one crosswise. The ribbons, which carry no aglets, are simply knotted with short ends. Six sections can be counted in the folded wrists of a marchioness's sleeve (Fig. 455) where the fasteners, as in Juana's effigy, appear to be flatly knotted ribbons. Weiditz records a sleeve (Fig. 456) with four or five lengthwise sections of purple rose banded with apple green, the edges joined with a few rose-colored fasteners. In these examples, little emphasis has been given to the exposed chemise sleeve. But it must be pointed out that in a lady's dress sleeve of dark olive-green material, hanging over a box rail at a tournament (Fig. 457), the three sections are separated, transversely and vertically, with conspicuous puffs of white. The chemise sleeve is so large that even after forming all those puffs it can allow a generous fullness to hang from the wrist.

Dress

A term frequently used in the late fifteenth century for a dress of rich material was *brial*. In medieval times, when men wore long skirts, this term identified a male garment also; the man's skirt stopped at or above the ankles, whereas a lady's covered her feet. The venerable word appears in Queen Isabel's accounts and the inventory of Queen Juana. In the costume of two dolls associated with Juana a *brial* was worn over a chemise and an underskirt *(faldrilla)* and under a *mantilla*.[476]

Briales were not exclusively luxurious garments of great ladies. Queen Isabel's treasurer (1483, 1484) provided woolen material *(paño)* for those of a nurse's maid and a slave. But these were exceptions. Most entries specify a velvet, black, mulberry, or the very expensive crimson; an even more costly brocade, white, crimson, green, brown; or the familiar *cebtí* (probably a silk), crimson, black, green, mulberry, yellow. In brocaded satin velvet *(brocado raso de pelo),* the cost of 11 varas to make one *brial* for Queen Isabel (1487) rose to 104,390 maravedis. For that sum three men could have bought themselves a good horse each, bringing three ambitious wives into the category where they too would have the right to wear silk and velvet.[477]

Could it be that the *brial* was cut in princesse fashion? Covarrubias says (1611) that this "ancient Spanish dress" was something like a *monjil*, for which Alcega's pattern shows the back of waist and skirt in one piece.[478] The 11 varas most commonly required for a woman's *brial* suggest that the dress carried a train (Fig. 458). Tailors making this garment, as well as others of figured material, were required to cut the pieces with the pattern right side up and with the figures matched.[479]

In listing three *briales* Juana's inventory mentions several details. A dress of figured crimson velvet

had a stomacher *(puerta),* sleevelets *(manguitos),* and sleeves *(mangas)* in which it would seem that the full upper part *(musequí)* was extended to hang long behind the wrist *(hecho una punta).*[480] Though it is difficult to find illustrations of it, the *puerta* must be mentioned because in the documents it is associated with a dress body. Juana had a number of *puertas* in silk or velvet, some lined with *grana.*[481] Possibly this detail is represented by the black triangular panel which Salome wears with a crimson and gold brocade dress (Fig. 300).

A *brial* could be lined with frieze, with buckram *(bocaran, bocací),* frieze and buckram, with frieze and linen *(lienzo).* For Queen Isabel (1487) 9 varas of buckram were required to line a *brial* of drawn-gold cloth. For fifteen-year-old María (1497) buckram (2 varas) was used only in the skirt-foot *(ruedo)* of a black velvet *brial.* When Juana was eleven (1490), the body *(cuerpo)* of her cloth-of-gold *brial* was lined with ½ vara of inexpensive holland.

As trimmings, there appear borders or purfles *(perfiles)* of ermine; strips *(tiras)* of fabric contrasting with the dress material; ribbons (160 varas of drawn-gold *cintas* weighing 18 ounces for one of Queen Isabel's *briales,* 1489); fabric-covered hoops *(verdugos);* also pearls, seed pearls, and gold ornaments. Queen Juana's crimson velvet *brial* carried 355 tree trunks *(tronquitos)* of gold at the skirt hem *(cortapisa)* and 121 smaller ones on stomacher, sleeve tops, and sleevelets. The crimson velvet *jeto* that adorned another dress of cloth of gold must be related to the French *get,* "narrow band of fabric or fur making a border".[482]

The right good end of a *brial* was to enter the service of the Church. Twelve and a quarter varas of black velvet for a *brial,* which had belonged to the Duchess of Alburquerque (1479), became a funeral pall. From her *brial* of brown brocaded satin were made a chasuble, a stole, and an amice, besides a mantle for an image of the Virgin.[483]

In *El crotalón* a camp follower, returning from the conquest of Orán (1509), uses the money of her dead captain to dress like a lady; among her expensive new clothes are *briales.* They are mentioned again at the end of the book (1546) as something of which light women were to be deprived.[484] But by the time Charles V had arrived in Spain, the *brial* must have ceased to be fashionable. It has not been found among the clothes mentioned in *Questiõ de amor,* in the accounts of Isabel de Portugal, or in descriptions of the weddings of 1541. Evidently it had been displaced by the *saya.*

A loose-fitting dress called *hábito* also character-izes our period. It was a favorite with Queen Isabel; in about twenty years she had fifty such dresses. Nurses and attendants were given habits of Courtrai woolen. The same fabric made costumes for the Infantas to wear during Holy Week (1486, 1487). In habits and mantles of black cloth, María (aged 9) and Catalina (aged 6) mourned their brother-in-law Prince Afonso of Portugal; forty-four court ladies and attendants also mourned him in such "pairs of clothes" paid for by the Treasurer (1491). Queen Isabel wore habit and tabard of black *contray* to mourn Ferrante, king of Naples (1494). As funeral clothes were traditionally loose fitting, the associa-tion of the habit with mourning reinforces its identi-fication as an ample garment.

But it appears also in handsome and colorful fab-rics. At Queen Isabel's court, velvet habits were often seen, black preferred, and after that crimson; then green, mulberry colored, or tawny. Next in favor came woolens, and then silks. Within the easy dimensions of a habit there was room for a fur lining; silk or velvet also was used. More wide sleeves are described than narrow. Gold trimming took the form of solid ornament—Arabic letters (1488), little clubs (*bastoncicos,* 1490)—or of embroidery on strips of *cebtí* (1493).

Worn under a mantle, the habit is illustrated in a terra-cotta statue (Fig. 459) somewhat earlier than our period. Its fabric, patterned as with a curly pile, perhaps crushed velvet, must have been supple, for the front fullness is gathered at the neck into small folds and bound with a narrow band. From the neck the garment flows in soft, unbroken box pleats almost to the feet, which are hidden by folds of a very long skirt underneath. Full sleeves are gathered tightly at the wrist. Narrow sleeves appear in a habit (Fig. 460) of handsome black and gold brocade faced with green at the hem. Sleeveless, a full-fronted dress (Fig. 11), also of black and gold brocade, is lined with crimson velvet and piped with gold at neck and armholes. The folds of a train are arranged in front of the feet.

Charles V's bride brought with her from Portugal eleven habits, of which in Spain several were con-verted into *sayas.* In contrast with the dresses previ-ously described, the *saya* must have had a fitted body to which the skirt, cut separately, was joined at the waistline. It will be remembered that in our period the man's jerkin *(sayo)* began to be seamed through the middle. Alcega's *Geometria* was pub-lished decades later (1580), yet its emphasis on the separate cut of *saya* body and skirt[485] may be taken as significant.

Baeza's accounts provide *sayas* for a laundress's helper, for a poor woman, for Moors—one of them turned Christian—but mostly for slaves until 1493, when such dresses were being made for servants and attendants. Four and ⅔ varas of cotton *(vitre* woven at Vitré, Brittany) were allowed for a maid's *saya* (1498). Infanta Catalina in 1500 had velvet *sayas,* and Queen Isabel's tailor (1502) was paid for 8½ varas of red woolen grogram *(cordellate)* at 144 maravedis the vara for a French *saya,* which is char-acterized (1515) as having wide sleeves. For court ladies' *sayas* no fabric was too handsome. In 1503, the year when Juana was battling frenziedly to re-join her husband in Flanders, this "Most Serene Princess" was offered, in the hope of distracting her no doubt, 13¾ varas of Genoese crimson velvet, at 2,655 maravedis the vara, for a French *saya.* Isabel de Aragón's trousseau (1515) included *sayas* requiring 13 to 17½ ells or varas each of velvet, damask, or satin. Two with wide sleeves used bro-caded velvet or gold-brocaded satin.[486]

In the Empress's accounts, parts associated with the *saya* body (*cuerpo, corpiño, corpecico*) are neck-band (*cabezón*), stomacher (*puerta, conportina*), and sleeves; with the skirt (*faldamento*), forepart (*delantera*) and foot (*ruedo*). For *conportina* I have found no relevant definition, but since its root must be related to that of *puerta,* one may suppose that it performed a similar function in the dress body. The Empress's *sayas* were lined in part, sometimes with buckram, black or reddish, often with damask, taffeta, satin, velvet, or cloth of gold or silver. Where body, sleeves, forepart, or skirt-foot were lined also with precious material, the buckram must have served as interlining.[487] A white taffeta lining is reported only for sleeves and *conportinas* in a *saya* of white silk *(cotonía de seda),* possibly a concession to summer heat. The body lining could differ from that of other parts: in a brown velvet *saya* given to the Marchioness of Astorga, the body was lined with brown taffeta, while the more visible sleeves, forepart, and skirt-foot were given cloth of gold.[488] Queen Juana's inventory mentions for three-year-old Infanta Catalina (1510) a *saya* of black velvet (5½ varas) lined with *grana;* body and skirt with taffeta also.[489] The trousseau record of Isabel de Aragón (1515) describes a wide-sleeved, black velvet *saya* as lined with ermine.[490]

The *saya* body, which fitted closely, may have opened under one arm. It met the skirt in a seam

458   ca. 1496–1502   **459**   1464–1467   **460**   ca. 1485–1495

461   ca. 1500–1510   **462**   1502   **463**   1507–1510

at the normal waistline (Fig. 463) or below it in front. The seam might be covered with a cloth belt (Fig. 391) or with a jeweled chain (Fig. 393).

Saya sleeves, unsewed, are mentioned in an inventory (1507). Later there are references to the wineskin *(borracha)* type (Fig. 448), but the most frequently cited style is the "pointed" *(de punta* or *de media punta),* also known as "French or half French" (see Figs. 313, 454). Savoyan *sayas* had sleeves made of strips or panes (see Fig. 442). The term *saboyana* would seem to relate to the fact that the Empress's sister Beatriz married into Savoy (1521).

In the *saya* skirt, waistline fullness often was set in pleats across the front (Fig. 306). Pleats can be indicated also for the whole skirt (Fig. 462). In a crimson dress (Fig. 463) soft pleats that begin at the waistline are lost lower down. Catherine of Aragon at her first wedding (1501) wore a dress "with many plights, moch litche unto menys clothyng",[491] which recalls the pleated skirt of a man's jerkin (Fig. 71). The length of the *saya* skirt varied from one that dragged slightly (Fig. 306), through a fair amount of train (Fig. 461), to one long enough to require assistance in the street (Fig. 307). This lady's crimson dress reveals in front a yellow underskirt.

Dress *(Brial)*

458 ARCHDUCHESS ca. 1496–1502, from figure of Juana la Loca, queen of Spain as archduchess of Austria, in *Horae diurnae, Hours of the Infanta Juana. f*3 (London. The British Library)

Dress *(Hábito)*

459 POTTERY VENDER 1464–1467, from figure of St. Justa by Lorenzo Mercadante (Sevilla. Cathedral, Puerta del Bautismo)

460 ATTENDANT ca. 1485–1495, from *Birth of the Virgin* by Pedro Berruguete (Montserrat. Monastery, Museo)

Dress *(Saya)*

461 LADY ca. 1500–1510, from figure of Empress's attendant in *St. Catherine's Conversion of the Empress and the Imperial Minister,* retable of St. Catherine, wing exterior, by the Tránsito Master (Barcelona. Museo de Arte de Cataluña)

462 LADY 1502, from figure of Melibea in *Tragicomedia de Calisto y Melibea.* Salamanca, 1502. Title-cut (The Hispanic Society of America)

463 ATTENDANT 1507–1510, from *Birth of the Virgin,* main-retable shutter, inner side, by Fernando de Llanos (Valencia. Cathedral)

The maids' dresses are rose-colored; all the cloaks suggest black. Escorting the group is a bearded gentleman clad in black cloak, blue jerkin, rose stockings, and black shoes.

Considerable attention was paid to the skirt-foot *(ruedo).* In 1502 an attendant of Queen Isabel received, for *sayas* of mulberry cloth, white frieze to trim the skirt-foot and *lienzo de naval* to line it. A *saya* skirt, lifted to facilitate movement, exposes the inner face (Fig. 461), which explains the care taken with a lining. Sometimes for the Empress the skirt material was repeated inside, as for a black velvet *saya* and a white damask one. More commonly the material varied: in a *saya* of crimson figured velvet, crimson satin formed the *ruedo* lining. Many times there was contrast: cloth of gold exposed against mulberry velvet, yellow taffeta against blue damask.

In addition to the *saya* there was a woman's garment called by the same term as a man's jerkin— *sayo.* One that required 10, 12, or 13 varas of *cebtí* would have been of floor length or longer. A *sayo,* possibly for the Queen (1495), that used only 6¾ varas of black satin was called "short" *(corto).* For her household the *sayo* is most often described as *mantonado* or *morisco,* either of which could require 12 or 13 varas of silk or velvet. *Mantones* are defined as two bands trimming a waist at front and back, of the same material as the waist, three fingers wide at the shoulders and narrowing toward the point where they meet at the waistline.[492] *Sayos mantonados* were heavily embroidered with gold or silver, perhaps in such bands. A *medio sayo, mantonado* or *morisco,* consisted of two contrasting fabrics, brocade with Rouen cloth, *cebtí,* satin, or velvet. Queen Juana had a *sayo morisco,* made with alternate gores *(jirones)* of blue velvet or blue *ceti,* which carried 2,728 pieces of gold (130 ounces) shaped into little wings like those of marsh hens *(alicas como rrallones, ralos).* Her *sayo morisco* of crimson velvet, gored *(jironado)* with green *ceti,* was trimmed with gold cords and garnished at the skirt-foot with strips of crimson velvet that had been embroidered with gold in flat stitch *(pasado).*[493] Isabel de Aragón's *sayo morisco* (1515) contained 7 varas of white brocade and 7 of crimson satin. The bipartite use of colors can be illustrated in a Moorish garment at Granada (Fig. 498).

The necklines of dresses have been dealt with in Figures 373–381. As mentioned, there comes a time when the low neck or the partlet with its insistent crossline dies out. Then the dress material runs

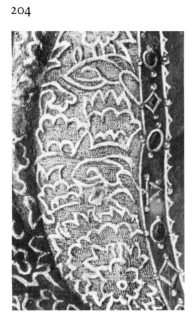

464   ca. 1490

465   1497–1503

466   1506

467   ca. 1490

468   ca. 1500–1515

469   ca. 1500–1515

470   ca. 1480

471   ca. 1520

472   1526

continuously to a high-collared neck. I have found no illustration of this change earlier than the copy (Bruxelles. Musées Royaux des Beaux-Arts) of a Moro portrait (ca. 1552) of the Empress's daughter Juana. But it must have occurred earlier: among the Empress's clothes are many *sayos altos,* which may be interpreted as high-necked dresses. Like the *saya,* they have bodies, linings, sleeves, skirts, and foreparts. Unusual materials are net, worked in or trimmed with gold, and *calicud* from India, padded or quilted *(colchado).*

In its reports of ladies attending hunt or joust at Naples, *Questiõ de amor* seldom details the style of their *sayas* but pays generous attention to trimmings, mainly appliqué. A *saya* of mulberry velvet and tawny brocade, quartered, is grilled in each quarter with strips of the opposite fabric set over white *pestañas.* On Laurencia's yellow cloth dress are applied lozenges of blue satin, each of which carries a smaller lozenge of stamped silver on blue satin over red velvet. The Marchioness of Persiana

---

Dress embroidery

464 QUEEN—DRESS FABRIC ca. 1490, from figure of Isabel I, queen of Castilla and Aragón, in *The Virgin of the Catholic Kings* (Madrid. Museo del Prado)

465 LADY 1497–1503, from figure of wise virgin in *The Wise and the Foolish Virgins,* choir stall, by Master Rodrigo (Plasencia. Cathedral)

466 COURT LADY 1506, from *Funeral Procession of Phelipe el Hermoso* (Écaussines. Château de la Follie, Collection of Comte Charles-Albert de Lichtervelde)

Dress hem-band embroidered

467 QUEEN ca. 1490, from figure of Isabel I, queen of Castilla and Aragón, in *The Virgin of the Catholic Kings* (Madrid. Museo del Prado)

468 LADY ca. 1500–1515, from figure of St. Lucy, tomb of the Duchess of Alburquerque (The Hispanic Society of America)

469 DUCHESS ca. 1500–1515, from effigy of Mencía Enríquez de Toledo, duchess of Alburquerque (The Hispanic Society of America)

Dress bands and strips

470 ATTENDANT ca. 1480, from *Birth of the Virgin* by Pedro García de Benabarre and Workshop (Ainsa. Parish Church)

471 LADY ca. 1520, from figure of listener in *St. Felix Preaching,* retable of St. Felix, by Joan de Burgunya (Gerona. Church of San Félix, Sala de Museo)

472 LADY 1526, from figure of St. Mary Magdalene in *Jesus Preaching,* retable of St. Mary Magdalene, by Pere Mates (Gerona. Cathedral, Tesoro)

---

appears in a chessboard of crimson velvet squared with gold galloons *(fresos)* three fingers wide; every velvet square bears a small gold column.[494] In addition to such columns, silversmiths wrought in gold oak and fern leaves, Arabic letters, small knockers, feathers, little clubs, and branches. One hundred ten and ½ ounces of hammered-gold ornaments adorned a tabard of Infanta Isabel (1487). At Arbeca (Lérida) Phelipe el Hermoso's scribe (1503) saw a young countess wearing a crimson velvet coat laden with gold letters made by silversmiths; he neglected to record the message.[495]

Embroidery was another fashionable form of embellishment. Effort was spent most lavishly where the result would be seen, on the outer garments tabard and coat *(ropa),* but the technique must have been the same, whether on dress or coat. Gold thread—drawn, spun, or *de orilla*—as well as silk and spun silver, was used for the work. Nothing is said of designs, except for the mention of Arabic letters. On a tabard of woolen material *(limiste)* for Infanta Isabel (1486), the four ounces of gold thread used may have been applied directly on the cloth. Usually, however, when a garment was of woolen such as *grana* or *contray,* the embroidery would be done on bands of satin, *cebtí,* velvet, or brocade. On a crimson *cebtí* habit for Queen Isabel (1493), strips cut from ½ vara of the same fabric were worked with 9 ounces of drawn-gold thread and 5 ounces of *de orilla* gold. Metallic threads were stitched *(punteados),* or rather couched, with silk. Six names of Queen Isabel's embroiderers are given, men working at 2 *reales* (62 maravedis) per day. Seventy days were required to embroider a *marlota* of mulberry satin, possibly for the Queen (1484), with 7⅛ ounces of gold thread and one ounce of stitching silk.

Illustrations representing embroidery on the body of a dress are not easy to find. A raised floral design in gold (Fig. 464) may have been embroidered; its background indicates a sort of netted surface, also in gold. Relief panels of four addorsed C-scrolls round a Greek cross, repeated in long verticals (Fig. 465), could represent appliqué. A cross, almost the saltier raguly of Burgundy, appearing in several vertical lines and in another following the hem (Fig. 466), must have been executed in stitchery. What a gaily clad young woman is doing in the gloom of a funeral procession is a mystery; the Burgundian cross suggests an association with Phelipe el Hermoso. Her dress can be found again in Album Ob II (ƒ20, *Dama Hazpanta*) at the Cabinet d'Estampes,

473   1477   **474**   1514   **475**   ca. 1560

476   1477   **477**   ca. 1488   **478**   ca. 1521

Bibliothèque Nationale, Paris. That skirt is green patterned with black, while at the waist has been added a scarlet cloth draped diagonally like those in Figures 485 and 500.

The richly decorated hem-band *(cortapisa)* is abundantly illustrated. Using letters as ornament may have stemmed from the men's example. Associated with a saint or a queen, however, the letters probably expressed piety or respect, rather than sentimentalities. In an early example (Fig. 467) the letters are in gold—a few strange characters followed by D...OES:O—on a plain brown strip edged with pearls. A gold band carrying black letters—EME:RIPAINA:POPL:FIDS—edges a crimson and gold dress (Fig. 303). In a figure of Saint Lucy the hem letters (Fig. 468), which have been read as her name, may be interpreted also as STAMILISTA. The decoration of a duchess's hem-band (Fig. 469) suggests pearls and precious metal set with jewels, a reminder of the 355 gold ornaments that adorned a *brial* hem of Queen Juana. On a large-figured dress of crimson and silver (Fig. 306) the gilt hem-band carries shaded crescents. As late as 1539–1543 (Toledo. Cathedral, upper choir stall) the decorated *cortapisa* persists, though rendered simply in incised dots and fleurets.

Very popular as trimming for women's wear, as well as for men's (see Figs. 66, 87), were bands *(fajas)* or strips *(tiras)* of silk or velvet contrasting

---

Skirt open over forepart

473 LADY 1477, from figure of Grammar in Torre, Alfonso de la. *Vision delectable. f*3 (Paris. Bibliothèque Nationale)

474 HARLOT 1514, from figure of Elicia in *Tragicomedia de Calisto y Melibea.* Valécia, 1514. XVIII auto (Madrid. Biblioteca Nacional)

475 MARCHIONESS ca. 1560, from effigy of María de Córdoba, marchioness of Las Navas (Madrid. Museo Arqueológico Nacional)

Skirt divided into panels

476 LADY 1477, from figure of Reason or Truth in Torre, Alfonso de la. *Vision delectable. f*21 (Paris. Bibliothèque Nationale)

477 DAUGHTER OF A POET ca. 1488, from *St. James and St. George* in Marcuello, Pedro. *Devocionario de la Reyna d.ª Juana, à quien llamaron la Loca. vºf*127 (Chantilly. Musée Condé)

478 LADY ca. 1521, from figure of Hispania in *Figürliches Musterbuch für Kunstmaler* by Niklaus Manuel Deutsch (Basel. Kunstmuseum, Kupferstichkabinett)

---

with the dress material. In English usage such bands were known as "guards",[496] perhaps because they followed seam lines. Bands often were set over the "eyelash" band *(pestaña)*. In an early example of plain bands (Fig. 470), narrow strips appear in groups of three, dark on light, while later wide and narrow are combined—rose-red on gold-yellow (Figs. 312, 471), black on crimson (Fig. 481), red on orange (Fig. 472).

Charles V noted this trimming and undertook to control it (1537): "On *sayas* women may not wear bands more than four fingers wide, and not more than eight of them from top to bottom; or in place of each band, two or three strips *(ribetones)* requiring no more silk than one band. . . . Of silk *pestañas* women may have as many as they wish on their coats *(ropas)*. But this provision is not to be understood as extended to public women, who may not wear silk at all." Women whose clothes did not satisfy these commands did not lose the use of them immediately, but might wear them four months longer. Tailors and embroiderers, however, had to conform at once or be fined.[497]

Forepart

The forepart *(delantera)*, which was handsome, filled the empty space of a skirt open at front. In English costume the forepart was "often mounted on a coarse underskirt".[498] I have found no Spanish reference to such support, but one *delantera* did have laces of gold cord. This garment comes into view in the trousseau of Isabel de Aragón (1515), for whom were purchased 3 ells of double black taffeta for lining the forepart and the sleeves of a black satin *saya.* The Empress had many foreparts. The most elaborate, made of white crimped *(escarchada)* cloth of silver and worth 230 ducats (86,250 maravedis), carried bows of white velvet adorned with spun-gold thread, among which were scattered diamond-shaped points of hammered gold set on white linen with an edging of white velvet.[499] One of the Duchess of Medina Sidonia's guests (1541), daughter of a cardinal, wore with a tawny satin *saya* a forepart of crimped cloth of gold, veiled first with a netting made from the tawny satin and then with one of gold bands or fringes *(franjas).*[500]

Illustrations begin earlier than available texts. Grammar (Fig. 473) with a plain light-rose dress wears a green and white, large-figured forepart (perhaps of brocade), trimmed with four groups of three bands each. Elicia's (Fig. 474) suggests cloth of gold or silver under zigzag bands of dark velvet. The Empress's red and gold brocade forepart (Fig. 313) harmonizes with her *saya* of crimson figured velvet. A late type of this dress appears in the effigy of a lady who died in 1560 (Fig. 475). Though the sculptor has detailed no ornament for the forepart, he has provided a curious decoration for the *saya* skirt—a length of sheer material tied into five puffs *(papos)* with rather heavy cords. *Papos* of silk and silver cloth and little roses of linen and baroque pearls, each *papo* or rose set over a lozenge of gold cord, decorated a white satin forepart of the Empress.[501]

Skirt

In another phase of the open skirt, it is cut into several panels. Reason's rose-colored skirt (Fig. 476) is divided into four over an apple-green underskirt, which is banded with blue-green and hemmed with a gold band figured in black. Other panels (Fig. 477) hang over a hoop skirt. Panels tied together with ribbons (Fig. 478) happily coincide with a textual reference. At Naples the Marchioness of La Chesta wears a *saya* with gores *(jirones)* of drawn-gold and drawn-silver thread woven in checks. "The gores, loose, were tied with blue ribbons over a lining of crimson damask."[502]

Dresses—*brial, saya*—could carry the hoops *(verdugos)* that make so striking a feature of women's costume in our period. Mounted on the outside of the skirt, the hoops sometimes cast a definite shadow (Fig. 301). They are visible on dresses (Figs. 479–480), or the dress skirt is lifted (Fig. 316) or parted (Fig. 477) to expose them on an underskirt. For hoops, which began to appear in the 1460's or 1470's, there is concrete gossip to explain their origin. Palencia, a contemporary courtier-historian, writes that it was with the intent of concealing the aftermath of an indiscretion that his queen adopted a skirt of extravagant width and kept it rigidly distended with very hard hoops *(aros)*, which she concealed by having them sewn inside. Her example was followed by ladies of her court, all of whom could have been suspected of being in an advanced state of pregnancy.[503] This queen, the beautiful but unfortunate Juana de Portugal, died in 1475. Talavera in that same decade uses in relation to skirts the term *verdugos*, which signifies "smooth twigs put out by a tree that has been cut or pruned"; the inference is that such twigs were used for hoops.

An editor of his text later says plainly, "They were called *verdugos* in the beginning . . . because they were made of osiers *(varillas de mimbre)* with which formerly executioners scourged evildoers."[504] Here is a favorite device of disparagers, associating a disapproved fashion with an unsavory character.

Talavera has more to say about hoop skirts. He speaks of woolen cloth being packed about the hips, which thus were overheated, while below, about the legs, the hoops stood out, making a hollow space that admitted winter cold. He, too, thought the garment had been invented to conceal adulterous pregnancies and blamed it for causing miscarriages and abortions.[505] Nevertheless his confessant, Queen Isabel, was devoted to the skirt, which in her time was made with the hoops outside, furnishing decoration not only because of their relief but also because of the textural or color contrast of their coverings.

When Queen Isabel (still a princess), seated in a royal chair on the *estrado,* received Burgundian ambassadors (1473), she was wearing a *brial* of crimson velvet bearing hoops covered with green *cebtí,*[506] a favored color combination. Cloth-of-gold hoops stiffened another *brial* of hers. Of those furnished for underskirts, Baeza records both the fabric and the color. *Cebtí* is cited 28 times out of 46, mostly crimson, green, or white in that order, and then brown, orange, yellow, blue, or silvered *(plateado)*. Velvet *verdugos* were used on *cebtí,* brocaded satin, cloth of silver, or *grana;* white damask or satin on crimson or green velvet, on mulberry velvet or brocade, or on crimson brocaded velvet. I have not found the hoop skirt mentioned in Queen Juana's inventory, but the adjectives *verdugada* and *verdugado* appear in the accounts of Isabel de Portugal. As both masculine and feminine forms are used, it would seem that nouns have been omitted— *[faldrilla, saya] verdugada, [sayo] verdugado.*

The five *verdugadas* that the Empress brought from Portugal each had 14 hoops.[507] When her skirts were of taffeta, the hoops generally were of the same taffeta, but if the skirts were of satin or damask, the hoops would be of same-colored velvet. A new feature appears, the half-hooped skirt *(media verdugada),* in which probably only half the skirt length bore hoops, or perhaps they were placed only across the front. The Empress's wardrobe mistress *(camarera mayor)* was given such a garment of blue damask with hoops of blue velvet. The Empress herself had a half-hooped skirt of brown satin with hoops of brown velvet and a forepart, also of the velvet, to cover them.[508] The use of a concealing forepart and the generally monochrome effect of such skirts in her time suggest that hoops were losing importance as a decorative device. Carmen Bernis states that in the mid-1530's ladies of high standing were wearing their hoops concealed, while those of lower degree were still making of theirs an ornamental feature,[509] plainly visible (Fig. 552).

The hoop skirt is abundantly illustrated. Worn in full view, six hoops, gold covered, distend a skirt of gold and black brocade (Figs. 310, 479). The hips are padded, doubtless with the wool that Talavera decried. One of Salome's companions has red hoops on a green dress. A relief (Fig. 480) shows Queen Isabel arriving in a hoop skirt at the surrender of Moclín (Granada). She can hardly be having a comfortable ride with the hoop-backs crushed between her legs and the barrel of her mount. Another Salome (Fig. 316), having drawn up her brown and gold dress, reveals a green velvet skirt with paired, rose-covered hoops. A camp follower in Charles V's expedition to Tunis (Fig. 552) wears a skirt which, in the tapestry seen at the Sevilla Alcázar, is yellow-beige with crimson shadows between the hoops.

In 1501 the English noted that Catherine of Aragon and her ladies wore "benethe ther wast certayn rownde hopys, beryng owte ther gowns from ther bodies, aft^r their country man^r."[510] This fashion caused such consternation in Italy that by 1507 authorities at Treviso near Venice had passed a statute prohibiting the use of "foreign" dresses with hoops.[511] French ladies succumbed to the *vertugade* during the reign of François I, English to the "verdingale" or "farthingale" before mid-century.[512] Spanish descendants of the *verdugada* were the *guardainfante* (17th century) and the *miriñaque* (19th century).

A Spanish poem published in 1544 illustrates the passion that a *saya verdugada* could inspire:

A matron of good reputation,
but given to dress and pomp,
suffered from desire
for a stylish dress with hoops—
    very graceful
and elegant it seemed to her—
she had seen on the way to church.
She began to be melancholy,
appeared to be greatly fatigued,
    did not eat,
but constantly sighed and groaned.

Her husband,
oppressed and sorely afflicted,
sent for a physician,
Who
came to see the matron,
proceeded to take her pulse
and then with learned questions
to seek the evident cause.
Upon the husband's return
    very gently
he told him: Have no fear
that your wife will presently die
of this sickness, or that there are
no merchants in Toledo.
Buy her without misgiving
six varas of fine *grana*
and another four of crimson
    velvet
and put them in a place
where she may rejoice to see them,
together with some pearls.
Immediately
everything was there,
not a moment of delay,
and he, with this hope alone,
from being almost dead
    revived.
As soon as ever she saw it,
her eyes lit up with joy,
and, all her troubles ended,
she was twice as well as before.[513]

Tucks could divide a skirt into sections that look almost like flounces. A skirt of dark wine-red velvet (Fig. 482) is divided evenly with two tucks and hemmed with rose cloth touched with red. In a crimson skirt, apparently of wool (Fig. 483), two tucks are stitched at the hips and one appears at the knees; the hem carries a plain band of like depth and a velvet edge-strip *(ribete)*. A skirt of gold brocade (Fig. 484) is divided by two tucks above the knees; its hem is jeweled.

The skirt named *basquiña* had prolonged currency from the late fifteenth century until well into the nineteenth. One patterned in Alcega is cut in four pieces, on the straight of the goods at front and back and on the bias at each side. The length is 1½ varas and the hem appears to measure over 3 varas.[514] Covarrubias defines the *basquiña* as a closed skirt put on over the head.[515]

In Baeza's accounts the material most frequently mentioned for this garment is *grana,* the handsome woolen fabric woven with a twill, which in red frequently was imported from London or Florence at

479   ca. 1470–1480

480   1489–1495

481   ca. 1520–1530

482   ca. 1474–1477

483   ca. 1490–1500

484   ca. 1500

485   1495

486   ca. 1500

487   ca. 1520–1530

1100 to 1500 maravedis the vara. Queen Isabel's little girls had the *basquiña* in *grana* (about 1 to 2 varas) or in holland, which speaks of summer heat, until María was twelve and Catalina nine (1494), when they had it in yellow *cebtí* or satin (5½ varas). For these and for several other silk *basquiñas* the trimming was strips of crimson velvet. Black velvet bands were the favored decoration for those of red woolen, a combination remembered still in Gallegan regional dress. But Queen Juana's *basquiña* of *grana* carried strips of white brocaded satin bordered with black velvet points.[516] *Grana* skirts for María and Catalina (1499) were provided with findings *(aparejos)* which included frieze for lining, and wool *(lana)* probably for hip padding. In the same year Margarita de Austria, leaving Spain, was given a *basquiña* of white fustian (9⅓ varas) lined with black

buckram. One of black camlet (1507) was lined with red buckram.[517]

Basquiñas in the Empress's accounts are divided between silks and woolens, which latter include the white *grana de Toledo*.[518] She provided such a skirt for a pawn of Charles V, his niece Princess Kirstina of Denmark, whom he married off at thirteen (1534) to the Duke of Milan three times her age. This *basquiña* was among the most handsome at court. Made of red silk *(grana de polvo de Valencia)*, it was trimmed with bands of cloth of gold woven with silver loops *(altos)* and piped at each side with crimson velvet. The bands ran in pairs at front, back, and sides, and another pair along the hem, the placement shown in Figure 481. For the Princess's fool *(loca)* there was a *basquiña* in green Cuenca cloth trimmed with two bands and one piping of green velvet.[519] Kirstina was a leader of fashion; in Lorraine, where she married next (1540/41), she set a style of headdress and coiffure.[520]

Underskirt

As terms relating to skirts the Spanish Academy admits *falda* and *faldillas,* the forms entered in Covarrubias, but not *faldrilla*, which in our period meant "underskirt". Since *faldrilla* is the characteristic entry in the documents, I have used that form. Covarrubias speaks of *faldillas* as "open" in contrast with the closed *basquiña*. He says that women wore *faldillas* over the chemise, putting "one skirt over the other", that is, wearing more than one at a time. Thus many would be needed. I have reckoned over 200 entries for the *faldrilla* in Baeza's accounts and even more in the Empress's. Queen Juana is credited with only five.

In Queen Isabel's household, woolen *faldrillas*—of *grana*, frieze, green *palmilla* from Cuenca, cloth of Courtrai—were generally given to a slave, a servant, or a court attendant, though a few of cloth were supplied to the Infantas. For royalty silks or velvets were the usual fabrics. The material for Queen Isabel's *faldrillas* could run to 11 varas each, the same as for a *brial*. Most of the Queen's were black. A dozen times in the *Cuentas* materials are issued for completing or for enlarging a *faldrilla*. Half of one for Infanta Catalina (1488) was cut from new crimson velvet, the other half from a brocade *cota*, a reusing of material that was to become drearily familiar to her during her wilderness years as a young widow in England. Even the Empress's *faldrillas* not infrequently had been *sayos* or

Hoop skirt

479 PRINCESS ca. 1470–1480, from figure of Salome in *Banquet of Herod*, retable of St. John the Baptist, by Pedro García de Benabarre (Barcelona. Museo de Arte de Cataluña)

480 QUEEN ON HORSEBACK 1489–1495, from figure of Isabel I, queen of Castilla and Aragón, in *Surrender of Moclín*, choir stall, by Master Rodrigo (Toledo. Cathedral)

Skirt trimmed with straight bands

481 LADY ca. 1520–1530, from *Castilian Lady* in *Dessins français du XVIe siècle*, Album Ob 23, *f*45 (Paris. Bibliothèque Nationale, Cabinet des Estampes)

Tucked skirt

482 LADY ca. 1474–1477, from figure of Saint in *The Flagellation of St. Engracia* by Bartolomé Bermejo (Bilbao. Museo de Bellas Artes)

483 ATTENDANT ca. 1490–1500, from *Birth of the Virgin*, main retable, by Pedro Berruguete (Paredes de Nava. Church of Santa Eulalia)

484 LADY ca. 1500, from figure of St. Apollonia (Palencia. Cathedral)

Skirt banded with zigzags or points

485 LADY 1495, from choir-partition relief by Master Andrés and Master Nicolás (Nájera. Monastery of Santa María la Real)

486 QUEEN ca. 1500, from figure of Herodias in *The Beheading of St. John the Baptist*, Hispano-Flemish School (Madrid. Museo del Prado)

487 WOMAN ca. 1520–1530, from *From Burgos (Bovrgoy)* in *Castilla* in *Dessins français du XVIe siècle,* Album Ob 23, *f*27 (Paris. Bibliothèque Nationale, Cabinet des Estampes)

marlotas once (or were about to become such), or a church vestment, a traveling bed, a petticoat for a daughter, a pair of hose for her son. It is no wonder that few, if any, garments of this period have survived, when even royalty thus used up every bit of the life in their dress materials.

Silk *faldrillas* were made warm with linings and padding. Of the findings given to Archduchess Juana (1496) for a habit, a waist *(cos),* and a *faldrilla,* a third or more would have gone into the last, or ⅔ vara of white frieze and 6 varas of dyed linen with perhaps half of the 4 pounds of wool intended, probably, for padding false hips *(caderas postizas).* Buckram sometimes took the place of linen, apparently 2 pieces (10 varas) for a *faldrilla.* An ermine lining was supplied to Infanta Isabel (1488). The Empress's *faldrillas* could be lined with damask or holland, but the material most commonly cited is red buckram.

On a *faldrilla* of expensive London *grana* (1491) a duke's daughter had hoops, as well as trimming strips, of black velvet. No adornment was provided for underskirts of the lower orders. The Infantas' carried hoops. For Queen Isabel (1488) crimson velvet hoops were mounted on a cloth-of-silver *faldrilla.* She wore them of *cebtí* also, white, mulberry, or green, but in later years her underskirts carried only fabric strips contrasting in color or texture. The Empress had a blue velvet *faldrilla* trimmed with gold braid. A white satin one bore on its white velvet skirt-foot puffs *(papos)* of the satin[521] (see Fig. 475).

Also associated with the *faldrilla* was appliqué in the form of points *(puntas)*—white damask for Princess Isabel (1490) and crimson velvet for Archduchess Juana (1496). Queen Juana's *basquiña* trim of white brocaded satin bands bordered with the sharp punctuation of black velvet points is illustrated in black on the gold of Herodias's underskirt (Fig. 486). The point-trimmed skirt appears in a woodcut for the month of May (Li, Andrés de. *Reportorio de los tiempos.* Burgos, 1493) and on a choir stall of ca. 1510–1520 (Sevilla. Cathedral). Large black points, recorded for a yellow skirt (Fig. 487), are seen also in Aesop's *Libro del . . . fabulador* (Toledo, 1547. *v°f*XXIX. British Library copy). A zigzag band of 1495 (Fig. 485) or of 1514 (Fig. 474) may be taken as related.

Underskirts of such handsome materials and conspicuous trimming must have risen to the surface where they would be visible. They probably have been seen in the illustrations: under a lifted dress skirt (Figs. 316, 458, 461) or through openings between free panels (Fig. 476).

Another skirt which Covarrubias places as being worn under the *saya* or the *basquiña* is the *manteo,* which still survives as an outer skirt in Leonese and Gallegan regional dress—a wrap-around of woolen banded with velvet; in Galicia it is called *mantelo.* The Empress's accounts record two kinds of *manteo:* one for covering *(de cubrir),* probably used as a cape, and the other for underneath *(de debajo).* Except those of white taffeta or fustian, her listed *manteos* are of woolen—cloth, frieze, or serge *(estamente)*—and the colors are red, white, rose, orange, blue, brown, or green. Only three carry any kind of trimming, red or brown ribbons. No sixteenth-century illustration of this underskirt has been found.

Waist

Coming to the waist, we find it in Baeza's accounts with the name of *cos.* For Infanta Catalina aged 3 (1488), only ½ vara was required. For a woman, 1½ to 2 varas were provided. One vara is reported for sleeves of the Queen (1492); sleeves are mentioned half a dozen times.

A cursory count of *coses* listed shows 44 of black velvet and 25 of crimson *cebtí.* Of fabrics in all colors, *cebtí* (66) and velvet (61) lead over satin (39), brocade (21), and woolen (1). Black (80) and crimson (57) surpass by a wide margin mulberry (22), green (11), white (10), brown (1), tawny (1), and blue (1). *Grana* lined *coses* for the younger infantas (1487), and linen *(holanda* or *bretaña)* served a few times. Embroidery was lavished on waists for the Queen and her daughters, ounces of gold stitched directly on green satin or on crimson or mulberry *cebtí,* or worked on black or mulberry brocaded satin, probably in strips, to be applied over crimson *cebtí* or mulberry satin. Such status symbols cannot have languished unseen.

Queen Juana's color preferences for her twenty-seven *coses* were those of her mother's household—black or crimson. For fourteen garments, sleeves are recorded, some garnished with crimson velvet (strips on white *ceti* or edge-strips on cloth of gold). In one case crimson *ceti* sleeves were combined with a black body. A *cos* of tawny *ceti* was embroidered with points *(puntas),* with "P's" (for Phelipe, no doubt), and with leaves of gold. The richest adornment was that of 839 little shells stamped from hammered gold for a *cos* of black velvet lined with holland. Bernis compares the *cos* to the man's doublet (*jubón*) and suggests that a tight sleeve appearing at the wrist inside a wide dress sleeve (as in Figs. 438, 450, 454) may represent this waist.[522]

Another small waist was the *corpecico* for which Isabel de Aragón (1515) required but 1 vara of satin or damask. Dozens of *corpecicos* or *corpiños* are registered in the Empress's accounts. For these, velvet remained first choice (17), but running close were taffeta (16) and satin (15). Black was still favored (26) with red next (11) and then brown or white (5 each). Twenty-five of these waists, almost half, were lined, sixteen with taffeta chiefly black. Trimmings were few and modest—strips of black velvet or of the garment fabric, except that pinked bands of cloth of gold gleamed on a *corpecico* of red satin.

The waist called *gonete* required for the Queen or Infanta Isabel 2 varas of velvet or *cebtí*, unless long sleeves were intended (1485), in which case 2 varas were added. In color black and in fabric velvet were favored for this garment also, with crimson and *cebtí* running second; as an exception Infanta Isabel (1484) had one of blue velvet with sleeve facings (*vueltas*) of blue *cebtí*. A lined *gonete* must have been coveted in winter; besides silk, *grana* or fur was used. For the Infanta at sixteen (1486), 18 rabbit skins were given out to line a *gonete* of unknown material. In 1495, the year before Juana married, her standard had risen to 40 sables within crimson brocaded velvet. For a *gonete* of crimson velvet with "wide" sleeves (1515) Isabel de Aragón required 240 ermines.

Waists worn evidently with separate skirts are not uncommonly seen in paintings and sculptures. These garments generally have a peplum. The *gonete* may be illustrated in a fitted waist with shallow peplum (Fig. 488), which is worn in conjunction with *cofia y tranzado*. Another such waist, shown in back view (Fig. 489), is made of crimson velvet and embroidered in gold. This type of peplum is seen also in the French drawings (Figs. 394, 487). In a waist of rose brocade, figured in darker rose (Fig. 490), the peplum begins under the breasts and runs down to a deeply curved edge, which carries a narrow border of white picked out with black (Arabic letters?) and hung with gold tassels. It is worn over a blue-gray skirt and a white chemise embroidered in black. Tassel-hung waists of similar length are provided for a figure of Salome (1521) by Alejo Fernández (Marchena (Sevilla). Church of San Juan) and also for a statue (1525–1530) of Queen Isabel (Bruges. Cheminée du Franc).

A waist of the Empress, said to be like a *cos*, carried the name *saino*, which as a garment term is unknown to the Spanish dictionary but is near to the Portuguese *sainho*, diminutive of *saio*. Perhaps of Portuguese origin, the waist is listed most often in white, whether linen, silk, or wool. One of holland was quilted (*embutido*), another backstitched (*pespuntado*); one of satin was quilted with cotton (*colchado*). Of the Empress's 30 white *sainos* or *saynos*, only one was of velvet, the fabric she favored for black or colored waists of this type. One of mulberry velvet had sleeves *de borracha* (see Fig. 448). The accounts mention linings of cotton (*cotonía*), frieze, damask, or taffeta. Trimmings were an occasional *pestaña* or *ribete*. Some high-necked *saynos* are reported, one of black velvet with "half-French" sleeves. Carmen Bernis has found the *sayno* listed subsequently in dowries recorded at Madrid.[523]

A "little *sayo*" (*sayuelo*) goes back to Queen Isabel's time. That for Infanta Catalina (aged 1, 1486) required a single vara of black satin; that of brocade for Juana (aged 15, 1494) was lined with 42 ermines. A more helpful measure is the 6 varas of black *cebtí* allotted to four *sayuelos* for Moorish women turned Christian (1492). Queen Juana had one of wool, made with narrow sleeves and lined with black satin, and a wide-sleeved one of *grana* banded with black velvet. Those of the Empress were of wool, *grana* (2) or white (2). Bernis, from documents available to her, concludes that the *sayuelo* was much used by wives of artisans and farmers.[524]

Garments with derivative names like *sayno* and *sayuelo* would seem to correspond to the waist with knee-length peplum, which is similar in its proportions to the man's jerkin (*sayo*). A knee-length peplum cut in a deep curve front and back (Fig. 491) is edged with a narrow, plain band and a wider band of pleating. Another long peplum (Fig. 492) is fitted over the hips; the fullness rippling at the hem may be due to a circular cut or to inserted gores. A waist of purple rose banded with apple green (Figs. 319, 493) has its long peplum pleated across the back and held tight at the waistline with a gilt-touched belt.

Overdress or short dress

With the peplum extended into a three-quarter-length skirt, the garment was really an overdress or perhaps a "short dress" (*saya corta*). In an early example (Fig. 494) embroidery of linked-scroll de-

488   1495   **489**   ca. 1490–1500   **490**   ca. 1525–1530

491   ca. 1520   **492**   1527   **493**   1529

494   ca. 1500–1515   **495**   ca. 1520   **496**   ca. 1520–1530

sign borders the low-cut neckline, and a wider, more elaborate pattern adorns the skirt hem. Long tubular sleeves are open almost to the shoulder along the front, where the edges are joined with unagleted laces; the wrist is turned up in a cuff. Each wide chemise sleeve is drawn out between two laces to hang in front of the dress sleeve. In another overdress (Fig. 495) the skirt is open at the front and the edges, bordered with narrow bands, are joined with laces whose ends cannot be seen. The waist top rises to a hood-front with folds like those in Figures 350, 351. In a third such dress (Fig. 496) the skirt, lighter in tone than the waist, is divided at the side and the edges are joined with dark, apparently agleted laces.

Underdress

As for the underdress called *cota*, documents give little clue beyond listing its handsome material. One

---

Waist with peplum

488 WOMAN 1495, from choir-partition relief by Master Andrés and Master Nicolás (Nájera. Monastery of Santa María la Real)

489 ATTENDANT ca. 1490–1500, from *Birth of the Virgin*, main retable, by Pedro Berruguete (Paredes de Nava. Church of Santa Eulalia)

490 LADY ca. 1525–1530, from figure of St. Barbara in *St. Catherine and St. Barbara*, retable of the Immaculate Conception, by the Pulgar Master (Granada. Church of San José)

Waist with long peplum

491 LADY ca. 1520, from figure of St. Mary Magdalene in *Marys at the Tomb* (Valladolid. Museo Nacional de Escultura)

492 LADY 1527, from figure of Delphic Sibyl on dustguard, retable of the Virgin, by the Alcira Master (Gandía. Church of Los Jesuitas)

493 LADY OF HIGH RANK 1529, from *[Thus Women in Spain Look from Behind]* in Weiditz, Christoph. *Das Trachtenbuch. f58* (Nürnberg. Germanisches Nationalmuseum)

Overdress

494 QUEEN ca. 1500–1515, from figure of St. Catherine, tomb of the Duchess of Alburquerque (The Hispanic Society of America)

495 LADY ca. 1520, from effigy (southeast of Burgos. Abbey of San Quirce)

496 ATTENDANT ca. 1520–1530, from *Birth of the Virgin*, choir-book miniature (Granada. Cathedral)

---

for Queen Isabel (1487) required 9 varas of black brocaded velvet (75,555 maravedis), so it cannot have been so long as the *brial*. Queen Juana's scribe records "a *cota* of green *ceti* which is a *faldrilla*", perhaps with a body or waist attached. Other *cotas* of hers include a body *(corpecico)* and sleeves. A dozen silk *cotas* were lined with woolen cloth, several woolen with silk. Their usual trimming was the band called *jeto*, mainly of black or crimson velvet. The Empress omits the garment, but at one of the 1541 weddings it surfaces again, made of black velvet and worn under a *saya* that is short enough to reveal seed-pearl embroidery on the foot of the *cota*.[525]

Moorish Garments

THE EFFECT OF MOORISH taste on garments worn by Christian ladies has been noticed; the *camisa morisca* and the *sayo morisco* probably were so designated because of their rich decoration rather than because of their exotic cut. We have noted also the use of Arabic letters in embroidery and of the popular Moorish headdresses, *alhareme* and *almaizar*. Now we come to body garments of Moorish origin.

Drawers

Unmentionables in our period were mentioned but not illustrated for noble ladies of Spain. The Duchess of Alburquerque's inventory (1479) includes linen drawers and their white silk cords, presumably for tying about the waist. There are also 9 white ribbons carrying white and gold aglets that had belonged to drawers.[526] The Empress had drawers of yellow satin trimmed with strips of cloth of silver, together with blue and white silk stockings *(medias calças)*.[527] The garments and the name *zaragüelles*, from the Arabic *sarāwīl*, had been borrowed from the Moors. The length is uncertain. Navagero (1526) describes Moorish women's *Zaragolles* at Granada as "of cotton or linen *(tela)* tied on *(attaccatta)*". In Algiers such drawers were reaching to the ankle, in Morocco to below the calf of the leg. Mármol Carvajal (ca. 1571) says that at Fez, when Moriscas from Andalucía went out, they

497   1529

Moorish garments

497 DRAWERS *(ZARAGÜELLES)* 1529, from *In This Manner Moriscas Dress in the House with Their Children* in Weiditz, Christoph. *Das Trachtenbuch.* f100 (Nürnberg. Germanisches Nationalmuseum)

498 HOUSE COAT *(MARLOTA)* 1529, from *In This Manner Morisca Maidens Are Dressed in the House* in Weiditz, Christoph. *Das Trachtenbuch.* f103 (Nürnberg. Germanisches Nationalmuseum)

wore very long *zaragüelles*, very wrinkled about the legs. But he could have mistaken for wrinkled drawers-legs what actually were stockings, described by Navagero as "all pleated with the creases set transversely, so that they make the leg very large."[528]

In the Moriscan "house dress" that Weiditz recorded at Granada (Fig. 497) full white drawers are tied at the waist over a red body garment and met at the knees with yellowish stockings pleated horizontally. The fact that the Empress's *zaragüelles* were accompanied with stockings suggests that her drawers also reached to the knees, and that drawers and stockings may have been joined, perhaps with agleted laces as men's upper- and netherstocks could be joined.

Ladies' use of drawers was earlier in Spain than in England or France, which did not have the example of Moors immediately before them. The custom

498   1529

evidently was not criticized at the Spanish court as a usurpation of male prerogative, which was the case in Italy at this time. "Galley breeches" *(calzoni a la galeota)* such garments were called at Ferrara,[529] where Lucrezia Borgia had made them fashionable.

The drawers recorded for Queen Juana, bluntly termed "breeches" *(calzones),* were lined with white fur,[530] a touch of comfort in the long winters of her imprisonment. Court ladies for whom drawers are not listed may have contented themselves with their long chemises, as did peasant women still in the 1920's.

Marlota

The Spanish lady's *marlota* (from the Arabic *mallûta*) must have been much like the man's, a loose-fitting coat hanging to below the knees, made with sleeves and sometimes a collar. That Weiditz sketched this garment at Granada (Fig. 498) is generally agreed.[531] His *marlota* is bipartite, yellow at the girl's right, intense blue at her left. He complicates the situation by making her right sleeve purplish and the left crimson, matching neither the *marlota* nor the underdress, which is crimson at her right and green at her left. The armscyes receive attention, being bound with a narrow band, which makes one wonder further whether the sleeves belong to the body of the *marlota*. However, the Duchess of Alburquerque (1479) left a *marlota* which did have sleeves and also armscye decoration, six buttons at each shoulder. These were seed-pearl buttons, of which there were 6 more on each sleeve and 12 down the front. There had been 13, but one was ground up as medicine for the Duchess during her last illness. For this *marlota,* of crimson velvet embellished with pearls and seed pearls all about the skirt-foot, the sleeves, and the neckband, the Duchess owed 70,000 maravedis when she died.[532]

The first *marlota* entry that I have found in Baeza's accounts is an item (1484) providing 15½ varas of coarse half holland for the tailor to make a trial garment, as though he had no pattern or previous experience in making a *marlota*. The next listing specifies 10 varas of black velvet, 5 ounces of fine gold, and ½ ounce of silk thread to be sent to the embroiderer, who turns out to be a passementerie maker *(cordonero)*. He spent twenty days making gold braids and couching *(asentar)* them on the velvet. For a crimson *marlota* an embroiderer devoted twenty days and an ounce of gold *de orilla* to the sleeves alone. On one of mulberry satin another man put in seventy days' work, using 7⅛ ounces of gold thread with one ounce of silk for the stitching *(puntear)*. There is no statement that these garments were intended for the Queen herself, but in 1485 Baeza is definite: 10 varas of mulberry *cebtí* with 11¼ of green *cebtí* for a lining are assigned to Her Highness.

Moorish ladies had the *marlota* in wool. The dowry of Isabel Romaymia recorded at Granada in 1525 lists one of red cloth trimmed with gold passementerie and buttons, its velvet sleeve-facings embroidered with gold thread and seed pearls; another of tawny cloth was silvered *(plateada)*. A new *marlota,* bought for her with 40 of the bridegroom's gift of 65 ducats, is of expensive, figured red velvet *(alto y bajo)*. We know about these *marlotas* because the Inquisition in 1566 confiscated Isabel Romaymia's dowry, along with property of her silk-merchant husband, and she petitioned to get it back, which suggests that after forty years her bridal clothes still had value.[533] Spanish ladies' *marlotas* availably recorded were generally of silk or velvet. I have found no mention of their being worn on public occasions and therefore conclude that they must have been luxurious house coats.

Queen Juana's inventory omits the *marlota;* it is possible that with her its place was taken by the *sayo morisco,* which often was bipartite and of which she had several richly trimmed. The Empress brought from Portugal three satin *marlotas,* black, crimson, or tawny, but as soon as she came to Granada (1526) one of white taffeta was made for her, trimmed with a band *(faja)* and an edge-strip *(ribete)* of white velvet. She left a number of *marlotas,* most of satin or taffeta, with a few of damask, velvet, or *sarga* (a twill of silk or fine wool), or of cloth of gold or silver. I have counted six white, four each black, crimson, or tawny; of other colors there was one each. Details mentioned for these garments are sleeves (sometimes pleated), skirt-foot, and front. Perhaps a third of the sleeves are lined with contrasting material of matching color; skirt-foot and front also could be lined. Trimmings include passementerie *(cairel),* bugle beads *(cañutillos),* buttons, gold cords, fabric bands, and applied lozenges. The Empress's *marlota morisca,* of green satin and crimson velvet covered with twisted cords of spun gold, was priced at 40 ducats. Among the *marlotas* she gave away was a black satin one to her son's wet nurse and another of two-faced velvet, blue and crimson, to her niece, Kirstina of Denmark.[534] A duchess of Villahermosa as late as 1540 had a black velvet *marlota* in her trousseau.[535]

Rabelais mentions such a garment (1530) as "beautiful" and "purfled with gold". Éléonore d'Autriche at the French court (1532) had a *merlocte* of crimson-violet satin trimmed with crimson velvet. In the late sixteenth century the word *marlotte* was still current in France for a garment which has been identified as a long coat or overdress, made with short, puffed sleeves and fastened just under the throat.[536]

Accessories

Waistcloth

For a minor feature of the period, a waistcloth of varying depth, illustrations have been found but no Spanish references. The Portuguese have a word for something like it: *saio,* defined as "cloth rolled about the waistline, held in place with a crude band, buttons, or hooks."[537] An early Spanish example— red, belted with white, over a green dress (Fig. 499)—extends from just under the arms to below the waistline, which it parallels. How it is kept

499   ca. 1500

500   ca. 1512–1516

501   1529

502   ca. 1489

503   1519–1520

504   ca. 1531

505   ca. 1520–1530

506   1529

507   1539–1543

standing is not clear, perhaps with buckram. The same thing appears three times in a *Birth of the Virgin* at Cuenca (Cathedral, Chapel of San Roque). A notch, which marks the center front of the waistcloth in Figure 499, is shown in the Cuenca *Birth* at back, together with a long *tranzado*. Another type of waistcloth, longer but not so deep, is lapped in front with both ends hanging diagonally (Figs. 485, 500), an arrangement which lends to Saint Catherine in the latter Figure a swashbuckling air not belied by the long sword she harbors. In a later example, where the cloth again is placed horizontally (Fig. 501), the depth has shrunk to a band, and excessive length is taken up with folds contained within a belt.

Sash

An accessory many times mentioned is the sash designated by the word *faja*, used also for "trimming band". When Infanta Isabel was about thirteen (1483), she was allowed for a sash 1½ varas of green *cebtí* or of the doubly expensive crimson *cebtí*. The next year for a sash of black satin she received 2 varas, the length generally prescribed for a woman's. Queen Isabel and her household preferred silk sashes—my count gives 74 of *cebtí*, 30 of satin, 1 of damask. Heavier materials also were used, *grana* for 26, velvet for 5, cloth for 2. Black sashes were the most popular: 49 black to 28 crimson, 15 mulberry, 11 green, 3 white, 3 blue, 1 yellow.

Cebtí and satin would be easily crushed, and many crushed sashes are illustrated. An early example (Fig. 502) is tied in front at the waistline in one standing loop with ends falling. This style, which enjoyed a long vogue, can be found in men's costume of the period also. Short ends generally are finished plain, although a few show fringe. On Juana la Loca's effigy, long ends (Fig. 503) carry a fluted ball and an urn-shaped ornament. A later example (Fig. 504) is of gold cord.

The sash might be taken as a symbol of control:

> That wife of the shoemaker,
> Devoted to slippers,
> Spends all of his money
> On cosmetics and trifles.
> Her husband is foolish
> To let her go on so,
> Unable to tighten
> The sash or the girdle.[538]

In the 1520's it was sometimes allowed to slip below the waistline and tie over the abdomen. One sash arranged thus (Fig. 505) is narrow, perhaps of cord, and the single loop stands erect. A fabric sash (Fig. 506) is tied in two loops, the ends short and plain. Another in the same position (Fig. 507) has one loop erect and long ends finished with ball and fringe.

Sashes bore their share of decoration: strips *(tiras)* of black velvet (1485); gold and silk embroidery on black velvet (1492); black *cebtí* applied on drawn gold (1495). Queen Juana had one of white *ceti* on which were worked "Pharaohs" in gold thread,[539] another design taken probably from playing cards, like the clubs used on a habit or on chopines. Sashes could also be striped like that of Queen Isabel in the wooden effigy at Granada (Fig. 305), where the colors, retouched in the eighteenth century, are red, rose, white, gold, vermilion, and green. These sash-ends are finished with a round medallion and a gold tassel.

Waistcloth

499 QUEEN ca. 1500, from figure of St. Catherine, retable of *The Apotheosis of the Virgin* (The Hispanic Society of America)

500 QUEEN ca. 1512–1516, from figure of St. Catherine, choir stall (Zamora. Cathedral)

501 WOMAN 1529, from *Thus Go the Old Women in Santander* in Weiditz, Christoph. *Das Trachtenbuch. f*117 (Nürnberg. Germanisches Nationalmuseum)

Sash at waistline

502 LADY ca. 1489, from figure of Fortitude, tomb of Alvaro de Luna, by Master Sebastián (Toledo. Cathedral, Chapel of Santiago)

503 QUEEN 1519–1520, from effigy of Juana la Loca, queen of Spain, by Bartolomé Ordóñez (Granada. Royal Chapel)

504 QUEEN ca. 1531, from portrait of François I and Éléonore d'Autriche, French School (Hampton Court Palace)

Sash worn low

505 LADY ca. 1520–1530, from figure of saint in *Saint with Donors* (Madrid. Collection of Eduardo Lucas Moreno)

506 WOMAN OF SEVILLA 1529, from *In This Manner Women Go About . . . in Sevilla* in Weiditz, Christoph. *Das Trachtenbuch. f*60 (Nürnberg. Germanisches Nationalmuseum)

507 QUEEN 1539–1543, from figure of crowned saint, choir stall, by Felipe Vigarny (Toledo. Cathedral, Upper Choir)

508   1467–1481

509   ca. 1480

510   1507–1515

511   1482–1495

512   ca. 1490–1500

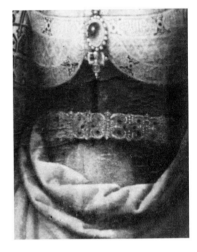

513   ca. 1530

514   ca. 1470–1475

515   1489–1493

516   ca. 1535

Belt

Leather belts were worn. Queen Isabel at a meeting with English ambassadors (1489) "was girt with a belt of white leather made in the fashion that men are accustomed to wear. Its pouch *(gibecière)* was garnished with a great balas ruby, large as a foil button, and set among five rich diamonds and other precious stones the size of a bean. The rest of the belt carried large precious stones in great number."[540]

In the available illustration of a woman's belt with pouches (Fig. 510), the latter hang from straps to about the knees, whereas men's purses were fastened to the belt or to short straps (Figs. 218–223). Evidently the Queen preferred a style that would keep her valuables near at hand. The Segovia inven-

tory (1503) describes leather belts *(cintos)* but fails to specify whether they were men's or women's. Of three of cowhide, one was embroidered with silks and two carried pouches *(esqueros)*. A "Vizcayan" of red leather, worked with colored silks, was adorned with silver-gilt motifs *(argentería)* and in the middle with the arms of Castilla and León. Another Vizcayan, lined with blue damask and embroidered all round with spun gold, carried the same arms, also in the middle.[541] A woman's belt that suggests the possibility of leather and buckles at front (Fig. 508) hugs the waistline; the long end hangs to above the ankles. Queen Isabel's short belt (Fig. 509) also buckles at front.

A fairly wide example, possibly of velvet (Fig. 511), is bordered with lines and figured through the middle with pseudo-Arabic characters. One of green velvet, narrower (Fig. 512), is embroidered with gold and set with jewels. Queen Isabel must have owned another belt, called *cinta de ceñir*, of old, green velvet, on which were mounted 15 large, round bosses *(tachones)* of chalcedony, every boss secured with 3 small nails of silver gilt, like little stars. Alternating with the bosses were ":Y:"'s in silver gilt, each set with a green stone and a red one of jasper.[542] Queen Juana had fabric belts ornamented with gold motifs, sometimes enameled. Of two in black velvet two fingers wide, one carried 33 little crosses, each with 2 pendent fleurs-de-lis or small carnations; the other carried 60 pieces, each of 3 little pillars and their arches. Two *ceti* belts were about three fingers wide: a crimson adorned with 60 pieces, bowknots and crosses of St. Andrew; a white with 50 M's and crosses.[543]

Salome's belt of gold, pearls, and rose-colored jewels (Figs. 316, 418) bears letters that appear to read "YCQEMV." A metallic one (Fig. 513), in which confronted C-scrolls set with red stones alternate with spindles, corresponds to the gold belts *(cintas de oro)* that were sent to Infanta María (1500) after she had become queen of Portugal. Each of hers was formed of a set of like pieces—57 square bosses, 97 Moorish spurs, 147 leaf clusters, or 166 open spheres—of 22-carat gold enameled in vermilion, white, green, brown, and black, and elaborated with small details such as bows, carnations, and tree trunks.[544] For one of Queen Juana's *cintas de oro* a buckle and an end *(cabo)* are mentioned, together with 16 principal pieces of gold and precious stones. Such belts have been described by Priscilla Muller with thorough attention to detail.[545]

Plain belt

508 LADY 1467–1481, from figure of St. Mary Magdalene, choir stall (León. Cathedral)

509 QUEEN ca. 1480, from figure of Isabel I, queen of Castilla and León, in sketch of retable for Church of San Juan de los Reyes, Toledo, by Juan Guas (Madrid. Museo del Prado)

510 WOMAN 1507–1515, from *Jesus and the Woman of Samaria*, choir stall, by Felipe Vigarny and others (Burgos. Cathedral)

Elaborate belt

511 ATTENDANT 1482–1495, from *Birth of the Virgin*, retable of Cardinal Mendoza, by the Luna Master (Guadalajara. Church of San Ginés)

512 ATTENDANT ca. 1490–1500, from *Birth of the Virgin*, main retable, by Pedro Berruguete (Paredes de Nava. Church of Santa Eulalia)

513 QUEEN ca. 1530, from figure of St. Catherine by Fernando Yáñez de la Almedina (Madrid. Museo del Prado)

Glove

514 QUEEN ca. 1470–1475, from figure of St. Helen, queen of Constantinople, in *Identification of the True Cross*, retable of the Holy Cross, by Pedro Berruguete (Paredes de Nava. Church of San Juan)

515 QUEEN 1489–1493, from effigy of Isabel de Portugal, queen of Castilla and León, by Gil de Siloe (Burgos. Monastery of Miraflores)

516 LADY ca. 1535, from figure of bystander in *Bullfight at Avila, 1534* (or *Valladolid, 1537*) by Jan Cornelisz Vermeyen (Madrid. Collection of Doña María Menéndez Pidal)

Glove

> . . . Germany . . . Champaigne,
> All that's worth nothing? We shall go to Spain,
> There we can surely satisfy our need.
> The leather's soft, the violet gives scent,
> Thus, madame, my very formidable friend,
> With Spanish leather I'll see that you are gloved.[546]

Spanish gloves were popular at home also. From 2 to 4 dozen pairs might be ordered at a time for a daughter of Queen Isabel. In 1490 her treasurer paid for 146 dozen in one lot for Princess Isabel, besides the expenses of a man sent to Ocaña (Toledo) to fetch them. They cost 1 real (31 maravedis) each pair or 10 reales the dozen. The Marchioness of El Cenete preferred those of Ocaña as being finer (más delgados) than others and once ordered 12 dozen for herself. Gloves de Perrillo, believed to keep hands white and smooth, were so popular that shops selling them occupied one whole side of the Plaza at Ocaña. On August 13th, 1506, the Marchioness of Mantua wrote to a friend at Rome: "I hear that a great quantity of Ocaña gloves, of which we are in need, have recently been brought from Spain." She asked the friend to get a Spaniard to inspect the gloves, because Spaniards could best judge their quality, and then to ship some by the earliest possible means. Later, in 1506, an abbot sent her from Rome fourteen pairs of Ocaña gloves.[547] Valencia and Ciudad Rodrigo also are cited as glove-making centers.

Of gloves described, Infanta Isabel (1488) had them in otter (nutria) lined with crimson cebtí and accompanied with silk ribbons. Marten tails made a pair for Queen Juana. A Barcelona glove maker who died in 1491 left 16 pairs of women's gloves, probably of leather, perforated (trepats) and garnished (cordats) with fringe of different colored silks. In the basement of his house was found a large assortment of skins, kid (cabrit) and calf (vedell) tanned and prepared.[548]

There are not many Spanish illustrations of women's gloves in our period. In the first example (Fig. 514) the seam of the thumb piece is quite visible; at the outer side the cuff runs to a point and ends in a tiny ball. In the gloves of an effigy (Fig. 515) rings are threaded over the fingers, which fit fairly well; glove-hand and cuff are loose. In the retable of Los Corporales, after 1492 (Daroca (Zaragoza). Colegiata, Museo), Queen Isabel has yellow-brown gloves with a pointed cuff carrying a small pendant;

her daughter's are gray tan. Such gloves, draping in easy folds about the wrist, are obviously of a single thickness there.

The next style includes a turnback cuff, giving a double or triple thickness at the wrist. Isabella d'Este (1506) describes Valencian gloves as "very strong (zaldi) inside and folded with the reverse outside", [549] probably making a cuff. A bystander at the bullfight obviously has adopted the straight stiff cuff (Fig. 516). Such gloves are better illustrated in the Moro portrait (1551) of María de Austria, the Empress's daughter (Madrid. Museo del Prado). The gray-brown hand is trimmed with a yellow cuff, which is slashed at the edge, forming small tabs. Following a style that Charles V had used twenty years earlier (Fig. 214), several fingers are slashed to admit rings with heavy settings. While an Italian portrait (ca. 1515) shows a lady's glove trimmed with but one row of fine slashes at the wrist, in German examples the cutting is extravagant. Cranach's Judiths have their glove fingers slashed at every knuckle, and the hand also across the back.

Gloves were included with the proper costume for a Valencian lady fleeing the plague:

> The gloves must be delicate
> And very little worn,
> Indeed oiled thoroughly
> And lastingly perfumed
> With exciting odors,
> You know, of balsamic resin
> With fragrant oil of balm.
> I believe, as I saw it there,
> They'll tell you of it in Valencia.[550]

The Empress liked her gloves to be yellow, and to keep her Majesty supplied with that color the wife of Prince Felipe's tutor wrote to her mother at Valencia: "The Empress wishes to try a recipe that she has for an oil that turns gloves yellow, and therefore she has told it to me in great secrecy, in order that I may beg your ladyship to have it made, [but] not to show it to anyone or to let anyone know what it is for. . . . I beg your ladyship to have it made by the recipe that accompanies this [letter] . . . and to make it in good quantity so that there may be some for me also. And be so kind as to send it the very soonest possible, for Her Majesty desires it urgently; since she spoke to me about it, she has asked two or three times whether I have written. . . .

"Recipe. . . . First they will have a quantity of oil of orange blossom, fresh and very good, and afterwards they will take of the yellow of rosebuds, of orange blossom, of white lily, and of the yellow of white musk-rose buds, and ox gall *(pedrafel)* if it is available. . . . All these things will be ground very thoroughly in a mortar, and afterwards they will be dissolved in the above-mentioned oil. When all has been well mixed, place it in a clean vessel on the fire and bring it to a boil; afterward, strain it through a fine cloth or a veil and squeeze it hard in order that all the virtue of the powders and their yellow may remain in the said oil as, the yellower it is, the better. If ox gall cannot be found, it doesn't matter much; make do with the other things."[551]

The Empress's accounts available here record only knit gloves *(de aguja):* two pairs of wool and white silk, assessed at two ducats for both—one pair with embroidery of red wool *(grana),* the other with a white insertion *(randa)* worked at the wrist. Two other pairs of wool and silk, all white, trimmed with a narrow insertion at the wrist and lined with white untwisted silk *(seda floja),* were valued at 1½ ducats together.[552]

Ladies' gloves, as everyone knows, served as favors in tournaments. When King Fernando and Queen Germana entered Valladolid (January 1509), they found two knights stationed at the city gate to beg a glove from each of the Queen's ladies, because three knights in her service wished to enter the lists against all who would appear.[553]

Point or lace

Ladies as well as gentlemen used laces or tagged points *(agujetas),* which frequently appeared on open sleeve edges and at the armscye (Figs. 450, 415). They also joined free skirt panels (Fig. 478), drew slashed edges together, closed the opening of a partlet (Fig. 388), or secured chopines (Fig. 543).

Quantities of ribbon were supplied to make points. The amount of 20 varas is frequently entered by Baeza; for Infanta Isabel alone (1488) seven "pieces" of ribbon were required at one time. A "piece" might contain 35, 40, 70, or even 80 varas. If the price for tagging points from a certain piece of ribbon is rated at one maravedi each point, and if the whole length of the ribbon is divided by the probable number of points tagged, a length of 13 or 14 inches is several times arrived at; sometimes it comes to 21 inches. Baeza records "wide" ribbons to be used for points in contrast with "narrow" for braiding. The entries are indefinite: "wide"

(1490), "wide in colors" (1490, 1493), "wide black" (1497, 1499). "Narrow ribbon" for points appears in 1493. The ribbon called *de medio listón* (1488, 1490) must have been half as wide as the *listón* which, according to the Academy dictionary, was narrower than the *colonia* of about 2 fingers' width.

Ribbons without aglets also were used as ties. In the long tubular sleeve of a saint (Fig. 520) the front edges are brought together—after the cascade of the chemise sleeve has been pushed aside—and tied with wide ribbons, each in one erect loop. The edges of a queen's slashed, gold-patterned dress sleeve are tied over a full, white chemise sleeve with rose-colored ribbons (Fig. 521), which are knotted without loops and hung at the ends with gold tassels. In another effigy sleeve (Fig. 522), sections are held together with narrow ribbons tied in a knot without loops.

Aglet

On points of this period the aglets *(cabos, clavos),* usually of gold, were short; those of a queen (Fig. 517) seem to measure about an inch in length. Round, twisted, set with small pearls, possibly enameled, they finish ties of generous width. Salome's gold aglets (Fig. 518), also round and short, are plain. Éléonore d'Autriche, even with a gorgeous dress, wears modest aglets on ties of cord (Fig. 519). Points did not need to match a dress. With green sleevelets Salome's ties are rose lavender. Jeweled pins or buttons might be used as a substitute (Fig. 393). In a later period (1551–1615) the aglet changed, becoming two or three times as large and much more elaborate. The very large examples illustrated in Figure 422 must have been taken from the copyist's own time.

The ladies of Queen Isabel's household used many aglets. Sixty-five for Infanta Isabel (1483) required 7,600 maravedis worth of gold and 62 maravedis for the making of each, bringing the cost of one aglet to 179. The charge for making 20 enameled pairs (1488) was 143 per pair. For tagging *(clavar)* points the price sometimes works out to one maravedi each—204 for tagging 17 dozen points (1487)—but it could be more or less—186 for 15 dozen (1484), 100 for 12 dozen (1488). For Infanta Isabel (1488) the price was 5 each in a set of 36.

In Queen Juana's inventory 577 aglets have been counted, all of gold, large or small, enameled, twisted, enameled and twisted, square, or split

517   1489–1493

518   ca. 1500

519   ca. 1530

520   ca. 1500–1515

521   ca. 1521

522   1525

(rajados). Fourteen of the last were on 7 gold cords *(torzales)*. A "small French coat" belonging to her carried 118 larger and smaller gold aglets, while another of black *ceti,* lined with white fur, had 46 at two slashes and 22 on the sleeves. Square gold aglets number 104 on a coat of black velvet lined with ermine.[554] The gold and red silk cords *(torzales)* tying slashes in Belisena's dress at Naples end in aglets made of pearls.[555]

The Empress's aglets are listed on 9 pages of her book of accounts, and there are 2 pages of missing aglets entered under Deficits. Small aglets *(cabitos)* were numerous, 3,000 being mentioned in one entry, 458 of them on white satin sleeves that had been sent to her sister-in-law, queen of Hungary. Each of the 3,000 was set with 3 seed pearls *(aljófar),* besides being fashioned with coronets *(coronetas)*

and finials *(remates)* of gold and 3 little gold settings *(engastecicos)* between the pearls, "so that each little aglet had 4 gold settings *(engastes)*." Gold roses brought by the Empress from Portugal and 1,230 ducats from the Spanish treasury had been used in making them. Many aglets were triangular in section, some round. They could be plain, garnished with filigree grains, or enameled rose pink *(rosicler)* and white, or black and white. Forty-four aglets, each set with a large baroque pearl and worth a ducat were among the missing. Over 100 had been used in chopines. Two pairs of those were enameled "in medium relief". The Empress gave 24 pairs, three-sided, plain, to Charles V's niece Kirstina. After Isabel's death, aglets of hers were sold: 100 plain ones to Juana Manuel, 88 triangular and twisted to the Countess of Chinchón.[556]

Tagged point

517 QUEEN 1489–1493, from mantle arm-opening on effigy of Isabel de Portugal, queen of Castilla and León, by Gil de Siloe (Burgos. Monastery of Miraflores)

518 PRINCESS ca. 1500, from sleevelet edge on figure of Salome in *The Beheading of St. John the Baptist*, Hispano-Flemish School (Madrid. Museo del Prado)

519 QUEEN ca. 1530, from sleeve panes in portrait of Éléonore d'Autriche, queen of France (Chantilly. Musée Condé)

Untagged lace

520 QUEEN ca. 1500–1515, from overdress sleeve on figure of St. Catherine, tomb of the Duchess of Alburquerque (The Hispanic Society of America)

521 QUEEN ca. 1521, from dress sleeve on statue of Isabel I, queen of Castilla and Aragón, by Felipe Vigarny (Granada. Royal Chapel, Museo)

522 MARCHIONESS 1525, from dress sleeve on effigy of Leonor Manrique de Castro, marchioness of Ayamonte, by Antonio Maria Aprile and others (Santiago de Compostela. Church of San Lorenzo)

Footgear

TALAVERA RECOUNTS types of ladies' footgear in one accusing breath: footed hose *(calzas con pies)*, slippers or pumps *(servillas)*, gaiters *(avampiés)*, buskins *(borceguíes)*, shoes *(zapatos)*, cork-soled shoes *(alcorques)*, sabots *(zuecos)*—each could contribute to sinful female indulgence. In another breath he names boots *(botas)*, mules *(chinelas)*, overshoes *(galochas)*, and later, on a rising note of tension, chopines *(chapines)*.[557] Whatever their type, he knew them all, though in public they must generally have been inconspicuous. Women's skirts were so long that painters and sculptors tended to ignore all but shoe toes, swallowing up the rest in a mass of folds.

Hose

There is plenty of documentary evidence about women's footgear. Hose were of concern even to a lady fleeing from the plague:

Of the hose I will not speak
Because of their hidden place,

But their quality is such
They do not fail to match
All that has gone before.[558]

Those for Queen Isabel's household were cut from *grana* or red grogram *(cordellate)* or from holland. For her eldest daughter at sixteen (1486), ⅞ vara of *grana* made two pairs of hose, while 1½ varas of holland apparently made one pair. Red hose and also white are illustrated in Torre's *Vision delectable* (1477), mauve or pumpkin yellow in Berruguete's *Birth of the Virgin* (1490). The Empress's inventory (1539) mentions hose knitted *(de aguja)* of red wool *(grana)* with embroidered designs, clocks evidently, at the middle or with frills *(lechuguillas)* at the top, as well as of black silk with stripes of gold worked from top to bottom. Her hose of holland were quilted with cotton *(acolchadas)*.[559] In this period changes can be observed, from long hose *(calzas largas)* of rose-red London cloth for one of Princess Isabel's attendants (1490) to stockings *(medias calzas)* of blue and white silk for the Empress (1529–1538), and from seamed cloth to elastic knitting.

Slipper

The slipper name *servilla* Covarrubias derives from the word for "female servant" *(sierva)*, a slipper being "light for those who have to run from here to there". In 1599 *xervilla* was defined as "pumpe or pinsen to were in pantofles"; another slipper *(zapatilla)* is mentioned (1524–1527) as being worn with *galochas*.[560] Under Queen Isabel, not servants but her daughters received *servillas*. Oliver Asín relates them to the Arabic *šarbīl*, " 'a somewhat closed slipper of fine leather and very thin sole' "; for this type at Sevilla an insole is included.[561] The Segovian inventory (1503) mentions *servillas* of *grana*; Queen Juana had them of leather. It is possible that one appears inside a chopine on a royal effigy (Fig. 523): rows of dots running over the toe suggest a slipper of tooled leather. Husbands at the turn of the century presented *servillas* and chopines to their wives; with the same types a friar rewarded his night's companion, daughter of a sacristan. Moriscas of the 1560's wore them matched in color and fabric, of green or mulberry velvet, of velvet and goatskin.[562]

Weiditz, one of the few artists of the period to record the whole foot, has a Valencian lady walking in pumps (Fig. 524). Brown and slashed over the toes, they were probably of leather which would

523   1489–1493

524   1529

525   1507–1510

526   1477

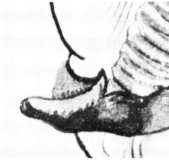

527   1529

528   1530–1550

529   ca. 1500–1510

530   1524

531   1529

532   ca. 1474–1477

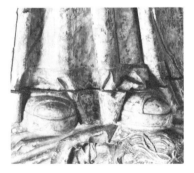

533   ca. 1499

534   1529

bear such slashes. They meet the ground with a flat sole, without even a heel piece to raise the foot.

Slipper, Sandal

523 QUEEN—SLIPPER AND CHOPINE 1489–1493, from effigy of Isabel de Portugal, queen of Castilla and León, by Gil de Siloe (Burgos. Monastery of Miraflores)

524 WOMAN—PUMPS 1529, from *Thus Women in the Kingdom of Valencia Go Walking in the Streets* in Weiditz, Christoph. *Das Trachtenbuch.* f109 (Nürnberg. Germanisches Nationalmuseum)

525 ATTENDANT—SANDALS 1507–1510, from *Purification of the Virgin,* main-retable shutter, inner side, by Fernando de Llanos (Valencia. Cathedral)

Shoe

526 LADY—SHOES AND MULES 1477, from figure of Arithmetic in Torre, Alfonso de la. *Vision delectable.* v°f12 (Paris. Bibliothèque Nationale)

527 MOORISH WOMAN—SHOE 1529, from *Thus a Morisca in Granada Travels with Husband and Child across Country* in Weiditz, Christoph. *Das Trachtenbuch.* f106 (Nürnberg. Germanisches Nationalmuseum)

528 LADY—SHOE 1530–1550 (Barcelona. Museo de Indumentaria, Rocamora Collection)

Mule

529 LADY—MULE ca. 1500–1510, from figure of Saint in *Martyrdom of St. Margaret,* retable of St. Margaret, by the Paredes Master (Paredes de Nava. Church of Santa Eulalia)

530 LADY—MULE AND SHOE 1524, from figure of St. Mary Magdalene in *The Crucifixion,* retable of St. Vincent, by León Picardo (Burgos. Cathedral, Museo Diocesano)

531 WOMAN—THICK-SOLED MULES OR RUDE CHOPINES 1529, from *Thus in Galicia Women Go to the Spinners' House and to the Field* in Weiditz, Christoph. *Das Trachtenbuch.* f18 (Nürnberg. Germanisches Nationalmuseum)

Pantofle

532 LADY—GILDED SURROUND ca. 1474–1477, from figure of St. Engracia by Bartolomé Bermejo (Boston. Isabella Stewart Gardner Museum)

533 LADY—REINFORCED SURROUND ca. 1499, from effigy of María de Perea from Ocaña (London. Victoria & Albert Museum)

534 MOORISH GIRL—WIDE INSTEP BAND 1529, from *In This Manner Morisca Maidens Are Dressed in the House* in Weiditz, Christoph. *Das Trachtenbuch.* f103 (Nürnberg. Germanisches Nationalmuseum)

Buskin

In equal numbers with *servillas,* buskins often were supplied to ladies of the court. Infanta Isabel had both to walk the Stations of the Cross (1484). Women's buskins probably looked much like men's (Figs. 192–194). They could be wide, or narrow pinching the feet, of a thousand colors, with or without bands (Talavera); they could be soled with goatskin, lined with cloth or fur; be 1/3 vara high (1552). Cordovan (goatskin) made the best buskins, but sheepskin would do for women.

Sandal

The sandal, not mentioned by Talavera, appears occasionally in illustrations. At Valencia scenes of the life of the Virgin show it worn by attendants. In one pair (Fig. 525) narrow straps run back and forth across the foot from loops at the sole edges, while down the instep lies a broader piece which narrows abruptly to pass between two toes. Another pair is gilded. Red sandals are worn by a Muslim woman in number X of the Tunis tapestry series designed by Vermeyen (Madrid. Royal Palace).

Shoe

Talavera gives considerable space to shoes *(zapatos),* which generally were of leather—deerskin, chamois, cowhide, goatskin, sheepskin. They could be of deerskin and white, or be of various colors; have very long points or be blunt-toed *(romos);* be closed or open; be worn with or without overshoes *(galochas)* or cork-soled *alcorques.* They could be fastened with a cord *(de cuerda),* be with or without buckles *(puertas),*[563] be trimmed with gold or silk passementerie *(caireles),* be embroidered in silk, carry one or many bows. In Queen Isabel's household shoes were given to slaves (1485), to Moorish women (1488), to the Infantas (1486, 1491). The Segovia inventory (1503) lists shoes in black, white, or yellow. For Queen Juana only one pair is recorded and that old, of velvet trimmed with silver gilt *(argentería).* Documents give little clue as to distinctions between men's and women's shoes. They were sized in points *(puntos),* 4 and below for children, about 6 or 7 for women (1552). Shoes must have been fragile, or the Infantas walked a great deal; María and Catalina each (1496) were provided monthly with 4 pairs of shoes and 3 pairs of buskins.

Worn with vermilion hose, white shoes reaching almost to the ankle (Fig. 526) show one seam at the side with perhaps additional stitching over the instep. This type continued into the sixteenth century. Moorish footgear was visible, skirts being of calf length and hose coming to an end above the ankle. A Moorish shoe (Fig. 527) is rendered in brown with horizontally pleated blue hose. Navagero says that at Granada (1526) Moorish women used "on the feet not pantofles but *escarpines* small and fitted".[564] *Escarpines* is Fabié's translation (1879) of *scarpe, scarpa* being the general word for "shoe" in Italian. On the basis of Weiditz's drawings, a better term might have been *zapatos*. Percyvall (1599) calls the *escarpín* both "a kind of socke and a pumpe".

St. Mary Magdalene wears a shoe slashed in the quarter (Fig. 530). There exists an actual shoe of black goatskin (Fig. 528) cut at the toe in short, staggered slashes. The sole measures 18.7 cm., which is little more than the 18.5 cm. of a chopine insole (Fig. 546). The seam joining quarter and vamp is partly covered with a broadening strap, in which a buttonhole is cut to receive a square knot of leather thong. Under the heel two pieces of leather have been added, one between sole and quarter, one underneath the sole. The term for these pieces would be *taco* or *tacón,* which originally signified "mending piece for a shoe sole" and ultimately came to mean "heel". But that was after our period.

Mule

With soles of only moderate thickness, the yellow overshoes in Figure 526 can hardly be *alcorques* which required at least two layers in the sole, one of cork and another of leather to surround and contain the cork. They can hardly be *galochas,* which are defined as having soles of wood with leather instep bands *(empeines)* and which appear as early as 1397.[565] They seem more like mules *(chinelas)* which were soled, not with cork, but with two or three layers of leather and were easy to slip on and off. One example (Fig. 529) has an open-toed vamp and another (Fig. 530) a band over the instep. I have found no mention of *chinelas* in Baeza's accounts, but the term does appear in Palencia (1490).[566]

A Gallegan woman wears a pair of thick-soled mules or rude chopines (Fig. 531) suitable for a

muddy road. The shoes are red, and the soles are shaped with almost straight sides instead of being slanted like those of the luxurious chopine.

Boot

Inside the overshoes the woman may be wearing boots, of which I have found no other possible illustration. Covarrubias says that the woman's boot was called *botín.* Women's *botines* of red and white leather were recorded at Segovia (1503). A Granada ordinance (1523) mentions for women little boots *(botinicos)* of cordovan with tongue of cordovan or calfskin, certainly not of sheepskin. At Sevilla (1525) the *botinico* had an insole, and *botines* of cordovan could be of all colors; they could not be of sheepskin unless they were black, the skin dressed with tallow. Queen Juana had 2 pairs of *botines* and 15 *botinicos,* 4 of the latter black.[567]

Pantofle

The popular pantofle *(pantuflo)* was built on a cork platform. Associated with ladies, it does not appear in Baeza's records, but it is included in Queen Juana's inventory—12 pairs from Valencia and an old pair of black leather. At Granada (1523) pantofles could be "half or whole" *(medio o entero).* With outer parts of goatskin, they should have the insole cut from calfskin and unlined, or from goatskin and lined, but not with paper. Customers (1524) who brought to the maker their own material—velvet, silk, or leather—could have it cut in their presence. The Empress had pantofles of velvet, black, crimson, or mulberry-colored, the latter lined with *grana.* She had also six pairs from Valencia.[568]

At Zaragoza (1553) women's *pantuflas* could be "closed and low-cut" *(cerradas y escotadas).* Of goatskin, black or in colors, they were made 2 to 3 fingers high and of any length required for a price of 5 *sueldos* (90 maravedis). Five fingers high, they cost 7 *sueldos* and 6 *dineros* (132 maravedis). Farm women were expected to afford them brocaded and 3 fingers high for 7 *sueldos.*[569]

A pantofle containing probably a single layer of cork is illustrated in our period. Saint Engracia wears one (Fig. 532) in which the gilded surround bears Roman letters, R F M - N O V, in dark brown; the instep strap and its buckle also are gilded. For Queen Isabel in her intarsia portrait at Plasencia Cathedral (Fig. 565), similar buckled footgear is indicated. An effigy shows pantofles (Fig.

533) secured with a band over the instep, the sole reinforced with a layer that rises to a point at the front. A Moorish girl wears over bare feet pantofles (Fig. 534) with a sole of cork and a thinner, outer sole of yellow leather; the black vamp band carries yellow, pinked edges.

Chopine

For the chopine *(chapín),* "shoe of important women",[570] there is a wealth of illustration. Actual examples exist. Furthermore, the high cork sole lifted a skirt hem above the floor, and painters could see the shoe. It was worn over a slipper out of doors. With difficulty one envisions this impractical, luxurious shoe coping with the muddy or rutted streets of its time. Chopines generally made women take short, difficult steps. A great lady at Barcelona, as she treads her "prisoner's pace",[571] is helped along by a male escort (Fig. 307). In another scene (Fig. 552), the wearer of cream-colored chopines has a man for support at each side. But a chopined spinner (Fig. 550) is presented as swinging along in a tremendous stride, an uninhibited example that would seem to be the mischievous exception proving the rule. Arrived at church, a lady would take off her chopines before sitting down to hear a sermon. Lying empty on the church floor (Fig. 543), they recall a sixteenth-century poem:

When women are come to pray
Or to chant the morning hymns,
Their chopines frequently
Go flying off and stray
Into the choir.[572]

Examples of the chopine, imperfect but probably the earliest in existence, have been recovered from piles of rubbish under a stair at the Alhambra. With the benevolent cooperation of Señor Don Jesús Bermúdez Pareja, curator of the Museo Nacional de Arte Hispanomusulmán, five fragments of cork could be matched into one platform. In the principal fragment (Fig. 535) four corks varying in thickness had been fitted together and pegged firmly with sharp-pointed pieces of cane. There must originally have been a fifth layer, for one cane protrudes. The usual tendency of a platform was to widen at the sides, narrow toward the ends, rise toward the heel, and diminish from top to bottom. Such a platform would be covered with leather, frequently goatskin. The outsole was flat and oval (Fig. 547), in contrast with the waisted sole of Italian chopines.

A leather cover that had lost its corks and its outsole consisted of four pieces: insole, side or surround, and two vamp sections. In its making, the vamp sections would be interlined, lined, finished along the upper edge with overhand stitching, and pierced with holes for lacing. Surround and vamp sections would be laid against the insole and sewn to it with coarse fiber thread, linen or hemp, in stitches perhaps ½ cm. long, after which the surround could be turned right side out and slipped over the cork platform. Surround ends were not sewn but lapped, the seam being placed sometimes at the shoe front, as on the effigy of Queen Juana at Granada. In another fragment with only one vamp section remaining, the outsole had been cut large enough to allow the lower edge, folded in, to be turned up for a centimeter all round. This edge, somehow shrunk to fit smoothly, was sewn to the surround with fiber cord in blind stitches about 1.5 cm. long.

In a chopine retaining its corks but lacking the outsole (Figs. 536, 537), the insole showed 2 layers of leather. Surround and vamp sections were of goatskin lined throughout with coarse canvas. Further interlined with 6 layers of thin paper and one of leather, the vamp sections had as inner lining another layer, possibly sheepskin. The outer goatskin had been drawn over the top edge, which was about ½ cm. thick, to meet the inner lining and was there sewn overhand with stout fiber thread. Each vamp section was pierced with two rows of 6 holes, but the unagleted lace—intricately braided cord of gray-tan linen or hemp covered with interlaced threads of crimson silk—had not been run through the outer rows of holes. In actual use the lace probably went first down an outer corner hole, came up through the next inner hole, crossed the instep gap and went down the corresponding inner hole on the other side, came up again through another corner hole and then, making a right-angled turn, went down the next outer hole and so on, through all 24 holes. When the lacing was complete, the two ends would be left in the same outer row, as in the chopines taken off by a lady seated in church (Fig. 543). Her laces are finished with aglets.

Decoration of the chopine, blind tooling with touches of black and gilt (Figs. 536, 537), may offer a clue as to its date. The ancient guilloche design, outlined with dots and toned black around gilt centers, runs midway down the length of the insole and also lies near the upper edge of the surround. Below the surround guilloche is a plain gilt band

535   ca. 1500

536   ca. 1500

537   ca. 1500

538   ca. 1500

539   1200–1250

540   ca. 1470–1475

541   ca. 1500

542   1529

543   ca. 1520

544   ca. 1550

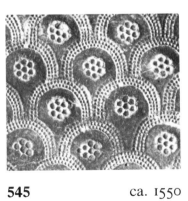

545   ca. 1550

but faintly visible in the photograph,[573] and below the band, in a design of black with gilt edges, long leaves spread gracefully at each side of a crouching animal (Fig. 538). At one end, leaves curve over a motif like a stoppered flask overbent with lobed leaves. Outlined with small dots, the designs are reserved against a background of dots and circles. On the vamps appear several rows of triangles of dots, two black bands, and a few black dashes with rounded ends.

Associated with the Alhambra, this chopine may be expected to show Hispano-Moresque influence. Similar tooling in dots and circles is found in a bookbinding of about 1480–1490 assigned to that style.[574] In this binding, and in another covering a manuscript of 1474, such work occurs in borders, not in backgrounds. The motif above the animal could be a stylization of the bird that hovers over crouching hare or running dog in fifteenth-century Mudejar tiles. The flask-like ornament seems related to a foliated pine-cone design in a Hispano-Moresque textile of the thirteenth century (Fig. 539). Though these comparisons weight the evidence toward a fifteenth-century date for the Alhambra chopine, it might be wise to leave it where Oliver Asín has placed it—"perhaps of the fifteenth century, if it is not of the sixteenth".[575]

Besides leather and metals, fabrics were used for chopine vamps and surrounds. For this purpose Baeza seems never to have bought sheepskin or goatskin, which doubtless was provided by the shoemaker, but often paid for velvet, a half vara for each pair of chopines. Black was the most popular, crimson next, and then green, mulberry-colored, and blue. Of silks, satin and *cebtí* were used. Other items furnished were buckles and aglets, *caireles,* braids, gold thread, sole leather, and cork. Five and one-half ounces of silver-gilt ornaments as well as gold and silver embroidery thread were allowed for 2 pairs of velvet chopines, a black and a crimson, for Infanta Isabel (1487). The year of her wedding (1490) she had 2 *cebtí*-covered pairs, a green and a mulberry-colored, embroidered with drawn-gold thread to the weight of about 23 ounces, at a cost, including labor, of 17,860 maravedis, more than three quarters the price of a team of mules.

For Queen Juana about 70 pairs of chopines were kept in her wardrobe. Velvet was her favorite covering in mulberry color, green, crimson, or tawny. Pairs in brown or blue *ceti* also are listed. Trimmings include silver-gilt ornaments and bugles of gold and silver or of gold only.

Among the chopines of the Empress Isabel were silvered shoes from Valencia, but in others not specifically from that city the material was velvet—mulberry-colored, white, tawny, crimson, or green—and the usual trimming was gold bugles with silver sometimes added. In comparison with the almost 24 ducats (8,930 maravedis) spent on a pair for Princess Isabel (1490), the highest price paid for the Empress's chopines was 7 ducats. One such pair of tawny velvet worked with gold bugles had bows of silver at the middle *(entremedias).* Another

Chopine parts

535 LADY—CORK FRAGMENTS ca. 1500 (Granada. Museo Nacional de Arte Hispanomusulmán, Alhambra)

536, 537 LADY—LEATHER COVER, SIDE and TOP ca. 1500 (Granada. Museo Nacional de Arte Hispanomusulmán, Alhambra)

Chopine ornament

538 LADY—SURROUND DESIGN ca. 1500, from drawing by Manuel Ocaña, *Planos de la Alhambra,* no. 82 (Granada. Museo Nacional de Arte Hispanomusulmán, Alhambra)

539 FOLIATED PINE-CONE DESIGN 1200–1250, from Hispano-Moresque textile of gold and silk (Burgos. Museo de Telas Ricas)

Chopine cover

540 QUEEN—LETTERED SURROUND ca. 1470–1475, from figure of Saint in *St. Helen Forcing Judas to Reveal the Hiding Place of the Cross,* retable of the Holy Cross, by Pedro Berruguete (Paredes de Nava. Church of San Juan)

541 PRINCESS—JEWELED SURROUND ca. 1500, from figure of Salome in *The Beheading of St. John the Baptist,* Hispano-Flemish School (Madrid. Museo del Prado)

542 WOMAN—PAINTED SURROUND 1529, from *In This Manner Women in the Kingdom of Castilla Go about the Streets and to Church* in Weiditz, Christoph. *Das Trachtenbuch.* f23 (Nürnberg. Germanisches Nationalmuseum)

Chopine details

543 LADY—AGLETED LACES ca. 1520, from figure of listener in *St. Felix Preaching,* retable of St. Felix, by Joan de Burgunya (Gerona. Church of San Félix, Sala de Museo)

544, 545 LADY—CHOPINE OF LEATHER TOOLED WITH IMBRICATED DESIGN and DETAIL OF DESIGN ca. 1550 (Barcelona. Museo de Indumentaria, Rocamora Collection)

546   ca. 1550

547   ca. 1550

548   ca. 1550

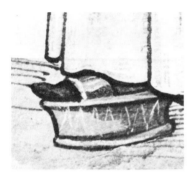

549   1529

550   ca. 1570

551   ca. 1515–1525

552   1535

was covered at the ends with crimson velvet; in the middle, embroidery of spun gold on crimson velvet was applied over white satin. At the sale of the Empress's effects after her death (1539), chopines were purchased by the Count of Olivares and by one of the Portocarreros,[576] great personages of Spain.

Chopines could be even more richly adorned. A pair of the 1470's (Fig. 540) are as bright as the gown brocade, which must have been of gold. Surround ends are laced together over the heel of the platform, and the sides bear an inscription in Roman letters, M . . . , C V E. The Duchess of Alburquerque (1479) left a pair of crimson satin chopines with vamp sections wrought of silver-gilt filigree, each bearing 7 enameled clubs (bastones), perhaps the same knotty stock that appeared on playing cards. The front (delantera), also of filigree, carried 8 enamels.[577] In a chopine worn by Salome as she receives the head of John the Baptist (Fig. 541) the surround, bright with gold, is adorned with large pearls set about a green or a rose-colored stone. The open-toed vamp also is luminous with gems and pearls. For the silver chopines made at Sevilla, makers were warned not to use tin plate or any other base metal in vamp sections or insoles.[578]

The chopines of a Castilian lady (Fig. 542) probably were painted. Her platform surrounds are divided with narrow gilt bands into four zones, in which rows of triangles, gray, crimson, or white, alternate with rows of circles, gray or white. Similar decoration appeared in Cataluña. With black slippers a Barcelona lady's chopine vamp bands are crimson (Fig. 307), while three horizontal crimson bands separate rows of black circles and zigzags on a beige surround; the circles suggest the tacks that sometimes were set in decorative patterns on this shoe. The maids' chopines have crimson vamp bands and insole with beige surround carrying brown zigzags and outsole. At Valencia, if a chopine was painted, whatever the color, it had to be varnished. The custom of painting saints' pictures on chopine surrounds was not encouraged by Valencian authorities.

Rich adornment continued for a long time. In Calderón's play, El conde Lucanor (1615), the Duchess of Tuscany drops off on stage a chopine made with gold welt (virilla) and diamond-headed nails. The Count's servant wishes to sell the glittering bauble, but Lucanor has it returned to the Duchess with his portrait painted on the outsole,[579] an inviting oval with its smooth, flat surface, as can be seen in Figure 547.

Parts of a chopine are named in a Valencian document of 1389 copied in 1563: lespicio, "now called capellada" (vamp piece); plantelles (insoles; in 1523 at Granada the insole was called palmilla); taloneres (heel or back pieces); and brāques, which could have meant "surrounds". The obvious equivalent of the last term is "branches", but its appearance here may be owed ultimately to the Basque word branka (ship's prow), such a shape being not unrelated to that of the chopine. Revisions of the document, recorded in 1563, identify soles (outsoles), rebatuts (overhand seams), cohes de capellades (ends or tails of vamp pieces), gires (welts).[580]

Sevillian ordinances published in 1527 mention two types of chopine, open and closed. The "open", which was fraudulently called chinela, had but one capellada (vamp piece),[581] perhaps the single band set well back across the instep. A Valencian lady (Fig. 549) has such a band in vermilion touched with gold securing a vermilion chopine zigzagged with gold; it is worn over black slippers. The swinging spinner (Fig. 550) has stout red bands to secure brown chopines over black shoes and gray hose.

Plural vamp pieces (capelladas) of the "closed" shoe suggest two sections laced together as in the early example (Figs. 536, 537). In a later shoe with four holes in a row (Fig. 544), the ribbon lace ends

---

Chopine with closed uppers

546, 547 LADY—TOOLED AND PAINTED CHOPINE and ITS OUTER SOLE ca. 1550 (Solsona. Museo Diocesano)

548 LADY—CHOPINES BANDED WITH LEAD ca. 1550 (Solsona. Museo Diocesano)

Chopine with open upper

549 NOBLEWOMAN 1529, from In This Manner Noblewomen in Valencia Go to Church When It Is Hot in Weiditz, Christoph. Das Trachtenbuch. f89 (Nürnberg. Germanisches Nationalmuseum)

550 SPINNER ca. 1570, from figure of woman of Villarreal in Album Ob II, f28 (Paris. Bibliothèque Nationale, Cabinet des Estampes)

Chopine wearer

551 DUCHESS ca. 1515–1525, from effigy of Francisca Manrique de Lara, duchess of Cardona (Cardona. Castle, Church)

552 CAMP FOLLOWER 1535, from The Army Re-embarking at La Goleta, cartoon for tapestry XII in the Conquest of Tunis series designed by Jan Cornelisz Vermeyen (Wien. Kunsthistorisches Museum)

are drawn out at two outer corner holes and tied in a bow that lies parallel to the instep opening. In this handsome chopine of brown ungilded, uncolored goatskin, the surround, insole, and vamp sections are decorated with a tooled imbricate pattern (Fig. 545) of small dots enriched with larger dots and circles. The surround ends lap at front.

In another example (Fig. 546) the vamp pieces appear to be lined with cowhide. The front lapping of the surround ends is secured with a nail. On each side, the tooling consists of a line of dot-triangles above a design of leafy scrolls, flowers, and a vase, outlined with small dots and reserved against a background of dots and circles. Once the chopine carried a metal band; in the space formerly protected, there is color, still bright. The design seems to have been covered in gold leaf and painted with red glaze, which retains an enamel-like quality. Motif edges are defined with white, and a wavy line of white makes a narrow border low on the surround. The turned-up rim of the outsole (Fig. 547) fits so smoothly and firmly that it must have been glued; no stitches to the surround could be detected. Chopine makers at Valencia used starch as an adhesive, possibly made of rice as it is contrasted with the bookbinders' paste of fine-sifted wheaten flour. Sevillian ordinances (1524) required that outsoles be of calfskin or cowhide.[582]

Two chopines (Fig. 548), apparently made on the same last to be worn interchangeably, still are bound with leaden bands secured with nails also of lead, which does not rust. Other metals are mentioned in an old dictionary, where the chopine is described as "bound about with Tin, thin Iron, or Silver".[583] The insole length of these chopines, 18.5 cm., would seem too short even for the small foot of a Spanish lady, and a wearer's toes must often have overhung the cork platform (Figs. 549, 550).

The chopines in Figures 546–548 entered the Museo Diocesano at Solsona from the collection of a priest who had obtained them at nearby Cardona over a century ago. In her recumbent effigy (Fig. 551) the wife of the second duke of Cardona has her feet covered with a long skirt, but through the fabric can be detected the forms of tall, straight-fronted shoes, each resting on the back of a small dog. Francisca Manrique de Lara was married in 1498; her husband, Fernando Folch de Cardona, succeeded to the title in 1513 and died in 1543. It seems likely that the Solsona chopines existed in Duchess Francisca's time.

The height of chopines depended on the layers of cork that could be pegged together. Writing in 1438, the Archpriest of Talavera, who had visited Valencia in the previous decade, noted the height as about a *jeme* (13.5 cm.). Fernando de Talavera, forty years later, found that chopines could be "an elbow length tall". Hardly enough cork existed, he complained, to satisfy the demand.[584] Daughters of Talavera's Queen kept the height modest. Of chopines received from Valencia for Infantas María and Catalina (1497), six pairs were a hand high, another six but 3 fingers high. Envoys sent by that ardent widower, Henry VII of England, to measure the charms of the young Neapolitan, Juana de Aragón, managed at Valencia (1505) to see her chopines and found them 6 fingers wide and a foot high.[585] Covarrubias agrees with Talavera that chopines could add an elbow length to a woman's height, which would seem an impossible dimension did there not exist an actual example from sixteenth-century Venice—with a platform of wood instead of cork—measuring 49 cm. (Paris. Musée de Cluny). A commentator on Talavera's outcry reports (1638) that the number of cork layers had reached 24; how they were pegged together is not stated. He confesses that he would rather watch ladies atop their chopines than men on very high stilts and marvels at the ease with which chopine wearers went up and down steps.[586] It is no wonder that a satirical phrase developed, *ponerse en chapines* (to raise oneself above one's condition).[587]

Though the kingdom of Valencia is not listed as one of the major cork-producing regions, the capital city was long famous for its platform shoes (*tapins* in Valencian). A sixteenth-century writer who saw the world in the dress of a Spanish lady found the West Indies in her pearls and corals, Milan in the gold of her trimmings, and Valencia in her chopines.[588] Dozens of pairs made in that city were procured for Queen Isabel's daughters. The captive Juana had 37 pairs so identified in her hoard, and 25 are listed for the Empress. In the documents available no textiles are associated with these shoes; if a material is mentioned, it is gold or silver, which leads one to assume that Valencian chopines must generally have been made of gold- or silver-leafed leather. In the Naples of Alfonso V, Valencia was known for the gilded leather of its shoes.[589] "Ever since the craft was established [at Valencia] only goatskin could be gilded, and no chopine maker, secretly or openly, could make gilded chopines or cause them to be made of anything but metal-leafed goatskin. Also, only good hide from a steer flank was suitable for soles. And let no chopine maker presume to put in old corks, or even to have old corks in his house."[590]

Oliver Asín with his emphasis on the Hispano-Roman and the Hispano-Arabic industries of cork-shoe making, and Carmen Bernis, with the statement that chopines were known in Spain in the fourteenth century (her earliest Italian reference is from 1494), would seem to have disposed of the popular notion that cork-platform shoes were introduced from Venice. Corominas also stresses the native character of the Hispanic chopine, thanks to the abundance of cork in the Iberian Peninsula.[591]

Outer Garments

Mantle

The outer garment of simplest cut was the mantle *(manto)*, a long, sleeveless cloak open at center front, which goes back to the Iberians. Nearer our period is a description dated 1467 and a corresponding effigy (Fig. 553). The sculptor's contract reads, "a long mantle that drags on the floor . . . to be closed with a rich brooch *(firmale)* on the breast"; the painter's instruction prescribes, "the mantle black".[592] The paint is gone, but the effigy mantle remains, softly pleated into a narrow band at the rather low neckline and fastened with a brooch at center front. The right side is slit for the arm to pass through, but there is no visible opening for the left arm, which hugs the drapery caught up under it. Behind the knees the mantle-foot lies on the floor. The style with one arm-slit *(manera)* continues for fifty years, the latest illustration I have found (Fig. 555) dating from 1512–1516. The *capa* so popular with men counted for much less with women, while the *manto* for men, according to Bernis, was almost exclusively an item of ceremonial apparel.[593]

All classes of women wore the *manto*, combined often with a habit. In 1479 a bridegroom was permitted to give his bride a *brial*, a coat, and a mantle.[594] A woman on horseback in tapestry XII of the Tunis series (Madrid. Royal Palace) is well wrapped in her mantle. Baeza provided mantle material for nurses of the Bragança princes (1483, 1484) and for

a servant of Prince Juan's nurse (1490). The little Infantas had mantles for Holy Week (1486, 1487), and with such garments they mourned their Portuguese brother-in-law (1491). Queen Isabel (1500) gave the Countess of Cabra cloth for a mantle, a gift or part of a gift that was made to her yearly. Mantle material was generally woolen, *paño* or *contray,* and the amount 3½ to 5 varas. The hue, when mentioned, is black, except that Infanta Isabel (1489) had one of tawny color. In a group of donors (Burgos. Church of San Gil) the mother and the married daughter wear black mantles, while two other daughters appear in crimson dresses. Margarita de Austria going home as a widow (1499) took along mantles of black twill *(sarga),* probably of narrow width and therefore silk as 14 to 16 varas were required for each one.

The silk garment could show rich color. Three ladies in the Duke of Cardona's family (1503) wore mantles of crimson satin lined with ermine when they met Phelipe el Hermoso.[595] Of the three mantles of Venetian satin or damask (9 varas each) that Isabel de Aragón had as a bride (1515) only one was black; the others were mulberry crimson *(morado carmesí).*[596]

The most gorgeous mantle represented appears on the effigy of Queen Isabel's mother (Fig. 554). Over a fabric apparently enriched with seed pearls, quatrefoils in relief (Fig. 556) are raised still higher with a twisted cord along the edge. At the center of each quatrefoil is a four-petaled figure, probably representing hammered gold, with a pearl at each petal point. Other raised edges and their cords intersect forming an octagon, within which a five-petaled rose is set over ten sharply triangular points radiating from the center; rose and points also suggest gold. Numberless pearls follow the lines of the cords. In the border (Fig. 557), a background of narrow strips, possibly of gold in the woven original, carries a design of raised, confronted scrolls alternated with quatrefoils, each of which includes pearls and a square jewel in a four-petaled setting. With all this elaboration the sculptor felt that the fabric was still pliable enough to be rendered in narrow folds. For the same Queen's kneeling statue the artist suggests, over the mantle surface, a raised grill-work of star design (Fig. 558) with a jeweled ornament in each enclosed space. In contrast with these garments, Queen Juana's and Empress Isabel's mantles—each left three—were not deemed important enough to describe.

553   1467–1477   **554**   1489–1493   **555**   ca. 1512–1516

556   1489–1493   **557**   1489–1493   **558**   1496–1499

559   ca. 1474–1477   **560**   ca. 1500–1515   **561**   ca. 1528

The most that other illustrated mantles achieve is a worked border (Fig. 559). That of the Duchess of Alburquerque (Fig. 560) suggests raised embroidery of running leaf-scrolls, each centered on a five-petaled flower, which is worked over a band of narrow strips woven diagonally in an overall effect of tiny lozenges. The band is edged on one side with diagonal stitches made with wider strips. In the garment being copied, these strips could have been of gold. On Queen Isabel's mantle at Granada, a painted border (Fig. 561) suggests embroidery of confronted C-scrolls enclosing a sort of anthemion, which appears also on the *prie-dieu* cushion. The mantle itself is painted gold with a lining of rose-red, and the border design is reserved in gold on blue or black. In documents the trim recorded is an edge-strip of black velvet.

Covarrubias says definitely that it was with the mantle that a woman covered herself, including her head, when she left her house. Vives, writing in 1523, warns girls: "Going out of doors, the damsel should be careful not to expose her breasts and her throat, or to walk revealing herself at every step with the *manto,* but to cover her face and breasts. At the most, uncovering one eye so that she may see the road where she is going." His well-meant effort was too late by a generation or two to spare Gómez Manrique delicious suffering at the sight of a sinuous, graceful figure wrapped in a mantle:

> Away my heart flew
> Where I first saw your form,
> At once I was warm
> Knowing it was you.
> Although you were wrapped,
> My vision was true—
> That mantle of black
> Could never hide you.
>
> Through it appeared
> Your charm and your air,
> The drapery fair
> Your grace magnified.
> Then sore was the smart
> And troubled I grew,
> When after my heart
> My eyes followed too.[597]

A few illustrations show the mantle worn over the head, as in Figure 563. More comfortable would have been the hood *(cogulla)* with which a mantle of black *contray* was made for Queen Isabel (1498), and which may be illustrated in the effigy of another lady (Fig. 562). Here the front edge is turned back about the face, and both arms emerge to view, the slits decorated with a cusp-edged passementerie of pearls, cord, and braid.

Other mantles had a collar. St. Engracia's long, black velvet mantle—lined with emerald-green damask and trimmed with a band of gold work and round red and square green stones (Fig. 559)— has a flat collar of the damask. The mantle is fastened with a crosspiece of the banding (Fig. 573).

Coat

The coat *(ropa)* also opened down the front; buttons and buttonholes *(ojales)* or a buckle *(hevilla)* were supplied to close it. In the men's section *ropa* was translated "gown", but to avoid confusion here "coat" is used, inasmuch as "gown" for women has lost its former meaning of "overgarment". The Spanish coat was of rich materials; brocade often is mentioned for Queen Isabel and her daughters. They had *ropas* and *ropas francesas,* but how the two types differed is not indicated. For *ropas* were allowed 8 varas of black velvet (1485) or 13¼ varas of green satin (1487), both for the Queen; for the French type, 8 varas of especially rich, brown bro-

Mantle with arm-slit

553 LADY 1467–1477, from effigy of Isabel de Cuadros by Egas (Guadalupe. Monastery, Church)

554 QUEEN 1489–1493, from effigy of Isabel de Portugal, queen of Castilla and León, by Gil de Siloe (Burgos. Monastery of Miraflores)

555 LADY ca. 1512–1516, from figure of saint, choir stall (Zamora. Cathedral)

Mantle fabric

556, 557 QUEEN 1489–1493, from effigy of Isabel de Portugal, queen of Castilla and León, by Gil de Siloe (Burgos. Monastery of Miraflores)

558 QUEEN 1496–1499, from kneeling statue of Isabel de Portugal, queen of Castilla and León, by Gil de Siloe (Burgos. Monastery of Miraflores)

Mantle border embroidered

559 LADY ca. 1474–1477, from figure of St. Engracia by Bartolomé Bermejo (Boston. Isabella Stewart Gardner Museum)

560 DUCHESS ca. 1500–1515, from effigy of Mencía Enríquez de Toledo, duchess of Alburquerque (The Hispanic Society of America)

561 QUEEN ca. 1528, from statue of Isabel I, queen of Castilla and Aragón, attributed to Diego de Siloe (Granada. Royal Chapel)

562   ca. 1500   **563**   ca. 1513   **564**   1552

565   1497   **566**   1529

caded velvet (the Queen, 1487) or 9 of crimson velvet (Princess Isabel, 1490). Sleeves may have been tied on: a separate entry was made for coat sleeves of black, brocaded satin for Princess Isabel (1487), and six pieces of ribbon were to be made into agleted laces (1496) for *ropas.*

This garment served as background for impressive ornament. Queen Isabel, for trimming coats (two or three) that she would wear at festivities

for her first daughter's wedding (1490), requisitioned 30 marks (240 ounces) of gold "besides certain other marks" (worth altogether not far from 1,000,000 maravedis) to be worked into decorative motifs. Goldsmith-wrought motifs *(piezas labradas)* identified by name are ferns, oak leaves, little knockers *(aldabillas),* stems or branches *(ramillos),* feathers, and eagle-shaped rattles? *(ruidores de aguilas),* which last were tied with 21 ounces of gold cord

Mantle worn over the head

562 LADY ca. 1500, from effigy of María Manuel (Burgos. Museo Arqueológico Provincial)

563 LADY ca. 1513, from effigy of María de Herrera (Santa María del Campo. Parish Church)

Coat

564 QUEEN 1552, from portrait of Catalina de Austria, queen of Portugal, by Antonio Moro (Madrid. Museo del Prado)

565 QUEEN 1497, from figure of Isabel I, queen of Castilla and Aragón, choir stall, by Master Rodrigo (Plasencia. Cathedral)

566 WOMAN 1529, from *Thus Women in the Kingdom of Valencia Go Walking in the Streets* in Weiditz, Christoph. *Das Trachtenbuch. f*109 (Nürnberg. Germanisches Nationalmuseum)

---

on a coat of crimson and white *cebtí* (1487). Ornaments were secured with ribbon also, or stitched on with silk. Gold thread made fringes and insertions *(randas)*. Silks served as hem-bands *(cortapisas)*—white damask on a brocade coat, crimson satin on a green brocaded velvet, and mulberry satin on another brocade. The twenty brocade coats of Princess Isabel's trousseau (1490) were in different colors, four in metallic cloth woven of drawn-gold thread *(oro tirado),* and six of silk enriched with pearls and gold ornaments. Her gold-trimmed coats (1488) were wrapped in coarse linen. Gold letters adorned the crimson velvet coat of the Duchess of Cardona's daughter (1503).[598]

Woolen cloth was used occasionally. Queen Isabel (1495) had a black cloth coat trimmed with black velvet. A coat of white *paño* was provided for the daughter of the Queen's wardrobe keeper (1486). For the return to Flanders, Margarita de Austria (1499) received two of *grana* (5 varas each). *Grana* lined a crimson *cebtí* coat for Infanta Isabel (1486), and the furrier furnished linings.

Queen Isabel's embroiderer mounted gem stones *(piedras)* as well as gold motifs *(piezas)* on a coat to be worn at Epiphany (1484). Such trimming is notable on a French coat of tawny *ceti* lined with crimson velvet belonging to Queen Juana, the description of which[599] makes plausible every detail of her grandmother's mantle (Figs. 556, 557). On each side of the front blazed 3 large baroque rubies and 3 large diamonds. The rubies were set in "spiders" *(arañas)* of gold, enameled in white with points of crimson *(quirimires),* the diamonds in roses enameled white and green and in points of

quirimires. Between each pair of jeweled motifs appeared a wheel *(torno)* of pearls set upon a rose of white or green and white enamel, 6 wheels in all. The right sleeve carried 16 rubies, 7 diamonds, and 23 wheels, the left 13 rubies, 10 diamonds, and 24 wheels, all set on roses except that 4 rubies were in spiders. In addition the fronts and the sleeve openings carried 116 large gold motifs in the form of tree branches or trunks *(troncos)* shaped into bows.[600] In Queen Juana's inventory I have counted 36 *ropas francesas* and 75 *ropas.* For both types there is mention of "wide" or "narrow" sleeves and of "open" sleeves with gold aglets. Many of the French coats were trimmed with the band called *jeto,* and almost half had a *puerta,* which must have been a front piece like a stomacher. Each sleeve of the jeweled coat had two slashes *(golpes)* in the upper part, one to the back *(parte de fuera)* and one to the front *(parte de dentro),* and two in the lower part similarly placed. The jewels and the bows evidently were placed over or near these slashes. A French coat with long skirt is described as Flemish in style, two *ropas* of black cloth with a long train as Flemish mourning. Juana's favorite coat material was black *ceti* and then, black velvet; crimson lagged far behind. Almost a third were of woolen material. Many coats were lined with silk or velvet, the sleeves getting the best treatment. Fur linings also were recorded: ermine (2), marten (6), unidentified pelts *(peñas)* in white (5).[601]

The Empress's coats, like Prince Juan's, were called by the augmentative term *ropón.* Her favorite material for this garment was colored satin—crimson, tawny, brown *(pardo),* mulberry—and next taffeta, in which black played a large role. There were half a dozen coats of frieze, one of black cloth, one of cloth of gold. For linings, besides the favored taffeta, warmer materials are evident—Breton linen quilted, brown plush, the crushed velvet called *vedijudo,* and fur. Trimmings were modest, the narrow edge-strip *(ribete),* the wider *faja,* or the pinked-edged *pestaña.* In addition can be noted some passementerie and cording. The Empress had no French coats, but almost a third of her collection were called *saboyanos,*[602] which recalls the fact that her sister Beatriz (1521) had married the Duke of Savoy. Lucrezia Borgia wore *roboni alla spagnola.* The Italian *roba* generally was lined with fur,[603] but for the Empress's coats I find only three allusions to fur linings, and those of marten.

Illustrations of the lady's coat in this period are not plentiful. One may take it that Queen Isabel's

567   1488

568   ca. 1500

569   after 1498

570   1529

571   1529

572   1529

long overgarment of large-patterned brocade (Fig. 565), collarless, with long, moderately wide sleeves and high belt, is a *ropa;* at least so it has been called in our day. A shorter coat, worn by a Valencian lady (Fig. 566), hangs from the shoulders, beltless. Purplish touched with silver in the drawing, this garment also is collarless, cut low at the neck where it buttons. The sleeves are complicated. A full, brown inner sleeve carries an outer one of the purplish material cut into sections, at least six, each finished with a slashed tan border. In the lady's left sleeve, corners of four sections center upon a round medallion, while at the back, gray laces with flying ends serve to join other sections. The right sleeve, in the upper part, shows two sections attached to a trimming band; lower sections hang loosely.

A codex of ca. 1540 illustrates a dark-colored coat in which the sleeve fullness is concentrated in a large puff at the top. The sleeve is open all along the back, giving egress to white pull-outs, three in the puff and two in the foresleeve. The skirt, which in front ends well above the hem of a light-toned hoop skirt, lengthens at back to a train.[604]

By mid-century the *ropa* had developed a collar

Monjil

567 COUNTESS 1488, from figure of Juana Pimentel, countess of Montalbán, main retable, by the Luna Master (Toledo. Cathedral, Chapel of Santiago)

Tabard

568 PRINCESS ca. 1500, from figure of Saint in *St. Ursula and the Eleven Thousand Virgins* by the Segovia Master (Madrid. Museo del Prado)

Loba

569 BRIDE after 1498, from figure of Maria in *The Marriage of Marco Coppola and Maria Piccolomini* in Ferraiolo *[Cronaca della Napoli aragonese]* *f*92 (New York. The Pierpont Morgan Library, M 801, *f*84–150)

570 YOUNG WOMAN, BACK 1529, from *Thus Go Damsels in Barcelona, Seen from the Back,* in Weiditz, Christoph. *Das Trachtenbuch. f*69 (Nürnberg. Germanisches Nationalmuseum)

571 YOUNG WOMAN, SIDE 1529, from *Thus Go Damsels in Barcelona, the Greater Part with Low-cut Shoes,* in Weiditz, Christoph. *Das Trachtenbuch. f*68 (Nürnberg. Germanisches Nationalmuseum)

572 WOMAN 1529, from *Thus Also They Go in Barcelona* in Weiditz, Christoph. *Das Trachtenbuch. f*67 (Nürnberg. Germanisches Nationalmuseum)

---

and buttoned part way down the front. The sleeves continued to be full at top above a fitted lower sleeve. As worn by a queen (Fig. 564), the garment of rich, greenish-black velvet is trimmed with gold braid or embroidered bands. There are openings at each side, but no pull-outs emerge.

Monjil

That the *monjil* was an overgarment is proved by the fact that at Infante Ferdinand's christening on a March day (1503) a lady-in-waiting to Queen Isabel wore over a *basquiña* a *monjil* of crimson velvet lined with ermine. The sleeves were slashed many times, and at all the openings were set ornaments of hammered gold.[605] Pisetsky defines the Italian *mongile* as "mantle with sleeves, probably of monastic origin",[606] which presents a logical picture. In the Queen's household women of all categories wore this garment. For Isabel herself Baeza dealt with thirty-five *monjiles* in twenty years. Black velvet was overwhelmingly the favorite material, then black *cebtí,* then black satin; about 8 varas was a common allowance for a woman. Some colored silks and velvets also are listed, and a few woolen *paños,* black, mulberry, blue, green, or tawny. *Contray* was used for servants as well as for the Queen. *Grana* went into linings, 1 vara of it to 3 of the black velvet for three-year-old Catalina's *monjil* (1488). A few silk or velvet linings are mentioned; more were of fur, mainly rabbit or ermine.

The *monjil* is reliably illustrated in a painting at Toledo (Fig. 567). The Duchess of El Infantado, ordering portraits of her parents to appear in a retable, specifies that her mother is to be painted as clad in "the modest headdresses her ladyship was accustomed to wear and with a velvet *monjil,* her mantle thrust aside so as to reveal much of the *monjil*".[607] The mantle covers more than we should like, but by tracing the area of lustrous gray velvet that lies over the brown and gold brocade of the *brial* and under the black mass of the mantle, one can perceive the *monjil's* long puckered sleeves, not very wide, and the generous folds of its skirt considerably shorter than the dress. One's impression is that the *monjil* was a full, loose-fitting garment open at front, extending to below the knees. Queen Juana left one of black *ceti,* lined with black taffeta, and two or three of *buriel,* a cloth woven of black-sheep's wool. One had narrow sleeves.[608]

By the time of the Empress the *monjil* had undergone development. Parts of it are mentioned as body (cuerpos), collar band (cabezón), vest or stomacher (portina, conportina), back pieces (cuartos traseros), sleeves, skirt (falda, faldamento), forepart (delantera), skirt-foot (ruedo), most of which were characteristic also of the saya. Sleeves varied considerably in the Empress's fifty monjiles: some were de punta (Fig. 454), others French or half French, de borracha (Fig. 448), or with pull-outs (papos). Crimson, white, tawny, or mulberry garments are listed, but black was still preferred in velvet, satin, or taffeta. Several were of black cloth, one each of gold or silver cloth. For lining, black taffeta was most used, though warmer materials are mentioned—yellow frieze, crushed velvet, fustian; marten appears once. Buckram occasionally went into the making.[609]

No measure of materials is indicated in the Empress's accounts, but in Queen Isabel's time velvets were issued in these proportions: 8–8½ varas for a monjil, 11 for a brial, and a top limit of 12½ for a habit. Change is evidenced in the fact that from the Empress's wardrobe a mulberry velvet monjil that had been transformed from a saya made two chasubles, whereas only one was obtained from a tawny satin habit.

Bernis says that before the second half of the sixteenth century the monjil, which had been full and rather short, became full and long like the habit. Tailors of 1522 still were required to know how to cut both these garments. The Empress sent one of each to a poor woman in Portugal.[610] But at the Sesa wedding (1541) Catalina de Mendoza appeared in a monjil instead of a saya. A French mongille of 1544 was made like a robe in front, buckram lined the top of the sleeves; it might have small pockets. Alcega's Libro de geometria omits the habit, and the monjil, which drags a train, looks like a dress, differing from the saya mainly in that it has a one-piece back flaring from shoulder to hem.[611] Later, the name monjil was applied to the hanging sleeve (manga perdida).[612]

Bernia

Women as well as men wore the bernia. Queen Juana had one of two-faced velvet, brown and green, trimmed with "locks" (guedejas) or tassels of spun-gold thread.[613] That in the Empress's wardrobe, of mulberry crushed (de vedija) velvet, carrying a salvaje (tassel?) of mulberry silk, was sent by her order to the Emperor.[614] The most interesting thing about this garment is its origin. A Spanish text of

1511, speaking of woolen materials, lists irlandas and bernias together; one of mid-century says, "Ireland is a very cold country, and there they make the shaggy bernias that are brought to Spain."[615] Rabelais (1530) gives the garment a Moorish cast, bernes à la Moresque, and Gay, who defines the berne as "woman's mantle without hood", sustains the Moorish relation as against the Irish.[616] Pisetsky describes the fifteenth-century sbernia of Italy as "short and sumptuous", the sixteenth-century type as "worn so as to leave one arm free", and quotes Vecellio, " 'a sbernia fastened with a brocca (brooch?)' " in connection with a late sixteenth-century engraving.[617]

Tabard

A woman's tabard appears about 130 times in Baeza's accounts. The tabard has been described as "a flowing overgarment, short and beltless, with a round opening to admit the head, not closed at the sides, and furnished with short, floating sleeves (ailerons)."[618] A painting of Queen Isabel and her eldest daughter (Fig. 311) illustrates garments that partly conform to this description. They are cut with a low neckline, which would go easily over the head, but with a fairly long skirt, which is divided at front and back instead of being open at the sides. The sleeves are open at the outer side and not under the arm, as in a herald's tabard. Mounted rubies, emeralds, and pearls set on gold galloon border the Queen's neckline. More jewels are suggested along the front edges and the hem of her tabard skirt and at the lower edge of its sleeve, which for the rest is bordered with simple, linear embroidery. To this garment, deep purple in color, the texture of velvet has been ascribed.[619]

The Princess's tabard is made of brocade in gold and crimson and is lined with gold and white brocade. A gold band carrying pearls and green jewels borders the low neckline. Other edges are gold embroidered in a linear design of scallops and waves, which at the left back is more carefully rendered as contiguous S-scrolls. The brocade of the dress is woven with green figures on a gold ground.

Another tabard (Fig. 568), lined with green, is of large-patterned brocade in tan, brown, and white. The full garment has a low neckline, but no openings can be seen in the skirt. One long hanging sleeve is pulled forward by the left hand. The other sleeve, open to the shoulder, hangs in a long straight tube. Bands jeweled with pearls, as well as with rose-red or green stones, trim the neckline, the sleeve-end, and the skirt hem. The underdress is dull purple.

Of the silk materials used for this garment, Baeza most often mentions damask, of which Queen Isabel (1495) ordered for one tabard 10 varas of black and for another 16 varas of blue. Rich velvet tabards were made for Infanta Isabel. A black (10 varas at 750 maravedis, 1487) carried 110½ ounces of hammered-gold ornaments from Zaragoza. One of crimson (7 varas at 3,000 maravedis, 1488) was lined with 240 ermines and adorned with almost 9 *marcos* (72 ounces) of hammered-gold pieces given by the King, her father. A notable decoration for an unidentified tabard (1487) comprised 11 varas of Arabic letters embroidered with 5½ ounces of gold thread on 1⅙ varas of expensive crimson velvet. The embroiderer worked twenty-two days to make these lettered bands, which must have been about 3½ inches deep.

Most tabards were made of woolen fabric—*buriel* for a slave (1484), *brunete* for nurses and attendants of the Portuguese princes (1483), *contray mayor* worth much more, 600 maravedis the vara, for nurses of the Queen's own children (1484). Her personal attendants fared even better. María de Medina (1493) had *contray mayor* at 1,000 maravedis. The wardrobe keeper's wife (1486) received *grana* at 1,400, almost as good as Infanta Juana's allotment (1485) at 1,600. Queen Isabel (1491) had a tabard of red *grana* dyed rose. In 1483 she acquired one of light-green Rouen cloth (5¼ varas at 600 maravedis), one of violet-red *grana* also from Rouen (5½ varas at 1,100), and one of red London *grana* (4½ varas at 1,300). The red one was trimmed with embroidered bands, 1½ varas of satin worked with 9 ounces of gold thread. For the violet-red tabard, ½ vara of black velvet was supplied to bind *(ribetear)* the edges. The popular red-and-green combination appears in crimson velvet binding a tabard of green Rouen cloth for Infanta María (1488) and in green velvet, one of *grana* for Juana (1488). When a tone is indicated for *contray* it is generally black, though cheap "mulberry tawny" (6½ varas at 576 maravedis) was provided for Infanta Isabel (1488), redeemed by 15 ounces of drawn-gold embroidery on expensive crimson velvet.

For the long journeys by horse or mule, traveling cloaks were a necessity; tabards "for the road" *(de camino)* were always of wool, two thirds of those listed being of *contray*. Some were left untrimmed; others had the edges bound with velvet, and there might be further decoration *(guarnición)*. Infanta Juana (1490) had a traveling tabard of expensive red *grana* with a trimming of gold embroidery on mulberry brocaded satin. In a like one for María (1490) crimson velvet was included as trimming, but there was no embroidery. The Queen's traveling tabard (1494) was made "with sleeves." Of cheap black *contray,* the tabard was worn for mourning the King of Naples. For renting a woman's at Sevilla, presumably as mourning, the price was 4 maravedis per day for a new one, 3 for an old.[620]

Queen Juana's inventory lists an "open" tabard of blue silk camlet made with a hood *(capilla).* Front, hood, and sleeve ends were embroidered with "quills" *(cañutillos)* of gold thread. A black velvet tabard in four sections *(cuartos)* and with long sleeves is called "Castilian". The whole garment, including the sleeves, was adorned with openwork, eyelets *(trepas),* and with 2,365 bows *(lazos)* of fine gold, stamped, burnished, and milled *(grafilados)* at the edges. Together with 60 other pieces, the total weight was over 30 *marcos* (240 ounces).[621]

The tabard must have lost favor before mid-century, for I do not find it included in the Empress's *Libro de cuentas.*

Loba

The *loba,* which with men became ultimately the wear of physicians and scholars, seems to have been comparatively short-lived with women. A longish, free garment, it could be open or closed, with sleeves or without. Baeza concerns himself with it for Queen Isabel and three of her daughters. Princess Isabel's *loba* of black cloth (1490) was lined with black *cebtí;* Infanta [María's] of black *cebtí* (1491) had a lining of black velvet. Two *lobas* are mentioned for the Queen, one of *contray mayor* (1491). The other of black cloth (1490) was lined with crimson *cebtí.* Thirteen varas for the *cebtí* lining are recorded and 6 varas or less for the cloth.

Of the *loba* sleeves mentioned occasionally, some cannot have been very large. One and one-half varas of black satin sufficed to provide sleeve linings for a cloth *loba* of Infanta Juana (1491) and also trimming for her matching *hábito.* A black damask *loba* (1523) had both sleeves and front lined with black velvet. In the Empress's garment of mulberry satin the sleeves were lined with the same satin. Women's *loba* sleeves might be called "wings" *(alas),*[622] which suggests free hanging panels like those of the man's tabard (Fig. 281).

The *loba* left by Queen Juana was made of black damask. Black *lobas* continue to appear in inventories—of cloth (1510), of *buriel* (1518), of damask (1523)—but richly colored fabrics are not unusual. Isabel de Aragón's trousseau (1515) included *lobas* of crimson or tawny velvet, of satin in white or mulberry crimson, as well as of black velvet, satin, or damask. One of hers was trimmed with 42 ounces of drawn-gold thread worked into 50 *aunes* of narrow braid or passementerie. Twelve to 14 *aunes* of silk material were required for each of Isabel de Aragón's *lobas*, whereas about 9 sufficed for *manto* or *monjil*.[623]

The Empress had half a dozen *lobas*—of white or blue damask, of mulberry satin, of mulberry cloth of gold, of black velvet or taffeta. Their most interesting feature is that they reflect her taste for a single color—the white damask *loba* is trimmed with a band of white velvet, the mulberry satin with mulberry velvet in two edge-strips.[624]

An open *loba* without sleeves (Fig. 577) is worn by a sister of the famous Cardinal Mendoza. Of large-figured brocade, its fronts are brought together under her enameled gold collar of flowerets and wattled twigs.[625] A sash, which secures the fronts, passes through the long armholes, leaving the back to flare from the shoulders. The fur lining is extended to bind the edges except at the skirt hem. On the kneeling Countess the *loba* has been drawn out to look almost as long as the dress, but in an upright position it probably would be revealed as shorter, much like the open, sleeveless *loba* worn by a bride at Naples (Fig. 569) when Spain was in the ascendant there. This blue-green garment over a gold-colored dress is followed on the same page by one of gold over a red dress. I have found no Italian equivalent; the *lòbbia* was a man's cape.

Weiditz sketched two sleeveless *lobas* at Barcelona. The younger woman's (Fig. 570), brownish gray with horizontal touches of gilt, is combined with a blue dress considerably longer and ending in a train. *Loba* neck and large armholes are bound with lighter-colored material. In the side view (Fig. 571), which does not fully explain itself, the fronts look as though they might be open, say to the waistline, with the top edges not quite aligned. This garment must have had a circular cut, since from a flat neck the front and the back hang in deep vertical folds. The older woman's *loba* (Fig. 572), which shows no front opening, is rose touched with silver. Through the large armholes, which seem to be narrowly bound, escape vermilion dress sleeves with white pull-outs. The *loba* skirt ends above the beige, crescent-patterned band which trims the red dress skirt and its train.

Capuz

Seated sidewise in a saddle trimmed with silver gilt, Queen Isabel (1486) on a chestnut mule rode into the Royal Camp at Illora. The mule's headstall and checkreins *(riendas falsas)* were embroidered in silks interlaced with golden letters, while the Queen wore a cloak *(capuz)* of *grana* adorned with Moresque work. Infanta Isabel, in a black *capuz* similarly enriched, rode with her. This garment "served the lady for going about outside," says an inventory (1511).[626] Queen Isabel and her two elder daughters had *capuces*, but not the little girls. Baeza cites seven "for the road" *(de camino)*, five of black or red wool and one of green *cebtí*. Three of these had sleeves, as did seven others, which recalls the tabard. If the woman's *capuz* was made like the man's (Figs. 275, 279), it was fitted close to the neck with perhaps a short front opening, which could be fastened with buttons, to ease its passage over the head. *Grana*—mulberry, red, or rose—was a popular fabric; eleven in these materials to twenty-two of four other woolen cloths and three of damask appear in Baeza. Infanta Isabel and the Queen each had a *capuz* in tawny cloth. Slaves got mulberry, and serving women, grayish brown. An illustration cited for this garment is from the figure of Queen Isabel on a coin of 1475, but the identification is questionable; Bernis has termed such a garment "tabard".[627]

Queen Juana, who had little occasion to go abroad, left only one *capuz* of black *ceti* with open arm-slits *(maneras)*. It is more surprising that the Empress also had but one, unless it means that the *capuz* was then out of style. Hers was of black velvet. The original lining of cloth of gold was given to a Navarrese friar, presumably for ornaments in his monastery church, and the *capuz* was relined with black taffeta.[628]

Capote

Another cloak *(capote)* of the Empress was made of tawny woolen and trimmed with "colored feathers from the Indies and in parts of it with little pieces that seem to be of gold."[629] The colored trimming must have arrived from Mexico, where natural feathers were worked by devoted craftsmen into brilliant ornaments that ranked with those of gold and jewels in the order of beauty.[630] This example gives the only glimpse that I have had of Spanish dress in our period being affected by ideas imported from the New World.

Furs

LADIES USED FUR mainly for lining and trimming. The separate fur piece, which in Italy was worn over the shoulders as early as the portrait of Juana de Aragón (1518), designed by Raphael (Paris. Musée National du Louvre), is described in Isabel de Portugal's *Libro de las quentas* (1529–1538)—"two martens were fastened together and trimmed with feet, forepaws, and head of gold for Her Majesty's *rostro* (face *or rather* neck)."[631] But in Spain, so far as I know, the fur neckpiece[632] was not depicted until Sofonisba Anguisciola included it in her portrait of Queen Isabel de Valois (ca. 1568), copied by Juan Pantoja de la Cruz (Madrid. Museo del Prado).

Talavera complained that whereas an old *sayo* or *manto* used to serve as lining for the new, in his time the material inside could cost more than that outside.[633] Precious linings doubtless were meant to be seen as well as to lend warmth. Queen Isabel I wore a half mantle of crimson satin so artfully arranged that its ermine lining was impressively visible to a foreign visitor (1489).[634] A girl could reveal expensive ermine by turning up her skirt hem (Fig. 576). On the other hand, the only indication of a fur lining, other than the bulkiness of a garment, might be a line of fine white hairs erect along the neckline (Fig. 378), between the dress brocade and the jeweled trimming.

Ermine

In Queen Isabel's circle ermine was favored. Baeza's accounts (1483–1504), combined with Isabel de Aragón's bridal list (1515), record ermine as lining outer garments *(monjil, mantilla, ropa, tabardo)* and dresses as well *(saya, hábito)*. Separate waists *(gonetes)* and sleeves also were lined with it. On a wide-sleeved, black velvet *saya* of Isabel de Aragón

were expended 6 timbers of ermine skins (240) worth a total of 42 ducats (15,000 maravedis). They could cost from 52½ to 77½ maravedis each. A *hábito* needed 120–360 skins, a *gonete* up to 240, a *monjil* 200–332, a *tabardo* 240, a *mantilla* 260–400. In a *monjil* for Infanta [María] at age nine (1491) ermines were eked out with 10 white pelts *(pellejas)*, probably of sheep. Queen Juana's inventory lists fur linings as though they had been taken intact out of their original garments and saved thus to be used again. In this state the substitution of white sheep fells for ermine at the tops of sleeves and in part of the skirt-foot became clearly evident.[635] The Empress's accounts show only a pair of sleeves and a *mantilla* lined with ermine.[636]

This fur was much used in trimming bands. Fifteen timbers of ermine skins (600) were dressed and cut into strips *(tiras)* for Queen Isabel (1495). How they were used is suggested by a wide band at a bateau neck (Fig. 362), a narrow one at dress hem (Figs. 458, 461) or sleeve edge (Fig. 458). Such bands also decorate the long armholes (Fig. 573) and the hem of Saint Engracia's surcoat of wine-red and gold brocade. In the painting of her arrest, likewise by Bermejo (San Diego. Fine Arts Gallery), the surcoat skirt is seen to be lined as well as trimmed with ermine.

Sable

Sables *(martas cebellinas)* made the perfect lining, warm yet light in weight. When the term *cebellina* is omitted, one cannot be quite certain that the pine marten *(marta)* is intended, especially when the fur is described as "fine, good, or very singular". However, martens of excellent quality are said to exist still in the Pyrenees and to be exported from France or Spain. Queen Juana had martens from Galicia. A fair test for distinguishing the two furs is the price. The "common marten" (1493) was valued at 108½ maravedis, whereas a sable could cost from 375 (1493) to the 1,460 paid for each of 2 "very fine" skins for Infanta Juana (1495). The Empress's inventory lists 147 martens with a total value of 350 ducats (892.8 maravedis for each skin), every one bearing a *firma* (mark of origin?), the skins sewed together (in pairs as in a timber?).[637] The Polish ambassador was careful to say it was *martas cebellinas* that his Queen had sent to the Empress. He had to wait a year for the chance to make an effective presentation—until after the birth of Felipe

573   ca. 1474–1477   **574**   ca. 1500–1515   **575**   ca. 1530

576   ca. 1490   **577**   ca. 1500

II (1527)—but then Isabel rewarded him by saying that the sables of his gift (three 40's) were very black and far superior to those that the Emperor had handed on to her from the Russians.[638]

No statement has been found as to how many sables were required to line a whole dress or outer garment. Forty sables at 1277.5 maravedis each must have made a complete lining for a *gonete* of expen-

sive crimson brocade belonging to Infanta Juana (1495), the year before she departed for the chill winters of Flanders. In the same year only 6 at a ducat each went into her crimson satin *saya* that carried also purfles of cat *(gato)*. Martens were combined with sables in the lining of a coat *(ropa)* for Margarita de Austria (1499). Probably the sables went into lining a part that was likely to show.

Ermine

573 LADY ca. 1474–1477, from figure of St. Engracia, wearing an ermine-trimmed surcoat, by Bartolomé Bermejo (Boston. Isabella Stewart Gardner Museum)

574 LADY ca. 1500–1515, from figure of St. Barbara, wearing an ermine jacket, tomb of the Duchess of Alburquerque (The Hispanic Society of America)

576 PRINCESS ca. 1490, from figure of Eudoxia, wearing an ermine-lined habit, in *Exorcism of the Princess Eudoxia*, retable of St. Stephen, by the Sinobas Master (Los Balbases. Church of San Esteban)

Lynx?

575 QUEEN ca. 1530, from water color of Éléonore d'Autriche, queen of France, wearing fur oversleeves (Paris. Bibliothèque Nationale, Cabinet des Estampes)

Sable or marten

577 COUNTESS ca. 1500, from figure of Mencía de Mendoza, wearing a fur-lined *loba*, in *St. Dominic and Doña Mencía de Mendoza, Countess of Haro* (Reggio Emilia. Civici Musei e Galleria d'Arte)

The 2 very expensive skins mentioned before were used at the sleeve wrists of a crimson *ceti sayón* for Juana (1495). This fur is suggested in the dark lining and in the bands at neck, fronts, and armslits of the patterned *loba* worn by a great lady (Fig. 577).

Marten

Martens are mentioned more frequently than sables. Princess Isabel (1488, 1490) had two habits lined with martens. For Queen Isabel (1494, 1495) they lined parts of two habits and part of a *monjil*, which probably included the sleeves as they often received special attention. In Queen Juana's *monjil* of crude *buriel*, the sleeves were lined with "very singular martens", while for the body only one skin of unknown quality is mentioned.[639] Empress Isabel left three pairs of sleeve linings comprising, respectively, 79, 83, and 66 martens; for her auction these collections were priced at 452, 250, and 130 ducats.[640] Her *manteos* required 27, 32, or 40 martens each. Of small accessories Queen Juana had a black *ceti* partlet *(gorguera)*, four buskins, and black *ceti* gloves lined with marten, and one pair of gloves made of marten tails. That Juana in Flanders (1505) spent her time buying martens and silks for new clothes every day is reported by a Spanish ambassador who did not succeed in seeing her.[641]

The *penilleras* of marten that entered into Juana's linings suggest strips of fur, since *llera (glera)* signifies "section of river bed" which probably would be long and narrow. In a marten-lined coat *(ropa)* the sleeves were of *penilleras*, which lined also a little coat *(roponcillo)* of hers, a *manteo*, and a corselet *(corselete)*.[642]

Empress Isabel had a coat lining of marten heads and paws. Martens and marten heads lined a bed coverlet of blue velvet, which was presented at her sale for 160 ducats. A coverlet of martens and mulberry velvet, passed on from Queen Juana's wardrobe, is described as though the velvet, not the fur, formed the lining.[643]

Squirrel

Squirrel is rarely mentioned for ladies of our period. I know of no illustration where the familiar heraldic design of "vair" appears in women's dress at this time. The plain gray fur at the cuffs and hem of Saint Engracia's dark wine-red velvet gown (Figs. 573, 532) shows characteristics of squirrel, possibly the *gris* of Siberian breed, of which 5,200 maravedis' worth lined a black velvet *monjil* (1487) for Juana de Mendoza, Infanta Isabel's chief attendant. Of the red-brown native squirrel *(esquirol, ardilla)*, Queen Isabel (1490) had 100 skins at 40 maravedis each to complete the lining of a crimson velvet *monjil*, and Infanta Juana (1493) received 266 at 35 maravedis to line a black velvet habit.

Otter

Otter *(nutria)* is cited as the material of gloves. For Infanta Isabel (1483) otter gloves cost 93 maravedis; lined with crimson *cebtí* (1488) they went up to 250.

Cat

No descriptive adjective defines the kind of cat whose fur has been mentioned, but it must have been wildcat *(gato montés)*. Queen Isabel's household used it for purfles on garments of crimson velvet and white camlet (1490) and of crimson *cebtí* (1495). Black cat went on black velvet (1494). A single skin cost 124 maravedis in 1500. Isabel de Aragón (1515) had a lining of cat in a black satin *monjil.* Pisetsky, speaking of such a lining for Bianca Maria Sforza, says that then the domestic cat was rather a rare animal.[644]

Muskrat, genet, lynx

Muskrats *(almizcleras)* lined a *mantilla* of crimson *cebtí* for Queen Isabel (1495) and another for Queen Juana. Black genets appear in the Empress's accounts lining a short tippet *(beca)* of crimson velvet. There also we find a lynx *(lobo cervato)* coat lining, complete with hood and sleeves, valued at 400 ducats.[645]

Rabbit

Less expensive rabbit and lamb also were good wear in winter. Rabbit skins cost from 62 to 108 maravedis each, most often 80 or 86. They were black, white, or grayish brown *(pardillo)* and were sometimes sheared *(tundidos)*. Queen Isabel (1494) took 90 black skins of the cheapest kind for a *monjil*, the garment most often associated with rabbit lining. María and Catalina at thirteen and ten years (1495) were given only 50 each to line their *monjiles* of black satin. Juana had 19 skins for a *gonete* (1495) and 4 were issued for a single velvet sleeve (1500).

Lamb

Not often recorded, lamb can be identified by the terms *romania* (Rumanía) and *corderina*. Talavera gives an idea of this fur by saying that Adam's and Eve's tunics probably were not of unborn lamb *(abortón)* or of very delicate lamb fells *(corderinas)*, but rather of crude or hard *(cuesqueras)* and graceless fells like those worn by shepherds and charcoal makers.[646] Queen Isabel (1500) ordered for her attendant Violante de Albión 5½ dozen Navarrese lamb fells at 43 maravedis each to line a *monjil*. The 3½ times as expensive Rumanian lamb was used to line habits and a black cloth mantilla for the Queen or her daughters.

Peña

Meaning "lining fur in general", *peña* is used by scribes who do not trouble to identify the type. Margarita de Austria's taste for black and white is shown in the fact that for her a coat of black twill *(sarga)* was lined with white *peñas*, a habit of white *sarga*

with black *peñas*. Juana la Loca had a French coat of black velvet lined with white sheep fells *(pellejas)*.[647]

Sheep fell

The most widely used fur was sheep fell. The Prior of Guadalupe Monastery gave Queen Isabel a coat of *pellico de carnero,* and she valued it so much that she said she did not take it off her body, but kept it always with her as her best shield against winter, like her beloved husband Don Fernando.[648] This monastery was famous for making luxurious coats *(zamarros)* of well-dressed sheep fells. Such coats are a recurring item in Baeza's accounts. One entry (1494) specifies that Infanta Juana had 8 varas of white satin and 4 of white damask for a *zamarro,* which implies an outer cover for the fells. Her inventory as queen mentions a coat with separate sleeves. Queen Isabel gave *zamarros* as presents to individuals and also for a time provided them annually for the female members of her household. In eleven years Baeza paid for 1273 *zamarros,* including 100 purchased at the Medina del Campo fair (1494) and 145 at Ocaña (1498). For the little Infantas a *zamarro* cost 365 maravedis. Bought in quantity for women, they were priced most often at 570 or 620. María de Medina, maid to Queen Isabel (1494), had a *zamarro* that cost 1,240 maravedis; for the nurse of Prince Miguel (1498), one carrying three trimming strips *(tressinas, tres tiras)* was provided at a price of 5 gold florins, or 1,425 maravedis. The Empress's *zamarros* were even more expensive, 5 or 6 ducats each. One had 3 strips and an edging *(ribete)* of tawny velvet. Another with 3 strips was fastened with buttons and frogs *(alamares)* of white silk.[649] No illustration of the garment has been found for this study.

Outer wear

Of expensive furs used as an outer fabric two illustrations can be presented. One is a sleeveless jacket (Fig. 574) cut on the lines of a fifteenth-century surcoat without the skirt. Horizontal strips of fur—probably ermine which was often used on surcoats—make up a narrow vertical panel at each side of an embroidered panel and form also, farther back, a curved band running continuously from over the shoulder down the front and over the hip. Each panel or band is finished with a plain binding. Leafy scrolls pattern the embroidery except for one four-sided motif, suggesting a jewel, near the top. At the low edge of each fur panel is a band marked with zigzags, probably more embroidery.

The second example is furnished by sleeves of Éléonore d'Autriche. Indicated in the Hampton Court picture (Fig. 442) as of light-tan fur with darker spots, possibly lynx, they are detailed in a water color (Fig. 575) made from a full-length portrait once in the Gaignières Collection, Paris. The sleeves seem to be shaped in a triangle which hangs by one corner from a spot at the top and back of the armscye, while the lower two corners meet over the forearm.

NOTES

Full bibliographical entries for works cited in more than one note are given in References.

1 An account of the Prince's household was first requested in 1535 by Charles V, who wished to found a similar establishment for his son Felipe (Fernández de Oviedo y Valdés. *Libro*, p. IX).

See also Tudela, José. *Almazán, corte de los Reyes Católicos.* In *Celtiberia.* 1962. v. 12, p. 187–193.

2 Fernández de Oviedo y Valdés. *Libro.* p. 35–36, *tr.*

3 *Ibid.* p. 61–63, *tr.*

4 Baeza. v. 2, p. 138, 216.

The yearly income of a high nobleman ran between three and forty million maravedis, 8,000–106,666 ducats (Fernández Alvarez, Manuel. *La sociedad española del Renacimiento* [Salamanca, 1970] p. 147).

Under Fernando and Isabel the maravedi originally was a copper coin. Three hundred seventy-five maravedis equaled one ducat. A *sueldo* or an *escudo* was worth 18 maravedis, a *real* 31, a *florín* 265, a *dobla* 365, a *castellano* 485 (Baeza. v. 1, p. 45, 209, 214; v. 2, p. 137, 239). A *marco* weighed about 8 ounces. In 1483 the gold *marco*, divided into 50 *castellanos*, was worth 24,250 mrs.; the silver, 67 *reales*, amounted to 2,077 mrs. (Clemencín. p. 524).

Gonzalo de Baeza, treasurer of Queen Isabel, recorded her expenditures from 1477 until she died (1504). In the many subsequent statements drawn from his accounts, the year and the name of the person concerned are indicated in the text, but no volume or page numbers are given in the notes. For a complete entry see *References.*

5 Fernández de Oviedo y Valdés. *Diálogos.* p. 70–71.

6 Padilla. p. 44, 45; Maura y Gamazo, Gabriel, 1. duque de Maura. *El príncipe que murió de amor.* Madrid, 1944. p. 166–169; Anghiera. v. 1, p. 332.

7 Between 9 and 10 varas were required for the two mourning garments issued to each of the hundred poor, and over 1,000 varas of *jerga* were purchased, most of it from Moors. Ten days after the death, that is, on October 16th, *jerga* was left off and a different mourning called *luto* was put on. Hundreds of varas of *luto* (possibly black, as Palencia (1490. Art. *Pulla*) speaks of *vestiduras negras de luto*), were purchased for chaplains, chapel assistants, and for women and servants who did not take *jerga*. Cheap white cloth and grayish brown *(pardillo)* were bought by the piece or the half piece, also *buriel*, a crude material probably woven of black-sheep's wool. Certain widows in the royal service had mantles of *buriel* (*Documentos relativos á la enfermedad y muerte del príncipe D. Juan.* In Fernández de Oviedo y Valdés. *Libro.* p. 243–247).

8 Comines, Philippe de. *Las memorias . . . de los hechos y empresas de Lvis vndecimo y Carlos octavo, reyes de Francia.* Amberes, 1643. v. 2, p. 454, *tr.* (ch. CXC).

Even after quoting Comines and his mention of black

mourning, Gil González Dávila says, "Our histories add that great and small dressed in white *jerga*, which was the last time that this kind of mourning was used in Castilla" (*Historia de las antigvedades de la civdad de Salamanca.* Salamanca, 1606. p. 408, *tr.*).

In 1502 Isabel and Fernando issued a pragmatic on mourning and wax which forbade the use of *jerga* in mourning any dead person, no matter how exalted his rank. The approved fabric was sheared cloth (Spain. Laws, statutes, etc. *Pragmaticas y Leyes. f-v°* fclxj).

9 Resende. *fcxxj, tr., -fcxxij.*

10 Lalaing. p. 173.

11 Ferrari. p. 154–155, *tr.*

Further accounts of the *juego de cañas* are given in Münzer, Jerome. *Viaje por España y Portugal en los años 1494 y 1495.* Madrid [1924] p. 85–86.

12 Bernis Madrazo. *Las miniaturas de "El cancionero de Pedro Marcuello".* In *Archivo español de arte.* 1952. v. 25, p. 14.

13 *Deuxième voyage de Philippe le Beau en Espagne, en 1506.* In *Collection des voyages des souverains des Pays-Bas.* Bruxelles, 1876. v. 1, p. 437, *tr.*

14 Alcocer, Pedro de. *Relación de algunas cosas que pasaron en estos reynos, desde que murió la reina católica Doña Ysabel, hasta que se acabaron las comunidades en la ciudad de Toledo.* Sevilla, 1871. p. 19.

15 Rodríguez Villa. *Crónicas.* p. 476, 477, *tr.*

16 *Ibid.* p. 366, *tr.*

17 *Ibid.* p. 464, *tr.*

18 *Ibid.* p. 465, *tr.*

19 Fernández de Oviedo y Valdés. *Diálogos.* p. LXII, *tr.*

20 Vital. p. 151, *tr.*

21 Santa Cruz. v. 1, p. 169, *tr.*

22 Vital. p. 222–223, *tr.*

23 Igual Ubeda, Antonio. *El imperio español.* Barcelona, 1954. p. 115–116.

24 Santa Cruz. v. 1, p. 258, *tr.*

25 Fernández de Oviedo y Valdés. *Relación.* p. 453, *tr.*

26 Great Britain. Public record office. *Letters.* p. 938.

27 Jenkins, Marianna Duncan. *The state portrait, its origin and evolution.* [New York] College Art Assn. of America in conjunction with The Art Bulletin, 1947. p. 42; Armstrong, Edward. *The Emperor Charles V.* London, 1910. v. 1, p. 22.

28 Boehn. v. 2, p. 44; Schneider, Hugo. *Le costume militaire suisse du XVIe siècle.* In Congrès international d'histoire du costume. 1st, Venice, 1952. *Actes.* [Milano, 1955] p. 110.

29 Blau, Friedrich. *Die deutschen Landsknechte.* Görlitz, 1882. p. 13, *tr.*

30 Pellicanus, Conradus. *Das Chronikon des Konrad Pellikan.* Basel, 1877, quoted in Boehn. v. 2, p. 118; Repond, Giulio. *Le costume de la garde suisse pontificale et la renaissance italienne.* Rome, 1917. p. 12; Bleckwenn, Ruth. *Beziehungen zwischen Soldatentracht und ziviler modischer Kleidung zwischen 1500 und 1650.* In *Waffen- und Kostümkunde.* 1974. v. 16, p. 107, Fig. 2.

31 Boehn. v. 2, p. 31-33.

32 Lazarillo de Tormes. *f-vºf*29, *tr. (Tractado 3.º).*

33 Aretino, Pietro. *I ragionamenti* [dedicated to François Ier, 1535-1538] Milano [1960] p. 344, *tr. (2.a parte, 1.a giornata).* See also the Spanish translation in Croce (p. 155).

34 Croce. p. [173] *tr.*

35 Fernández de Oviedo y Valdés. *Las quinquagenas.* v. 1, p. 175, *tr.*

36 Ferrari, quoted in Croce. p. 107.

37 Teresa, Saint. p. 193, 194, note 68.

38 Zúñiga. p. 18, 22.

39 Brantôme. v. 2, p. 12, *tr.*

40 Sandoval. pt. 2, *vºf*32 (bk. 18, I).

41 Talavera, Hernando de, abp. of Granada. *Instrucion . . . por do se regiesen los oficiales, oficios y otras personas de su casa.* In R. Academia de la historia. *Boletín.* 1930. v. 96, p. 809.

42 Teresa, Saint. p. 194, note 76.

43   *Haced llanto, caballeros,*
    Que será bien empleado;
    Dejad las barbas crecer . . .
    Ni dejeis cabello entero . . .

Torres Naharro, Bartolomé de. *Muerte de Fernando V el Católico.* In Durán. v. 2, p. 79 (no. 1037), *tr.*

44 Sánchez Cantón. *Retratos imperiales.* In [Toledo (City). Hospital de Santa Cruz] *Carlos V y su ambiente.* Toledo, 1958. p. 17; Idem. *Los retratos de los reyes de España.* Barcelona [1948] p. 111.
Julius II (pope, 1503-1513) is credited with a distinct innovation when he decided to grow a beard in order to inspire greater respect (Reynolds, Reginald. *Beards.* Garden City, New York, 1949. p. 181). Clement VII, who crowned Charles V at Bologna (1530), also was bearded. François I and Charles V must have taken up the fashion almost together. In May 1535 Henry VIII "commanded all about his Court to poll their heads, and to giue them example, hee caused his owne head to bee polled, and from thence forth his beard to bee notted [polled] and no more shauen" (Stow. p. 570).

45 Baumgarten, Hermann. *Geschichte Karls V.* Stuttgart, 1886. v. 2, p. 480.

46 Rodríguez Villa. *El emperador.* p. 160.

47 Zúñiga. p. 21, 22.

48 Norris. v. 3, bk. 1, p. 313.

49 La Celestina. *vº*sig.h⁵ *(Auto IX).*

50 Lazarillo de Tormes. *f-vºf*36, *tr. (Tractado 3.º).*

51 *Hechos del Condestable.* p. 191.

52 Bernis Madrazo. *El tocado masculino en Castilla durante el último cuarto del siglo XV: Los bonetes.* In *Archivo español de arte.* 1948. v. 21, p. 26, *tr.*

53 Rubio *and* Acemel. p. 16.

54 "From the fifteenth century and forward the word *grana* was ascribed to a twilled fabric of wool, except for that woven at Valencia, which was of silk. . . . *Grana* was never other than red in its different hues" from blood red, *colorada,* to mulberry, *morada* (Herrero García, Miguel. *Para la historia de la indumentaria española.—noticia de algunas telas.—La grana.* In *Hispania,* Madrid. 1941. v. 1, no. 5, p. [106] 107, *tr.*).

55 Sevilla (City). Archivo de protocolos. v. 5, p. 229 (no. 735).

56 Toledo (City). Ordinances. p. 49.

57 Bernis Madrazo. *Indumentaria* II; Cunnington. *Handbook.*

58 Brantôme. v. 1, p. 15.

59 Segovia (City). Alcázar. p. 117, 118.

60 Sevilla (City). Ordinances. *f*CCIIII.
Caps or bonnets that were to be black, mulberry-colored, tawny, or olive-green had first to go through a bath of bright blue *(celeste de azul subido);* blacks underwent two baths of the blue (*Ibid. f*CCIIII). At Toledo (1531) knots had to be tied in the yarn before the first bath so that afterward the quality of the blue could be tested (Toledo (City). Ordinances. p. 46).

61 *Ibid.* p. 46, 47, 56.

62 Toledo (City). Biblioteca pública. *Catálogo de la colección de manuscritos Borbón-Lorenzana, por Francisco Esteve Barba.* Madrid, 1942. p. 457, pl. [30, 31]

63 Sevilla (City). Archivo de protocolos. v. 1, p. 120 (no. 466), 136 (532).

64 Díaz del Castillo, Bernal. *Historia verdadera de la conqvista de la Nueva España.* Madrid, 1632. *f*13.

65 Vallejo, Juan de. *Memorial de la vida de Fray Francisco Jiménez de Cisneros.* Madrid, 1913. p. 99.

66 Manrique. p. 330, 337.

67 Quintero Atauri, Pelayo. *Sillerías de coro en las iglesias españolas.* Cádiz, 1928. p. 77, note 1.

68 Sevilla (City). Ordinances. *vº*CCXII, *f*CCXIII.

69 Fernández de Oviedo y Valdés. *Relación.* p. 417, 442.

70 Bradford, William. *Correspondence of the Emperor Charles V. and his ambassadors.* London, 1850. p. 354.

71 Teresa, Saint. p. 194, note 69.

72 Delicado. sig.E¹ *(Mamotreto. XIX).*

73 Fernández de Oviedo y Valdés. *Relación.* p. 427.

74 Muñoz de San Pedro y Higuero. p. 7, 35.

75 Vital. p. 148.

76 Bernis Madrazo. *Modas moriscas.* p. 205.

77 Segovia (City). Alcázar. p. 120.

78 *Inventario de la Capilla Real de Granada,* quoted in Bernis Madrazo. *Modas moriscas.* p. 206 and note 2.

The *almaizar* is described and a tapestry inset is illustrated in May, Florence Lewis. *Silk textiles of Spain.* New York, 1957. p. 18, 252, Fig. 8.

79 Alcega. 1580. *v°f*29-*f*30.

80 Girón. p. 101, 102, *tr.*

81 Gay. v. 2, p. 333, Art. *SAYON.*

82 *Ibid.* v. 2, p. 333, Art. *SAYON.*

83 *L'entrate del Re don Carlo d'Austria in Hispagna in questo anno 1517* (Biblioteca de Tarragona), quoted in Bernis Madrazo. *Indumentaria.* II. p. 24, 112 (no. 58).

84 Vital. p. 150, 151, *tr.*

85 *Questiõ de amor.* Sevilla, 1528.
By an unknown Spaniard; completed at Ferrara April 17th, 1512; published in Menéndez y Pelayo, Marcelino. *Orígenes de la novela.* Madrid, 1907. v. 2, p. [41]–98. (*Nueva biblioteca de autores españoles.* v. 7)

86 Spain. Laws, statutes, etc. *Declaracion.* sig.a⁴.

87   *No me ha dexado alegria*
        que dexe su compañia.

   Questiõ de amor. *f*xj *(Aqui el autor cuenta. . . .),* *f*xxxv, *v°f*xxxv, *v°f*xxxiiij *(Los atauios delos capitanes. . . .),* *f*viij, *tr. (Respuesta de vasquiran a Felisel.).*

88 A description of such ornaments comes from Hungary. "The studdings of garments, circular or square, and decorated with geometrical, floral, human and animal motifs, were embossed on thin silver sheets over bronze blocks (Figs. 3, 4). These spangles were either sewn onto the edges of the garment or else scattered all over its surface. The custom was most in vogue in the thirteenth and fourteenth centuries . . . similar studdings preserved in the convent of St. Andrew at Sarnen in Switzerland . . . originate from the wedding-dress of Ágnes, the Dowager Queen of Hungary [ca. 1300, pl. 7 in color]. The material . . . has been cut up . . . but even so this unique relic . . . is aglow with some one thousand and three hundred fine silver spangles" (Héjj-Détári, Angéla. *Old Hungarian jewelry.* [Budapest, 1965] p. 19); Hall, Edward. p. 519.

89 [Muñon, Sancho de] *Tragicomedia de Lisandro y Roselia* [Salamanca, 1542] Madrid, 1872. p. 146, *tr.*

90 Bernis Madrazo. *Indumentaria* II. p. 58 (28–29), 100, Art. *PUERTA;* Torquemada. *f*113, *tr. (Colloqvio V. De los vestidos).*

91 Bernis Madrazo. *El traje.* p. 231.

92 Vital. p. 151, *tr.,* 170, *tr.,* 201, 202.

93 Oznaya. p. 339–343.

94 Granada (City). R. Audiencia y chancillería. *v°f*221 (19), *f*147 (6), *f*222 (30).

95 Sevilla (City). Ordinances. *v°f*CLX [i.e. CLXV] *v°f*CLXIIII.

96 Granada (City). R. Audiencia y chancillería. *v°f*151 (4).

97 Bernis Madrazo. *Indumentaria* II. p. 94, Art. *JUBON.*

98 Vives. *Diálogos.* p. 3.

99 Toledo (City). Ordinances. p. 200.

100 Alcega. 1580. *f*21.

101 Sevilla (City). Ordinances. *v°f*CLX [i.e. CLXV] *f-v°f*CLXIIII [i.e. CLXVI] *f-v°f*CLXVII.

102 Peña Cámara. p. 293.

103 Great Britain. Public record office. *Calendar . . . Venice.* v. 3, p. 31, 34.

104 Spain. Laws, statutes, etc. *Quaderno de las cortes que en Valladolid tuuo su magestad del Emperador . . . el año de 1523.* Burgos, 1535. *v°*sig.biij-sig.biiij.

105 Girón. p. 100, *tr.*

106 Padilla. p. 19 and note *.
Pietro Martire d'Anghiera, who was in Barcelona at the time, says that it was the King's gold collar that took the blow (*Epistolario.* v. 1, p. 227). However, as the aim was made at the point where the neck joins the head, and as a gold collar generally lay at the base of the neck or lower, it would seem correct to give the credit to the doublet collar.

107 Sevilla (City). Ordinances. *v°f*CLX [i.e. CLXV]

108 Girón. p. 100–101.

109 Torquemada. *v°f*112, *tr. (Colloqvio V. De los vestidos).*

110 Giovanni di Paolo. *Figure di Beate* (detail of "Paradiso"), dated 1445. Siena. Pinacoteca (Pisetsky. v. 2, Fig. 96, p. [225]).

111 Talavera. *Tractado.* *v°f*61, *tr.*

112 Serrano y Sanz, Manuel. *Inventarios aragoneses de los siglos XIV y XV.* In R. Academia española. *Boletín.* 1922. v. 9, p. 266.

113 Lazarillo de Tormes. *f*15 *(Tractado 2.º).*

114 Gay. v. 2, p. 195, *tr.,* Art. *PALETOT;* Cunnington. *A dictionary.* p. 154, Art. PALTOCK; Norris. v. 3, bk. 1, p. 22.

115 Bernis Madrazo. *Indumentaria* II. p. 99, Art. *PALETOQUE;* Pérez Pastor. v. 2, p. 259.

116 Bernis Madrazo. *El traje.* p. 231.

117 Talavera. *Reforma.* *v°f*3–*f*4.

118 Idem. *Tractado.* *v°f*60–*f*61, *tr.*

119 Oznaya. p. 366, *tr.*

120 Vives. *Diálogos.* p. 139, 141, *tr.*

121 Clemencín. p. 309.

122 Fernández de Oviedo y Valdés. *Libro.* p. 65, 25.

123 Vital. p. 170.

124 Bernis Madrazo. *El traje.* p. 194, *tr.*

125 Vital. p. 170, *tr.*
Étoffer—estofar, aforrar un vestido (Fernández Cuesta, Nemesio. *Diccionario de las lenguas española y francesa.* Barcelona, 1885. v. 1, p. 768, Art. *ÉTOFFER*).

126 Gay. v. 1, p. 360–361, Art. *CHEMISE.*

127 Segovia (City). *Alcázar.* p. 121.

128 Sevilla (City). Ordinances. *f*CLXIIII [i.e. CLXVI] *tr.*
An ordinance of 1546 at Granada required that new canvas, doubled, be placed at the waistbands *(pretinas)* where points were attached. In cloth hose, bands *(virones)* of linen had to be inserted from the waistline down to the turn of the buttock *(talle de la nalga)* to protect the lining. The seams of silk-fabric hose and the edges of silk trimmings were waxed, which would prevent raveling (Granada (City). R. Audiencia y chancillería. *v°f*220 (1, 3, 5), *f*221 (11)).

129 Fernández de Oviedo y Valdés. *Libro.* p. 26, 44, 65; Vives. *Diálogos.* p. 141; La Celestina. *v°*sig.k[6].

130 Rey Soto, Antonio. *La imprenta en Galicia: el libro gótico.* Madrid, 1934. p. 105.

131 Alós, Ramón d'. *Inventaris de castells catalans (sigles XIV-XVI).* In *Estudis universitaris catalans.* 1910. v. 4, p. 168.

132 Vital. p. 212, 213.

133 Fernández de Oviedo y Valdés. *Relación.* p. 446.

134 *La marvillosa coronación.* p. 129.

135 Fernández de Córdoba y Salabert. v. 1, p. 149.

136 Stow. p. 867.

137 Rodríguez Villa. *El emperador.* p. 749.

138 Since the horse martingale is called *gamarra* in Spanish, the word *martingala* must have originated outside the Peninsula.

   Notes on Rabelais by Jacob Le Duchat (1658–1735) and others shed light on "the Martingale Fashion, *wherein is a Spunge-hole with a Draw-bridge for the Fundament, in order to dung the more easily.* . . . This sort of Breeches which was still in Use in *Rabelais's* Time, took its Name from the *Martegaux* [Martigaux], the People of *Martegue* [Martigues] in *Provence,* who were the first Inventors of it, and the Author assigns them to such Guttlers and four Feeders as the Pedant *Janotus,* because these same *Martingale* Breeches having, behind, an Opening covered with a Piece of square Cloth, which moved up or down like a Draw-bridge, perfectly well suited those great Eaters, who oftentimes can't untruss other Breeches fast enough" (Rabelais. v. 2, p. 59, note 114).

139 Pisetsky. v. 2, p. 339.

140 Salazar, Eugenio de. *Cartas.* Madrid, 1866. p. 27.

141 Brantôme had seen Spanish soldiers on the move use the martingale rather than "dally so much with untying and retying laces" and described it as a "drawbridge" *(pont-levis)* when worn by a mounted Frenchman who served in Italy under Louis XII and François I (v. 1, p. 210, *tr.*).

142 Rodríguez Villa. *El emperador.* p. 749.

143   *Tan ben e tan gen si causseron
      Que diseras c'ab el nasqueron.*

   From *Flamenca,* quoted in Jaberg, Karl. *Zur Sach- und Bezeichnungsgeschichte der Beinbekleidung in der Zentralromania.* In *Wörter und Sachen.* 1926. v. 9, p. 141, *tr.*

144 Pisetsky. v. 2, p. 339; v. 3, p. 138.

145 Bernis Madrazo. *Indumentaria* II. p. 55 (nos. 7–10).

146 Oznaya. p. 373.

147 *La maravillosa coronación.* p. 127, *tr.*

148 Isabel de Portugal. *Relacion* I. sig.9, p. [3]

149 Cunnington. *Handbook.* p. 32.

150 *Relación . . . de las grandes fiestas . . . en Flandes [1549]* In *Relaciones de los reinados de Carlos V y Felipe II.* Madrid, 1950. v. 2, p. 206.
   A statement attributed to Holinshed's *Chronicles* is quoted as follows: "In reference to Spain, [William] Harrison [between 1577 and 1587] wrote: 'The Spaniards now wear trunk hose . . . and beneath them curiously wrought stockings,'" which Grass takes to have been "hand 'knit-silk stockings'" (Grass, Milton N. *History of hosiery.* [New York] 1955. p. 118).

151 Peña Cámara. p. 293.

152 "Design'd for some Lady. Such was the Gallantry of the *French* at that Time, and so continued almost to the End of the XVIth Century . . . *their Breeches were so close, there could be no Pockets made in them: but instead thereof they had a swindging Codpiece, with two Wings on each Side, which they fastened with Points, on either Side one: and within this large Space, which was between the said two Points, Shirt and Codpiece, they put their Handkerchiefs, an Apple,* an Orange, *or other Fruit, as also their Purse, &c. and it was not at all uncivil, when they were at Table, to make a Present of the Fruit, which they had for some Time kept in their Codpiece, any more than it is now-a-days to offer Fruit out of one's Pockets* (Rabelais. v. 2, p. 132–133, note 9).

153 Sánchez Cantón. *Floreto.* p. 72–73.

154 Hermosilla, Diego de. *Diálogo de la vida de los pajes de palacio.* Valladolid, 1916. p. 18.

155 Pisetsky. v. 3, p. 137.

156 Navarra. Laws, statutes, etc. *v°f*LIX; Spain. Laws, statutes, etc. *La prematica. v°*sig.Biiij-sig.B[5].

157 Laver. *Early Tudor.* p. 7. In Laver, ed.

158 Evans. p. 62, pl.62.

159 Kelly, Francis M. *and* Schwabe, Randolph. *A short history of costume & armour.* London [1931] v. 2, p. 3.

160 Reade, Brian. *The dominance of Spain,* 1550–1660. p. 15, pl. 1. In Laver, ed.

161 Sevilla (City). Ordinances. *v°f*CLVI, *f-v°f*CLVII, *f*CLIX.

162 Sevilla (City). Archivo de protocolos. v. 1, p. 125 (no. 487); Haring, Clarence Henry. *Trade and navigation between Spain and the Indies in the time of the Hapsburgs.* Cambridge, 1918. p. 124.

163 Sevilla (City). Ordinances. *v°f*CLIX, *v°f*CLVII.

164 La Celestina. *v°*sig.i[8], *tr. (Auto XII).*

165 Covarrubias y Orozco. *v°f*148, Art. *BORZEGVI.*

166 Ballesteros-Gaibrois. p. xx (no. 91), XXI, (95 y 96), XXIV (113).

167 Cunnington. *Handbook.* p. 39.

168 Rodríguez Villa. *El emperador.* p. 758.

169 Talavera. *Tractado. f*63.

170 Durán. *Romancero general.* v. 1, p. 52 (no. 103).

171 Sevilla (City). Ordinances. *f-v°f*CLV; Toledo (City). Ordinances. p. 59.

172 Vargas Machuca, Bernardo de. *Libro de exercicios de la gineta.* Madrid, 1600. *f-v°f*11.

173 Tapia y Salcedo, Gregorio de. *Exercicios dela gineta.* Madrid, 1643. pl. 8, p. 17–18; etching by María Eugenia de Beer.

174 Toledo (City). Ordinances. p. 59, *tr.*

175 Castillo. Valēcia, 1511. *v°f*ccxxj.

176 Palencia. *v°f*lxxxxvj, Art. *Coturni.*

177 Navarra, Spain. Laws, statutes, etc. *f*LIX.

178 Covarrubias y Orozco. *f*294, Art. *CHINELA.*

179 [Sindbad, the philosopher] *El libro de los engaños, edited by John Esten Keller.* Chapel Hill, 1953. p. 8.

180 Oliver Asín. p. 138, *tr.*

181 Spain. Laws, statutes, etc. *Pragmaticas y Leyes.* ƒclix.

182 Toledo (City). Ordinances. p. 59.
   In 1928 sheets of cork cut from the tree were boiled to soften them and to increase their bulk.

183 Zúñiga. p. 21, *tr.*

184 Carreres Zacarés, Salvador. *Más pantuflos.* In *Correo erudito.* [1941] año 2, entrega 11, p. 45; Ballesteros-Gaibrois. p. LVII (no. 308).

185 Fernández de Oviedo y Valdés. *Diálogos.* p. 70.

186 Castiglione. *vº*ƒxxvij (bk. 1).

187 Granada (City). R. Audiencia y chancillería. *vº*ƒ166 (10).

188 Sevilla (City). Ordinances. ƒCXCVIII.

189 Spain. Laws, statutes, etc. *La prematica.* *vº*sig.B¹.

190   *Capelo galochas guantes*
        el galan deue traer
        bien cantar y componer
        en coplas y consonantes

   Castillo. Valēcia, 1511. ƒlj.

191 Milán. *vº*sig.Ev, *vº*sig.E⁷.

192 Muñoz de San Pedro e Higuero. p. 36.

193 Sáez. p. 535.

194 Mendez de Silva, Rodrigo, quoted in Díaz Ballesteros, Miguel. *Historia de la villa de Ocaña.* Ocaña, 1868. v. [1] p. 108.

195 Rodriguez Moñino. v. 3, p. 301.

196 Sevilla (City). Ordinances. *vº*ƒCCXXXIII.

197 A. *Los guantes.* In *El Museo universal.* 1862. año 6, p. 91.

198 Great Britain. Public record office. *Calendar . . . Venice.* v. 3, p. 19.

199 Rodríguez Villa. *Las cuentas del Gran Capitán.* In R. Academia de la historia. *Boletín.* 1910. v. 56, p. 285, *tr.*

200 Guevara. *Epistolas.* pt. 2, ƒcxvj-ƒcxvij, *tr.* *(Letra [XX] para micer perepollastre).*

201 Great Britain. Public record office. *Calendar . . . Venice.* v. 3, p. 328.

202 Cervantes Saavedra. ƒ173, *tr.* (ch. XXXI).
   In a passage which Gay dates 1560, Garzóni reports: "Spanish gloves are treated with oil of jessamine and with ambergris, after they have been well washed with a little malmsey wine and anointed with a little odoriferous grease. Or indeed with powder of cypress, with pomade, with oil of cedar, with oil of benzoin, and with some grains of musk, with select cinnamon, cloves, storax, nutmeg, oil of lemon and civet. Or indeed with water of orange flowers and of musk rose. Or indeed with goat tallow *(becco)* mixed with oil of jessamine, of *martella*, of lemon, camphor, and white lead *(biacca).* Or indeed with oil of sweet almonds, roots of white lily, rose water, oil of musk, oil of fruit stone *(spico, spicchio?)*, white ambergris, oil of storax, and similar things" (Garzóni, Tommaso. *La piazza vniversale.* Venezia, 1616. *vº*ƒ281, *tr.*, *Discorso LXXXVI*); Gay. v. 1, p. 760, Art. *GANT.*

203 Gay. v. 1, p. 760, Art. *GANT.*

204 Castiglione. ƒlxxvij (bk. 2).

205 Almela y Vives. p. 16–17.

206 Fernández de Oviedo y Valdés. *Las quinquagenas.* p. 319–320, *condensed and tr.*

207 Sánchez Cantón. *Floreto.* p. 17.

208 Muñoz de San Pedro e Higuero. p. 36, 38.

209 [Braamcamp Freire, Anselmo] *Inventario da Guarda-roupa de D. Manuel.* In *Archivo histórico portuguez.* 1904. v. 2, p. 387–388.

210 Sevilla (City). Ordinances. *vº*ƒCCXXXIIII.

211 Puiggarí y Llobet. p. 320.

212 Gay. v. 1, p. 658, *tr.*, Art. *ESCARCELLE.*

213 Pisetsky. v. 2, p. 378.

214 Fernández de Córdoba y Salabert. v. 1, p. 150.

215 Gay. v. 1, p. 777, *tr.*, Art. *GIBECIÈRE.*

216 Puiggarí y Llobet. p. 320.

217 *Nouveau Larousse illustré.* Paris [1898–1904] v. 4, p. 841, Art. *GIBECIÈRE.*

218 Vives. *Diálogos.* p. 143, *tr.*

219 Covarrubias y Orozco. ƒ238, *tr.*, Art. *CORCHETE.*

220 Leloir. p. 3, Art. *AGRAFE.*

221 Vives. *Diálogos.* p. 3, 5, *tr.*

222 Amador de los Ríos. p. 47; Fernández de Córdoba y Salabert. v. 1, p. 81.

223 Sevilla (City). Ordinances. *vº*ƒCCXXXIII, *tr.*

224 Granada (City). R. Audiencia y chancillería. ƒ221 (11, 12), ƒ151 (2).

225 Guevara. *Libro.* ƒcxxxv (ch. v).

226 Granada (City). R. Audiencia y chancillería. ƒ152 (14), ƒ171 (5), ƒ152 (2, 5).

227 Bernis Madrazo. *Indumentaria* II. p. 74, Art. *AGUJETAS.*

228 Juana la Loca. *Inventario.* p. 199.

229 Gay. v. 1, p. 361, Art. *CHEMISE.*

230 Vital. p. 170.

231 Aḥmad ibn Muḥammad, al-Makḱarī. *The history of the Mohammedan dynasties in Spain.* London, 1843. v. 2, p. 160–162, 165.

232 Dozy, Reinhart Pieter Anne. *Spanish Islam.* London, 1913. p. 452.

233 Girón. p. 101–102, *tr.*

234 Bernis Madrazo. *Modas moriscas.* Fig. 15.

235 Anghiera, Pietro Martire d'. *Incipitur Legatio Babylonica.* [dated . . . alexandria . . . 1502; printed, ca. 1515?] *vº*sig.A.7.

236 Dozy, Reinhart Pieter Anne. *Dictionnaire détaillé des noms des vêtements chez les Arabes.* Amsterdam, 1845. p. 113, Art. [djobbah].

237 Bernis y Madrazo. *Modas moriscas.* p. 215–216.

238 Ricard, Robert. *Espagnol et portugais "marlota", recherches sur le vocabulaire du vêtement hispano-mauresque.* In *Bulletin hispanique.* 1951. v. 53, p. 136, 152.

239 Alcega. 1580. v^of62, tr.

240 Castillo. Toledo, 1527. v^ofxlviij.

241 Vital. p. 248, tr.

242 Durán. Romancero . . . moriscos. p. 130.

243 Pérez de Hita. v^of115–f121.

244 Durán. Romancero general. v. 1, p. 23 (no. 49), 46 (85),
51 (97), 78 (152), 79 (153); Idem. Romancero . . . moriscos.
p. 31, 40, 60, 147.
    See also Matulka, Barbara. The novels of Juan de Flores
    and their European diffusion. New York [1931] p. 266–282:
    Fiometa's Sepultura, color symbolism; British museum.
    Dept. of manuscripts. Additional 10431. Der spanische can-
    cionero des Brit. mus. . . . von Dr. Hugo Albert Rennert.
    Erlangen, 1895. p. 76–77. (Offprint, Romanischen For-
    schungen, v. 10)

245 Madrid (City). Museo del ejército. Catálogo. [Madrid, 1953]
v. 1, p. 211; Amador de los Ríos. p. 62–64.

246 Bernis Madrazo. Modas moriscas. Fig. 13.

247 Durán. Romancero . . . moriscos. p. 32, 130, 131, 147.
    For description of mid-sixteenth-century marlotas see
    Martínez Ruiz. p. 67–72.

248 Covarrubias y Orozco. v^of194, Art. CAPELLAR.

249 Bernáldez. p. 238–240 (ch. LXXXIV).

250 Manrique. p. 329, 336, 337.

251 Fernández de Córdoba y Salabert. v. 1, p. 149.

252 Bernis Madrazo. Modas moriscas. Figs. 10, 16.

253 Alcega. 1580. f63, tr.

254 Dihle, Helene. Neue Forschungen zur spanische Tracht. In
Zeitschrift für historische Waffen- und Kostümkunde. 1939.
v. 6, pt. 10, pl. II, 8.
    The marlota is reproduced in pl. III, 6.

255 Durán. Romancero general. v. 1, p. 23 (no. 49), 51 (97),
118 (227).

256 Pérez de Hita. v^of69, f73–f75.

257 Evans. p. 63.

258 Bernis Madrazo. Indumentaria II. p. 24–25.

259 Romano, Giuseppe. Cronaca del soggiorno di Carlo V in
Italia (dal 26 Luglio 1529 al 25 Aprile 1530). Milano, 1892.
p. 203, quoted in Bernis Madrazo. Indumentaria II. p. 25,
112 (no. 81).

260 Questiõ de amor. f-v^ofxxx (Como las damas salieron. . . .).

261   No se puede mi passion
            escreuir
            pues no se puede sufrir.

    Idem. f-v^ofix (Aqui el autor cuenta . . . .), fiiij, tr. (Las
    cosas q̃ Flamiano mostro. . . .).

262   El fuego que el alma abrasa
            avn que se encubre
            con la pena se descubre.

    Idem. fiiij, v^ofiiij, tr. (Las cosas q̃ Flamiano mostro. . . .).

263   Las cuentas de mis pesares
            se han de contar a millares.

    Idem. fxxxij, tr. (Como los mantenedores. . . .).

264 Vital. p. 200–203.

265 Milán. sig.Aiiij, v^osig.Av, sig.A⁶, A⁷, A⁸, tr., sig.Ciij.

266 Beaulieu, Michèle and Baylé, Jeanne. Le costume en Bour-
gogne de Philippe le Hardi à la mort de Charles le Téméraire
(1364–1477). Paris, 1956. p. [41] tr.

267 Vital. p. 201, tr.

268 Crónica del Rey Don Juan II by unknown. Comiença la
Cronica del serenissimo rey Juan el segundo. Logroño, 1517.
v^oflxxxiii (año xxiiii), fccl (Generaciones).

269 Hechos del Condestable. p. 42; Questiõ de amor. fiiij (Las
cosas q̃ Flamiano mostro. . . .).

270 Lazarillo de Tormes. f26, v^of28, f29 (Tractado 3.°).

271 Milán. v^osig.C⁷, sig.Diij.

272 Questiõ de amor. fxj, ix, v^ofx (Aqui el autor cuenta. . . .),
fxxij (Lo que passo acabada la egloga.).

273 Great Britain. Public record office. Calendar . . . Venice.
p. 414, 416–417; Idem. Letters. p. 521.

274 Fernández de Oviedo y Valdés. Relación. p. 462–463.

275 Vital. p. 170, 202.

276 La maravillosa coronación. p. 127.

277 Fernández de Córdoba y Salabert. v. 1, p. 150.

278 "At night when, in Florence, it is the custom to go out a
great deal, there are worn . . . capes termed 'in the Spanish
style', that is, with a hood at back. He who wears it in
the daytime, if he is not a soldier, is considered a rascal,
a man of wicked life" (Varchi, Benedetto. Storia Fiorentina.
Firenze, 1858. v. 2, p. 85, tr. (bk. 9)).

279 Girón. p. 101.

280 Sevilla (City). Ordinances. v^ofCLXIIII.

281 Bernis Madrazo. Indumentaria II. p. 81, tr., Art. CAPA.
For an illustration of the Gallegan cape see Ibid. Fig. 142.

282 Fernández de Córdoba y Salabert. v. 2, p. 183.

283 Bernis Madrazo. Indumentaria II. p. 81, Art. CAPA.

284 Almela y Vives. p. 7.

285 Girón. p. 101.

286 Bernis Madrazo. El traje. pl. V (no. 36), p. 221.

287 Vandevivere, Ignace. La cathédrale de Palencia et l'église
paroissiale de Cervera de Pisuerga. Bruxelles, 1967. p. 27–
28, pl. CXVIa in color.

288 Fernández de Oviedo y Valdés. Diálogos. p. 70, 71.

289 Ortiz de Zúñiga, Diego. Annales eclesiasticos y secvlares
de la . . . Civdad de Sevilla. Madrid, 1677. p. 489 (bk. XIV).

290 Sevilla (City). Ordinances. fCLXIIII [i.e. CLXVI]
fCLXVII.

291 Fernández de Oviedo y Valdés. Libro. p. 27.

292 Questiõ de amor. v^ofx, fxj, v^ofxj-fxij (Aqui el autor
cuenta. . . .).

293 Spain. Laws, statutes, etc. Pragmaticas y Leyes. fclix.

294 Bernis Madrazo. Indumentaria II. p. 89, Art. ESCUBA;
Fernández de Córdoba y Salabert. v. 1, p. 150.

295 Girón. p. 101.

296 Menéndez Pidal, Ramón. Poesía popular y romancero. In
Revista de filología española. 1914. v. 1, p. 361, 362.

297 Zúñiga. p. 18.

298 Sáez. p. 534.

299 Girón. p. 101, *tr.*

300 Bernis Madrazo. *Indumentaria* II. p. 90, Art. *GABAN.*

301 Valdés, Juan de. *Diálogo de la lengua.* Madrid [1969] p. 123, *tr.*

302 Covarrubias y Orozco. *f-v°f*432, Art. *GAVAN.*

303 Guevara. *Libro. f*cxxxv (ch. v); Covarrubias y Orozco. *f*193, Art. *CAPA.*

304 Segovia (City). Alcázar. p. 119.

305 Girón. p. 101, *tr.*

306 Sandoval. pt. 1, *v°f*5 (bk. 1, XIII).

307   *Claro descubre mi pena*
             mi tristeza y el agena.

     *Questiõ de amor. v°f*iij, *tr. (Las cosas q̃ Flamiano mostro. . . .).*

308 Spain. Laws, statutes, etc. *Las pramaticas. v°f*CLVI [i.e. CLXI]

309 Sevilla (City). Ordinances. *v°f*CLXX.

310 Girón. p. 101.

311 Talavera. *Tractado. v°f*53-*f*54, *tr.*

312 Bernis Madrazo. *El traje.* pl. V (nos. 27–29), p. 214.

313 Correia, Gaspar. *Lendas da India.* Lisboa, 1860. v. 2, p. 409.

314 Zúñiga. p. 31.

315 Díaz Tanco de Frejenal, Vasco. *Los veinte triumphos.* [n.p., ca. 1535?] *f-v°f*lviii.

316 Alcega. 1580. *v°f*64–*v°f*65.

317 Bernis Madrazo. *Indumentaria* II. p. 77, Art. *BALANDRAN.*

318 Peña Cámara. p. 293.

319 Zúñiga. p. 21, *tr.*

320 Spain. Laws, statutes, etc. *Las pramaticas.* v *°f*CXXXVIII, *tr.*

321 Segovia (City). Alcázar. p. 118; Fernández de Córdoba y Salabert. v. 1, p. 149.

322 *Enciclopedia vniversal ilvstrada evropeo-americana.* Barcelona [1907?–30] v. 15, p. 1283, Art. *COTA DE ARMAS.*

323 "These chivalric characters with emblazoned tabards . . . came to be [a] familiar . . . adjunct in the Isabeline style" (Proske, Beatrice Gilman. *Castilian sculpture, Gothic to Renaissance.* New York, 1951. p. 141).

324 Santa Cruz. v. 2, p. 426, *tr.*, 445–446.

325 The Metropolitan Museum of Art owns several badges of recognition, of which one possibly is Spanish, that is, Catalan. It is an ovoid shield of bronze measuring 13 by 8.5 cm. The edge, turned back all round to a depth of about 1 cm. and reinforced with a bronze band of matching width, creates a hollow space which, when and if the badge had a back, could be used for carrying letters. Its charge is a gilt lion rampant to the dexter side on a blue enamel field. The edge band also is gilded (seen by courtesy of the Curator of Arms and Armor, Dr. Helmut Nickel. Badges of recognition are discussed in his *The man beside the gate.* In New York. Metropolitan museum of art. *Bulletin.* 1966. v. 24, p. 237–241).

326 Paz y Mélia. v. 11, p. 59, 64, 435.

327 Links. p. 28.

328 *Ibid.* p. 55.

329 Segovia (City). Alcázar. p. 118.

330 Covarrubias y Orozco. *f*262, *tr.,* Art. *ÇAMARRO.*

331 Zúñiga. p. 17, *tr.*

332 Escobar y Prieto, Eugenio. *Epistolario Guadalupense de los Reyes Católicos.* In *El Monasterio de Guadalupe.* [1917?] v. 2, p. 224.

333 Guevara. *Libro. f*cxxxv (ch. v).

334 Rodríguez Moñino. p. 301.

335 Manrique. p. 329.

336 Prat, Jean-H. *Fourrure et pelletiers à travers les âges.* Paris [1952] p. 166.

337 Sevilla (City). Ordinances. *v°f*CLXXII.

338 *Viaje de Turquía* (attributed to Andrés de Laguna *or* to Cristóbal de Villalón). In Serrano y Sanz, Manuel. *Autobiografías y memorias.* Madrid, 1906. p. 130. *(Nueva biblioteca de autores españoles.* v. 2)

339 Lévi-Provençal, Évariste. *L'Espagne musulmane au x°ᵐᵉ siècle.* Paris, 1932. p. 184.

340 *A new English dictionary.* Oxford, 1926. v. 10, pt. 1, p. 36, Art. *Timber, sb.²* "1503 . . . For xij tymir of gray grece to lyne the samyn, ilk tymir contenand xl bestis"; Fisher, Raymond H. *The Russian fur trade, 1550–1700.* Berkeley and Los Angeles, 1943. p. 68. (*University of California publications in history.* 31)

341 Paz y Mélia. v. 12, p. 79, note 1.

342 *La maravillosa coronación.* p. [125]

343 Bernis Madrazo. *Indumentaria* II. Fig. 53.

344 Garzóni, Tommaso. [*La piazza vniversale.* Sp. tr. with additions by Cristóbal Suárez de Figueroa] *Plaza vniversal de todas ciencias, y artes.* Perpiñan, 1629. *f*375.

345 Talavera. *Auisacion. f*23–*v°f*24.

346 Ribadeneyra, Marcelo de. *Historia de las islas del Archipiélago Filipino, y Reino de la Gran China* [Barcelona, 1613] Madrid, 1947. p. 372, quoted in Teresa, Saint. p. 203, note 189.

347 Diego Angulo Iñiguez considers this dais to be actually a *gloria,* "a double pavement in communication with a furnace heated red by burning straw to produce a layer of hot air under a room floor. . . . Sometimes the double floor runs under a whole room; sometimes, as in Berruguete's painting, it is reduced to the dais" *(Pintura del Renacimiento.* Madrid [1954] p. 91, *tr. (Ars hispaniae,* v. 12)).

     A diagram and further description of the *gloria* are given in Flores, Carlos. *Arquitectura popular española.* [Madrid, 1973] v. 3, p. 69, 70, 72.

348 Talavera. *Auisacion. v°f*24–*f*26.

349 Cotarelo y Mori, Emilio. *La dama castellana a fines del siglo XV.* In R. Academia española. *Boletín.* 1916. v. 3, p. 81.

350 In Las Hurdes (Cáceres), as recently as 1928, women traveled in such a saddle, few roads for wheeled vehicles then existing there.

351 Machado. p. 170–184.

352 Carriazo. p. 46–47, 48–49; Bernáldez. p. 279–280 (ch. XCV); *Chronica.* ƒ307 (ch. CXXVIII).

353 Resende. *ƒ-vᵒƒ*lxvij, *tr.* (ch. CXVIII).

354 *Chronica. ƒ-vᵒƒ*307 (ch. CXXIX).

355 Eximeniç, Francesch. *Libre deles dones* [Sp. ᵗʳ by Alonso de Salvatierra?] *Este deuoto libro se llama Carro de las donas.* Valladolid, 1542. bk. 2, *ƒ-vᵒƒ*xlv (ch. lxv).

356 Ochoa y Ronna. p. 19.

357 *Ibid.* p. 16–17.

358 Spain. Laws, statutes, etc. *Las pramaticas. vᵒƒ*CXLI-ƒCXLII, *tr.*

359 Molinet. p. 62.

360 Sánchez Cantón. *Floreto.* p. 52.

361 The story that Margarita de Austria brought a carriage with her into Spain is not confirmed by Molinet, her librarian and biographer. He says that a gentleman of Phelipe el Hermoso's entourage (1502), lord of Boussu, "kept his cart going *(fit roller sa charrette)* beyond the [Basque] mountains, which had not been done in the memory of man, and at which the country people could not have been more astonished, never having seen such a cart on their borders" (Molinet. p. 181, *tr.;* Lalaing. p. 150).
    Larousse illustrates the *charrette anglaise* as a light, two-wheeled cart.

362 Molinet. p. 159.

363 Faria e Souza, Manoel de. *Evropa portuguesa.* Lisboa, 1679. v. 2, p. 501, *tr.*

364 Resende. *ƒ-vᵒƒ*cxxv, *tr.*

365 [Great Britain. Public record office] *Calendar of letters, despatches, and state papers, relating to the negotiations between England and Spain.* London, 1862. v. 1, p. 5, 12, 13, 39, 123, 129, 220–221, 226, 246–247.

366 Leland, John. *Joannis Lelandi antiquarii de rebvs Britannicis collectanea.* Londini, 1770. v. 5, p. 353–354.

367 *The Voyage.* p. 278, 288.

368 *Idem.* p. 288.

369 Mattingly. p. 48.

370 Green, *Mrs.* Mary Anne Everett (Wood). *Letters of royal and illustrious ladies of Great Britain.* London, 1846. v. 1, p. 139.

371 Lalaing. p. 179–180, *tr.*

372 Anghiera. v. 2, p. 83–84.

373 Mattingly. p. 66.

374 Sánchez Cantón. *Floreto.* p. 70–71; Fuente, Vicente de la. *Doña Juana la Loca vindicada de la nota de heregía.* Madrid, 1869. p. 15–16.

375 Prawdin, Michael [pseud. of Michael Charol] *Juana la Loca.* Barcelona [1957] p. 109–110.

376 Anghiera. v. 2, p. 278, *tr.*

377 Rodríguez Villa, Antonio. *La reina Doña Juana la Loca; estudio histórico.* Madrid, 1892. p. 238, *tr.*

378 Sandoval. pt. 1, ƒ15, *tr.* (bk. 1, XXXIIII); Sánchez Cantón. *Floreto.* p. 73.

379 Juana la Loca. *Inventario.* p. [171]–375.

380 Sandoval. pt. 1, ƒ17 [i.e. 10] (bk. 1, XXIII).

381 Castillejo, Cristóbal de. *Diálogo y discurso de la vida de corte.* In Castro y Rossi, Adolfo de. *Poetas líricos de los siglos XVI y XVII.* Madrid, 1854. v. 1, p. 227, *tr.* (*Biblioteca de autores españoles.* v. [32])

382   *Las tres hazen compañia*
         allalegria.
    *Questiõ de amor. ƒ*ix, *vᵒƒ*ix, *tr., ƒ*x *(Aqui el autor cuenta. . . .), ƒ*xiij *(Delas cosas que Flamiano y Belisena passaron. . . .).*

383 Idem. *vᵒƒ*[xvij] *(Lo que eneste tiempo . . . cañas.).*

384 Idem. *vᵒƒ*xxvij *(Lo que se concerto. . . .), ƒ*xxviij, *vᵒƒ*xxviij *(Como las damas salieron. . . .), vᵒƒ*xxxij *(Aqui da razõ el auctor. . . .).*

385 Vital. p. 94–95, 121, 129–130.

386 Osório. p. 141, 232.

387 Anghiera. v. 3, p. 315, *tr.,* 320, *tr.,* 324.

388 Osório. p. 234–236.

389 Góis, Damião de. *Crónica do felicíssimo rei D. Manuel.* [Lisboa, 1567] Coimbra, 1955. v. 4, p. 229.

390 Anghiera. v. 4, p. 251.

391 Sousa, Luís de, frei. *Anais de D. João III.* Lisboa [1951] v. 1, p. 73–76.

392 Andrada. p. 42, 48–51, 210–211.

393 Anghiera. v. 4, p. 374.

394 Llanos y Torriglia, Félix de. *Discurso. . . . Contribución al estudio de la reina de Portugal . . . doña Catalina de Austria.* Madrid, 1923. p. 24, 25, *tr.*

395 This painting has been assigned to two weddings, the third of Manuel I (1518) and that of João III (1525). At the left an elderly gentleman's white robe bears on the hem a clear inscription: D. ALVARO. DA. COSTA. PRIMᴿᴼ· Pᴰᴼᴿ· DESTA CASA. Alvaro da Costa was the name of the ambassador who in September 1517 went to Spain to arrange for Manuel I to marry Infanta Leonor.
    Reynaldo dos Santos reports the painting as dated 1541 and states that the habit of dating, rare at this period, was peculiar to Garcia Fernandes (*Os primitivos portugueses (1450–1550).* Lisboa, 1958. p. 37). The portraits of the bride and the groom resemble those of Catalina de Austria and João III. João, 23 when he married, is shown with a beard in some portraits. Manuel I, nearing 50 in 1517, was then represented as clean shaven. It would seem that in 1541 the painter used likenesses of the reigning pair to represent their predecessors. The Queen's dress resembles somewhat that shown in one type of portrait of Isabel de Portugal (Fig. 386), who married in 1526.

396 Andrada. p. 49, 295, 296.

397 Great Britain. Public record office. *Calendar . . . Venice.* v. 3, p. 459, 460, 470.

398 Fernández de Oviedo y Valdés. *Relación.* p. 434–435, 441–442.

399 Fernández de Córdoba y Salabert. v. 2, p. 206.

400 Full details of Isabel de Portugal's wedding journey, drawn from several contemporary sources, are given in Carriazo. p. 60–86.

401 Paz y Mélia. v. 11, p. 316, *tr.*

402 Great Britain. Public record office. *Calendar . . . Venice.* v. 3, p. 374, note *; Braamcamp Freire, Anselmo. *Ida da Imperatriz D. Isabel para Castela.* In Academia das ciências de Lisboa. *Boletim da classe de letras.* 1918–1919. v. 13, p. 563, *tr.;* Flórez, Enrique. *Memorias de las reynas catholicas.* Madrid, 1790. v. 2, p. 869, *tr.*

403 Guevara. *Epístolas.* pt. [1] *vºf*xxix, *f*xxx *(Letra [XIII] para el marques delos velez).*

404 Uhagón y Guardamino, Francisco Rafael de, marqués de Laurencín. *Dos relaciones históricas.* In R. Academia de la historia. *Boletín.* 1926. v. 88, p. 53, 61–63.

After the passing of a king or a queen, certain of the royal clothes and other possessions might be reserved to the consort and the children or be given to friends and attendants, but a great many were sold at public auction *(almoneda).* Leaving debts unpaid was considered a serious obstacle to salvation, and hard cash was in short supply (Sánchez Cantón. *Inventarios reales. Bienes muebles que pertenecieron a Felipe II.* Madrid, 1956–59. v. 1, p. XII. *(Archivo documental español.* v. 10)

The Empress's sale went on for two years after her death (1539–1541), and some of the great families of Spain were represented among the buyers. Arrangements for the sale probably followed the same course as that for an auction held for her daughter-in-law (1569), of which exact details are known.

The first task after a royal demise was to draw up an inventory. That finished, quarters were rented in a convenient location, where things to be sold were arranged on shelves, tables, and trestles. The official in charge sent a crier *(pregonero)* to announce in clear, intelligible terms through streets, plazas, and markets that anyone who wished to buy at the royal sale should go to a certain address, where the things would be shown and sold to the highest bidder. The hours of one sale were from 8:00 to 12:00 A.M. and from 2:00 to 6:00 P.M. The *pregonero* would loudly announce and describe each object, and then buyers made their offers. All sorts of people attended—nobles, hidalgos, hangers-on at court, merchants, tradesmen, rustics, even monks and curates. A great noble might send an agent. Servants bought garments within their means or accepted them as quittance of back pay. Old-clothes dealers were excluded (Amezúa y Mayo, Agustín G. de. *Isabel de Valois.* Madrid, 1949. v. 3, p. 530–533).

405 Paz y Mélia. v. II, p. 317, *tr.*

406 Mignet, François Auguste Marie Alexis. *Rivalité de François Iᵉʳ et de Charles-Quint.* Paris, 1875. v. 2, p. 472–473, 488–490.

407 *Le journal.* p. 344, *tr.;* p. 345.

408 Boehn. v. 2, p. III.

409 *El crotalón.* p. 249, *tr.*

410 Saxl, Fritz. *Costumes and festivals of Milanese society under Spanish rule.* London [1937?] p. 20–21.

Saxl associates the doll (Wien. Kunsthistorisches Museum) with Gianello della Torre, an engineer from Cremona, Italy, who as Juanelo Turriano worked at Toledo for half a century until he died in 1585. Saxl's description tallies with another passage: "The gait . . . gave a certain air of distinction which no hidalgo could afford to neglect. The man's gait should be martial with great strides; the lady's delicate, rapid, with tiny steps" (Teresa, Saint. p. 207, *tr.*).

In the seventeenth century, Countess Aulnoy would write: "When Spanish ladies walk, they appear to fly; in a hundred years we could not learn this manner of moving along. They press their elbows against the body and go without lifting their feet from the ground, as when one glides" (Aulnoy, Marie Catherine Jumelle de Berneville, comtesse d'. *Relation du voyage d'Espagne.* La Haye, 1691. v. 2, p. 126, *tr.* (8th letter, March 29th, 1679)).

411 Talavera. *Tractado.* *f-vºf*65, *tr.*

412 Eximeniç, Francesch. *Libre deles dones.* Barcelona, 1495. *vºf*XIX (ch. xxiiij).

413 Juana la Loca. *Inventario.* p. 319.

414 Ballesteros-Gaibrois. p. XC-XCI (nos. 523–526).

415 Talavera. *Tractado.* *vºf*65.

416 Sánchez Cantón. *Floreto.* p. 35, *tr.*

417 Norris. v. 3, bk. 1, p. 334; Milan. Pinacoteca di Brera. *Catalogo.* Milano [1950?] p. 52, no. 310, pl. facing p. 64.

418 Pisetsky. v. 2, Fig. 105 (p. [241]), p. 288.

419 Hall, Edward. p. 508.

420 Great Britain. Public record office. *Calendar . . . Venice.* v. 3, p. 69.

The diffusion of the *tranzado* through western Europe is amply treated by Carmen Bernis in her *Modas españolas.* v. 1, p. 98–103.

421
    porque hidalgo el marido
    lleuaua vn rabo tendido
    y vn brial mucho trepado
    y vn tauardo de morado
    y vn trançado muy cumplido.
    . . . essa hija del sedero . . .
    pues los dias de holgar
    lo mas que trae es prestado
    pone se de gran trançado
    por algun nescio engañar.

Reinosa. *vº*sig.a¹, sig.aiij, *tr.*

422 Isabel de Portugal. *Libro.* sig.cccxv *(cofias y trançados),* p. [1–3], sig.cccxviij *(cofias y trançados),* p. [1]

The treasurer's accounts for Isabel la Católica and the inventory of Juana la Loca's wardrobe have been published (see Baeza and Ferrandis Torres). But most of the accounts of the Empress Isabel seem to be still in manuscript in the Archivo General at Simancas. The Hispanic Society has microfilms taken from five documents: *Dela Almoneda* [1539–1541] *Inventario . . . 1539, Libro de las quentas* [1529–1538] *Relacion* I [1532–1538] and *Relacion* II [1526–1529] (see *References* for fuller entries).

The *guarda mayor* was responsible for listing the Empress's clothes, recording when they were cut out, when they were made into something else, when they were given away. There was a book that the Empress signed when a gift was made by her order. The *camarera mayor* also kept a check on the clothes, occasionally coming up with a record *(fe)* when no other evidence was available. Garments were sewed in many towns, Burgos, Palencia, Ocaña, Sevilla, Valladolid. The *guarda* must have found the job tedious, for at least once he was driven to say that it did not matter whether the different accounts matched, whether a skirt *(faldrilla)* was of mulberry cloth of gold or of brown cloth of silver. Sometimes *cota* was written instead of *faldrilla* and had to be corrected. There are also lists of garments missing—the Deficits *(Alcances).*

The inventory of Queen Isabel became available too late for citation in this book. The garments she left are briefly described in Torre y del Cerro, Antonio de la. *Testamentaría de Isabel la Católica.* Barcelona, 1974. p. 80–174: *Joyas de oro (agujetas)* through *Entrega . . . bonetes, sonbre-ros . . . .* Some pieces are recorded as given away to become church vestments or ornaments. For the many that were sold, the name of the buyer and the price are listed.

423 *Relación de las fiestas.* p. 164–168; *Memoria de la ida.* p. 146, 148, 152–153; Villar y Macías, Manuel. *Historia de Salamanca.* Salamanca, 1887. v. 2, p. 227.

424 Talavera. *Tractado.* v^of65, *tr.*

425 Villalobos, Francisco López de. *Libro intitulado Los problemas* [and other works]. Caragoça, 1544. v^oXVI.
    Subsequent references explain the duration of this custom. In *Don Quixote* (1605) the innkeeper hangs a comb in a pied ox's tail, which the barber borrows to wear as a disguising beard (v^of136, ch. XXVII). An English traveler in the next century found a hostess of Castilla la Vieja keeping her combs in a cow's tail (Swinburne, Henry. *Travels through Spain, in the years 1775 and 1776.* London, 1779. p. 410).

426   Yo vi al sol que sescondia
        de embidia de vnos cabellos
        e alos dos nos peso vellos
        a el que su luz perdia
        [a mi en ser tan lexos dellos]
        no me puso espanto cierto
        el ver quan presto cego
        mas que dalli no quedo
        para siempre ciego e muerto
        como yo.

    Castillo. Toledo, 1527. v^oclxxviij.

427 Covarrubias y Orozco. f32, *tr.,* Art. *ALBANEGA;* Talavera. *Tractado.* v^of65.

428 Delicado. v^osig.B ii *(Mamotreto. VII).*

429 *El crotalón.* p. 178.

430 Vives. *[De institutione]* v^ofxxiij-fxxiiij.

431 *Memoria de la ida.* p. 150.

432 Rodríguez Villa. *Bosquejo.* p. 242.

433 Machado. p. 174, *tr.*

434 *Libro de las joyas.* p. 35.

435 Isabel de Portugal. *Libro.* sig.cccxv *(trançados y cofias),* p. [2], sig.cccxvij *(cofias y trançados),* p. [1, 2]

436 Bernis Madrazo. *Indumentaria* II. p. 77, Art. *BEATILLA.*

437 Gil Ayuso. p. 231.

438 Bernis Madrazo. *Indumentaria* II. p. 96, Art. *MANTELLINA.*

439 Isabel de Portugal. *Libro.* sig.ccIxxxij *(mantellinas),* p. [1–3], sig.cccl *(mangas y mantellinas de lienço),* p. [1]; Idem. *Inventario.* f170.

440 Machado. p. 170–171, *tr.*

441 Segovia (City). Alcázar. p. 118.

442 Weiditz, Christoph. *Das Trachtenbuch.* Berlin und Leipzig, 1927. pl. LXXV *(f52).*

443 *The Voyage.* p. 278.

444 Bernis Madrazo. *Indumentaria* II. Fig. 140.

445 Juana la Loca. *Inventario.* p. 322–323.

446 Segovia (City). Alcázar. p. 120, 124.

447   Con vn gentil alhareme
        discretamẽte tocada
        por q̃l viẽto no le queme
        y mas por fin q̃ se teme
        ser conoscida y mirada
        El sombrero dun color
        qualquiera para el camino
        guarnescido por mejor
        con borlas doro muy fino

    Castillo. Valẽcia, 1511. fclxxj.

448 Talavera. *Tractado.* f66.

449 *Ibid.* f66.

450 Gil Ayuso. p. 230–231.

451 Juana la Loca. *Inventario.* p. 271–277.

452 *Dote da Infanta D. Beatriz, Duqueza de Saboia (An. 1522).* In Vasconcelos, Joaquim António de Fonseca e. [*História da ourivesaria e joalharia portuguesa, sacra e profana.* Porto, 1882] p. LXVII.

453 Isabel de Portugal. *Dela Almoneda.* sig. *Data de gorgueras . . .* p. [1, 2]; Idem. *Libro.* sig.cccxix *(gorgueras . . .),* sig.cccxx *(gorgueras . . .),* p. [1, 2], sig. cccxxij *(gorgueras . . .),* p. [1]

454 In the hip-length portrait of Queen Isabel, attributed to Antonio del Rincón (Madrid. Museo Naval), embroidery motifs of the partlet are definitely castles and lions.

455 Lisbon (City). Museu nacional de arte antiga. *Pintura portuguesa.* Lisboa, 1956. pl. 18, *Pope Cyriacus Blessing Saint Ursula and Prince Conan.*

456 Pérez Pastor. v. 2, p. 416.

457 *Relación de las fiestas.* p. 164–168.

458 *Memoria de la ida.* p. 146.

459 *Libro de las joyas.* p. 40.

460 Carmen Bernis (*Indumentaria* II. p. 92, Art. *GORGUERIN,* Fig. 125) identifies the collar of the Countess of Haro with the *gorguerín* of pearls and diamonds or other precious stones that was worn by friends of the Countess of Niebla (1541). In the Empress's *Libro de cuentas* the *gorjalin* or *gorjerin* can be of linen quilted *(embutido)* and made with neckband and frill, as well as of drawn silver with a frill of gold (*Libro.* sig.cccxix *(gorgueras y gorjerines),* p. [3]).

461 Madrid (City). Instituto de Valencia de Don Juan. p. 146, Fig. 190, halftones 36–38.

462 Gómez-Moreno, Manuel. *El panteón real de las Huelgas de Burgos.* Madrid, 1946. p. 86.

463 Madrid (City). Instituto de Valencia de Don Juan. p. 137, 139, *tr.,* Figs. 171–174.

464 Rodríguez Villa. *Bosquejo.* p. 240.

465 Isabel de Portugal. *Libro.* sig.cccxlvij *(camisas),* p. [3, 5], sig.cccxlviij *(camisas),* p. [1, 2]; Bernis Madrazo. *Indumentaria* I. p. 190, 198, pl. 1.

466 Isabel de Portugal. *Libro.* sig.cccxlvij, p. [4] *(mangas de lienço),* sig.cccxlviij-ix *(mangas de lienço),* p. [1, 2]

467 Sánchez Cantón. *Floreto.* p. 76.

468 Juana la Loca. *Inventario.* p. 285–286, 288–291, 292–293; Isabel de Portugal. *Libro.* sig.ccxx-ccxxvj *(mangas de oro y seda),* sig.cccxlvij, cccxlix-cccl *(mangas de lienço, de sinabafo),* sig.ccxx, p. [1–3]

469 Oliveira Marques, António Henrique R. de. *A sociedade medieval portuguesa; aspectos de vida quotidiana*. Lisboa [1964] p. 57.

470 Bernis Madrazo. *Indumentaria* I. p. 207.

471 "Painted in the second third of the sixteenth century by order of the [fourth] duke [of Villahermosa] D. Martín de Gurrea y Aragón, grandson of Doña María [López de Gurrea], probably the portrait of this lady and some further portraits were taken from others of half length. . . . The high erudition and exquisite taste of the duke D. Martín are sufficient basis for affirming that whatever was added to the original types is most exact and conforms entirely to the clothes and ornaments of those same personages, whose clothes, kept for many years by their descendants, must without doubt have been consulted" (Carderera y Solano. v. 2, pl. LXVII, text, *tr.*).

472 Bernis Madrazo. *Indumentaria* I. p. 201.

473 The cap-sleeve with jeweled band is found in Flemish paintings as early as 1434 (Jacques Daret. *The Nativity*. Castagnola, Switzerland. Castle Rohoncz Collection).

474 Was this the style that François I borrowed from Éléonore? Though she entered Bordeaux wearing Spanish clothes, she left the city "in a litter, dressed as a French lady with her hair in the Spanish style" (*Le journal*. p. 345, *tr.*).
  "The new Queen arrived in France with her national Spanish costume, which was worn by all her attendants as well" (Chantilly. Musée Condé. *Crayons français du XVIe siècle. Catalogue . . . par Étienne Moreau-Nélaton*. Paris, 1910. p. 86, *tr.*).
  Henry VIII owned a picture of " 'The Frinshe queene Elonora, in the Spanyshe arraie, and a cap on her headd, with an orange in her hand' " (Norris. v. 3, bk. 1, p. 273).
  "Eleanor kept this fashion until 1537, when Francis sent home her Spanish attendants and begged her to adopt French styles" (Roblot-Delondre, Louise. *Portraits d'infantes*. Paris et Bruxelles, 1913. p. 22, note 3, *tr.*).

475 Carderera y Solano. v. 2, pl. LXXXVI [i.e. LXXVI] text.

476 Juana la Loca. *Inventario*. p. 269.

477 Spain. Laws, statutes, etc. *Las pramaticas*. *f*CXXXIX.

478 Alcega. 1580. *v*°*f*76.

479 Sevilla (City). Ordinances. *v*°*f*CLXIIII.

480 Juana la Loca. *Inventario*. p. 286.

481 *Ibid*. p. 296.

482 Gay. v. 1, p. 775, *tr.*, Art. *GET*.
  Queen Juana's inventory lists with the furs 43 varas of *jetos*, some wide, some narrow; marten and leopard? *(leopas, leopardo?)* are mentioned specifically (p. 304, 303, 305). Also used for *jetos* were *ceti*, brocade, and velvet (p. 280–292).

483 Rodríguez Villa. *Bosquejo*. p. 238.

484 *El crotalón*. p. 163, 249.

485 Alcega. 1580. *v*°*f*74-*v*°*f*75.

486 Gil Ayuso. p. 233–234, 236.

487 Isabel de Portugal. *Libro*. sig.ccxxvij-ccxxxv *(sayas)*.

488 *Ibid*. sig.ccxxviij, p. [4], sig.ccxxxiiij, p. [2]

489 Juana la Loca. *Inventario*. p. 284.

490 Gil Ayuso. p. 238.

491 *The Voyage*. p. 288.

492 R. Academia española. v. 4, p. 489, Art. MANTÓNES.

493 Juana la Loca. *Inventario*. p. 284, 286.

494 *Questiõ de amor*. *v*°*f*ix, *f*x *(Aqui el autor cuenta. . . .)*, *v*°*f*xxix *(Como las damas salieron. . . .)*.

495 Lalaing. p. 251.

496 Cunnington. *A dictionary*. p. 99, Art. GUARDS.

497 Spain. Laws, statutes, etc. *Declaracion*. *v*°sig.aij, *tr.*

498 Cunnington. *A dictionary*. p. 81–82, Art. FOREPART.

499 Isabel de Portugal. *Libro*. sig.ccxxxvj *(delanteras de sayas)*, p. [2]

500 *Memoria de la ida*. p. 152.

501 Isabel de Portugal. *Libro*. sig.ccxxxvj *(delanteras de sayas)*, p. [3]

502 *Questiõ de amor*. *f*xxx, *tr.* *(Como las damas salieron. . . .)*.

503 Palencia, Alfonso Fernández de [1423-ca. 1492]. *Crónica de Enrique IV*. Madrid, 1905. v. 2, p. 171–172.

504 Talavera. *Reforma*. *f*5, *tr.*

505 Idem. *Tractado*. f 84, *f*85-*v*°*f*86.

506 Clemencín. p. 327.

507 Isabel de Portugal. *Relacion* II. sig.7, p. [1] *(verdugadas)*.

508 Idem. *Libro*. sig.ccliij *(verdugados)*, p. [3]

509 Bernis Madrazo. *Indumentaria* II. p. 63 (no. 94).

510 *The Voyage*. p. 288.

511 Pisetsky. v. 3, p. 69.
  This author suggests that the hoop skirt may have come to Italy by way of France, but since Naples long was in constant touch with Spain, the skirt must have gone to Italy directly from Spain.

512 Kelly, Francis M. *Shakespearian dress notes—II*. In *The Burlington magazine*. 1916. v. 29, p. 357.

513
  Vna dueña diz que honrrada,
  muger de pompa y arreo,
  adolecio de desseo
  de vna saya verdugada
  muy loçana,
  a su parecer galana,
  que yendo a la yglesia vio . . .
  començosse a entristecer
  y mostrar muy fatigada,
  no comia,
  mas sospiraua y gemia . . . .
  El marido
  congoxado y affligido . . .
  embio por vn doctor . . . .
  El qual . . .
  a la muger se llego
  y los pulsos le toco . . .
  despues de esso procediendo
  por sus preguntas sabidas
  las causas bien entendidas . . .
  al marido se boluio . . .
  y muy quedo
  le dixo: no tengays miedo
  que de este mal muera ya
  vuestra muger, o no aura
  mercaderes en Toledo . . . .
  Compralde sin mas recelo . . .
  seys varas de fina grana
  y quatro de terciopelo
  carmesi,

y ponganselas alli,
porque se alegre de verlas,
y ciertas onças de perlas . . . .
   En vn punto
ya estaua alli todo junto
sin momento de tardança;
y el con sola esta esperança
estando casi defunto,
   rebiuio;
y ella, luego que lo vio,
se le alegraron los ojos,
y cessando los enojos
doblado sana quedo.

Castillejo. p. 378–379, *tr.*

514 Alcega. 1580. *f*58.

515 Covarrubias y Orozco. *f*396, Art. *FALDA.*

516 Juana la Loca. *Inventario.* p. 295.

517 *Libro de las joyas.* p. 59; Teresa, Saint. p. 198, note 128.

518 Larruga y Boneta, Eugenio. *Memorias políticas y económicas sobre los frutos, comercio, fábricas y minas de España.* Madrid, 1790. v. 9, p. [1]

519 Isabel de Portugal. *Libro.* sig.ccl *(basquiñas),* p. [2], sig.cclj *(basquiñas),* p. [4]

520 Brantôme. v. 2, p. 350.

521 Isabel de Portugal. *Libro.* sig.ccxxxviij *(faldrillas),* p. [1, 2]

522 Juana la Loca. *Inventario.* p. 297–299; Bernis Madrazo. *Indumentaria* II. p. 86, Art. *COS.*

523 Isabel de Portugal. *Libro.* sig.cclxxiiij-cclxxvj *(saynos de seda e paño e otras suertes),* sig.ccclj-ccclij *(. . . saynos de deshilado y rred y lienço),* sig.cclxxvj, p. [3], sig.cclxxvij, p. [1, *alcances*], sig.lxiij *(Alcances),* p. [2]; Bernis Madrazo. *Indumentaria* II. p. 104, Art. *SAYNO.*

524 Bernis Madrazo. *Indumentaria* II. p. 104, Art. *SAYUELO.*

525 Juana la Loca. *Inventario.* p. 288–290; *Relación de las fiestas.* p. 151.

526 Rodríguez Villa. *Bosquejo.* p. 240.

527 Isabel de Portugal. *Libro.* sig.ccclxxij *(calças y çaraguelles),* p. [2]

528 Navagero. *v°f*25, *tr.;* Haedo, Diego de. *Topographia, e historia general de Argel.* Valladolid, 1612. *f*27 [i.e. 28]; Torres, Diego de. *Relacion del origen y svcesso de los Xarifes.* Sevilla, 1586. p. 84–85; Mármol Carvajal, Luis de. *Descripcion general de Affrica.* Granada, 1573. v. 2, *f*103.

529 Pisetsky. v. 3, p. 71.

530 Juana la Loca. *Inventario.* p. 305.

531 Bernis Madrazo. *Modas moriscas.* p. 218, Fig. 11; Arié, Rachel. *Acerca del traje musulmán en España desde la caída de Granada hasta la expulsión de los moriscos.* In Instituto de estudios islámicos en Madrid. *Revista.* 1965–1966. v. 13, p. 110–111; Martínez Ruiz. p. 67.

532 Rodríguez Villa. *Bosquejo.* p. 236, 241.

533 Garrad, K. *La industria sedera . . . Apéndice.* In *Miscelánea de estudios árabes y hebraicos.* [Granada] 1956. v. 5, p. 99, 101, 103.

534 Isabel de Portugal. *Relacion* II. sig.9, p. [1]; Idem. *Libro.* sig.cclxx-cclxxiij *(marlotas),* sig.cclxx, p. [3], sig.cclxxi, p. [1], sig.cclxxij, p. [3, 4]

535 Villahermosa, Martín de Aragón y Gurrea, duque de. *Discursos de medallas y antigüedades que compuso . . . D. Martín de Gurrea y Aragón . . . con una noticia . . . por D. José Ramón Mélida.* [Madrid] 1902. p. XLVIII.

536 Gay. v. 2, p. 116, Art. *MARLOTTE;* Leloir. p. 270, Art. *MARLOTTE.*

537 *Grande enciclopédia portuguesa e brasileira.* Lisboa [1935–60] v. 26, p. 638, Art. *SAIO.*

538
Essa otra del çapatero
mucho puesta de xeruillas
que en afeyte y cosillas
echa todo su dinero
su marido es majadero
en dexalla assi traer
y no se sabe poner
la faxa y el ceñidero.

Reinosa. sig.aiij, *tr.*

539 Juana la Loca. *Inventario.* p. 301.

540 Machado. p. 171, *tr.*

541 Segovia (City). Alcázar. p. 165–167.

542 *Ibid.* p. 79.

543 Juana la Loca. *Inventario.* p. 186–188.

544 Clemencín. p. 342, 343, 344, 345.

545 Muller. p. 14–16.

546
. . . irai ge en Alemaingne . . . Behaingne,
Tout ce ne vault? Nous irons en Espaigne,
la pourons nous assouvir nostre affaire;
le cuir es doulx, la viollette flaire.
Ainsy, madame et ma tres redoubtee,
de cuir d'Espaigne vous en serez gantee.

La Marche, Olivier de. *Le triumphe des dames. . . . Ausgabe nach den Handschriften.* Rostock, 1901. p. 62, no. 113, *tr.*

547 Luzio *and* Renier. p. 682–683, *tr.*

548 Durán y Sanpere, Agustín. *Per a la història de l'art a Barcelona.* Barcelona, 1960. p. [81]–82.

549 Luzio *and* Renier. p. 683, *tr.*

550
Los guätes mucho delgados
de poco tiẽpo traydos
han de ser sobre engrassados
de contino perfumados
con olores encẽdidos
Ya sabeys dun benjuy
con olio de torongel
do creo por q̃ lo vi
quẽ valencia os diran del

Castillo. Valẽcia, 1511. *f*clxxj, *tr.*

551 Letter of Estefanía de Requesens to her mother, countess of Palamós, April 7th, 1536. In March, José María. *Niñez y juventud de Felipe II.* Madrid, 1942. v. 2, p. 297–299, *tr.*
   The New York Botanical Garden reports no record of pollen being used in dyes, but it is difficult to see how the "powders and yellowness" *(pólvores i grogor)* of white flowers could refer to anything but their pollen.

552 Isabel de Portugal. *Libro.* sig.ccclxxiiij, p. [1] *(guantes).*

553 Fernández de Córdoba y Salabert. v. 2, p. 185.

554 Juana la Loca. *Inventario.* p. 199–200.

555 *Questiõ de amor. v°f*xxviij *(Como las damas salieron. . . .).*

556 Isabel de Portugal. *Libro.* sig.xl-xlij, p. [1], sig.ccclx *(cabos y puntas de oro),* sig.xiii *(Alcances),* sig.ccclx, p. [2, 3], *tr.*

557 Talavera. *Tractado.* $f54,63$, $v^ of66$.

558   *Las calças no digo quales*
    por su lugar escondido
    mas de tal fineza y tales
    q̃ puedan ser biẽ yguales
    con todo lo referido

    Castillo. Valẽcia, 1511. $f$clxxj, *tr.*

559 Isabel de Portugal. *Inventario.* v^of176.

560 Percyvall, Richard. *A dictionarie in Spanish and English* [ed. by John Minsheu] London, 1599. p. 246; Delicado. sig.A⁴ *(Mamotreto. III).*

561 Oliver Asín. p. 140, *tr.;* Sevilla (City). Ordinances. v^ofCXCVII.

562 Reinosa. sig.a⁵, a⁶; Martínez Ruiz. p. 98.

563 The translation of *puertas* by the term "buckles" is based on Tilander's use of "buckle" for *porteta,* which he based on a phrase of 1528, "nin trayan *çapatos a cuerda* nin *de fiuiella"* (Tilander, Gunnar. *Fueros aragoneses desconocidos, promulgados a consecuencia de la gran peste de 1348.* In *Revista de filología española.* 1935. v. 22, p. 141, 125).
Fibiella, antecedent of *hebilla,* means "buckle".

564 Fabié y Escudero, Antonio María. *Viajes por España de . . . y de Andrés Navajero.* Madrid, 1879. p. 298–299, *tr.;* Navagero. v^of25.

565 Corominas. v. 2, p. 634, Art. *GALOCHA.*

566 Palencia. v^oflxxxxvj, Art. *Coturni.*

567 Segovia (City). Alcázar. p. 165; Granada (City). R. Audiencia y chancillería. $f166$ (8); Sevilla (City). Ordinances. f-v^ofCXCVII; Juana la Loca. *Inventario.* p. 366, 367.

568 Granada (City). R. Audiencia y chancillería. v^of166 (10), $f167$ (18); Isabel de Portugal. *Libro.* sig.ccclxx *(chapines),* p. [3], sig.ccclxxj *(chapines y pãtuflos),* p. [4]

569 *Pregon de las tassas de los officiales y jornaleros y alquileres de mulas* [Çaragoça, 1553] sig.Aiij (facsim. in Sánchez, Juan M. *Pregón de tasas y jornales).* In *Archivo de investigaciones históricas.* 1911. año 1, p. [143]

570 Covarrubias y Orozco. $f174$, *tr.,* Art. *CALÇADO.*

571 "And tread on cork stilts, a prisoner's pace" (Hall, Joseph, bp. of Norwich. *Satires.* Chiswick, 1824. p. 110 (Book IV, Satire VI, first published 1598).

572   *ni al tiempo que estan rezando*
    o cantando sus maytines,
    que alli suelen los chapines
    alguna vez yr bolando
    por el coro.

    Castillejo. p. 390.

573 Regarding this band, Señor Bermúdez quoted a statement that the gilt had not been achieved with gold leaf, but rather with a technique like that used in making the leather wall hangings known as *guadamaciles,* in which sheepskins metal-leafed with silver or tin were glazed with yellow to simulate gold. That industry, said to have originated at Ghadames in Tripoli, was established at Córdoba in the Middle Ages. Existing examples of sixteenth-century *guadamaciles* show dot-and-circle punchwork in rather coarse scale used as background.

574 Waterer, John W. *Leather craftsmanship.* New York, Washington [1968] Fig. 122.

575 Oliver Asín. p. 145, *tr.*

576 Isabel de Portugal. *Inventario.* v^of179-v^of180; Idem. *Libro.* sig.ccclxxj *(chapines y pãtuflos),* p. [1, 3]

577 Rodríguez Villa. *Bosquejo.* p. 239.

578 Sevilla (City). Ordinances. v^ofCXCV.

579 Calderón de la Barca, Pedro. *El conde Lucanor.* In his *Qvarta parte de comedias nvevas.* Madrid, 1672. p. 398 [i.e. 397]-399.
For other literary references to the chopine see Ashcom, B. B. *"By the altitude of a chopine".* In *Homenaje a Rodrí-guez-Moñino.* Madrid [1966] v. 1, p. 17–27.

580 *Llibre del mustaçaf.* fCCClxviiij; Corominas. v. 1, p. 509, Art. *BRANQUE;* Aizkíbel, José Francisco de. *Diccionario basco-español.* Tolosa, 1883. v. [1] p. 136, Art. *BRANKA; Llibre del mustaçaf.* f-v^ofCCClxxj, fCCClxxij.

581 Sevilla (City). Ordinances. v^ofCXCV, fCXCVI.

582 Tramoyeres Blasco, Luis. *Instituciones gremiales, su orígen y organización en Valencia.* Valencia, 1889. p. 255; Sevilla (City). Ordinances. v^ofCXCV, fCXCVI.

583 Stevens, John. *A new Spanish and English dictionary.* London, 1706. Art. *Chapín.*

584 Martínez de Toledo, Alfonso. *El arcipreste de talauera que fabla delos vicios d'las malas mugeres E conplexiones delos onbres.* Toledo, 1500. fXXI; Talavera. *Tractado.* v^of54, v^of66.

585 [Uhagón y Guardamino, Francisco Rafael de, marqués de Laurencín] *Relaciones históricas de los siglos XVI y XVII.* Madrid, 1896. p. 9–10.

586 Covarrubias y Orozco. $f220$, Art. *CODO;* Paris. Musée de Cluny. *Catalogue et description des objets d'art de l'antiquité, du moyen age et de la renaissance . . . par E. du Sommerard.* Paris, 1884. p. 530, no. 6653; Talavera. *Reforma.* f-v^of12 [i.e. 15].

587 Though in the time of Isabel la Católica many such shoes were provided for the young unmarried Infantas, the phrase "to put into chopines" came to mean "to marry off a daughter". "Chopine of the Queen and of the Infantas" referred to the gift that Castilla made to a queen or a princess on the occasion of her wedding. That of an infanta could amount to 290,000 doblas, while a queen's, levied on the common people, came to 150,000,000 maravedis (over 400,000 doblas), paid in seven installments, four months apart.

588 Cerda, Juan de la. *Libro intitvlado, Vida politica de todos los estados de mugeres.* Alcalá de Henares, 1599. $f478$.

589 Montalto, Lina. *La corte di Alfonso I di Aragona: vesti e gale.* Napoli, 1922. p. 28.

590 *Llibre del mustaçaf.* v^ofCCClxviiij-v^ofCCClxx, *condensed and tr.*

591 Oliver Asín. p. 127; Bernis Madrazo. *Modas españolas.* v. 2, p. 33; Corominas. v. 2, p. 23.
For an extended history of the chopine see Anderson, Ruth M. *El chapín y otros zapatos afines (The chopine and related shoes).* In *Cuadernos de la Alhambra.* 1969. no. 5, p. [17]-41.

592 Rubio *and* Acemel. p. 16, 23, *tr.*

593 Bernis Madrazo. *Indumentaria* II. p. 97, Art. *MANTO.*

594 Serrano, Luciano. *Los reyes católicos y la ciudad de Burgos (Desde 1451 a 1492).* Madrid, 1943. p. 212.

595 Lalaing. p. 251.

596 Gil Ayuso. p. 236.

597 Covarrubias y Orozco. *f*538, Art. *MANTO;* Vives. *[De institutione]* v*°f*xxxv-*f*xxxvj;

>   El coraçon se me fue
>   donde vuestro vulto vi,
>   e luego vos conosçi
>   al punto que vos mire;
>   que no pudo fazer tanto
>   por mucho que vos cubriese
>   aquel vuestro negro manto
>   que no vos reconosçiese.
>   Que debaxo se mostraua
>   vuestra graçia y gentil ayre,
>   y el cubrir con buen donayre
>   todo lo magnifestaua;
>   asy que con mis enojos
>   e muy grande turbaçion
>   alla se fueron mis ojos
>   do tenia el coraçon.

Manrique. v. 2, p. 219, *tr.,* revised from version by Alice J. McVan in *Translations from Hispanic poets.* New York, 1938. p. 12.
   The mantle covering all but one eye is well illustrated in Vecellio, Cesare. *Degli habiti antichi e moderni.* Venice, 1590. *f*283, *CITELLA SPAGNVOLA,* a woodcut probably based on a design of earlier date.

598 *Chronica,* v*°f*307 (ch. CXXIX); Lalaing. p. 251.

599 Juana la Loca. *Inventario.* p. 277–280.

600 For illustrations of the *tronco* motif see Muller. Figs. 3, 4, 6.

601 Juana la Loca. *Inventario.* p. 279, 280–284.

602 Isabel de Portugal. *Libro.* sig.cclxi-cclxij *(ropones),* sig.cclxvi-cclxix *(. . . rropones).*

603 Pisetsky. v. 3, Fig. 32 (p. 65); v. 2, p. 263.

604 Bernis Madrazo. *Indumentaria* II. Fig. 139.

605 Sandoval. pt. 1, *f-*v*°f*5 (bk. 1, XIII).

606 Pisetsky. v. 2, Fig. 108 (p. [245]), *tr.*

607 *Escritura de obligación . . . a 21 de diciembre de 1488.* In *Archivo español de arte y arqueología.* 1929. v. 5, p. 120, *tr.*

608 Juana la Loca. *Inventario.* p. 294, 302.

609 Isabel de Portugal. *Libro.* sig.cclvj-cclx *(mongiles).*

610 Bernis Madrazo. *Indumentaria* II. p. 98, Art. *MONGIL;* Sevilla (City). Ordinances. v*°f*CLXIIII; Isabel de Portugal. *Libro.* sig.cclx *(mongiles),* p. [4]

611 *Relación de las fiestas.* p. 168; Gay. v. 2, p. 139, Art. *MONGILLE;* Alcega. 1580. *f-*v*°f*76.

612 R. Academia española. v. 4, p. 597, Art. MONGIL.

613 Juana la Loca. *Inventario.* p. 295.

614 Isabel de Portugal. *Libro.* sig.cclxxxvj *(manteos),* p. [2]

615 Spain. Laws, statutes, etc. *Las pramaticas.* *f*CCV, CCVII, CCXIII; Sánchez Cantón. *Floreto.* p. 256.

616 Rabelais. *Œuvres de Rabelais collationnées . . . sur les éditions originales.* Paris [19–?] v. 1, p. 292; Gay. v. 1, p. 149, Art. *BERNE.*

617 Pisetsky. v. 2, p. 255, *tr.;* v. 3, Fig. 36-*a destra* (legend), *tr.*

618 Leloir. p. [396], Art. *TABAR ou TABARD, tr.*

619 León Salmerón, Africa *and* Diego y González, J. Natividad de. *Compendio de indumentaria española.* Madrid, 1915. p. 99.

620 Sevilla (City). Ordinances. v*°f*CLXX.

621 Juana la Loca. *Inventario.* p. 294.

622 Spain. Laws, statutes, etc. *Pragmaticas y Leyes. f*clix.

623 Gil Ayuso. p. 233–236.

624 Isabel de Portugal. *Libro.* sig.cclxxviij, p. [1], sig.cclxxix, p. [1] *(lobas).*

625 Muller. p. 11, Fig. 5.

626 Bernáldez. p. 220–221 (ch. LXXX); Roca, Joseph María. *Inventaris.* In R. Academia de buenas letras, Barcelona. *Boletín.* 1929–30. v. 14, p. 293, *tr.*

627 Angulo Iñiguez, Diego. *Discurso. . . . [Isabel la Católica: sus retratos, sus vestidos y sus joyas]* Santander [1951] p. 45, Fig. 7; Bernis Madrazo. *Pedro Berruguete y la moda.* In *Archivo español de arte.* 1959. v. 32, p. 18, note 37.

628 Isabel de Portugal. *Relacion* II. sig.5 *(abitos),* p. [2]; Idem. *Libro.* sig.cclxxviij, p. [3] *(otras Ropas que se trayeron de portugal).*

629 *Ibid.* sig.cclxxviij, p. [3] *(otras Ropas), tr.*

630 López de Gómara, Francisco. *Historia general de las Indias . . . con la conquista de Mexico.* Medina del Campo, 1553. pt. 2, v*°f*xlvi; García Granados, Rafael. *Antigüedades mejicanas en Europa.* Méjico, 1942. p. 8, 9, 16.

631 Isabel de Portugal. *Libro.* sig.clxxj *(forros de martas . . .),* p. [4], *tr.*

632 For descriptions and illustrations of such fur pieces see Muller, p. 103, Figs. 166, 167.

633 Talavera. *Tractado.* v*°f*57.

634 Machado. p. 171.

635 Juana la Loca. *Inventario.* p. 305.

636 Isabel de Portugal. *Libro.* sig.clxx, p. [3] *(otros aforros).*

637 Idem. *Inventario. f*145.

638 Paz y Mélia. v. 12, p. 77.

639 Juana la Loca. *Inventario.* p. 302, *tr.*

640 Isabel de Portugal. *Dela Almoneda.* sig. *martas y aforros,* p. [1]

641 Fuensalida, Gutierre Gómez de. *Correspondencia.* Madrid, 1907. p. 388.

642 Juana la Loca. *Inventario.* p. 303.

643 Isabel de Portugal. *Libro.* sig.clxx *(aforros de martas),* p. [1], sig.clxxj *(Dacta forros . . .),* p. [1]; Idem. *Dela Almoneda.* sig. *martas y aforros,* p. [1]

644 Pisetsky. v. 2, p. 259.

645 Isabel de Portugal. *Libro.* sig.clxx, p. [3] *(otros aforros).*

646 Talavera. *Tractado.* v*°f*58-*f*59.

647 *Libro de las joyas.* p. 56, 57; Juana la Loca. *Inventario.* p. 282.

648 Reyes Huertas, Antonio. *Pastores y conquistadores.* In Roca Piñol, Pedro. *La estética del vestir clásico.* Tarrasa, 1942. p. 52.

649 Isabel de Portugal. *Libro.* sig.clxx, p. [4] *(çamarros).*

REFERENCES

R. Academia española, Madrid. *Diccionario de la lengua castellana.* Madrid, 1734. v. 4.

[Alcega, Juan de. *Libro de Geometria, Practica y Traça.* Madrid, 1580]

_____. *Libro de Geometria, pratica, y traça.* Madrid, 1589.

Almela y Vives, Francisco. *Carlos I en la ciudad de Valencia.* Valencia, 1959.

Amador de los Ríos, Rodrigo. *Notas acerca de la batalla de Lucena y de la prisión de Boabdil en 1483.* In *Revista de archivos, bibliotecas y museos.* 1907. v. 16, p. [37]–66.

Andrada, Francisco d'. *Chronica do . . . rey destes reynos de Portugal, dom João o III deste nome.* [Lisboa, 1613] Coimbra, 1796. v. 1.

Anghiera, Pietro Martire d'. *Epistolario.* Madrid, 1953–57. 4 v. (*Documentos inéditos para la historia de España.* v. 9–12)

Baeza, Gonzalo de. *Cuentas de Gonzalo de Baeza, tesorero de Isabel la Católica.* Madrid, 1955–56. v. 1, 1477–1491; v. 2, 1492–1504.

Ballesteros-Gaibrois, Manuel. *Valencia y los reyes católicos (1479–1493).* Valencia, 1943. v. 1.

Bernáldez, Andrés. *Historia de los Reyes Católicos Dⁿ Fernando y Dª Isabel.* Sevilla, 1870. v. 1.

Bernis Madrazo, Carmen. *Indumentaria española del siglo XV: La camisa de mujer.* In *Archivo español de arte.* 1957. v. 30, p. 187–209. Cited as *Indumentaria* I.

_____. *Indumentaria española en tiempos de Carlos V.* Madrid, 1962. Cited as *Indumentaria* II.

_____. *Modas Españolas medievales en el Renacimiento Europeo.* In Waffen- und Kostümkunde. 3. series. 1959. v. 1, pts. 1 & 2, p. 94–110; 1960. v. 2, pt. 1, p. 27–40.

_____. *Modas moriscas en la sociedad cristiana española del siglo XV y principios del XVI.* In R. Academia de la historia, Madrid. *Boletín.* 1959. v. 144, p. [199]–228.

_____. *El traje masculino en Castilla durante el último cuarto del siglo XV.* In Sociedad española de excursiones, Madrid. *Boletín.* 1950. v. 54, p. [191]–233.

Boehn, Max von. *Modes and manners.* London, Bombay, etc. [1932] v. 2.

Brantôme, Pierre de Bourdeille, seigneur de. *Œuvres complètes.* Paris, 1848, '42. 2 v.

Carderera y Solano, Valentín. *Iconografía española.* Madrid, 1855 and 1864. v. 2.

Carriazo, Juan de Mata. *Amor y moralidad bajo los Reyes Católicos.* In *Revista de archivos, bibliotecas y museos.* 1954. v. 60, p. [53]–76.

_____. *La boda del emperador.* In *Archivo hispalense.* 1959. 2.a época, v. 30, p. [9]–108.

Castiglione, Baldassare, conte. *Il Cortegiano;* [Sp. tr. by Juan de Boscán] *Los qvatro libros del Cortesano.* Toledo, 1539.

Castillejo, Cristóbal de. *Diálogo de mugeres* [Venice, 1544] In *Revue hispanique.* 1921. v. 52, p. [361]–427.

Castillo, Hernando del, comp. *Cancionero general.* Valēcia, 1511.

_____. *Cancionero general.* Toledo, 1527.

La Celestina by unknown, reputedly by Fernando de Rojas. [*Comedia de Calisto y Melibea?* Burgos? 1499?]

Cervantes Saavedra, Miguel. *El ingenioso hidalgo Don Quixote de la Mancha.* Madrid, 1605.

Chronica. De los muy altos y esclarecidos reyes Catholicos don Fernando y doña Ysabel de gloriosa memoria by Antonio de Lebrija *or rather* by Fernando de Pulgar. Valladolid, 1565.

Clemencín, Diego. *Elógio de la Réina católica Doña Isabel.* Madrid, 1821.

Corominas, Juan. *Diccionario crítico etimológico de la lengua castellana.* Madrid [1954] v. 1, 2.

Covarrubias y Orozco, Sebastián de. *Tesoro de la lengva castellana, o española.* Madrid, 1611.

Croce, Benedetto. *España en la vida italiana durante el renacimiento.* Madrid [1925]

El crotalón de Christophoro Gnosopho. In Menéndez y Pelayo, Marcelino. *Orígenes de la novela.* Madrid, 1907. v. 2, p. [119]–250. (*Nueva biblioteca de autores españoles.* v. 7)

Cunnington, C. Willett & Phillis. *Handbook of English costume in the sixteenth century.* London [1954]

Cunnington, C. Willett *and* Phillis, *and* Beard, Charles. *A dictionary of English costume.* London [1960]

[Delicado, Francisco] *Retrato de la Loçana andaluza.* [Venice? 1528. facsim.: Valencia, 1950]

Durán, Agustín. *Romancero de romances moriscos.* Madrid, 1828. (*Coleccion de romances castellanos anteriores al Siglo 18.* v. 1)

_____ *Romancero general, ó Coleccion de romances castellanos anteriores al siglo XVIII.* Madrid, 1849, 1851. 2 v. (*Biblioteca de autores españoles.* v. 10, 16)

Evans, Joan. *Dress in mediaeval France.* Oxford, 1952.

Fernández de Córdoba y Salabert, Luis Jesús, 17. duque de Medinaceli. *Series de los más importantes docvmentos del archivo y biblioteca del exmo. señor Dvqve de Medinaceli . . . publicados . . . por A. Paz y Mélia.* [Madrid, 1915–22] 2 v.

Fernández de Oviedo y Valdés, Gonzalo. *Diálogos,* quoted (from a manuscript copy made in 1686) in Carriazo. *Amor.* p. [54]–76; quoted also in Rodríguez Villa. *Crónicas.* p. LIX–LXXI.

_____ *Libro de la camara real del prínçipe Don Juan e offiçios de su casa e seruiçio ordinario.* Madrid, 1870.

_____ *Las quinquagenas de la nobleza de España.* Madrid, 1880. v. 1.

_____ *Relacion de lo sucedido en la prision del rey de Francia, desde que fué traido en España.* In *Coleccion de documentos inéditos para la historia de España.* Madrid, 1861. v. 38, p. 404–530.

Ferrandis Torres, José. *Inventarios reales (Juan II a Juana la Loca).* Madrid, 1943. (*Datos documentales para la historia del arte español.* v. 3)

Ferrari, Antonio de, *Galateo. La Giapigia e varii opuscoli.*

Lecce, 1867. v. 1, p. [103]–167: *Dell' educazione dell' italiani.*

Gay, Victor. *Glossaire archéologique du moyen âge et de la Renaissance.* Paris, 1887–1928. 2 v.

Gil Ayuso, Faustino. *El equipo de boda de doña Isabel de Aragón, año 1515.* In Cuerpo facultativo de archiveros, bibliotecarios y arqueólogos. *Anuario.* 1934. v. 2, p. [225]–248.

Girón, Pedro. *Crónica del emperador Carlos V.* Madrid, 1964.

Granada (City). R. Audiencia y chancillería. *Ordenanzas.* Granada, 1672.

Great Britain. Public record office. *Calendar of state papers and manuscripts, relating to English affairs, existing in the archives and collections of Venice.* London, 1869. v. 3.

_____ *Letters and papers, foreign and domestic, of the reign of Henry VIII.* London, 1870. v. 4, pt. 1.

Guevara, Antonio de. *Epistolas familiares.* Valladolid, 1539–41. 2 v. in 1.

_____ *Libro llamado Menosprecio de corte y alabança de aldea.* In his *Las obras.* Valladoli, 1545. v^ofcxxiiij-fclij.

Hall, Edward. *Hall's chronicle; containing the history of England, during the reign of Henry the Fourth, and . . . to the end of the reign of Henry the Eighth.* London, 1809.

Hechos del Condestable don Miguel Lucas de Iranzo (Crónica del siglo XVI). Madrid, 1940.

Isabel de Portugal, empress of the Holy Roman Empire. *Dela Almoneda dela Emperatriz nῤa Señora Que esta En gloria* [1539–1541] MS. in the Archivo General, Simancas (Valladolid). Contaduría Mayor, 1.a época, Leg. 550.

_____ *Inventario de las ropas y alhajas de la S ^{ra} Emperatriz fecho en toledo año 1539.* MS. in the Archivo General, Simancas (Valladolid). C. y S. Reales, Leg. 67.

_____ *Libro de las quentas de la Recamara de la emperatriz nra señora q̃ Esta en gloria* [1529–1538] MS. in the Archivo General, Simancas (Valladolid). Contaduría Mayor, 1.a época, Leg. 464.

_____ *Relacion delas Ropas dela enperatriz nra. s^q q̃ seã deshecho en castilla y delo q̃ se a tornado a hazer* *dellas* [1532–1538] MS. in the Archivo General, Simancas (Valladolid). Contaduría Mayor, 1.a época, legajo 465. Cited as *Relacion* I.

———— *Relacion . . . delas rropas q̃ se traxeron de portugal quando su mag. vino a castilla y delas q̃ sean hecho en ella hasta principio del año de mdxxix años* [1526–1529] MS. in the Archivo General, Simancas (Valladolid). Contaduría Mayor, 1.a época, legajo 465. Cited as *Relacion* II.

Le journal d'un bourgeois de Paris sous le règne de François Ier (1515–1536). Paris, 1910.

Juana la Loca, queen of Spain. *Inventario de D.ª Juana la Loca* [1509–1555] In Ferrandis Torres. p. [171]–375.

Lalaing, Antoine de. *Voyage de Philippe le Beau en Espagne, en 1501*. In *Collection des voyages des souverains des Pays-Bas, publiée par M. Gachard*. Bruxelles, 1876. v. 1, p. [121]–340.

Laver, James, ed. *The Tudors to Louis XIII*. London, Sydney, etc. [1952] (*Costume of the western world*. v. 3)

Lazarillo de Tormes by unknown. *La vida de Lazarillo de Tormes, y de sus fortunas y aduersidades*. Anvers, 1554.

Leloir, Maurice. *Dictionnaire du costume et de ses accessoires des ARMES et des ÉTOFFES des origines à nos jours*. Paris [1951]

Libro de las joyas de oro e plata . . . y otras cosas de Azienda de . . . doña Margarita princesa de Castilla. In Ferrandis Torres. p. [29]–61.

Links, J. G. *The book of fur*. [London] 1956.

Llibre del mustaçaf. Valencia, 1563. MS. in the Archivo Municipal, Valencia.

Luzio, Alessandro *and* Renier, Rodolfo. *Il lusso di Isabella d'Este marchesa di Mantova*. In *Nuova antologia*. October 16th, 1896. v. 65, p. 666–688.

Machado, Roger. *Journals . . . embassy to Spain and Portugal* [1488–1489] In Great Britain. Public record office. *Chronicles and memorials of Great Britain and Ireland during the middle ages*. London, 1858. no. 10, p. [157]–199 (English tr., p. 328–368).

Madrid (City). Instituto de Valencia de Don Juan. *Catálogo de bordados, por M.ª Angeles González Mena*. Madrid, 1974.

Manrique, Gómez. *Inventario*. In his *Cancionero. Publícale con algunas notas D. Antonio Paz y Mélia*. Madrid, 1885. v. 2, p. 326–339.

La maravillosa coronación del . . . Emperador . . . en la ciudad de Bolonia. In *Relaciones de los reinados de Carlos V y Felipe II*. Madrid, 1950. v. 2, p. [125]–131.

Martínez Ruiz, Juan. *La indumentaria de los moriscos, según Pérez de Hita y los documentos de la Alhambra*. In *Cuadernos de la Alhambra*. 1967. no. 3, p. [55]–124.

Mattingly, Garrett. *Catherine of Aragon*. London [1963]

Memoria de la ida de la condesa de Niebla a su casa [Año 1541] In *Relaciones de los reinados de Carlos V y Felipe II*. Madrid, 1950. v. 2, p. [145]–155.

Milán, Luis. *Libro intitulado el Cortesano*. Valencia, 1561.

Molinet, Jean. *Chroniques*. Paris, 1828. v. 5. (Buchon, Jean Alexandre. *Collection des chroniques nationales françaises*. v. 47)

Muller, Priscilla E. *Jewels in Spain, 1500–1800*. New York, 1972.

Muñoz de San Pedro e Higuero, Miguel, conde de Canilleros. *Documentación familiar de Diego García de Paredes*. In *Revista de estudios extremeños*, 1956. v. 12, p. [3]–58.

Navagero, Andrea. *Il viaggio fatto in Spagna, et in Francia*. Vinegia, 1563.

Navarra, Spain. Laws, statutes, etc. *Las ordenanças, leyes de visita, y aranzeles*. Estella, 1557.

Norris, Herbert. *Costume & fashion*. New York [1938] v. 3, bk. 1.

Ochoa y Ronna, Eugenio de. *Epistolario español. Coleccion de cartas de españoles ilustres antiguos y modernos*. Madrid, 1870. v. 2. (*Biblioteca de autores españoles*. v. 62)

Oliver Asín, Jaime. *"Quercus" en la España musulmana*. In *Al-Andalus*. 1959. v. 24, p. [125]–181.

Osório, Jerónimo. *Da vida e feitos d'ElRei D. Manoel* [tr. of his *De rebvs, Emmanvelis regis Lvsitaniæ*. Olysippone, 1571] Lisboa, 1806. v. 3.

[Oznaya, Juan de] *Historia de la guerra de Lombardia, batalla de Pavia*. In *Coleccion de documentos inéditos para la historia de España.* Madrid, 1861. v. 38, p. 289–403.

Padilla, Lorenzo de. *Crónica de Felipe I.° llamado el Hermoso.* In *Coleccion de documentos inéditos para la historia de España.* Madrid, 1846. v. 8, p. [5]–267.

Palencia, Alfonso Fernández de. *Uniuersal vocabulario en latin y en Romance.* Apud Hispalim, 1490.

Paz y Mélia, Antonio. *El embajador polaco Juan Dantisco en la Corte de Carlos V (1524–1527).* In R. Academia española, Madrid. *Boletín.* 1924–25. v. 11, p. [54]–69, [305]–320, [427]–444, [586]–600; v. 12, p. [73]–93.

Peña Cámara, José de la. *El hatillo de un marinero de la carrera de Indias (1530).* In *Correo erudito.* [1941] año 2, entrega 8, p. 293–296.

Pérez de Hita, Ginés. *(Historia De las Gverras Civiles de Granada).* [n. p. (Paris?) 1606?]

Pérez Pastor, Cristóbal. *Noticias y documentos relativos a la historia y literatura españolas.* Madrid, 1914. v. 2.

Pisetsky, Rosita Levi. *Storia del costume in Italia.* [Milano, 1964–66] v. 2, 3.

Puiggarí y Llobet, José. *Estudios de indumentaria española . . . de los siglos XIII y XIV.* Barcelona, 1890.

Questiõ de amor by unknown. Sevilla, 1528 (December 6th, 1526).

Rabelais, François. *The works of Francis Rabelais.* Dublin, 1738. v. 2.

Reinosa, Rodrigo de. *Aqui comiençan vnas coplas delas comadres.* [Burgos? ca. 1501? facsim.: Madrid? ca. 1880?]

Relación de las fiestas y regocijos que se han hecho en las bodas del duque y duquesa de Sesa [Año 1541] In *Relaciones de los reinados de Carlos V y Felipe II.* Madrid, 1950. v. 2, p. [157]–169.

Resende, Garcia de. *Choronica qve tracta da vida [e] grandissimas virtvdes . . . do Christianissimo Dom Ioão ho Segundo.* Lisboa, 1596.

Rodríguez Moñino, Antonio. *Viaje a España del Rey Don Sebastián (La entrevista de Guadalupe).* In *Revista de estudios extremeños.* 1947, v. 3, p. [3]–75, [279]–358.

Rodríguez Villa, Antonio. *Bosquejo biográfico de Don Beltrán de la Cueva, primer Duque de Alburquerque.* Madrid, 1881.

_____ *Crónicas del Gran Capitán.* Madrid, 1908. (*Nueva biblioteca de autores españoles.* v. 10)

_____ *El emperador Carlos V y su corte según las cartas de Don Martín de Salinas, embajador del infante Don Fernando (1522–1539).* Madrid, 1903.

Rubio, Germán *and* Acemel, Isidoro. *El maestro Egas en Guadalupe.* Madrid, 1912.

Sáez, Liciniano. *Demostracion histórica del verdadero valor de todas las monedas que corrian en Castilla durante el reynado del señor Don Enrique IV.* Madrid, 1805. p. 528–536: *Relacion de los inventarios . . . [de] don Alvaro de Zúñiga,* 1468.

Sánchez Cantón, Francisco Javier. *Floreto de anécdotas y noticias diversas que recopiló un fraile dominico residente en Sevilla a mediados del siglo XVI.* Madrid, 1948. (*Memorial histórico español.* v. 48 bis)

Sandoval, Prudencio de. *Dela vida y hechos del emperador Carlos Qvinto.* Valladolid, 1604–06. 2 pts.

Santa Cruz, Alonso de. *Crónica del emperador Carlos V.* Madrid, 1920–21. v. 1–2.

Segovia (City). Alcázar. *Libro de las cosas que estan en el tesoro de los alcaçares de . . . Segouia . . . el qual hizo gaspar de grizio . . . por mandado de la dicha Reyna [Isabel] . . . e puso por ynventario . . año [1503]* In Ferrandis Torres. p. [69]–169.

Sevilla (City). Archivo de protocolos. *Catálogo de los fondos americanos.* Madrid, Barcelona, etc., [1930], Sevilla, 1937. v. 1, 5.

Sevilla (City). Ordinances. *Recopilacion de las ordenãças dela muy noble y muy leal cibdad de Seuilla.* Seuilla, 1527.

Spain. Laws, statutes, etc. *Declaracion de la pregmatica que su magestad del Emperador . . . mando hazer . . . A cerca de los trajes y vestidos.* Valladolid, 1537.

_____ *Pragmaticas y Leyes hechas y recopiladas por mandado delos muy altos, Catholicos y poderosos Principes, y señores el Rey dõ Fernãdo, y la Reyna doña Ysabel.* Medina del cãpo, 1549.

_____ *Las pramaticas del Reyno. Recopilacion de algunas bulas . . . cõ todas las pramaticas: y algunas Leyes del reyno.* Alcala de Henares, 1528.

_____ *La Prematica q̃ su Magestad ha mandado hazer . . . para el remedio dela gran carestia que hauia enel calçado.* Alcala de Henares, 1552.

Stow, John. *The Annales, or Generall Chronicle of England, begun first by maister IOHN STOW, and after him continued . . . vnto the ende of this present yeere 1614.* Londini, 1615.

Talavera, Fernando de, abp. of Granada. *Auisacion ala uirtuosa y muy noble senora dona maria pacheco condessa de benauēte de como se deue cada dia ordenar y occupar para q̃ expienda bien su tiempo.* MS. in the library of the Monastery of El Escorial.

_____ *Reforma de trages . . . ilvstrada por . . . Bartolome Ximenez Paton.* Baeça, 1638.

_____ *Tractado p̃vechoso q̃ demuestra como en'l uestir y calçar comūmēte se cometē muchos peccados* [1477] MS. in the library of the Monastery of El Escorial.

Teresa, Saint. *Obras completas.* Madrid, 1951. v. 1, p. [131]–585: *Tiempo y vida de Santa Teresa* by Efrén de la Madre de Dios.

Toledo (City). Ordinances. *Ordenanzas para el buen régimen y gobierno de la muy noble, muy leal e imperial ciudad de Toledo.* Toledo, 1858.

Torquemada, Antonio de. *Los colloqvios satiricos.* Bilbao, 1584.

Vital, Laurent. *Relation du premier voyage de Charles-Quint en Espagne,* In *Collection des voyages des souverains des Pays-Bas, publiée par MM. Gachard et Piot.* Bruxelles, 1881. v. 3, p. 1–303.

Vives, Juan Luis. [*De institutione.* Sp. tr. by Juan Justiniano] *Libro llamado Instrucion de la muger christiana.* Caragoça, 1555.

_____ [*Linguae latinae exercitatio.* Sp. tr. by Chr. Coret y Peris] *Diálogos.* Madrid, 1792.

The Voyage, &c. of the Princess Catharine of Arragon to England. In *The Antiquarian Repertory.* London, 1808. v. 2, p. 248–322.

Zúñiga, Francesillo de. *Cronica.* In Castro y Rossi, Adolfo de. *Curiosidades bibliográficas.* Madrid, 1855. p. [9]–54. (*Biblioteca de autores españoles.* v. 36)

ACKNOWLEDGMENTS

GRATEFUL acknowledgment is made to all persons and institutions granting permission to reproduce works of art in their collections.

Credit for photographs not supplied directly by institutions or private owners is to be given to the following: A. C. L., Brussels, figs. 3, 50, 61, 97, 304, 327, 466; A. D. A. C., Barcelona, fig. 181; Alguacil, Toledo, fig. 508; Fratelli Alinari, Florence, fig. 135; Alonso, Palencia, fig. 484; D. Anderson, Rome, figs. 116, 144, 159, 176, 191, 223, 234, 235, 316, 368, 393, 399, 417, 432, 486, 564; Anderson-Spalding-HSA, New York, figs. 60, 131, 197, 336, 352, 354, 369, 440, 453, 455, 490, 522, 547, 553, 561; Foto Ars, Reggio Emilia, fig. 577; courtesy of Diego Angulo Iñiguez, Madrid, fig. 496; Direktion der Bayerischen Staatsgemäldesammlungen, Munich, fig. 401; Paul Becker, Brussels, figs. 23, 400, 424; Braun et Cie., Paris, figs. 214, 370, 519; reproduced by permission of the British Library Board, London, figs. 67, 98, 121, 160, 246, 264, 374, 423, 430, 441, 458; A. Bruckmann, Munich, figs. 532, 559, 573; Byne-HSA, New York, figs. 258, 260, 353, 495, 515; Comisión de Monumentos, León, figs. 5, 120, 168; Henry Cooper & Son, Northampton, figs. 9, 457; José Díez, Plasencia, figs. 426, 429, 465; Alejandro Ferrant, Zamora, fig. 500; Foto Garay, Valladolid, fig. 349; Photographie Giraudon, Paris, figs. 2, 151, 283, 303, 346, 376, 397, 431, 477; J. Gudiol, Barcelona, figs. 26, 43, 63, 76, 84, 101, 186, 269, 408, 435; Hemme Collection, fig. 125; Ideal Studio, Edinburgh, fig. 132; Instituto de Conservación y Restauración de Obras de Arte, Madrid, figs. 167, 200, 207, 284, 286, 287, 296, 350, 505, 509, 563; permission granted by Junta de Museos, Barcelona, fig. 528; the Lord Chamberlain, London (copyright reserved), figs. 129, 309, 334, 378, 442, 504; Tomás Magallón Antón, Madrid, fig. 247; David Manso, Madrid, fig. 516; Ampliaciones y Reproducciones Mas, Barcelona, figs. 4, 15, 18, 19, 21, 33, 34, 38, 41, 42, 45, 47–49, 51–53, 55–59, 62, 64–66, 68–71, 73, 74, 79, 82, 83, 86, 87, 91–94, 99, 103, 104, 107, 113–115, 117, 118, 122, 124, 127, 128, 130, 133, 134, 141, 145, 147, 150, 154–156, 158, 161, 162, 165, 166, 169, 171, 173, 178, 180, 182, 184, 185, 187, 189, 192, 193, 195, 198, 199, 201, 212, 215, 217, 218, 220–222, 225, 228, 236, 237, 241–244, 248, 249, 251, 252, 265, 268, 270, 273, 275–277, 281, 288, 290–292, 294, 295, 297, 298, 300, 302, 305, 310, 312, 314, 315, 318, 324–326, 328, 333, 339–342, 355, 356, 358–360, 362, 364–367, 371, 375, 377, 379, 381, 382, 384, 387, 389, 391, 392, 395, 396, 407, 411, 413–416, 420–422, 425, 428, 434, 437, 439, 443, 445, 446, 448, 449, 451, 459–461, 463, 470–472, 479, 482, 483, 485, 488, 489, 491, 492, 502, 503, 511–514, 521, 525, 528–530, 540, 543–546, 548, 551, 555, 556, 558, 565, 567, 576; Erwin Meyer, Vienna, figs. 13, 313; Ministerio de Educación y Ciencia, Madrid, figs. 203, 204, 438; Moreno, Madrid, *see* Instituto de Conservación; Arquivo do Museu Nacional de Arte Antiga, Lisboa, figs. 39, 110, 148, 231, 345; Alberto Palau, Sevilla, figs. 112, 279, 373; photograph granted and authorized by the Patrimonio Nacional, Madrid, figs. 89, 348, 383; photograph authorized by the Patrimonio Nacional, Madrid, figs. 158, 167, 200; Photo Club, Burgos, figs. 16, 17, 27–29, 31, 54, 90, 100, 142, 143, 174, 210, 219, 227, 255, 259, 261, 262, 267, 274, 293, 330, 347, 380, 403, 510, 517, 523, 539, 554, 557, 562: Dr. José Manuel Pita Andrade, Madrid, figs. 535–537; RAP, Lisbon, fig. 12; Ruiz Vernacci, *see* Ministerio de Educación y Ciencia; Schaeffer Galleries, Inc., New York, fig. 450; John D. Schiff, New York, figs. 139, 146, 152, 213; F. Serra, Barcelona, figs. 257, 402; Service de Documentation Photographique de la Réunion des Musées Nationaux, Paris, figs. 7, 32, 230; Sindhöringer, Vienna, fig. 388; permission granted by Staatlichen Museen Preussischer Kulturbesitz, Gemäldegalerie Berlin (West), fig. 214; Thyssen-Bornemisza Collection, Lugano/Switzerland, fig. 323; unknown, figs. 1, 75, 81, 102, 111, 125, 202, 238, 278, 285, 301, 433, 452, 480, 507; Crown Copyright, Victoria & Albert Museum, London, figs. 239, 533; Winocio Testera Pérez, León, figs. 175, 177; Wolfrum, Vienna, figs. 119, 172.

INDEX

The foreign words, together with their explanation in the text, constitute a glossary of terms.

A

C

G

N

S

DATE DUE	
NOV 02 2009	

GAYLORD   PRINTED IN U.S.A.